Out of Harm's Way

Out of Harm's Way

*The Extraordinary True Story
of One Woman's Lifelong
Devotion to Animal Rescue*

Terri Crisp
and Samantha Glen

POCKET BOOKS
New York   London   Toronto   Sydney   Tokyo   Singapore

The stories in this book are all based on actual events. I have learned, though, that during disasters it is especially easy to lose track of time; events sometimes fall out of sequence, and a lot of the details become a blur. Whenever possible, Samantha and I contacted the people we included in the stories, and between all of us, we remembered what happened as best we could. I apologize for forgetting the names of some of the people; so in those cases, we came up with new names. To disguise their identities, several other people mentioned in this book were given other names too.

POCKET BOOKS, a division of Simon & Schuster Inc.
1230 Avenue of the Americas, New York, NY 10020

Library of Congress Cataloging-in-Publication Data

Crisp, Terri.
    Out of harm's way : the extraordinary true story of one woman's lifelong
devotion to animal rescue / Terri Crisp with Samantha Glen.
        p.   cm.
    ISBN: 0-671-52277-9
    1. Wildlife rescue—United States.   2. Crisp, Terri.   I. Glen, Samantha.
II. Title.
QL83.2.C75   1996
639.9'092—dc20   95-47938
[B]   CIP

First Pocket Books hardcover printing April 1996

10 9 8 7 6 5 4 3 2

POCKET and colophon are registered trademarks of
Simon & Schuster Inc.

All interior photos, unless otherwise noted, courtesy of author's collection.

Printed in the U.S.A.

*This book is dedicated to all the animals
that have died during disasters.
I wish we'd learned sooner how
we could have saved them.*

Acknowledgments

This is my thank you to several people who are at the top of my "Who Made the Biggest Difference in My Life" list.

First, I have my mom and dad, Ginny and Mac McKim, to thank. Throughout the years they have allowed me to explore who I wanted to be, providing me with a safety net should I stumble. They've never let me down, and I hope this book will make them proud of what they have been instrumental in creating.

If my English friend, Samantha Glen, hadn't been born with an extra heaping of persistence, there would not even be a book.

I met Samantha in 1993, shortly after my return from the Midwest floods. She had read an article that appeared in *The Wall Street Journal,* about the relief efforts I was coordinating for animals in St. Charles, Missouri. That article prompted Samantha to call United Animal Nations while I was still in Missouri. She identified herself as a writer interested in talking about the possibility of working on a book about my adventures with animals.

Being in the middle of a disaster, I had no time to discuss a book. I told Samantha that if she wanted to talk with me, she'd have to wait until after I got home.

"I thought I'd give you forty-eight hours to recover before I called," the woman with the captivating British accent responded after I answered the phone. "Terri, this is Samantha Glen. Welcome home."

She wanted to fly in from Colorado, where she was vacationing. At first I hesitated. I had been in Missouri for a month, and things at home in California were almost as big a disaster as the one I'd left. What I really wanted was just to be left alone for a while.

"I only need a few hours," Samantha insisted.

I suspected she would keep after me until we found time to meet, so I finally agreed to see her the following day.

One of the first people off the plane was a tall woman in her midforties who came through the door with a lively step, wearing a freeflowing denim dress and carrying a backpack slung over her shoulder.

"Hi, love," she said with an enthusiasm that reached all the way down through her outstretched hand.

We had lunch on the bougainvillea-covered patio of a Mexican restaurant in the mission town of San Juan Bautista. It was a lovely place to talk, and Samantha wasted no time bringing up the subject of the book. I was still resistant to the idea. Writing a book would require a great deal of time, and I didn't have much of it to spare.

But Samantha once again persisted.

"Let me make a suggestion," she said. "If we do this book, I think a third of the royalties should go for the animals."

I immediately thought of United Animal Nations and the Emergency Animal Rescue Service Program. If a book could give the program I was working so hard to help create the financial foundation it had been missing, maybe I could find time for it.

I have always loved to write. In fact, it's a passion of mine that only animals could replace.

I had a feeling that someday I'd put down on paper the stories I'd collected during all the different disasters, but I never expected something on this grand scale. Pages run off on my own printer, with spiral binding, seemed more likely. But Samantha gave me a dream grander than I'd ever imagined.

Almost two years have passed since Samantha and I met, and the book is now complete. It was Samantha's persistence and her love of animals that made it happen, and I will always be grateful to her. She has made a tremendous difference for animals in her own way, and she should be proud of what she made possible.

For just over a year and a half, Samantha and I worked on the book, devoting enormous amounts of time, energy, and emotion to the project.

Acknowledgments

It feels good to finally get all the stories out of my head and onto paper. Samantha deserves the credit for that, because I might not have gotten around to doing it until years later ... if ever. Samantha and I became best friends because of this book. I learned a lot from Samantha during the time we worked together. There were some pretty intense moments—laced with laughter, tears, shouting, and hugs.

This book has made the last two years of my life richer, and I must thank my husband, Ken, for all the time he allowed me to bury myself in my passions—while he did fun things like chauffeur kids around, wash clothes, clean house, and shop for groceries. He is a good and decent man for whom I have the deepest respect and love. I keep telling myself I must have done something really right to have gotten him.

I thank my daughters too. Jennifer has been a part of my life the longest—almost sixteen years. She helped me grow up when I needed to, and she remains my best buddy. I hope we continue to grow up together—laughing along the way.

Amy and Megan are still too young to fully understand why Mom spent so much time the last six months sitting at her desk, saying, "Okay. I'll be there in just a minute"—and then spent another hour without moving from her chair. I'll always treasure the times when they would sneak into my room while I was writing and quietly ask, "Mommy, can you read your book to us?" They have been my inspiration.

I've spent a lot of time away from my family in the past two years while developing the Emergency Animal Rescue Service Program and working on this book. I just hope my life will be an example to my daughters—proving to them that dreams do come true.

This acknowledgment would not be complete if I did not include Meredith Bernstein, our agent, who believed in this book as much as Samantha and I did. She showed us the ropes, and we couldn't have had a better guide.

It was Linda Marrow, our editor from Pocket Books, who really went to bat for us. Samantha and I will never forget that she was the first to fall in love with this book. We were unknown entities when we walked into the conference room at Pocket for the first time, but because she too loved animals, she fought for this book—and now there is an entire team at Pocket promoting it. Thanks as well to Mary Baumann Pesaresi, whose thoughtful insights and suggestions inspired us to do better. Thanks to Alan Glen, Samantha's husband, who believed in the dream, and whose support and encouragement

Acknowledgments

helped make it a reality. And of course, thanks to Sebastian, our part-Siamese cover model, who was rescued in 1985 during Hurricane Gloria.

When I watch the credits following a movie, I'm amazed at how many people it takes to create a motion picture. I am now equally amazed at how many people work behind the scenes to create a book. These are those people, whom I applaud for the job they do so well and for their shared love of animals:

GINA CENTRELLO, Publisher; KATE COLLINS, Associate Editor; AMY DURGAN, Publicist; LIZ HARTMAN, Director of Publicity; PAOLO PEPE, Art Director; AMY PIERPONT, Editorial Assistant; LISA RASMUSSEN, Sales Marketing Director; JULIE RUBENSTEIN, Executive Editor; PAM SABIN, Director of Advertising and Promotion; KARA WELSH, Associate Publisher.

Contents

Contents

In Between Disasters

Hurricane Andrew

Midwest Flood

Contents

Introduction

Why Am
I Doing This?

Was it destiny that I would help animals, or did my commitment to them begin with that first rescue at the Sears and Roebuck store in Santa Monica, California?

It was a drizzly Friday evening in early September, 1961. My parents had dragged me and my brother to Sears so they could shop for a new washing machine. It was a rather dull outing for a seven-year-old child, so I did what all curious kids do when they get bored. I wandered off. While on my quest for an adventure, I discovered the animals.

Kids have a natural ability to find toy departments, and I quickly found the one at Sears. But it wasn't the toys that captured my attention. On a shelf against the back wall were the stuffed animals: dogs, rabbits, teddy bears, elephants, and pigs, lying topsy-turvy, one on top of the other. Jumbled together on the dirty floor were cats, turtles, ducks, and monkeys that looked as if they'd been kicked and stepped on all day by people who didn't care enough to pick them up. These animals may have only been stuffed, but when you're seven and a half, there's not always a distinction between what's pretend and what's real.

Carefully, I set about scooping up each mistreated creature and placing it upright on the metal shelves, taking a moment to hug and brush the dirt off the ones that had come from the floor. As I stood in front of my furry friends, trying to find the perfect spot to place the last calico kitty and an alligator with bulging purple eyeballs, I felt a contentment that has repeated itself many times in my adult life.

Straightening stuffed animals on a department store shelf may not have the significance of retrieving animals struggling to stay afloat in rising floodwaters or comforting others injured by flying debris in a hurricane or washing crude oil off dying sea otters—but I was responding to a child's view of neglect.

Today the animals I help are living creatures. When I talk with people about what I do, they ask, "Why do you save animals in disasters?" I respond with two reasons.

First, I don't know how, to *not* help animals. Whether it's a dog running scared along a busy city street or a stuffed purple-eyed alligator lying buried under a stuffed elephant and giraffe, responding to the needs of animals is as natural to me as breathing. Animals are a part of my identity.

But the second reason I help animals in disasters is because it has to be done. My first disaster was a flood in Alviso, California in 1983. As I discovered one animal after another, abandoned by their owners to an almost certain death, I was amazed at people's indifference toward these helpless creatures. How could people rationalize saving their television set, but not their dog?

I was further shocked to learn that the local animal welfare organizations had no plan to help animals during disasters. They tried to respond, but their good intentions to rescue, provide emergency veterinarian care, and food and shelter were inadequate and often too late. As a result, animals died needlessly.

That first disaster opened my eyes to a problem I could not ignore. In 1983 I was just a naive volunteer who wanted to rescue drowning animals. Three years later, after my second disaster, I could no longer ignore the reality that animals would continue to die in these situations if people didn't learn how to do the job right.

Somebody had to do something. Somebody had to see that the same mistakes were not repeated. How that was going to be accomplished, I wasn't sure, but I knew I couldn't stand by and do nothing.

In 1988 I became the only United Animal Nations disaster volunteer. Today, it is my full-time job to recruit and train volunteers across the country to effectively implement the United Animal Nation's Emergency Animal Rescue Service Program—a nationwide disaster plan that has saved thousands of animals and will continue to save more. As director of the EARS Program, I am making sure animals are no longer overlooked during disasters and that in nondisaster times steps are taken to become better prepared for the next crisis.

Is destiny directing my life? I often wonder if I was put on this earth to help animals. Undoubtedly my passion for animals has fueled my determination, but I feel there is more to it. The sequence of events in my life no longer seems to be mere coincidence. Whatever the explanation, I will not quit. Each animal is a reason unto itself for me to continue pushing for the guarantee of help I know it deserves. I have bagged too many dead animals during disasters who died because people didn't care. This can no longer continue.

Animals need to be loved. They also need people who are willing to go beyond doing what is easy, to ensure their survival. It is my sincere hope that this book encourages others to act on behalf of the animals and do something that will make a difference for them.

Getting Started

1

Paddington

I often wonder what direction my life would have taken had Paddington not entered it. For a long time I thought I'd grow up to be a high school art teacher. I certainly never expected to have a career helping animals. I'd always loved animals, but my involvement with them didn't go much further than the dogs I grew up with and the occasional stray I'd bring home. Fifteen years ago, I couldn't bear to hear about a suffering animal. I wanted to believe that every dog and cat was loved and well cared for as my own were. It wasn't until I met Paddington that I began to realize how naive I was.

She literally jumped into my life one hot and smoggy August afternoon in 1978. I was working as an administrative assistant for Catholic Charities of Santa Clara County at the time, a job that finally paid enough so I could afford my first apartment. My office was nearby on the first floor of a once stately Victorian mansion.

The windows across from my desk opened out onto a neglected yard that was shaded by a sprawling oak tree. I'd become acquainted with the fat gray squirrel that lived in the upper tree limbs and some days came down and visited me at lunchtime. In the past months I'd discovered he was particularly fond of Ritz crackers.

On this particular day, a late afternoon rain had fallen, cleansing the air. I had opened the windows to breathe in the delightful smell of the earth after its shower and then gone back to looking up some addresses in the file cabinet when I heard it.

It was the lightest sound. A faint *thwopp* like a baseball hitting a catcher's mitt. I swung around just in time to see a bundle of fur land, sliding, atop the eight urgent letters I'd spent most of the day typing. The letters flew from beneath the paws across the glass-topped desk and onto the floor in all directions.

The tortoiseshell cat sank slowly to her stomach. She resembled a child who knew she had just done something wrong and was waiting for her scolding. I glanced at the muddy prints decorating my hard work, but it was the cat I was concerned about.

She was all eyes and belly, swollen with pregnancy. The rest of her was testament to days, maybe weeks, of a starvation existence.

"You poor thing," I whispered as I moved slowly toward her. "Where did you come from?"

San Jose State University was across the street from my office. I'd learned that it was not uncommon for students to dump their cats when the school year ended. I wondered if she was another one of the discards that I frequently saw wandering the neighborhood. It was obvious that no one had taken care of her for some time. As I began to pet her forehead, the golden eyes blinked with exhaustion.

She didn't object when I picked her up and placed her on a wadded up sweater in an empty box. She didn't move when I went into the staff kitchen and warmed some chicken broth I found in the cupboard.

Dipping my finger in the warm liquid, I held it against her mouth. Feeling the sandpaper roughness of her pink tongue against my skin gave me such an incredible feeling of being needed . . . of being loved. As the cat lapped up the last few drops of the broth, I knew this cat was going home with me.

I'd never seen a cat give birth. All the pets I'd grown up with had been spayed or neutered. I learned at an early age that there were too many unwanted dogs and cats in this world. The next morning, in her chosen spot in the middle of my waterbed, I saw my first litter of kittens being born.

Spring, my German shepherd mix, who'd been my best buddy since tenth grade, sat with me as we watched the three kittens arrive one at a time. The new mother licked each kitten clean and then stretched out so they could suckle. Before she dozed off, she looked up at me. I could hear her purring. I knew she was saying thank you.

4

The most amazing part was that the cat allowed Spring a chance to be a mom too. She had never had puppies, so when the cat didn't object to her helping to clean the kittens, Spring was quite pleased. It was a job Spring continued to do in the weeks that followed. These were probably the cleanest, most mothered kittens born that year.

I named our new friend Paddington. I found homes for the two marmalade kittens and kept the tortie, named Farina, because she looked just like her mother. My new companions settled nicely into my life.

Spring and the two cats would always be at the door to greet me when I came home. The trio would follow me from room to room. They'd talk to me. Cuddle up beside me when I read. Share my popcorn when we watched TV. I didn't have a lot of friends because I'd only lived in northern California for a year, but who needed friends when you had these guys to love you. I believed that my life was complete . . . until I met Doug.

He was the new roommate of one of the guys I worked with. A local boy with an easy, quiet charm. We met at an office party and I found I enjoyed his attention. I also liked the way he looked, nearly six feet tall, well-built, with sandy hair. I was especially pleased when he told me he liked animals.

I married him in naiveté eight months later.

It didn't take long for things to start going wrong, though. He kept changing jobs. I'd catch him in lies. Then came the late nights out with his buddies. I was learning that we had different ideas about what it meant to be married.

I kept hoping things would get better, but they only got worse.

Then came the demands. My cats could no longer be in the bedroom at night. He complained that they curled up on the pillow and purred too loud. He couldn't sleep, he said. I compromised and made them their own special bed in the living room.

But when he threw them outside and said, "Cats belong outdoors," he violated an area, where, for me, there could be no compromise. This time it was Doug who gave in.

In April of 1980 our daughter, Jennifer, was born. I had always wanted to be a mom, but the joy I should have been feeling was clouded by the recent death of Spring and my deteriorating marriage. The likelihood of becoming a single parent was becoming a very real possibility . . . and I was scared.

It was my grandmother who nudged me into doing what deep inside I knew I had to do. The week before my twenty-sixth birthday I was lying in bed, staring at the ceiling, wishing for a miracle, when I heard the phone ring.

"Uncle Kenny and I would like to take you to Lake Tahoe next weekend. It'll be our birthday present to you," my grandmother said.

"Thanks, but I really don't feel like going anywhere," I replied, wishing I could just hang up the phone.

"We'll be at your house at seven o'clock Saturday morning. Unless you want to wear your pajamas, I suggest you get up and be ready when we get there." There was no arguing with my grandmother.

It only took a weekend. Removing myself for even a couple of days from that troubled marriage made me realize I didn't want to live this way anymore. And more important, I didn't want Jennifer to be exposed to the constant turmoil. When I returned home Monday afternoon, it was to tell my husband to pack and move out.

He harassed me for months after that, but I never regretted my decision. It felt so good to be in charge of my life once again. I learned that the responsibility of being a single parent to an eighteen-month-old child wasn't as difficult as I had imagined. In fact, we were doing just fine . . . Jennifer, Paddington, Farina, and I.

Paddington and Farina continued to meet Jennifer and me at the door when we arrived home. At the end of a long day I looked forward to their greeting. They'd purr and rub against my leg, asking to be picked up. But not this particular evening. Before I could put my key in the lock, my front door swung open. Something was wrong.

Doug crossed my mind immediately, but I felt certain that he had returned all his keys. Could he have kept one though? Paddington and Farina were not at the door as I slowly peered into the dimly lit living room. I called their names, but no cats appeared. Frantically I checked each room and all their favorite hiding spots, but they were gone. I was devastated.

Leaving Jennifer with a friend, I searched the neighborhood until late that night, calling their names. I knocked on every door. I looked under cars, in dumpsters, over fences. I asked everyone I passed if they had seen two black-and-tan cats. No one had seen them. I finally returned home . . . alone. Collapsing on the couch, I cried myself to sleep.

The house seemed so empty when I woke up the next morning. I called Doug. I offered money. I threatened. I screamed. I pleaded. I cried. He snickered and slammed down the phone.

My younger brother, Todd, has always been protective of me, and he decided it was time he intervened. He paid Doug a visit, and after that I was never bothered by my ex-husband again.

But Paddington and Farina were still missing.

It was desperation that made me go to the Humane Society. When I was six, I had gone with my dad to an animal shelter to look for our boxer, Duchess, who had a bad habit of jumping our backyard fence. As we passed cage after cage of lost and abandoned dogs and cats, I felt an overwhelming sorrow for these animals. I couldn't bear to look into their pleading eyes. I begged my dad to let me take them all home. "We don't have room for all these animals," was his reply. How I wished we had a big house with a big backyard so that we could give all the dogs and cats at the shelter a home.

We left without finding Duchess, and I was unable to convince my dad to adopt even one of the shelter dogs. I will never forget how awful it felt to leave all those poor animals behind. I promised myself at that time, that I would *never* step foot in an animal shelter again.

The Humane Society of Santa Clara Valley was only a mile from my house. Maybe Doug had had some faint shred of remorse and dropped Paddington and Farina off at the shelter. I knew that animals were held for only a short time. I hoped I wasn't too late.

When I walked through the doors, I saw that the shelter was full of both people and animals. The animals were being hugged, talked to, petted, played with. Dogs, with their tails wagging, were going out the door with new owners. Cats peered out of cardboard carriers, which had lettering on the sides that read, "I'm going home." Glossy posters encouraged people to spay and neuter their pets. The people behind the counter were friendly. The place was clean. This was nothing like the place that I had visited as a child.

A sign over a door in the back identified it as the CAT ROOM. I figured that was where I should start my search. I wove my way through the crowd, stopping once to pet a golden retriever puppy who was pulling a youngster at the other end of a brand-new neon-pink leash.

"Let me show you this terrific kitten. He has the most darling personality," a young woman said to me as I walked into the cat room. Her badge identified her as a volunteer.

"I'm here to look for my cats, not to adopt one," I said, barely able to hold back the tears.

She put the kitten back in his cage and offered to help me look. For half an hour we checked every possible place where Paddington and Farina might be, even the dead animal file, but no luck. The sympathetic volunteer encouraged me not to give up and promised she would keep an eye out for them.

As I went to leave, I passed a bulletin board hanging in the hallway. In the center was a bright yellow poster announcing a volunteer training class the following Saturday. All week I thought about the volunteer who had so kindly helped me search for Paddington and Farina. She, too, was genuinely disappointed that we hadn't discovered them in a cage waiting to be taken home. Knowing that someone else understood how devastating it is to lose a beloved pet had helped me. I decided I wanted to be able to comfort other people who'd lost a pet too.

The volunteer class was taught by Kathy Snow, who, for half the day, talked to us about the Humane Society and what role volunteers played in the organization. I was fascinated and soon realized how ignorant I was about the services they provide. My childhood experience had left a terrible impression, and as an adult, I still held the belief that shelters did no more than house animals until it was time to kill them. At the end of the class I realized how wrong I'd been.

Before we left, Kathy asked each of us what volunteer job we wanted to do. I wanted to do them all.

What I ended up doing was teaching the volunteer classes, something a volunteer had never done before. My job at the time at the California School Employees Association was to instruct new employees in the union's policies and procedures, so it seemed my skills could be best used in a training position.

From that day on I was like a sponge. I wanted to learn everything I could to help animals. I wanted to know the good and the bad. All my free time was spent at the shelter, asking the staff questions. I'm sure I was a real pain, but I had lots of catching up to do. I often wished I could quit my paying job and work at the Humane Society, but unfortunately its salaries wouldn't support me and Jennifer. So I kept on volunteering. . . .

I think about Paddington and Farina to this day, especially Paddy. I sometimes even drive through my old neighborhood thinking I might find them perched in a tree or sitting on a porch. I believe things happen for a reason. It was no accident that Paddington came into my life. I just wish she could have stayed longer.

If only I could thank her for what she gave me.

Alviso Flood
Alviso, California . . .

The late spring storm was not normal—but no one was complaining.

The San Francisco Bay area has had its periods of drought, so rain in any amount—at any time—is welcome. In 1983, though, the rain fell almost nonstop for days, causing concern for the residents of Alviso. This small community, located on the southern edge of the San Francisco Bay, sits like a teacup at the water's edge. It is here, too, that some of the major storm canals from Santa Clara County empty into the bay.

When water began to spew over the tops of the storm canals and fill the streets of Alviso—the residents began to evacuate.

2

First Disaster

The rain had not let up all night. It had been two days since the relentless storm had moved into northern California, and everything was soggy. The gutters along my street were now small rivers, ushering the fast-moving water toward overflowing storm drains. Intersections were turning into lakes that were best maneuvered in a boat, not a car. The morning weather forecast predicted clearing skies were days away.

It looked as though we were in for a real drenching.

I didn't care. It was ideal stay-at-home weather and the first day of my vacation. And for a change . . . I had no place to go.

I'd planned my time well. I had taken my parents up on their offer to have Jennifer stay with them for five days. Danielle Steele's most recent novel was on my nightstand, and I looked forward to the romantic escape it promised. The freezer contained a sinful amount of cappuccino ice cream, and I'd paid an exorbitant price for a basket full of red raspberries that waited in the refrigerator. I'd tuned in my favorite classical station, and the soothing music blended well with the sound of the rain outside.

My morning routine always begins with a cup of coffee. I poured myself a mug full and added a cloud of forbidden whipped cream with a sprinkle of cocoa on top. The first jolt of caffeine slid down my throat with more satisfaction than usual.

"We interrupt this program for the following news bulletin." The radio announcer went on to describe the seriousness of the situation.

"The water has already reached depths of six to ten feet in Alviso, and it only promises to get worse . . ."

I half-listened as I continued to sip my coffee and stare out at the rain.

Alviso was an easily overlooked place. I wasn't even sure if this small community on the southernmost tip on the San Francisco Bay rated a spot on a map. It had a small boat harbor that turned into a muddy mess when the tide went out. There was one tiny ma-and-pa grocery store, several restaurants, a bait shop, and lots of birds.

Occasionally Jennifer and I would pack a picnic breakfast and drive to Alviso. The mudflats were perfect for bird-watching. We'd sit cross-legged on our blanket at the edge of the flats and watch western sandpipers and short-billed dowitchers through our binoculars. Overhead the California gulls squealed and dive-bombed like gaggles of feathered biplanes. We'd toss bread into the sky, and the skillful birds would capture the morsels in midair.

As the morning would start to warm, we'd leave Alviso, passing through the ten-square block neighborhood of pink stucco houses, Quonset huts, and dusty green house trailers. There were two things we couldn't ignore as we drove toward the hill that led us away from the harbor: the smell and the dogs.

The source of the rank smell, which worsened as the day got hotter, was the local landfill that bordered Alviso toward the south. The fill was a favorite place for people to "dump" dogs, thinking the animals could survive by rummaging though the garbage for food. Most of the dogs ended up wandering the streets of Alviso . . . hungry.

Jennifer and I felt sorry for the dogs, so we'd always stop at the ma-and-pa grocery store and buy a big bag of dog food. We'd tear open the bag and leave it in a place where the dogs could find it. Sitting in our car, we'd watch the dogs approach cautiously. Sometimes as many as ten would show up to eat. If we got out of the car, they'd scurry in all directions.

The rain was beginning to come down harder, and from my apartment window I could see the clouds to the west. They were black. The situation in Alviso was definitely going to get worse before it got better. I began to wonder what would become of the stray dogs.

My fingers punched in the phone number I knew by heart.

"Humane Society of Santa Clara Valley, Officer Fowler." The matter-of-fact voice sounded tired.

I hesitated for a moment. It wasn't usual practice for a Humane officer to pick up the main phone line, especially John Fowler. He was very seldom at the shelter. His duties kept him busy in the field. In the year I'd volunteered at the Humane Society, I'd barely gotten to know John, but I knew he was a good officer.

"John, it's Terri," I said. "I heard about Alviso on the radio. Are you guys doing anything to help the animals?"

"I'll be going out to assess the situation as soon as I can get a boat. I think I've found one, but it won't be here until noon." As John spoke I could sense his frustration.

"Do you need any help?"

There was a long pause, as if John was trying to figure out what damage I could do. After all, I'd never done this kind of thing before. Maybe I'd just get in the way, but I at least had to offer.

"Do you have some waders and a life jacket?"

"No, but I could get some at the sporting goods store." I began to see how unprepared I was.

"If you can get the gear, be here before noon. I've gotta go. I've got another call."

After hanging up, I stayed in my chair. I could only stare out the window. My heart was racing, fueled by adrenaline. My mind was bouncing from one thought to the next. What was I getting myself into? Would I see animals that had drowned? What if I drowned? Something told me I should be scared, but the desire to help got me to the Humane Society before noon.

*   *   *

Out of Harm's Way

I got my first glimpse of the flood from the road overlooking Alviso that afternoon. It was worse than I had imagined. In the distance all that remained above water were the roofs of immersed houses and treetops. Utility poles outlined where the roads had been. People's belongings floated on the surface of the water. I'd seen floods on TV, but they'd been only glimpses. I was now right in the middle of one and I was scared.

John inched our van toward the checkpoint that had been set up near the junkyard, an eyesore that sat perched above the flooded neighborhood. The going was slow. I hadn't expected the level of activity that surrounded us. There were police cars, assorted military vehicles, official Red Cross cars, mobile television-transmitting vans, catering trucks, U-Haul trailers crammed full of evacuated belongings, all trying to maneuver their way in and out of Alviso. And in addition to the vehicles, there were the people.

The scene reminded me of a disturbed anthill. You could see the panic and disbelief in the faces of those who had suddenly had their lives disrupted. These people stared. Cried. Laughed. Swore. Some stood alone, shaking their heads. Others huddled with family and friends. I'd seen pictures of disaster victims, but they hadn't prepared me for the reality. I could only stare back.

When we finally reached the checkpoint, John rolled down his window. Two national guardsmen approached.

"We're here to find out if there are any animals that need rescuing . . ." Before John could continue, the taller of the two soldiers turned and pointed at a building ahead to our left.

"There's a malamute in that attic over there. Once in a while, it'll poke its head out that open window. I don't think it's in any danger, but it might be hungry. The owners evacuated yesterday morning."

"Any problem with us using our boat to get it?"

"You got life jackets and radio communication? Without them, I'm afraid we can't let you go in," the soldier said.

"Yeah. We've got both." John had known what we would need.

"Then go get that dog and any other animals you find that people didn't give a damn about. People like that ought to be shot." These guys were on our side.

*   *   *

1 4

Alviso Flood

The rain bounced off the surface of the water like tiny bullets. It would be a while before the clouds overhead finished dumping their load. I pulled my raincoat tighter around my neck and repositioned my wet feet. John had packed our boat with cages, dog and cat food, a first aid kit, rope, a catch pole, and two granola bars. We'd already rescued the malamute, with the help of the National Guard, and now we were off in search of more animals.

I was finding it hard to hide my impatience. My inexperience would have gotten us in trouble if John hadn't been in charge. While he had been carefully packing the boat, I had wondered if he needed to be reminded that there were animals in need of help and if we didn't get moving, they'd probably drown. I would have just launched the boat and gone . . . unprepared. John's day-to-day experience as a humane officer and his foresight allowed us to successfully rescue a lot more animals than I would have been able to, going in unprepared.

I looked at the square, average face beneath the sandy, balding hairline of the man who was now piloting our boat through the water. His stocky body leaned starboard, his eyes scanning the tree and rooftops for stranded animals. Occasionally he'd turn off the motor and our boat would drift while we listened, hoping to hear a cat meowing or a dog barking. All we could hear was the rain and the water lapping against the side of our boat.

Down one street and then another we traveled. Detouring down cul-de-sacs and alleys. We went through front and backyards, under trees, over cars buried beneath the water's surface, between buildings, behind garages. We were passing the house on the corner of Moffet and Eldorado streets, whose front yard I remembered always blossomed into a field of deep lavender irises every spring, when I heard John shout.

"Look! Over there." He was pointing to a small dog struggling to keep its head above water. The dog's paws paddled furiously, but it couldn't keep afloat. It kept gulping water and going under.

Not far from the dog was a truck with a portion of the cab roof still above water. "Why won't he swim to the truck?" I asked John, puzzled.

John just shook his head. He'd cut the engine and was using the fence to pull us toward the dog. As we got closer, I could tell it was a retriever puppy, maybe seven or eight months old. What I noticed next were his eyes. This was one scared puppy.

"Hold on, guy," John urged as he got within reach of the puppy.

John leaned so far over the side of the boat, I thought for sure we were going in for a swim too. His hands grabbed the puppy behind its front legs, and he pulled. But it remained in the water. Its head jerked violently sideways as it squealed in pain.

Now we understood why the puppy hadn't been able to swim to safety. A one-inch, rusted chain, attached to his tight leather collar, was sinking the puppy to its death as surely as any anchor.

"Goddamit! How could people be so stupid." As John cursed, he reached back into the water and grabbed hold of the puppy so he could keep its head above water.

"Don't just sit there. Get up here." John's orders were curt and sharp.

I scrambled to obey. I threw myself forward onto all fours and slipped and slid like a true amateur over the assorted supplies and equipment until I could wedge myself up alongside John.

"Grab him, keep his head up, and *don't* let go," came the command. The body of the cold and squirming puppy was now in my hands. I had to be strong. I couldn't let John see me cry.

John worked to undo the buckle on the collar, but the fastener was broken. When he attempted to ease the collar over the pup's head, it wouldn't budge. The little guy jerked with sudden panicked energy, and I held on tighter.

"Don't lose him," John said as he moved to the back of the boat.

My hands were becoming numb from the cold water, but I could feel the dog's skinny body begin to slip from my grasp. The wind was shifting. It drove the rain straight into my eyes. I couldn't see.

"John," I screamed, "I'm losing him."

"Hold on." John was pulling a toolbox out from under the backseat. "I'll have that puppy free in just a second."

That second seemed like forever.

John finally returned to my side with a pair of bolt cutters. He reached under the water and squeezed the rusted chain between the sharp edges. *Please work! Please work!* I prayed silently.

With one last squeeze, the chain finally snapped free and disappeared into the water. John didn't have to tell me what to do next. I pulled the exhausted puppy out of the water toward me and buried him under my rain jacket. I could feel him shivering. I hugged

1 6

him tighter. He responded by peeking his head far enough out of my rain jacket to reach up and lick me on the chin.

"*Aaah!* You're welcome," I said.

"Well, you rescued an animal Terri." I could only nod.

"Now, dry him off and get him in a cage. He's not the only one out here that needs our help." John was right . . . again.

3

Magic

John and I had become friends. I admired him for his animal-handling abilities, and he respected my determination to learn. Together, we made a good team.

By the third day of the flood, the sky had lightened and the rain had weakened into a drizzle, interspersed with brief periods of the most welcome sunshine. We began our morning in search of a poodle named Fritz that had been left by his owner, locked in the bathroom.

"I figured he could could climb on the back of the toilet if the water got too high," was the owner's explanation for leaving Fritz behind.

We were afraid he might be wrong.

The water had reached its crest, but it was receding slowly. As we headed in search of the poodle, we began to see new things along our way. Houses that we recognized only by the color or style of their roof were starting to have windows, porch lights, and doors. Mailboxes, fences, bushes, and swing sets were now protruding from the water. As we passed one house, John pointed to the wall that faced us.

"Look at the side of that place." I squinted in the direction John was pointing. My eyes were not accustomed to the sunshine that had just begun to peek through the clouds. I shaded my eyes with my hand to see better.

"Oh, yuck." Almost the entire side of the house was covered with snails.

"Not even floodwaters can kill them off," said John as we motored past. "I bet the cockroaches have all survived too."

I watched the snails until we turned the corner. In spite of not being particularly fond of them, I was amazed at how hard they had worked to stay alive. With agonizing slowness, the snails must have crept up the rough stucco surface, probably just millimeters ahead of the rising water.

By late afternoon we'd rescued twenty-seven animals, including Fritz. We'd found him shivering on the back of the toilet when we waded into the musty bathroom. The waterline had reached the bottom of the medicine cabinet. Fritz had definitely done some swimming.

We took all the animals we rescued back to our van, parked adjacent to the checkpoint, so our friends from the National Guard could keep an eye on them. When the van's cages were full, we'd call the Humane Society and they'd send a couple of kennel workers to transport the animals back to the shelter. Over the three-day period we'd rescued close to one hundred dogs and cats, and Pigsley, a three-hundred-pound hog.

Before we hauled our boat out of the water each afternoon, we'd make our evening feeding rounds. I was learning that in addition to having lots of stray dogs, Alviso had an abundance of cats too. Some of the felines were friendly but just too frightened to let us catch them. Most of them were wild. The cats had survived by climbing up on rooftops and clinging to tree limbs. We were their Red Cross, bringing food to these disaster victims.

We had just arrived at one of our feeding locations when a Coast Guard boat pulled up. We recognized the men on board. They had reported a stranded dog to us the day before.

"We've got another rescue for you. Apparently there are two Chihuahuas in a trailer behind the grocery store. You guys got time to get them?"

John looked up at the sky. I knew what he was thinking. We don't have much daylight left. "John, you go get the dogs. I'll stay here and feed this bunch."

"I don't know." John's concern about leaving me alone was evident.

"Oh, don't worry. I'll be fine. I promise I won't do anything *too* crazy." John had told me how important it is to work in teams when rescuing animals. This time he made an exception.

1 9

Out of Harm's Way

John helped me haul the bags of food onto the roof before he got back into our boat. "I'll be back before dark." That meant I'd see him again in less than forty-five minutes.

I didn't have to call the cats. The dinner bunch arrived from different directions, eager to eat. They circled and paced as I filled paper plates with mounds of dry food. Occasionally one would meow, as if to say, "Can you hurry it up." Several of the braver cats got impatient and decided to eat right out of the bag.

In addition to feeding cats at this location, there were six plump chickens and an obnoxious rooster. I'd already scattered some chicken feed to satisfy them. They were busy pecking away as I laid down exactly thirteen paper plates. It was important to give each of the thirteen cats plenty of elbowroom.

With my job done, and not expecting John to return for a while, I sat down, stretched my legs out in front of me, and leaned back on my elbows to watch the feast.

This was the first time I'd stopped all day, and I suddenly realized how tired I was. It had been a long time since my morning coffee. A jump start of caffeine would sure have hit the spot. But caffeine wouldn't remedy the sore muscles.

Every part of my body ached, my arms the worst. In three days they had pulled me up onto roofs, lifted forty-pound bags of dog food, rowed our boat into places too full of debris to risk using the motor, cradled frightened animals, and carried a seventy-pound dalmatian two blocks through ankle-deep water because he didn't want to get his paws wet. Bandages covered the cuts on my forearm from my encounter with a cactus. Purple-and-green bruises were visible on bare skin not yet covered by bandages. I was basically a mess, but I was proud of my war wounds.

As the clouds overhead took on hues of pink and yellow, I got up slowly to refill some of the paper plates. A few of the cats had already finished and left without so much as a "meow" of thanks. A bulging black-and-white cat sniffed around her plate for any morsels that may have fallen off. She was the first to get seconds. I suspected her belly was full of kittens and not just food. I was scattering some more feed for the chickens when a familiar sound from the yard next door made me stop. Somewhere nearby there was a duck.

Now, granted we were in a flood, which if you're a duck must not be that unwelcome, but this duck sounded as if it was in trouble. I moved closer to the roof's edge, hoping to get a better look into the next yard. All I could see was water and floating patio furniture.

Alviso Flood

Quietly I waited for the duck to make another sound so I could pin-point its location.

Five minutes passed and the sound I'd been waiting for finally came. I moved to the north corner of the roof, and from there I could see to the far corner of the next yard. In a narrow space between a lopsided garage and a buckled fence was an enclosure roofed with chain-link fencing. Across its entrance was a makeshift gate, partially hidden by oleander bushes. The duck had to be in there.

I looked at my watch and estimated it'd be another fifteen minutes before John returned and I had just about that much good daylight left. Should I wait? Could I do this one on my own? I had promised John I wouldn't do anything too crazy! Another plea from the duck helped me make up my mind.

For a brief moment I hesitated. I felt like a kid again standing on the edge of my uncle Jim's swimming pool trying to get the courage to jump in, knowing how cold the water would be until I got used to it. I wasn't intending to go for a swim, but I knew the distance between me and the duck meant I'd have to get wet.

I sat on the edge of the roof dangling my legs over the edge. John had warned me the first day not to wear my waders into water deeper then my knees. Many a fisherman has learned the hard way—you fall in deep water with waders on and you may not reach the surface again. My waders lay crumpled in a heap on the roof.

It was time to take the plunge. I turned around and lowered myself slowly into the murky water, trying not to think about the snake I'd seen slither past our boat earlier that day.

The water was colder than I had expected.

Holding on to the edge of the roof, I pulled myself through the eight feet of water toward the fence that separated the two yards. When I got to the corner of the roof, I dog-paddled the short distance to the fence. Bushes buried below the surface tore at my jeans. I grabbed the water-logged wooden fence and held on.

"Okay. Over we go," I said to myself. My arms pleaded with me to reconsider. With both hands in place I pulled myself up until my stomach was teetering on the fence. I swung one leg over and sat straddling the wobbly planks. Feeling under the water with my sock-covered foot, I found the fence had a wooden brace that ran its length. It was just wide enough to balance myself on as I scooted along the fence in a sitting position. As I moved along the back fence, which leaned toward the yard behind it, I added a few splinters to my war wounds.

Out of Harm's Way

The roof on the back side of the garage hung over the fence. I now had to get off the fence and up onto the roof. The sooner I accomplished this the better, because the fence was becoming less stable. My rear end was first in the air as my hands grasped the fence and my one leg struggled to balance on the brace. At the most inappropriate moment a floating water bug decided to take refuge on my sleeve. He was in luck. I had no spare hands to shoo him away.

When I felt confident I wasn't going to go headfirst into the water, I raised the top half of my body ever so carefully. As I straightened up, my arms extended out from my sides for balance as I swayed to the right and then to the left, and the fence leaned even further. The water bug clung to my sweatshirt, hoping he wasn't about to go for a swim again. Dripping wet, I stood still.

Wasn't it about time for the cavalry to show up? I hoped to hear the sound of John's boat approaching, but all I heard was the duck, reminding me he still needed help.

Pulling my left leg out of the water, I rested it on the top of the fence, while my right foot stayed planted on the brace. The image of a tightrope walker entered my mind. I may not have had a rope to balance on, but this fence was feeling just about as narrow. Bending forward, I reached for the corner of the roof. With a tight grasp on the wooden structure, I pulled myself toward my refuge. My left knee touched down on the shingled surface first. The right leg followed. With me safely on the roof, the fence finally gave way. Its timing couldn't have been better. The water had slowly eroded its supports, and the entire length of the back fence disappeared under the water.

Great! Now what do I do? I thought to myself. I'd have to figure out a new way back, but I didn't have time to think about that now. The duck's calls for help were getting louder and more insistent.

"Okay. Okay. I'm coming," I yelled to it.

Reaching the furthest corner of the roof, I bent down to peer over the edge. There he was. A large male mallard frantically swimming back and forth in the enclosed space below me. I now understood his predicament. He was trapped by the garage on one side, the fence on the other, the chain-link roof, and the closed gate. There was no escape from the pen.

I was surprised he was still alive. The space between the surface of the water and the man-made roof couldn't have been more then three inches high when the floodwaters had reached their crest. The duck must have continuously paddled as he struggled to keep his beak above water. There was now enough room for the mallard to swim, but this duck was ready to fly the coop.

It would have been nice if I could have opened the gate from up on the roof, but for some reason, nothing was to come easily for me that day. I realized I'd have to lower myself back into the water in order to free this duck, who by now was squawking nonstop.

A breeze was starting to stir, which reminded me how cold I was. I pulled my rain jacket tighter around my neck, but it couldn't prevent the shiver that started at my toes and moved to all parts of my soaked body. I rubbed my hands together, trying to warm them before I stepped down to balance on the side fence. Lowering myself into the water, I positioned myself at the entrance to the enclosure. I felt with my toes to see if I could reach the ground below me, but the water was still too deep. As I surveyed the situation the duck continued to voice his impatience.

With my left fingers hooked in the chain-link gate, I used my right hand to feel under the water for a latch. I dog-paddled to keep afloat. It didn't take long to locate the gate latch, which was not locked. Wiggling the metal rod, I freed the gate. Clinging to the gate with one hand and grabbing on to the frame of the garage door with the other, I very slowly pulled the gate out toward me. I was able to create a space just wide enough for the duck to squeeze through, and he wasted no time escaping. He paddled away and never looked back. Before he reached the end of the driveway, he spread his wings and took flight.

As he flew over the treetops, I hoped he'd always remain free.

I'd done it. I couldn't wait to tell John.

But then I realized my solo rescue was not yet over. I still had to get back to the roof where my waders and the bags of cat food were. I thought about staying put until John returned. It would definitely be easier to get back up to that roof with his help, but I was beginning to get really cold. The risk of hypothermia entered my thoughts.

Just as I was beginning to plot my return route, I heard a noise from within the enclosure. *Please don't be a snake,* was my first thought.

Closing the gate wouldn't do any good. A snake could slip through the chain link with no problem. My only escape was to climb the fence.

Before I could raise myself to safety, I heard the noise again, but this time I realized a snake was unlikely to be the cause. It sounded like the thumping noise a rabbit makes with its back legs. Feeling somewhat braver, I peered into the enclosure. The noise came from the back end of the pen, which was about thirty feet long. My view was obstructed by pieces of scrap plywood leaning against the garage. I'd have to go into the pen to get a better look.

Clinging to the gate again, I managed to increase the opening so it was wide enough for me to squeeze through. My rain jacket got caught on a piece of metal and tore as I passed through it. With it came another scratch. Using the sagging chain-link ceiling to hold on to, I pulled myself along like a monkey hanging from a play yard jungle gym. Halfway into the pen, I discovered the source of the noise.

On a shelf near the back was the largest tan-and-white rabbit I'd ever seen. The water was within inches of covering the shelf that barely supported the animal. In the darkening shadows it was hard to see, but the rabbit looked as if he was okay.

"Hey, guy, what are you doing in here?" I couldn't believe someone had gone off and left yet another animal behind.

"I bet you'd like something to eat." John had packed some rabbit food in the van that morning. "You cooperate, and I promise you dinner."

Slowly I moved toward the shelf. As I got closer I saw that the rabbit's fur was wet. He'd been in the water at some point. I hoped he wouldn't get scared and jump back in. Speaking softly to the trembling rabbit, I got closer and closer until I could reach out and touch him. He flinched slightly when he felt my hand against his back, but he didn't move. I worked my fingers up toward the area behind his ears and gently petted the damp fur for a few minutes.

"You ready to go with me?" I could see the rabbit's nose moving nonstop.

I was still in water too deep to touch bottom, so I had to use one hand to hang from the chain-link ceiling. With my free hand I pulled the rabbit toward me. His back feet kicked, but I used my arm to nestle him against my chest. I lowered my chin and quietly tried to reassure him. He calmed down.

I wasn't quite sure what to do next. I listened for the sound of John's boat again, but there was a lonely silence outside the pen. He must have run into some problems too, because he should have been back by now. It would be completely dark before too long. For the first time, I was scared. What if I got stuck in Alviso for the night? The thought of remaining in the floodwaters for much longer made me shudder.

"Okay, bunny, if we're going to get out of here, we'd better come

2 4

up with a plan real fast. Any suggestions?" The bunny remained silent. "You're a big help."

Getting out of the pen was my first priority. With all the plywood leaning against the garage, I still wasn't sure that there might not be a snake sharing these close quarters with us. I decided to move out before one made its presence known.

Retracing my path was a lot more difficult with a hefty rabbit in tow. I had moved him up onto my shoulder, and using my chin, I tried to keep him wedged in place. I needed both hands to pull us out of the pen. It was slow going, and several times I had to stop and use one hand to reposition the rabbit. The gate was still wide enough for both of us to finally squeeze through.

Once on the outside of the pen, I had to figure out how to get both me and the rabbit back to the roof where my stuff was. With the rear fence down, it was like crossing a river without a bridge. My legs were starting to get numb, and a painful kink in my neck wasn't going away. I was running out of time. I'd have to swim to the fence that separated the two yards.

"Okay, rabbit, now you really have to cooperate. We're going for a swim."

I decided I'd try floating on my back with the rabbit on my chest, its body buried under my rain jacket. Whether this would work or not, I wasn't sure, but I didn't know what other choice I had. I slowly lay back in the water and struggled to stuff the rabbit under my jacket. Finally with his nose pressed up against my chin, we set off.

Our progress was slow, and several times I bumped into the patio furniture floating on the surface of the water. I remember staring up into the sky at one point and seeing the first star of the evening peeking out from the clouds. I'd not seen any stars in a week. The ever-present rain clouds had kept them well hidden. This seemed like a pretty good time to make a wish. "Oh, please, someone up there, work your magic and guide me out of this."

Just then I bumped into the fence separating the yards. We'd crossed our river.

My free hand grabbed the wooden plank, and I hung on. My teeth were chattering by now, and I was losing feeling in my legs. The rabbit wiggled under my jacket. "Hold on, guy, we're almost there."

There was one more obstacle in our way. I had to get both of us over the fence. I feared I didn't have enough strength left in my arms to pull us up. I was also concerned that I couldn't balance both of us if I made it onto the fence. The last thing I wanted to do was drop the rabbit. His chances of surviving would not have been good. And I'd worked too hard to save this bunny to have him drown now.

Just then, something bumped into my hip. A gurgling sound rose from under the surface of the water. I think I should have been scared, but for some reason I just remained still. Right in front of me, as I watched, a ladder slowly appeared from the depths of the floodwaters. It lay on the surface, within reach. Someone had worked some magic. We had our way over the fence.

Working quickly, with renewed energy, I positioned the ladder against the fence. With minimal effort I climbed the rungs, my rabbit still safely tucked under my rain jacket. I had just gotten us positioned on the fence, when a welcome sound penetrated the silence. It was John's boat.

"Well, bunny, we're safe, thanks to some very special magic. Magic . . . that's what I'll call you." I cuddled my new rabbit as we waited to be rescued.

4

Survivors

It had been four days since the residents of Alviso had been evacuated. The teasing sun of the day before had once again disappeared, and overnight it poured. When my alarm went off at five-thirty, I knew I'd be returning to Alviso.

The weather wasn't the only determining factor for how much longer I'd be doing rescue work. John could have grounded me. When he found Magic and me the evening before, teetering on the fence, both dripping wet, he could have gotten mad and not allowed me on the water again—but he didn't.

After Magic and I were safely in the boat and John was sure we were both okay, he said something that confirmed that my solo rescue had not gotten me in trouble, "What were you trying to do, catch pneumonia? If so, your timing's lousy. I'd hate to lose you just when I got you broken in good."

My teeth were chattering too hard to respond, but I managed a grateful smile.

Before John and I went our separate ways later that evening, we agreed to met at the Humane Society the next morning to decide if there was a need to do any more rescues in Alviso. The word we got as we drove past the checkpoint was that if the rain stayed away

2 7

overnight and the floodwaters went down another two feet, the military would begin escorting some of the residents of Alviso back to their homes so they could collect some of their belongings. We hoped this included animals that we may not have found.

It was six fifteen when I parked my car on the street in front of the Humane Society. I saw John leaning inside the van, already starting to load empty cages, which the evening before had held dogs and cats that we'd saved from having to spend another night trying to stay dry. Seeing the cages reminded me of the large German shepherd who had refused to go into a cage and wanted instead to ride on my lap back to the shelter.

He had been our last rescue before we started our evening feeding rounds. John and I had just finished searching for a cat reported to be stranded at George Mayne Elementary School and were headed north on First when we saw the dog down one of the dead-end streets. He was in the water . . . but he wasn't swimming. This ninety-pound dog was stretched across the back of a partially submerged couch floating in the middle of the flooded roadway. To keep from falling off the couch, he had bitten into the foam padding.

We had no idea how long the dog had been clinging by his teeth to the couch, but how ever long, his jaws had to be getting sore. John wasted no time coming to the dog's aid. He swung the boat around and killed the motor to allow the current to push us toward the black-and-tan shepherd. I eased an oar out from under the seat and positioned it in case I'd need to maneuver us closer. John moved to the middle seat and grabbed the catch pole. While we readied ourselves for the rescue, the dog stared back at us, his teeth still firmly planted in his makeshift life preserver.

I could see in John's eyes he was trying to figure out how to get close enough to the dog without running the risk of scaring it into the water. I suspected he would try to get the loop from the catch pole around the dog's neck and, hopefully, then be able to pull it into the boat . . . without capsizing us. Not the best plan, but I was learning that there is no written guide that can prepare you to rescue animals from all the different predicaments they get themselves into. You learn by doing.

"Terri, can you use the oar and move us around the right end of the couch? I want to come up on him from the back side." John's voice was just a whisper.

I lowered the oar into the water and paddled in smooth, even strokes. We moved closer to the couch, and the dog didn't move. His unblinking eyes watched our every move. As we got almost within arm's reach of the couch, John began speaking to the dog in a soft soothing voice.

"Easy, boy. Just hang in there. We're not going to hurt you."

The dog must have believed John.

At that moment he let go of the couch and made a desperate leap for our boat. It happened so quickly there wasn't even time to grab on to the sides to brace myself, but my mind did register that I might be about to go for a swim. Thank goodness John insisted we always wear our life jackets.

Our boat teetered-tottered, and waves of water came in over the railings as cages rattled. The dog had landed, on his nose, atop a forty-pound bag of cat food. We all sat motionless as the boat continued to respond to this unexpected intrusion. This wasn't how we had planned to get the shepherd into the boat, but the dog's plan ended up working just fine.

Then, without warning, he pushed himself up, scrambled over the cages, and planted himself next to me. With his mouth inches from my face, I began to hope that this was a friendly dog. John reassured him again that we weren't going to hurt him. I hoped this dog had the same intentions toward me.

When I felt it was safe, I finally spoke. "Well, welcome aboard," I said as the dog stared at me and shivered. "Are you going to let me dry you off?"

I got no response or obvious objection, so I moved one hand very carefully toward the stack of towels we'd stashed in a plastic bag under the front seat. The dog just watched and shivered.

"Okay, now I'm going to wrap this around you," I said as I unfolded the pink towel and moved it toward the dog.

He didn't object as I draped the towel over his back. Nor did he object when I grabbed another towel and used it to start drying off his chest. Instead, he moved closer to my side. If he were a cat, I'm sure he would have been purring.

"Looks like you got yourself a new friend," John said as he slid the catch pole back under the seat.

"Yeah, it does."

"Are you here to work or daydream?" It was John tapping on my car window.

I stepped from my car and stretched. "Looks like we're going back out, right?"

"Uh huh. I heard on the radio that the plan to let residents back in to pick up some of their stuff has been postponed until tomorrow at the earliest. It all depends on the weather." John tipped his head back and looked at the clouds overhead. "Doesn't look like the weather intends to cooperate."

"How soon are we going out?"

"I have to make a few phone calls first," John replied as he looked at his watch. "Maybe twenty minutes?"

"Good. That gives me time to check on that shepherd we brought in last night."

"Which one?"

"You know. My new friend," I teased as I headed toward the kennels.

When we'd gotten to the Humane Society the night before, I'd helped one of the evening workers put the dog in the run furthest from the door. By then he was almost dry and definitely ready to eat and settle in for a good night's sleep. I stayed with him while he ate because he seemed to want the company. I'm sure it had been lonely floating on that couch all by himself. The last thing the dog did before I closed the gate was jump up, plant his paws on each of my shoulders, and give me a sloppy kiss on my cheek. It was one of many kisses I'd received from him as he sat on my lap on the way back to the shelter.

As I walked past all the other runs on my way to say good morning to my new friend, I stopped to also say hi to the other dogs. I scratched foreheads, ears, and noses that stuck out through the chain-link doors. Tails wagged and the chorus of barks was deafening, each dog wanting to be heard above the others. I knew what they wanted. They wanted a home.

When I finally reached the last run, it was empty. As I put my key in the padlock to unlock the door, I figured the dog was in the outdoor portion of the run and as soon as he heard my voice, he'd come running. I was right. But I didn't receive the greeting I expected.

Just as I was about to open the door, I heard a voice holler from the other end of the corridor. "I wouldn't go in there if I were you."

"Why?"

No sooner had I asked, than the shepherd came charging through the opening with his teeth showing and the hair up on his back. His deep growls clearly warned, "Stay out—or else."

His appearance told me this was the same dog, but his behavior was completely different. How could a dog that had been glued to me in the boat and then sat on my lap to the shelter become so vicious overnight? I tried talking to him, but he continued to lunge at the door and growl. The kennel attendant said the dog had responded the same way toward him when he'd tried to clean the run earlier. I had lost my new friend.

It was just about six forty-five when I walked into John's office. He was still on the phone, so I sat and waited, thinking about the shepherd.

"How's your new friend?" John asked when he hung up.

"Not good, I'm afraid."

"Does the vet need to look at him?"

"No. I'm afraid this is something the vet can't fix."

I then told John about the dog's change in behavior.

"I've seen this before. When a mean or aggressive animal gets caught in a life-and-death situation, and they see no other way out but to let you help them, they can change temporarily. Once they feel safe again, they usually revert back to being their mean, nasty old self."

"Really! They can actually go through a personality change?"

"Yeah. Something like that," John said as he grabbed his clipboard and a box of chocolate chip cookies. "You ready to go?"

"Sure."

All I could think about as we drove to Alviso was the dog who had given me sloppy kisses.

When we reached the checkpoint, two rain-gear-clad national guardsmen waved us through. The two soldiers looked tired and cold as we passed. Their usual morning greeting was replaced with a mere nod. They, like everyone else, were more than ready for the weather to take pity and allow the water to recede.

"Why don't you start loading the boat while I go check in at the command tent," John suggested. "I want to see if they have heard of any more stranded animals."

"Okay," I replied as I pulled my rubber boots on. "How many cages do you think we'll need?"

"Not many. I'd be surprised if we found more animals. What I think we'll start finding are the ones that didn't make it, so be sure you throw some of those heavy black-plastic bags in the boat."

We'd already needed to use some of the black bags. We'd filled several of them each day. They'd get unloaded by a kennel attendant at the Humane Society and taken to the walk-in freezer, where they'd be kept until a rendering company could collect them. These were the animals I really felt sorry for. Their life had ended, and it seemed no one cared.

"Excuse me, ma'am." I was unloading some chicken feed from the van when I heard the deep voice. When I turned around, a couple in their mid-thirties stood behind me.

"Yes. Can I help you?"

The man spoke first. "Are you the people rescuing animals?"

"Uh huh."

"We got a cat that we couldn't catch before we left our house. Could you help us get him? I imagine he's getting pretty hungry about now." The woman nodded as the man continued to speak. "We thought this water would have been gone by now, or else we'd have asked for your help sooner."

"Didn't we all think this would be over by now," I replied as I reached into the van to get my clipboard.

"What I need from you is your address."

"We're at two-six-one-four Catherine. It's a white-and-green house. Or at least it used to be," the woman said as I wrote the information down on a piece of paper.

"What does the cat look like?"

"He's black and white, and he's got a torn ear," the woman told me.

"Henry's a real mean cat. He'll beat the hell out of any cat that dares tangle with him." The man seemed proud of his bully.

"Where was he when you last saw him?" I asked, expecting to be told that Henry was an outdoor cat.

"He was in the wife's and my bedroom, under the bed. We'll be able to show you where when we go in."

"Wait. You won't be able to go in with us. The police aren't allowing any residents back in yet." I stopped writing as I spoke to the man, who now stepped a foot closer to where I was standing.

"Maybe you didn't understand, ma'am, but Henry's a real mean cat. Ain't nobody can handle him but me."

"Believe me, we've handled lots of mean cats, and I'm sure we'll do just fine with Henry," I was quick to respond.

"You mean to tell, you won't let me go in?" The man's voice got louder as he spoke.

"You got to let my husband go. That cat'll scratch your eyes out, he's so mean."

"It's not my decision. The police make the rules."

Just then I heard John's voice. "Is there a problem here?"

"Yeah, we got a problem. This lady says I can't go in with you guys to get my cat." The man looked relieved that he didn't have to speak with me any longer. "He's a nasty sucker, and you'll need my help to catch him." I'm sure he thought John would agree.

"She's right. No residents are allowed in, under any circumstances." John's reply was not what the man had wanted to hear.

"What's wrong with you people? You going to just let my cat drown?"

"No, we'll get him for you," John tried to assure the man, but he wasn't listening.

"Come on, Carol. We're just wasting our time with these jerks." The man turned to walk away. "To tell you the truth, I don't give a damn if the cat drowns," the man boasted as he and his wife walked in the direction of an old beat-up Buick.

"Are we going to get the cat?" I asked John as he started at the couple.

" Sure we are. And I bet you anything, their cat isn't mean."

"Why?"

"I think the cat was only an excuse to get in and check out their house," John said as he went to get in the van. "I guess if I were the guy, I might try the same thing, though."

John had not gotten any other reports of stranded animals from the officer at the command tent, so Henry became our first rescue of the day.

The wind had picked up since daybreak, and the black clouds to the west were headed in our direction. More rain was definitely on the way. As we passed the displaced residents of Alviso who lined the shore waiting to be able to go home, I felt sorry for these people. Many of them had had so little to begin with. Now they had nothing.

Alviso had become a ghost town except for the police boats that patrolled for looters. John had heard they'd caught two guys during the night wearing scuba gear, and dragging plastic garbage bags full of stolen property through the water.

When we turned onto Catherine, I started to look for a green-and-white house that, hopefully, still had the numbers 2614 above water. The second house on the left looked as if it might be Henry's home. A lopsided piece of wood with metal numbers nailed onto it confirmed we were at the right place. The house was in bad shape, and it wasn't just the flood that had caused the damage.

"Isn't it lovely," I said as John steered us in closer to the house.

"You'd think *Better Homes and Gardens* would want this one on their cover," John joked as he turned off the motor.

Out of Harm's Way

We circled the house, hoping to find an unlocked window to crawl through.

"Bingo! This one's open," John announced as he slid a window on the south side of the house up. "The only problem is, it's too narrow for me to fit through. You'll have to go in alone."

"Thanks. Give *me* the mean one," I said as I shrugged off my rain slicker and stuck a waterproof flashlight in the pocket of my flannel shirt.

As I poked my head into the window to see what lay inside, John grabbed the catch pole and a pair of cat gloves. The inside of the house looked as bad as the outside. I thought about making another *Better Homes and Gardens* joke, but I knew it was time to get serious. Not knowing where this cat was, I realized he might be close enough to see we'd just given him an escape route and come leaping in my direction.

"How much water is there?" John asked.

"It's about waist deep, I guess." And I knew it would be cold.

"Any sign of the cat?"

"No, but there's a million ants crawling all over everything that's above water."

"Now, don't think you have to rescue all of them too." John was definitely in a good mood today.

"Okay. I'm going in. Once I'm in, you can hand me the pole and gloves."

I squeezed through the narrow window feetfirst, using my feet to feel for the kitchen counter that lay beneath the window. I had to kick some pots and pans into the water to make room for my feet on the countertop. While I stood on the counter, John handed me the cat gloves, and I stuffed them down the front of my waders until I knew if I'd need them.

"You might want to use the catch pole like a blind person's cane to feel your way through the water," John suggested as he handed me the pole through the open window.

Equipped for my second solo rescue, I lowered myself into the cold water. An all too familiar shiver ran up my spine as I stood in the water and looked around to get a sense of the house's layout. From the kitchen I could see into the dining room and living room. Somewhere beyond them had to be the bedroom where Henry had last been seen. That was where I planned to begin my search.

Lowering the catch pole into the water, I slid it against the kitchen floor. I held onto the slimy doorjamb between the kitchen and dining

3 4

room as I pushed some cushions out of the way. On top of the water there were also picture frames, a clock, lampshades, and a calendar. But no cat.

I moved through the dining room and into the living room, where I spotted the hallway I'd been looking for. It was now time to start calling for Henry.

"Here, kitty! kitty! kitty!" I got no response.

Entering the hallway, I could see three doors. I guessed they opened into two bedrooms and a bath. For close to fifteen minutes I waded from one small room to another, calling for Henry. I scoured that house and finally came to the conclusion that the cat was dead. John agreed and said we might as well call it quits.

"Do you think there even is a Henry?" I asked John as I stood on the kitchen counter again.

"You know, I thought they were lying about him being mean. I never thought they could be lying about there even being a cat," John said. He reached his hand through the window to help me back out.

"I hope they were lying, because that means one less animal existed to die in this flood."

I was about to grab John's hand when I heard a noise that made me stop. "Hold on, John. I think I just heard something."

"Yeah. It's probably the ants begging to be saved."

"No. Shush. I swear I heard a cat meowing." Maybe it was my ears deceiving me again, but I had to be sure. "There! You hear that?"

"Sure enough. There's a cat in here somewhere," John replied.

"Where do you think it is?" I asked, scanning the cluttered kitchen.

"It's got to be *in* something. The sound is definitely muffled."

Another meow directed our search toward a closed door at the other end of the room. I'd seen it before, but chairs from a small kitchen table had been pushed up against it by the water, and I'd just assumed Henry wouldn't be inside.

I lowered myself back into the water and moved toward the door. The muffled meowing continued. Unscrambling the chairs, I piled them up in front of the refrigerator to give me room to work. Then I pulled the cat gloves out of my waders. I hadn't forgotten that Henry was supposed to be a real mean cat.

John sounded like a protective parent as he cautioned me from the window. "Now, be careful when you open that door. He may lunge for you. And get that catch pole ready."

I had to admit I was scared.

Then I thought about the German shepherd . . .

3 5

Maybe Henry's personality would be altered temporarily if he saw me as his only chance for surviving. I sure hoped so, otherwise I might be in for a new experience I wasn't sure I wanted to have.

My hand reached under the water to locate the door handle. It turned easily enough, but pulling the warped door toward me was not as easy. With both hands I grabbed the door handle and with all my weight leaned to the right. The door budged a few inches. Just enough room to peer inside and see what lay in wait.

I flicked on my flashlight and let the light probe the darkness. Behind the thin plywood door was a laundry room painted a sickly, outhouse green. The control panels of the washer and dryer were showing above the waterline.

"Do you see the cat?" John asked impatiently.

"No."

I stood motionless in the waist-deep water and listened. It took a while to hear from Henry again. This time he revealed his hiding spot.

"John, I think he's in the washing machine."

I tugged on the door a few more times and got it open far enough for me to fit through. John had put a cage on the counter that I retrieved and carried with me into the laundry room. There was just enough light in the room to see to work. I put the wire cage down on the dryer and opened the door on the top to make it easy, I hoped, to just drop Henry into the cage and slam the lid closed. A sudden meow from Henry made me jump. The adrenaline really started to flow.

I planted myself in front of the washer then and took inventory of the situation. Cage ready. Pole in hand. Gloves on. The only thing missing was a catcher's mask. It would have been nice to have had one should Henry go for my face as he came leaping out of the washer. John was always so well prepared, I'm surprised he hadn't thought to bring one.

Using my right hand, I reached for the lid of the washer. In my left hand I held the catch pole. Then I tried John's line. "Easy, boy. Just hang in there. I'm not going to hurt you."

Henry replied with a meow that I hoped meant, "And I'm not going to hurt you, either."

When I had the lid open an inch, I stopped. The smell that came out of the washer made me want to slam the lid shut and not open it again. Henry had obviously been in the washer for a while, without a proper litter box. It suddenly occurred to me that in addition to being a real mean cat, he was going to be a real messy one too. I'd have to tell John to pack clothespins next time, as well as a catcher's mask.

I made myself lift the lid higher ... and higher. It wasn't until I had it halfway open that I actually saw Henry. I knew it was him because I could see that his black-and-white ear was definitely torn.

He was sitting on the side of the washer closest to me, staring up and blinking. His eyes were unaccustomed to even the sparse light coming into the laundry room. I decided to take advantage of the situation, and I reached in and grabbed the "mean" cat. In one clean swoop I had Henry out of the washer and into the waiting cage.

"I got him," I screamed triumphantly to John. "And I did it without even a scratch."

Henry just sat in his cage meowing, wishing for a bath.

The rain finally quit, and the residents of Alviso started to return to their homes three days later. John and I did no more rescues after we found Henry. In the four days we'd saved eighty-six animals.

As the days passed, people began to show up at the Humane Society to reclaim their pets. The man who owned the German shepherd couldn't believe we'd ever gotten near Bullet. He used him to guard his welding shop.

I stopped at the shelter as often as I could to see the remaining flood animals, and during those visits, Henry and I became good friends. When I'd open the door to the cat room, I'd yell out, "Is there a Henry cat in this room?" and a white paw would shoot out from between the bars of cage number 27 and beckon me to hurry and come pet him. John was right. Henry was anything but a mean cat.

Three weeks after the flood, there were still nine animals left unclaimed. One of those was Henry. Registered letters were sent to the addresses where the animals had been picked up, informing the residents that they had ten days to reclaim their animal or it would be put up for adoption.

At six o'clock on the tenth day, Henry, the real mean cat, went home with me.

5

Growing

From the Alviso flood I took home Henry and Magic. In the months that followed, other animals found their way into my life. On one rainy morning Jennifer and I found a long-haired dachshund wandering in traffic. We tried to find her owners, but eventually Amber became ours. About a year after the disappearance of Paddington and Farina, an abandoned kitten moved into the juniper bushes that lined my driveway. Tigger was a perfect blend of my two lost friends. My family had grown to five, and it was time to move.

My landlord, Larry Fargher, had a duplex for rent in Santa Clara, and Jennifer and I went to see it late one afternoon in April. The neighborhood was welcoming, with trees lining both sides of the street. When we pulled up in front of the duplex, I knew immediately that I liked it. There was a key under the mat, so we let ourselves in. The two-bedroom home had all the extras I had wished for—a fireplace, a dishwasher, and a small yard. We moved in two weeks later.

Settling into our new home was fun. I enjoy decorating, so wallpaper was hung, new curtains were made, and shelves were put up to hold all my favorite antique trinkets. I shopped at garage sales on Saturday mornings and brought home treasures that I could fix and use. After I'd read Jennifer a bedtime story, I'd curl up on the couch in front of the fire with my latest cross-stitch project, which would eventually get framed and hung on the walls.

Warm weekend afternoons were spent planting in the backyard. Jennifer had her own shovel, and she would help me plant purple pansies and pink impatiens. Magic would keep his nose close to whatever we were doing. The backyard belonged to him, and he wanted to make sure any additions we made met with his approval. Amber would lie in the sun, sound asleep, while Henry peered down at us from the roof. He'd learned his lesson in the flood—always stay on high ground. Tigger would brush up against my leg as I knelt in front of the flower beds. She always had to remain nearby. I think she had a real fear of getting lost.

I had been divorced for two years when we moved. In that time, I learned I could be a good parent, even though I was doing it alone. There were days when it was really tough, but I survived them to enjoy all the time Jennifer and I spent together, giggling, coloring, riding bikes, baking, singing, and being silly. Each day we were on our own seemed to make me stronger, more confident of my abilities. I was growing up, something, I was learning, that didn't end when you stopped being a kid.

In the first few weeks we lived on Princeton Way, I became friends with the woman who lived across the street. Her name was Pat Marcum, and she loved animals as much as I did. We both were active at the Humane Society and did crazy things like baking hundreds of dog biscuits in my kitchen one Christmas to raise money for the shelter. Pat was the one who told me about the cats who lived in our neighborhood.

I had noticed them from the beginning. They had once been domesticated, but over time and without an owner to care for them, they had instinctively reverted back to being wild, or feral. On garbage-collection day you'd see them hanging out of the cans that lined the curb. At night you'd hear them fighting. Several cats used my front yard flower beds as a litter box, and on several occasions I almost hit cats as they darted across the road in front of my car. There were lots of them, and they didn't look as if they belonged to anyone.

I felt sorry for these cats. They were all thin, and many had bald spots, torn ears, permanent limps—the scars of a tough life. I'd already seen a number of dead cats in just the short time I'd lived in the neighborhood. I was sure some were victims of contagious cat diseases, since it was unlikely any of these cats had ever been vaccinated. When Jennifer and I took walks, I'd try and approach the cats, but they didn't want my help. They disappeared into the bushes or under houses or climbed onto roofs to remain out of my reach.

When I finally asked Pat about the cats, she told me they were a problem that had been growing for five years. A family that had lived midway down the block moved out of state and chose to leave their cat behind. She was an ordinary orange-and-white cat named Milly who, within weeks of being abandoned, gave birth to a litter of kittens. From that first litter, six more litters were born in the first year.

A lot of the kittens didn't survive. Disease, cars, dogs, injuries, and starvation killed most of them. The others just barely survived. With each litter the cats became less tame. People were starting to be afraid of them, especially the large black-and-white Tom that was nicknamed Devil Cat. He'd startled me several times when I'd come home after dark.

"Hasn't anyone ever tried to catch them?" I asked Pat as we sat on her porch one warm summer evening.

"You can't catch them. They're meaner than hell. They'd tear you apart if you tried." I knew Pat was right, but something had to be done. These cats were suffering, and more would follow if the cycle was not stopped.

Two tiny gray kittens ended the suffering.

It was 3:15 A.M. when I looked at the clock. I'd been asleep until the faint meow of a cat woke me. At first I thought it was Henry or Tigger, but I soon realized the sound was coming from outside my bedroom window. When the meowing didn't go away, I thought I'd better investigate.

I threw on my bathrobe and my Birkenstocks, and slipped out the back door quietly so as not to scare away the cat. The porch light provided just enough light to see. As I walked toward the area below my window, the pitiful meowing persisted. It wasn't until I was right next to the animal that I saw it.

Hidden under the jasmine bush was a tiny gray kitten. It couldn't have been more than six weeks old, and it was in bad shape. Its eyes were sealed shut with mucus. The discharge from its nose made it sneeze repeatedly. Its sides were indented. It was having trouble standing. I expected it wouldn't survive the night.

Instinctively, I went back into the house for a towel. In the garage I located an empty box. When I returned to the backyard to pick up the kitten, he tried to fight me, but he had no energy to spare.

I knew I couldn't bring him in the house because he would be contagious to my cats, so I set the box down by the front door while

I went in the house to change clothes, get Jennifer out of bed, and grab my keys. At 3:55 we were ringing the emergency buzzer at the Humane Society.

"What you doing here at this time of night, Terri?" asked the woman who answered the door.

"I found this kitten in my backyard. I'm afraid he's in pretty bad shape."

The woman peered into the box I was carrying. "Yep, I'm afraid he's not going to make it." In the short time it had taken us to drive to the shelter, the kitten's breathing had become more labored.

We went to the counter and filled out the paperwork I was familiar with. I'd shown hundreds of volunteers how to complete the animal-impound form, but that was during training classes. This time was for real, and I'd have to check the box at the bottom that said, "Euthanize."

With the paperwork completed, the woman carried the box into the back room. By the time I got home, the kitten would be dead.

The following weekend I was doing some weeding in the front yard when I found the second kitten. He, too, was gray, but he'd already died. Maggots wiggled from an open wound on the kitten's side and ants crawled across the matted fur.

"Oh, you poor thing."

I cried as I used my shovel to scoop the kitten into a plastic bag. As I drove to the Humane Society, I remembered the gray cat I'd seen lying in the street a few days earlier. I wondered if she could have been the mother to these kittens. What really bothered me was not knowing whether there were more kittens somewhere, slowly starving to death.

Saturdays are always busy days at the Humane Society. I took the dead kitten in the back way and gave him to one of the kennel attendants. Then I went to fill out an animal-impound form. I checked the "Deceased" box. Two deaths in one week. It was hard to take, especially when I knew how much the two kittens had suffered.

I completed the paperwork and handed it to the woman behind the counter. Before she turned away to drop the paper into the bin marked Dead Animals, I asked if she could help me with one more thing.

"I want to rent a cat trap." I couldn't believe what I had just said.

"Okay. Just fill out this rental agreement, and I'll go get you a trap."

My hand shook and my stomach tightened as I completed the paperwork. It would have been easy to stop, tear up the paper, and tell

4 1

the woman when she returned that I had changed my mind, but in my mind I kept seeing the dead kitten with the ants crawling through its fur. I had to do this.

For the rest of the weekend I trapped feral cats. The first one I caught was a brown tabby that couldn't have been a year old. He hissed while he did somersaults in the trap, trying to find a way out. I had read the brief handout the Humane Society had given me on trapping cats. It said to cover the trap with a towel after you catch the animal. I did, and within a few moments the frightened cat calmed down.

I placed the trapped animal in my car, and he didn't make a sound the entire time it took to drive to the shelter. I even looked under the towel once to make sure he hadn't somehow managed to escape. While I filled out the paperwork, he sat quietly in the trap, staring with frightened eyes at the activity around him.

The Humane Society would hold the cat for seventy-two hours in case someone was looking for him. I suspected no one would come. After the holding period I knew the cat would be euthanized. No one would adopt him. It was hard enough finding homes for cute, cuddly kittens.

I returned the trap Sunday evening with the last cat in it. Devil Cat had tried to resist the temptation to go into the trap, but hunger finally lured him in. In total, I trapped eighteen of the mangiest, sickest, thinnest, meanest cats I'd ever seen. The neighborhood no longer had a problem.

As I drove home from the Humane Society, I cried. My heart was sick, but my mind told me I'd done the right thing. All evening I kept thinking about the cats, asking myself, "What have you done?" At one point I even considered going down to the shelter, bailing them all out, and setting them free. But I knew I couldn't. The cycle had to end.

I was able to do something that weekend that I had never done before. For the first time, I had considered an animal's quality of life and made the tough decision to humanely euthanize that animal to end its suffering. I was no longer that kid lining up stuffed animals on the shelves at Sears—I was growing up.

6

An Exception

Trapping feral cats was not something I had planned on doing. Nor was it something I wanted to do . . . but few people were willing to do it. The Humane Society knew what I'd done in my neighborhood and asked if they could refer other people to me who, too, were troubled by feral cats. It seemed the problem that had existed in my neighborhood for five years was not unique. These cats existed in large numbers throughout Santa Clara County.

It was happening more often. The telephone would ring and it would be another person describing a situation I hated to hear. "We have this terrible problem. We're overrun with cats. We heard you could help."

In the end, it became apparent that these people didn't want to do the job themselves. They wanted me to remove the cats. It wasn't that the callers were cruel or insensitive. Most of these people loved animals. In fact, it was often their concern for animals that had led to the overabundance. A stray would turn up, and they'd feel sorry for it and feed it. They couldn't bring the cat inside, so the feeding dishes got placed outdoors. Within a short time there were a couple more cats showing up to eat. Then the kittens would start to arrive. Before these people knew it, they had more cats than they could handle.

Out of Harm's Way

Most of the cats ended up at the Humane Society, where they cowered in cages for three days and then were euthanized.

Joelle chose to do things differently. She lived in a large, two-story house in a very desirable section of the foothills overlooking the valley. As I drove my car up the long driveway, I wondered how many cats this lady was feeding. Joelle had not given me a lot of information on the phone. I guessed she had the money to feed an entire neighborhood.

"You must be Terri. I'm Joelle. Please come in." The woman who answered the door had a wide smile that made me feel welcome.

It was before most people's breakfast time, on a crisp Saturday morning, yet the woman who greeted me looked as if she were ready for a photo shoot for *Town and Country* magazine. This woman and her house were a perfect match. Both were immaculate.

"How about some coffee? I just brewed a fresh pot," Joelle asked as we stood momentarily in the foyer.

"I'd love some," I replied, and I followed her across the marble-tile floor that led into the warmth of a spacious country kitchen.

"My husband and daughter aren't up yet, so I thought we could chat in here." Joelle busied herself setting out delicate teacups and saucers on the butcher-block table that sat in an alcove on one side of the room.

I moved over to the table and pulled out a wicker chair, cushioned in a lovely floral print. From my seat I could look out onto a well-groomed lawn, dotted with leaves from the stately sycamore and eucalyptus trees whose branches intertwined to create a natural barrier. A redwood deck circled a large swimming pool. It was a lovely place to live.

Joelle set a tray down on the table with a hot pot of coffee, a pitcher of cream, a bowl of sugar cubes, and a plate of miniature danishes precisely arranged.

"Please help yourself."

As I poured my coffee and loaded it with cream and sugar, Joelle sat down across from me. "That is where I feed the cats." She pointed in the direction of the covered patio.

Outdoors, over to one side of the patio I counted four shiny metal feeding dishes and one large plastic dish that I imagined must be for water. Not far from the dishes were three plaid, circular pet beds.

"Is that where you feed the feral cars or your own cats?" I asked.

"I don't have any cats," Joelle responded. "Only George."

"George?"

Joelle nodded. "Let me get him."

She crossed the kitchen and opened a door on the other side of the room. Out bounced a large, black, curly poodle. He wasted no time investigating who this person was who had arrived so early on a Saturday morning. A big kiss with his juicy tongue meant I was welcome to stay. George eventually curled up under the table and dozed as Joelle and I continued to talk.

"So this is where you feed the ferals! Those are some lucky cats." I wished all the cats I'd trapped had been as well cared for.

"Well, when they started to show up here last winter, I just couldn't let them starve. And the nights can get so cold. I always sleep better knowing they have a warm place to curl up." It wouldn't have surprised me if Joelle provided the cats with electric blankets too.

"They were all out there just before you arrived. I gave them breakfast and they took off into the woods. That's where they spend most of their time."

"Joelle, do you mean you fed the cats this morning?"

"Well, yes. They looked so hungry . . ." Joelle dropped her eyes to the table and used a finger to brush some crumbs into a neat pile.

"If they've already eaten, I doubt I'll be able to trap them. They won't go into the trap unless they're hungry." I had told Joelle this when we talked on the phone.

"Look!" Joelle was pointing to the tree line that ran along the back of the property.

Walking purposefully across the grass toward us was a stubby, short-haired, black-and-white-spotted cat. "That's Big Boy."

Big Boy did not fit the description of most ferals. He looked solid and healthy. His coat shone, and there were no notches on his ears or scars across his nose. He carried his tail high and walked toward the house as if he owned it.

"Isn't he adorable?" Joelle was indeed fond of these cats. I began to wonder why, if she cared so much about them, she was having them trapped and taken away.

By now Big Boy was standing in front of one of the shiny silver bowls, finishing up what breakfast he hadn't finished earlier. I was now certain I wasn't going to be doing any trapping that morning.

"Joelle, I'm afraid I'll have to come back another time. If we are ever going to catch these cats, you'll have to give up feeding them for a day at least." I now knew how difficult it would be for Joelle to do this.

"Can you come back next Saturday?" Joelle asked.

"That should be okay," I replied.

"Good, because my vet will be in, and he'll be able to spay and neuter them all."

"You mean you don't want me to take these cats to the Humane Society?" Things were starting to make sense to me now.

"Oh, heavens no! I could never have these cats destroyed. I just want them fixed so I don't end up with more than the six I've got." Joelle's eyes filled up with tears as she looked at me from across the table.

I reached over and put my hand on top of hers. "Joelle, I wish everyone were willing to do what you're doing." Her face relaxed, and we both just smiled.

"I'll be back next Saturday, especially since I know what a great cup of coffee this establishment serves."

Joelle laughed, and then promised, "I won't feed the cats."

Over the next couple of months I managed to trap all of Joelle's cats. Each one was spayed or neutered and checked for feline leukemia. Not one tested positive, which really surprised the veterinarian. Before releasing them back into the yard, each cat got all its shots and a new breakaway collar and reflective tag.

Joelle's population has remained at six. It's too bad that there are so many cats in need of a safe haven. For ferals . . . a good home is even harder to find.

Lexington Fire
Los Gatos, California . . .

The conditions were ideal for a fire.

The parched hillsides that outline the San Francisco Bay area provided the fuel, and the hot gusts of wind would breathe life into the flames. It was a dangerous combination. On Sunday, July 7, 1985 an arsonist lit the match—the only missing ingredient—and ignited a disaster.

It started as a small fire in the mountains above Los Gatos. Fire crews responded quickly and predicted an easy containment and no property damage. It prompted little concern among the residents of this mountainous community as they went about doing what they normally did on a Sunday afternoon. After all, fires, earthquakes, and mud slides were part of the way of life in the mountains, the price one paid for seclusion.

Monday morning, as usual, the mountain dwellers descended from their wooded enclaves for jobs in the valley below as the winds picked up and the temperature climbed into the nineties. By the end of the day, the Lexington Hills fire had been upgraded to a major wildfire.

7

Trying It Again

I must have been a farmer in a former life. It feels good to me to get up with the sun. When Jennifer was still young, I cherished those few minutes I had to myself. I'd peek into her room to see if she was still asleep and then tiptoe down the hall. In the cool quiet of the early morning, I'd sit in the garden and sip my coffee. The view of the Santa Cruz mountains off in the distance was a peaceful respite from the chaos of living in the valley.

On this summer morning, though, something was wrong.

The thick fog that normally iced the range had changed to an alarming, orange haze. Along with it came the distinct smell of smoke.

The phone rang. As I walked into the house, I wondered who would be calling so early.

"Terri, have you heard? There's a major wildfire raging out of control above Los Gatos." It was Warren Brodrick, the executive director of the Humane Society, and he sounded worried.

"They're going to barricade all the access roads off Highway Seventeen. Right now they're trying to keep the flames from jumping the highway. There are animals that are going to need help."

My mind flashed back to Alviso. "What can I do?"

"Any chance you could get a couple days off work?"

"Let me make a call. I'll get back to you."

I'd been at Advanced Micro Devices for a year, and I was due a week's vacation. Frank, my boss, loved dogs so it didn't take much persuasion to get time off on such short notice. By nine o'clock I was on my way to the shelter.

It wasn't until I was in the car that it occurred to me: the Humane Society was asking for *my* help. It made me feel good.

This disaster was occurring in another area that I was familiar with. Highway 17 is the connecting road that twists through the mountains between Santa Clara and Santa Cruz counties. There had been many summer days when Jennifer and I loaded up our car, like half the other people who lived in the valley, and then moved at a snail's pace through the mountains on our way to the beach in Santa Cruz.

The higher elevations had always reminded me of the Pacific Northwest. Densely covered with redwood, pine, and acacia trees, the mountains provided magnificent scenery. I couldn't imagine what the peaks would look like bare, reduced to gray ash. I hoped this was a fire that could be put out quickly.

The Red Cross had set up an evacuation shelter at Los Gatos High School. This tiny community, nestled at the base of the mountains, was a collection of well-preserved examples of Victorian architecture. I was relieved to learn that the town was in no danger.

Humane officers Marty and Ted had been assigned to respond to the fire. I was disappointed that John Fowler had moved out of the area several months earlier. It would have been nice to work with him again, but I knew Marty and Ted, and we would work well together.

When we arrived at Los Gatos High School, it was overrun with people and vehicles. We eased the Humane Society van through a clutter of BMWs, VW vans, and dented Chevy pickups, looking for a place to park. Marty, the younger of the two officers, was a big-city boy from back east with all the patience of a New York minute. His palm lay on the van's horn as he tried to clear a path through the people who walked ahead of us ... oblivious of what was going on around them.

At the far end of the parking lot a noisy crowd stood face-to-face with a lone police officer. We could hear the angry exchanges as we approached. A slim man in a dark blue suit seemed to be speaking for the people. "What do you mean we can't go back to our homes? Why didn't anyone warn us how bad this was going to be?" he demanded of the officer.

"It happened too quickly. There wasn't time," came the irritated response.

A tall woman, who you sensed was used to getting her way, pushed her way to the front of the crowd.

"I *must* get to my house. My two dogs are alone. It won't take me but a moment to grab them." You could hear the desperation in the woman's voice.

"Sorry, ma'am, but no one gets in." The officer's reply angered the crowd even more.

We stood on the perimeter, listening. I leaned closer to Marty and whispered, "Do you think we can get that lady's dogs?"

"I don't know if they'll let us in, either. But I think it's time I find out." Marty moved forward into the middle of the angry group.

The authorities had to let us in—otherwise, who would save the animals?

The officer was once again trying to bring order to the crowd. "Listen! Do you hear me?" He was practically hollering to be heard above the noisy voices. "I wish I could let you in, especially those of you with animals, but it's not safe up there. You'll have to wait until this thing burns itself out."

Everyone started speaking at once. There was no calming them down. These people were angry, and understandably so. I couldn't imagine what I'd do if someone told me I couldn't rescue my animals. I suppose I'd try to sneak into the area or offer them money or just run my car through the roadblock, even though I'd probably get arrested—if they caught me.

Marty had worked his way up alongside the officer. I stood back and watched the two of them talk for a few minutes. Then the policeman walked over to his patrol car and called someone on the radio. He didn't talk long. When he finished, he turned to Marty and they talked a couple of minutes longer. The smile on Marty's face gave me hope that we had gotten the permission we needed. Marty put his hand out and shook the officer's hand. As he turned and looked to where Ted and I were standing, he gave us a thumbs-up.

"We must be going in, Ted." I was thrilled and frightened all at the same time.

It was now Marty who tried to get the crowd's attention. "Folks, can you listen up?" Marty's deep voice caught the people's attention. "I'm with the Humane Society of Santa Clara Valley. We're here to help people who need to have their animals rescued."

"Well, it's about time someone wants to help us." It was the dark-blue-suited man who spoke.

"Now, I can't promise you that we can save everyone's animals, but we'll certainly try," Marty said. The police officer looked relieved to have a break from the shouting and hollering.

"What I want you to do is write down your name, address, and what animals you want us to look for, and then give that information to the two people standing over there." Marty pointed at Ted and me. "They'll collect the information."

Some of the women started rummaging through their purses, while men searched their pockets for something to write with. Others just yelled out the information. Ted and I were overwhelmed.

"Commanche Trail. Third house in. We have three cats, two mutts, and a bluetick hound."

"I'm on Shady Lane, fourth up from the mailbox. There's a big oak tree in the front yard. Can't miss it. My mule should be staked out next to it."

"My Arabians are in my barn . . ." The man broke into tears.

"I'm down the road from the old schoolhouse. You'll see my sheep in the front pasture."

Marty took over crowd-control again like a boot-camp sergeant. "Hold on, everybody. We're not going to get anything accomplished this way. If you don't hand us, on a piece of paper, the information I asked for, *we will not* be able to save your animals." This time they seemed to understand.

"Why are there only three of you?" It was the dark-suited man again.

" 'Cause that's all we've got," Marty replied. You could tell he was becoming annoyed with this guy.

"You mean with all the money the government gives your agency, they can only afford to hire three of you?" It was a mean remark, and he'd directed it at the wrong person.

Marty was not the person to attack. Two steps and he was in the man's face.

"Let me give you some information, mister," Marty growled. "The government doesn't give us one bloody cent. We operate solely on the generosity of people. Obviously you've never contributed, yet now you're asking for our help."

"Let him alone, Mike," someone yelled.

"Yeah, let the man do his job."

The dark-suit backed down.

During our momentary reprieve, I felt a tug on my shirtsleeve. Standing next to me was a towheaded youngster about five years old. He stared up at me with big blue eyes.

"Lady, would you save my frog?" he asked in a soft voice.

I squatted down to his level. "What's your frog's name?"

"Kermit. I found him in the creek behind our house."

A woman approached and put her hands on the small boy's shoulders. "If you could get the frog, you'd sure make my son happy. We live at 485 Sunny Brook."

"I promise I'll try."

We were interrupted by the screaming urgency of a car horn. An ash-covered Chevy Suburban careened across the parking lot. The crowd moved backward to get out of the way of the vehicle. It screeched to a stop next to our van. A graying, middle-aged man jumped out, leaving the engine still running.

"I'm a vet," he said quickly. "I got most of the animals out of my clinic." You could see the crowded assortment of caged dogs, cats, and birds that filled his car.

"But I didn't have room for the rabbits I was boarding. The fire's close. There's no time to waste. I'm at the top of Summit Road. Let's go."

"I'm afraid I can't let you back up there," the police officer reinstated his authority. "Give these people the information, and they can try and get the rabbits out."

"I know where your place is. Did you leave it unlocked?" Marty sensed the urgency of the situation.

"Yeah." The vet looked exhausted.

"Terri, you come with me. Ted, you stay here and collect the rescue information." Marty reacted like a veteran, even though this was his first disaster.

The last thing I heard before I climbed into the van was that familiar voice, "Don't forget my frog, lady."

As we sped southwest toward the vet clinic, we could see the inferno roaring heavenward, smothering the midmorning sky with smoke and ash. The sun was a large, eerie orange ball, staring down at the destruction below. I'd never been this close to a fire, but it didn't take experience to know this was a bad one. The July heat, fifty-plus-mile-per-hour winds, and the steep terrain were going to make fighting it difficult.

We turned off Highway 17 and started up Summit Road. The officer at the roadblock waved us through. Along each side of the road were fire trucks waiting to be dispatched. They'd come from all parts of northern California, Oregon, and as far away as Washington. We passed fire crews of men and women working on the hillsides with chainsaws and shovels in a feverish race to cut firebreaks against the oncoming firestorm.

The fire was fueled, in part, by the sap from the manzanita bushes. The gelatinous residue fed the greedy fire, causing huge pine trees to explode like roman candles. The smell of the burning pine brought back memories of campfires I'd enjoyed on family camping trips. The *snap, crackle, pop* of the burning forest sounded like a nightmarish cereal commercial.

We reached the clinic . . . but not before the fire.

The back roof of the stucco building had ignited. Flames leaped three feet into the air. The hillside behind the clinic was a wall of flames. There wasn't a fire crew in sight.

Marty didn't hesitate. He roared toward the clinic, with his foot to the gas pedal. The gravel spewed away from beneath our tires as we screeched to a halt a few feet from the front entrance. We grabbed our bandannas, slapped them over our nose and mouth, and hit the ground running.

The heat was unbearable. My eyes stung. It was hard to breath. Burning embers fell around us like fireworks on the Fourth of July. And I had thought the Alviso flood had been dangerous.

Marty was peering through the front window of the clinic. Smoke was starting to seep into the waiting area. The vet had told us the rabbits were in a room just to the left of the front door.

"Do you think we should go in?" I asked.

"Yeah, I think we still have enough time to get at least some of the rabbits out."

I just prayed we weren't too late. If the rabbits had already died, it would be from the smoke, not the fire. Either way . . . it's a horrible death.

"Why don't you stay here?" Marty suggested. I appreciated his concern, but I couldn't let him go in alone.

"No, I'm coming. Four hands can grab a lot more rabbits than two."

Marty turned the doorknob and used his foot to push open the door. Smoke drifted out through the opening, but it wasn't bad yet.

"We need to stay low to the ground," Marty said as he took the lead.

The flames were brutally tearing apart the back part of the clinic

as we sneaked in the front. I had never realized how loud a fire is.
We could hear boards snapping, windows exploding, and the floor
creaking. Above it all was a sinister-sounding whistle. I wanted to
cover my ears.

The door to the side room was open a crack. Marty felt the door
before he pushed it open. It was warm. Slowly he shoved it open
the rest of the way. I couldn't wait. I peered over his shoulder into
the room.

There they were, eight white rabbits, all staring at us with their big
pink eyes.

The vet had left the cages open. He didn't want to leave the rabbits
confined just in case an escape route opened up. None of the bunnies
had fled.

"Can you carry four?" Marty asked as he started to grab the two
rabbits closest to him.

"Sure." After swimming with Magic through the water in Alviso,
this would be easy.

A loud crashing sound from the back of the clinic made us realize
we'd better grab the rabbits and get out of there fast. I got the four in
the bottom row of cages and Marty got the ones on top. With an
armful of bunnies, we retraced our steps out through the door and
into the lobby. In just the short time we'd been in the building there
was a lot more smoke.

"Move it," Marty screamed.

I didn't hesitate. We came running out of the building, the eight
rabbits crunched in our arms, their back legs dangling and tiny pink
noses wiggling. Marty opened the back door of the van and lifted the
lids on two carriers. They weren't real big, but there wasn't time to
find larger accommodations. We jammed the rabbits into the cages
the way a magician would stuff them into his magic hat.

We slammed the back door and hurried to climb into the van. What
we saw ahead of us made us stop. The entire clinic was now on fire—
including the lobby and the room off to the left.

"These rabbits were meant to live," I said. I couldn't believe how
close we'd come to losing them all.

As we cleared the pebbled parking lot, the ominous crack of burning wood thundered behind us. We pulled out on the street and
stopped. A fire truck barreled into the driveway at the other end of
the parking lot. They were too late. We watched as the clinic collapsed into the inferno that consumed it.

Out of Harm's Way

Marty and I were quiet as we drove back down the hill. I repeatedly dampened our bandannas with water from a thermos I'd brought with me. We mopped our faces again and again in a desperate effort to cool our reddened flesh. We'd been lucky. The rabbits had been even luckier.

We rescued thirty-five animals that day . . . including Kermit.

8

Pony Express

Tuesday morning we stopped first at the command center in Vasona Park to get an update on the fire. It was hardly daybreak when we arrived, but the hill dwellers had beaten us. They clustered around the makeshift bulletin board that listed the homes that had burned. The fire had been merciless during the night.

The blaze was still raging out of control, burning across the land faster than a charging bull. Fifteen thousand acres had already been destroyed. Fire crews from all over the western United States had been summoned to duty. We were running out of time. The fire was spreading to more heavily populated areas of the hillside, and we could be told at any time that it was too dangerous to try to save more animals. This might be our last chance to save any more.

We sat in on the center's morning briefing under a large tent and drank strong coffee. A weary fire captain with a soot-streaked face reported the fire was only twenty percent contained. He couldn't tell us when total containment might come.

It was a nasty fire, and some of those fighting it were being pulled off the front lines after developing rashes in their throats and nostrils from breathing smoke mixed with the oil from burning poison oak. We were advised to wear bandannas at all times in the fire area. There was no question I'd wear mine. I'd gotten into some poison oak once, and it was bad enough just having it on my arm. I couldn't imagine having it in my throat.

After the briefing, Marty, Ted, and I looked through the remaining rescue requests we had on our clipboards. There were still a lot of animals up in those hills—dogs, horses, pigs, cats, cows, parrots, and an iguana. I passed the iguana on to Marty. I don't do lizards, especially ones that are longer than my arm.

The three of us divided up the requests and split up so we could try to get all the animals out before the end of the day. In addition to being threatened by the fire, these critters would be starting to get hungry and thirsty.

The conditions had worsened by midmorning. The sun was blotted out by a thick haze of ash. My headlights directed me through a frightening fog. Visibility was reduced to several hundred feet, sometimes less. The steep roads and blind curves had become increasingly more difficult to navigate. I kept my fingers crossed that I wouldn't meet a fire truck on one of the narrow roads. If I did, I'd have no choice but to back down the winding road—something I really didn't want to have to try with the Humane Society's oversized van.

By noon I was headed back down toward the valley. I'd stopped at all the places on my morning list, and the van was full with six large dogs, ten cats, a goat, and a bird who knew every cussword in the book.

Accustomed now to scanning the terrain for anything alive, I slowed down when a cloud of dust caught my attention. The tiny whirlwind was spewing dust across what was left of a burned vineyard.

What is that? An injured animal? I decided I'd better stop and investigate.

The vineyard was about an acre of now-open field dotted with the stalks of once-fruitful plants. It saddened me to see how a fire can rage through and reduce vines and trees to mere blackened skeletons of what they once were.

A six-inch coating of ash blanketed the field, and near its center the unknown disturbance still churned. As I approached the commotion, I realized there was a sound accompanying it, a muted cooing song.

Just then, from the dust arose a large covey of quails. There must have been fifty of them twittering and chattering to each other, alarmed by my presence. As they disappeared into the neighboring orchard of burned pear trees, I remembered, *Birds clean themselves by rolling in dirt—these guys are having a great time.* I smiled as I walked back to the van, relieved that this was one group of mountain dwellers that didn't need rescuing.

I was nearing Highway 17 when I came across an animal that did need my help, though. The smoke hung closer to the ground here, making it more difficult to see. Even though visibility was limited, there was no missing the Mercedes four-door sedan, the driver, and the pony.

My foot hit the brakes about the same time the man saw me. He was a portly fellow with a red face, which lit up with relief when he saw me. "You're just the person I need," he exclaimed as I approached.

His eyes were kind and blue, with the mischief of a leprechaun lurking in them. "This animal should fit fine in that van of yours, young lady," he said.

"Wait a sec. How did you get up here?" I questioned. We'd been told all the residents had been evacuated.

"I just flew through the air with the greatest of ease," he began in the lilting accent of old Ireland.

I was too tired for jokes. "I mean it," I interrupted. "You're not supposed to be up here. It's too dangerous."

"Then why are you here?"

"Someone had to save the animals," I replied.

The crinkles smoothed out from the corners of his eyes, and a pained expression took over his jolly countenance.

"Okay, then, how about saving this one?" He looped his hand one more time through the lead attached to the Shetland pony standing by his side.

"I'm a doctor with a bad back. It's been giving me a bit of a problem here lately, so I was laid up in bed yesterday. Today, I decided it was time to leave."

"You mean you never evacuated?"

"The lady's quick, wouldn't you say?" The question was directed to the pony.

It amazed me that this man and his pony didn't seem to realize the seriousness of the situation. here we were in the middle of a fire that had already earned the reputation of being one of the most destructive to hit this area, yet the Irishman didn't even seem concerned. I couldn't imagine he didn't hear the drone of the water-dropping helicopters overhead or the urgent shouts from the fire-fighters who were working on the hillsides around us.

"What matters is we have to get you, and your pony, out of here." There was no more time for idle chitchat.

"This isn't my pony."

"Whose is it?" I asked.

"I have no idea. I just found it strolling along the road, dragging this rope behind it. I couldn't leave it here to get burned alive." The man stroked the pony's mane as he talked. "I'm sure you agree."

"I can't put him in my van. It's full of animals." I knew I was already way over my limit. With the uncertainty about how many more trips I'd be able to make into the hills, I'd crammed in as many animals as I could. My four-wheeled "Noah's Ark" was so full that I had had no other place to put the cursing parrot than on my steering wheel. Besides, I didn't think the Irish doctor and I could lift the pony into the van, especially with his bad back.

I silently explored our options . . . and we didn't have many.

The doc must have noticed my frustration, because his appearance changed. With some difficulty he stood up straight, brushed some ash from his shirt, and looked right at me.

"How about if I stay here with the pony while you go and unload the animals you already have in the van? Maybe then someone could come back with you and help us load the pony."

It was a plan that might have worked under normal circumstances, but it was too risky to use. The wind had picked up in the last hour, and for the first time I could see flames on the hillside above us. The fire had changed directions again. I was beginning to understand how unpredictable fires are and how fast they can move. I was afraid that if I left the man and pony behind, they wouldn't be there when I got back.

"No, I don't think there's enough time for me to leave and come back. The fire is too close. . . . I know." Why hadn't I thought of this sooner? "I can take the pony and lead him alongside the van, at least down to Highway 17."

"Nope, won't work. I already tried that. The sound of my car spooked him. I was afraid he'd struggle loose and I wouldn't catch him again."

I was beginning to fear we'd have to leave the pony behind and hope I'd be able to return later and find him. I couldn't tie him up or confine him. If the fire reached this area, I'd want him to be able to escape the flames.

"Well, I think there is only one thing we can do. We'll put him in my car," the doc said.

"What?"

"Yeah. With your help, I think we can get him into the backseat."

I looked inside the immaculate Mercedes. It was upholstered in luxurious taupe-colored leather. There was not a touch of imperfection in this vehicle. I doubted a child had ever ridden in the car, let alone a small pony.

"Are you serious?"

"Very much so. I believe this pony belongs to a child, and right now that child is probably crying his eyes out, thinking his pony is lost or dead. A special pony is hard to replace. I know—I had one. Cars are a dime a dozen."

I wanted to hug the Irish doctor . . . but there wasn't time. The fire had dropped down over the ridge and was headed directly toward us.

"Okay, let's give it a try." I walked over to the sedan and opened both of the back doors. The doc had led the pony to the road-side door, where he waited for instructions.

"Give me the lead, and you get on the other side of the car. I'll hand you the rope, and when I tell you to—pull. At the same time I'll be pushing." It was the best plan I could come up with, considering I'd never even loaded a pony into a horse trailer, let alone a Mercedes.

Our first attempt was unsuccessful. The pony got right up against the doorframe, but wouldn't step up into the car. So, I instituted plan B, another ad lib.

With the doc holding on firmly to the rope, I bent down and, one by one, picked up the pony's front legs and placed them in the car. I suspected the pony had never been loaded into a Mercedes before, and he, too, needed to be shown what the plan was.

With both feet in the car, I got behind the pony, and when I gave Doc the signal, he pulled and I pushed, and the pony actually moved . . . all the way into the car. Doc quickly closed the other door, and I jumped out of the way to close mine. He was in.

"We did it," I screamed above the roar of the helicopter that was now hovering nearby dropping water on the approaching flames. "I can't believe it. We actually did it." All three of us were surprised.

"Let's get out of here now," the doc yelled. "Or we'll end up getting fried."

"I want to thank you," I said. "You're quite a guy."

Out of Harm's Way

In his usual style, the doc replied, "You do what you have to do. And right now we have to get that scrunched-up pony out of here."

"Yeah," I said as I turned.

Before I climbed into the van, the doc had the last word, "Hey, you forgot to put the seat belt on the pony."

Our plan wasn't perfect . . . but the pony survived.

9

Priorities

A grueling ten hours had passed since I'd arrived at Vasona Park that morning. With a few hours of daylight left, and my van empty of rescued animals, I decided to make one last check at the Red Cross shelter. No one had yet told us that we couldn't go back for more animals.

A woman ran up to my van before I'd even parked. She appeared to be in her mid-thirties, with a smooth, blonde pageboy that framed wide, anxious eyes. I knew she was searching for a pet.

She grasped the bottom of my window frame as I stopped the van and blurted out, "I gave my address to one of your colleagues yesterday, but I haven't heard from anyone."

"I take it you need an animal rescued?"

"Yes. My kitten. She's only eight weeks old. The poor thing must be so . . . frightened." Her voice broke as she spoke.

I'd completed all the rescues on my clipboard, so I knew I didn't have the paperwork on this one. It had been hours since I'd seen Marty and Ted, so I wasn't sure how many more rescues they had left. Since I had the time, I decided to follow up on this one.

"Why don't you give me the information again, and I'll see if I can find your kitten," I told the woman as I pulled a blank piece of paper from my notebook.

"Where's your house?"

"Aldecroft Heights. A fireman told me early this morning there were still some houses that hadn't burned."

I could see the hope in her face. But I knew that when the wind changed that afternoon, the fire had headed back in the direction of the Heights . . . probably to burn what was left.

"My house isn't very big. You could search it in less than five minutes. The kitten likes to lie on the rug in my sewing room . . . especially when I'm in there working." The recollection brought more tears to the woman's eyes.

Her expression was a mirror image of those of all the other displaced people with whom I'd had contact in the past two days. I wanted so much to help them, to ease the anguish and frustration. I knew reuniting them with their animals helped, but it just didn't seem to be enough.

"What's the quickest way to your place?" I asked, looking at my map.

The woman used her finger to point out the best route. She directed me to go past Lexington Reservoir and then left onto Old Santa Cruz Highway. Another left at the dead end. As she gave me directions, I asked for landmarks. By now a lot of the street signs had melted.

"Okay. I think I have what I need," I said, attaching the paper to my clipboard. "Oh, one last thing. What's your name?"

"April. April Larkin."

I followed April's directions without getting lost. Old Santa Cruz Highway cut through the devastation. The fire had left nothing untouched. Fire crews were working to keep isolated hot spots from flaring up again. It seemed odd how much the landscape reminded me of winter. The burned trees mimicked the naked ones of December, and the ground looked as if it'd just received a dusting of dirty snow. The fierce heat reminded me it was still July.

As I got closer to Aldercroft Heights I could see that the homes I'd passed the day before were now gone. All that remained standing were the chimneys. From one of the houses, I'd picked up two elderly golden retrievers, Mac and Jake. The couple who owned them warned me that Mac would have baggage. Sure enough. He met me in the driveway carrying his favorite tree limb.

The Aldercroft Heights sign was gone when I reached the secluded neighborhood. The fire spared nothing. As I wound up the steep hillside, my gut told me what I'd find. There was no way April's kitten could have survived this inferno.

6 4

April had told me her house was exactly one mile up from the horseshoe curve. I watched my odometer. Eight-tenths. Nine-tenths. I was getting close. Too close. What I saw made me want to close my eyes. I stopped the van and covered my mouth with my hands. I wanted to scream.

The house was gone.

I leaned my head back against the car seat and stared at the ceiling. Tears ran down my cheeks. This was hard . . . really hard.

I don't know how long I sat there. But before I left, there was something I knew I had to do. I'd have to look for the kitten. Unfortunately, there wouldn't be a live kitten to place in April's arms. She had told me she'd wait at the Red Cross shelter until I returned. How could I tell her the kitten had died, much less that her whole house was gone?

Before I got out of the van, I grabbed the shovel from behind the seat and I stuffed a plastic bag in my back pocket. (I'd never seen a burned animal before.) I didn't know what to expect. I knew I didn't want April to see whatever remained of the kitten when she returned. I had to find it and bury it. I forced myself forward.

Through my boots I could feel the heat from the blanket of ash as I wandered through what had once been a home. I used my shovel to poke my way through the rubble. There was so little left, a teacup handle, a twisted metal frame, a chipped ceramic vase—but no kitten. My search was futile.

I was on my way back to the van when I heard something. I stopped, but all I recognized was the sound of an approaching helicopter and the persistent wind. After the helicopter passed over, I remained by the van, listening. Hoping. Was it a kitten I'd heard? I suspected not. It had to have been my wish for a miracle that teased my ears.

No! I was wrong. Somewhere nearby there *was* a cat, crying for help.

About then the helicopter was passing overhead on its return trip to scoop more water out of Lexington Reservoir to douse the southern flank of the fire.

"Get out of here! Move!" I screamed at the noisy copter. "Move!"

It seemed an eternity before it was quiet enough to be able to hear the faint meow again.

"Here, kitty! kitty! kitty!" I called frantically before the helicopter returned.

"Please, where are you?" I moved in no specific direction, hoping to hear again the meow that would lead me to the cat.

There it was . . .

The cry for help was coming from the dried-up creek bed across the road. I dropped my shovel and ran, tripping over blackened bricks and mutilated pieces of metal. At the charred edge of the creek I stood still and listened. My heart was beating fast and my hands were shaking.

"Here, kitty! kitty! kitty!"

"Meoooow."

Across the creek was the wasted remains of an aluminum ladder lying almost submerged in ash. The sound had come from there.

When I reached the ladder, I gasped. There, huddled next to the first rung, was the tiniest soot-covered kitten I'd ever seen. With the bluest of eyes, it looked up at me and meowed.

"Oh, you poor thing. Come here." I reached down and carefully picked up the kitten. Holding it in midair in front of me, I saw that its whiskers were singed and its paws burnt . . . but she was alive.

"Is your mom going to be glad to see you," I said, as I cuddled the kitten in my arms. Several times I moved her close enough to kiss her dirty pink nose. I could feel her fur dry my tears. The kitten continued to meow, but it was a relieved meow. She knew she was safe.

When I got into the van, I grabbed an extra bandanna and poured some water on it. I laid the damp cloth across my lap and placed the kitten on it. Immediately she started to lick the bandanna, sucking up some of the moisture. It had been three days since she'd had anything to drink or eat. I waited to feed her, not sure how much I should offer her.

As we descended from the Heights, the kitten began to purr. I stroked her forehead and tiny blotches of white fur began to appear through the black coating. She had started to groom herself, but I tried to discourage her. Ingesting that much soot couldn't be good for her. Before we reached Highway 17, the kitten was asleep.

As I got closer to the Red Cross shelter, I began to practice how I was going to tell April about her house. How do you break that kind of news to someone? Do you just come right out and say, "Your house burned. There's nothing left." This was something I'd certainly never expected would be a part of rescuing animals.

April was waiting, as promised. As she ran to my van, I held the kitten up so she could see it, and for a while I forgot the house in Aldercroft Heights. I just wanted to savor the joy of this reunion.

"Agatha!" she screamed. "Agatha!"

April was hysterical when I handed the kitten to her through my open window. She couldn't talk. Instead she just laughed and cried, and held the kitten tightly against her chest. Agatha just purred.

As all this went on, I got out of the van and waited for the inevitable question. When April began to calm down, I decided it was time to tell her.

"I can't tell you how happy I am that I found Agatha," I said, then hesitated. The next words were going to be the hard ones. "I just wish there might've been some way I could have saved your home too."

"It's gone'?"

I nodded. "I'm so sorry, April. There's nothing left." I couldn't hold back my tears.

April Larkin freed an arm and pulled me toward her.

"You saved what was important," she whispered. "You saved what was important."

Her words still echo in my heart.

Important Associations

10

Santa Clara University

Santa Clara University is considered one of the finest educational institutions in the United States. For me, it had become a peaceful oasis nestled in the heart of Silicon Valley.

The campus wasn't far from our duplex. On occasion, when the summer heat made our home unbearable, Jennifer and I would wander its shady grounds, admiring the Spanish-influenced architecture and the fragrant, well-tended rose gardens that graced the grounds with hues of scarlet, yellow, peach, and lavender. More than once I'd thought how nice it would be if my daughter could attend this school and what a wonderful place to be employed.

In 1986 I was working in Palo Alto. The strain of an hour-and-half-long daily commute prompted me to read the Sunday classifieds every weekend. Finally one day I saw an ad that led me to update my résumé and put it in the mail.

An interview followed two weeks later with the acting director of Human Resources at Santa Clara University.

The appearance of the woman who ushered me into her office epitomized that of today's successful businesswoman. Jeanne Greene stood tall and gave the impression of a woman who'd found her style and was comfortable with it.

After I was seated, she left to get us both coffee. While she was gone, I glanced around the office. I think you can tell a lot about a person from her office. This lady was neat and organized.

Jeanne returned a few moments later with a cup of coffee for each of us. We began the interview as I stirred cream and sugar into my cup.

My employment history was covered before we finished our first cups of coffee. She probed my reasons for looking for a new job, and I held nothing back. I enjoy interviews, especially when there can be an open exchange of information on both sides.

"Is there anything you'd like to ask me?" Jeanne said when I'd finished answering her questions.

"Would you mind my asking why your title is acting director?" I'd already sensed this would be a woman I'd like to work with. I hoped she wasn't planning to leave soon.

"When the position of HR director became vacant some time ago, I was moved into this position on an interim basis. We are about to begin a search for someone to fill the position, and I will be submitting my résumé for consideration." I was glad to hear that.

I asked Jeanne some more specific questions about the job, and the more she told me, the more I wanted the position. It sounded perfect.

There was one question I had left for last. This one could eliminate me from further consideration for the position, but I'd made up my mind that I wanted it out in the open.

"In my free time I volunteer at the Humane Society here in Santa Clara," I said. "My job is to train new volunteers before they begin working in the shelter." I thought it might help to mention this. Jeanne had told me the Human Resource assistant helped with new-employee orientations.

"In addition to training volunteers, I also rescue animals during disasters. I helped during the Alviso flood and the Lexington Hills fire." I continued to ease toward the big question.

"I remember seeing pictures on TV. It must have been horrible for the animals," Jeanne sympathized.

"It was. That's why I want to be able to continue to help."

Jeanne just nodded.

"During those disasters, I used my vacation time. If I was offered this position, would I be able to save up vacation and sick time to be used for this purpose?" I waited for a response, almost afraid to breathe.

Jeanne put down the pen that she had been using to make notes and rested her elbows on the edge of her desk. "This means a lot to you doesn't it?"

It was my turn to nod.

"I'm fond of animals myself," she said slowly. "I admire your dedication, and it would be unfair not to reward it. As long as your requests for time off don't interfere with your ability to meet the commitments of this job, I don't see why it would be a problem."

What a relief. Now I just prayed I'd be offered the job. . . .

Just before Thanksgiving, I started to work at Santa Clara University. As Human Resource assistant, I recruited for staff positions on campus, so I quickly became acquainted with the people at the university. The job was everything I'd expected and more.

Over Christmas break I really moved in. With Jeanne's permission I used the time to redecorate my office. In two days I transformed it from a sterile, white-walled, fluorescent-lit, standard interior, to a room people wanted to walk into. I expected to keep this job for a very long time, and I wanted my space to feel comfortable for me too.

Jeanne was pleased with the results. She loved the grass-cloth wallpaper I applied on one wall, the table lamp that lent a soft glow to the room, and the pictures and baskets that blended well with the books on my shelves. She teased that the only thing missing was a dog curled up beside my desk.

"Don't tempt me," was my reply.

Jeanne supported my animal activities and became a good friend. She covered for me when there was an animal emergency and on several occasions overlooked animals I'd brought into work. There was the orphaned kitten that needed feeding every couple of hours and the disabled pigeon I found on campus one afternoon and kept in the department bathroom until I could get him to the wildlife center. At night, when I sometimes worked late, she didn't mind me running home and getting Amber, who by now was getting old, and who, I knew, would not be with me much longer.

This was a very happy time in my life. It seemed I had everything I wanted, but it was another advertisement in the *San Jose Mercury News* that would bring even greater fulfillment to my life . . . more than I could have ever imagined possible.

11

United Animal Nations

In 1988 my involvement with animals was still not far reaching. I continued to put in long hours at the Humane Society, but something kept making me feel I had to do more. I couldn't get out of my mind what I'd seen and felt during the Alviso flood and the Lexington fire. Dead animals leave a lasting impression.

I kept reminding the administrative staff at the Humane Society that a disaster plan should be written. We hadn't had one during the flood or the fire and our response time and ability to save the lives of more animals was therefore reduced. John, Marty, Ted, and I had learned a lot. That information needed to be documented so that the mistakes we made would not be repeated.

The day-to-day emergencies at the Humane Society kept a plan from being written, even though the administrators agreed one was needed. In trying to get something down on paper, I wrote to some of the national animal organizations, thinking they would have some guidelines I could follow. They seemed a logical resource. After all, they exist to help animals, and it seemed to me that animals needed a lot of help during disasters.

"No. We have no printed materials we can send you," I was told again and again.

"No. It's not on our agenda to implement a disaster program at this time," was the official word from one of the organizations.

Another organization said, "No. We don't have anything like that, but if you get something written, we'd like to see it."

As I reached one dead end after another, I began to feel that no one cared what happened to the animals during disasters. Was it naive to believe that animals deserved better? I had just about given up hope when I saw an advertisement in the *San Jose Mercury News*.

The bold black letters were what caught my attention: **Fire. Quake. Flood.** Directly underneath were four pictures of a horse, lamb, dog, and cat with the information that each year in America, untold thousands of dependent animals suffer during disasters. Could this organization, which I'd never heard of, be the one to help? It was time to write another letter. I hoped the response I received this time would be different.

I sent my letter to Belton Mouras, president of United Animal Nations, in Sacramento. In the letter I told him of my experiences during the flood and fire and my wish to continue helping animals during disasters. I hoped he could provide me with some information on how my local Humane Society could be better prepared too. After all, it was July again, and the memories of the Lexington fire served to remind me that fires can happen at any time. I feared we were no better prepared than we'd been two years before.

Belton's reply was in the formal tone of an ex-military man. He would be pleased to talk with me, the letter said.

We arranged to meet at a restaurant halfway between us, The Ol' Hoosier Inn, in Stockton.

My hunch about Mr. Mouras had been correct. He strode into the restaurant with the straight-backed, measured strides of a man who'd seen a lot of years in the military. After recognizing each other, we shook hands and chatted as the hostess showed us to our table.

Over lunch Belton told me he'd been in the animal movement since 1960 and had been the founder and president of the Animal Protection Institute, which, too, was based in Sacramento. In 1987 the board of directors at API had wanted Belton to serve for only another year, he believed because of his age. After months of negotiations his contract expired and he left and founded United Animal Nations.

"I wasn't ready to go pick grave sites yet," he snorted.

I agreed with him. Belton carried his sixty-odd years well.

"Deanna, Deb, Vernon, Cathy, and Scott resigned over the next few months from API and came to work for UAN," he explained. "I put a great value on loyalty."

I was starting to get the picture. United Animal Nations was still in its infancy. Belton didn't have to explain that there wasn't a lot of money. I knew how tough it was to attract new members, who bring with them the donations. I didn't have money to give . . . but I had my time.

"Your ad stated you needed help," I said as the waitress cleared away our dessert plates. "I can't contribute money, but maybe I could help with the Emergency Animal Rescue Service Program and share whatever experience I've gained from the two disasters I've been through."

Belton took off his glasses and cleaned them with his napkin. He cleared his throat before he spoke again.

I learned the Emergency Animal Rescue Service Program was Belton's idea. He, too, had recognized that not enough was being done to help animals when fires, floods, earthquakes, or other natural or man-made disasters struck. The idea for the program existed, but the funding had not yet been established.

"We're still a young organization, so it's tough getting support," Belton explained.

"I guessed that."

"We can't afford to hire someone to run the EARS Program right now, even though we sure could use someone with your qualifications." As he spoke, he straightened his back against the red leather seat.

I leaned forward. "Belton, I'm not looking to get paid. I just want to help in any way that I can, to make sure something gets done to guarantee animals receive the help they need during disasters. I think the Emergency Animal Rescue Service Program can do that."

Extending his hand, Belton leaned forward. "Well, I think we just got our first EARS volunteer."

In August 1988 Yellowstone National Park was experiencing the largest wildfire it had seen in years. Belton called and asked if I was available to go.

"We're getting conflicting reports on the fire. Members are calling to find out what's happening to the wildlife. We need someone there who can find out what's going on."

It was the first time I had to ask Jeanne for time off to go to a disaster. She responded by covering all my appointments for the week

I was in Yellowstone. Then in October of that same year, UAN sent me to Barrow, Alaska, when the three gray whales got trapped in the ice floe. Jeanne again covered for me at work, and my parents filled in at home, while I spent five days observing how people and organizations who have differing opinions on issues *can* work together toward a common goal.

After each disaster I returned to my job at the university. Jeanne and other coworkers would listen for hours as I shared my adventures.

"What you're doing is what this university expects its students to do," Jeanne told me one evening after everyone else had gone home. "You found your passion and are doing something with it to make a difference."

When I drove home that evening, I realized, I think for the first time, how fortunate I was.

Two weeks later Jeanne had some sad news. Her husband's employer was transferring him to New Jersey. She would be gone in a month.

I was devastated. Losing Jeanne was going to be especially difficult. She had become my confidant, my supporter, my backup. I often relied on her soft words of advice. I would truly miss her.

Just before Christmas, the university hired a new director of Human Resources. From the beginning she made it quite clear that she wanted things done her way. Changes were to be expected. As they say, "A new broom sweeps clean."

But over the next few months tensions started to develop. Jeanne had encouraged her staff to treat people like individuals. The new operating procedures were impersonal. They contradicted everything I believe in. I couldn't treat people the way my new supervisor wanted me to. I knew something had to change.

Toward the end of February I was using my lunch hours to work on a hiring report the new director had requested. I was at my computer when I heard the click of the wall light switch in my office. What followed was the unexpected brightness of the overhead fluorescent light that hadn't been used since my first month at the university.

The director stood in my doorway. Her forefinger stabbed the air as she spoke. "From now on I want these lights on. This is a workplace, not your living room."

In shock, I looked at the woman glaring at me from across the room. I thought about all her other barked remarks, the slights, and the barely disguised disapproval of the last few months. I was fed up with her intimidation.

Without saying a word, I stood up and marched over to the light switch and turned the light off. Then I said, in the toughest voice I could conjure up, "This is my office and the overhead lights *will* remain off."

"Well, it won't be your office for much longer if your attitude doesn't change," and with that the director turned and walked down the hall to her brightly lit office.

I knew that I had to make a decision and soon. For weeks I'd been considering getting another job on campus or leaving the university to pursue my animal activities full-time. I knew that the new director would not give me time off to go to disasters, and I couldn't imagine not being there to help.

Friends and family thought I was crazy to even think about giving up my job at Santa Clara. They kept reminding me of the great benefits, the free tuition for me and Jennifer, and the guaranteed check I got every two weeks. When they didn't think they were getting through, they used the guilt routine. "Think about your obligations to Jennifer."

I was thinking about my daughter when I made the decision to turn in my two-weeks notice. Most of the people who were trying to tell me not to give up what I had were people who hated their jobs. On Friday they were already dreading coming back to work on Monday. I didn't want to live like that, and I didn't want Jennifer growing up to think she had to accept what was and not try to make things better.

I'd had my own part-time wallpaper-hanging business for a few years, and I knew it would support Jennifer and me nicely and allow me more time to help the EARS Program expand. My decision was accompanied with an inner satisfaction that said, "Yes. This is what you are meant to do." March 10, 1989, was my last day at Santa Clara.

Two weeks later, the *Exxon Valdez* ran aground on Bligh Reef, and I was on my way to Alaska.

Exxon Valdez Oil Spill
Valdez, Alaska . . .

It shouldn't have happened, the locals said when they heard the news. The sea was calm, winds were light out of the east, and the tanker had navigated safely past the narrows, the most dangerous section of Prince William Sound. That was where it had been predicted an ecological disaster would someday occur. Bligh Reef had never been considered a threat. A child could navigate a tanker past the small island.

It shouldn't have happened, but it did, at 12:04 A.M. on March 24, 1989. It was not a good Friday.

12

Beginnings

I recognized the familiar excitement of heading into another disaster as the tiny, four-seater plane, belonging to Wilbur Air, navigated the natural chute of mountains that guided us toward Valdez. What lay ahead for me here in Alaska? Would I be up to the challenges to come? From my earlier experiences in Barrow, I knew I was about to enter a different kind of world. Alaska was our last frontier, a world of ancient customs and culture and dramatic landscapes and climate.

My first sight of Valdez imprinted itself on my mind in black and white. As the plane descended toward the runway, there was no color to be seen . . . just an endless expanse of white, with specks of black rooftops. The books I'd read before leaving said Valdez resembled the quaint mountain villages of Switzerland, tucked up against the Alps. The flowers of summer were supposed to be spectacular. I could only imagine how lovely it must be, because I would be in Valdez for just five days.

"You know, we're lucky to be flying in here," said the pilot next to me. "The locals believe nature has been on their side since the spill. They can't remember a late March without blizzards and the omnipresent, low, soupy fog cover that can make this town disappear for days."

I hoped nature would continue to cooperate, in spite of what man had done to this pristine wilderness.

"Do you work for Exxon?" It was the pilot again. He'd been silent the first forty-five minutes of our trip, which made me think it took all his concentration to fly us safely through the towering mountain ranges.

"No. I'm here for United Animal Nations. I'm going to help clean the birds coated with Exxon's oil."

"Yeah. I hear there are a lot of them."

I'd contacted the International Bird Rescue and Research Center in Berkeley, California, right after hearing about the spill. They had been hired by Exxon to care for the birds being affected by it. When I asked if they needed any help in Alaska, they were quick to say yes. My contacts would be Jay Holcomb and Alice Berkner, with whom I'd already worked on two local spills in the San Francisco Bay area. United Animal Nations supported my going and were covering my expenses for a short period of time.

"I know where you want to go," the innkeeper at the bed and breakfast told me after I'd checked in. "I'll drop you there if you'd like." I suspected I could find the place on my own, considering the size of Valdez, but I welcomed the ride. I'd tried to get a rental car, but Exxon had already rented the few that existed.

When the car stopped in front of a barracklike structure, I was sure we were in the wrong place, but the innkeeper pointed toward the run-down-looking building, and said, "It's back there where you wanna go."

"Are you sure?"

"Yeah. That's where they're taking the birds. The building used to be dormitories for Prince William Sound Community College. They've been planning on fixing them up, but luckily for the birds, they haven't yet."

After thanking my driver for the ride, I left the warmth of the station wagon. Immediately I was reminded that I was in Alaska. The sub-zero temperature made my eyes water as I crunched through the frozen snow between me and the makeshift bird center. I couldn't wait to get indoors. My thin California blood wasn't used to this.

The bird center was a narrow building, about half a block long. Inside, a hall ran its length, giving access to ten rooms. Someone had used his very limited imagination and painted the walls a monotonous, grubby green. Daylight tried to find its way through two small windows, but fought a losing battle against the dull yellowness of the overhead fluorescent lights.

The hall was deserted except for a half dozen reporters who slouched against the walls, waiting for a story. When the gray whales had been trapped, I'd learned to recognize members of the media from observing them in Barrow, Alaska. The tools of their trade gave them away: cameras, the narrow reporter's notepads, and the multipocketed tan vests that held all their other paraphernalia.

I realized I must be where there was some Exxon-related activity, or these guys wouldn't be here. My eyes fastened on a flash of yellow at the far end of the hall. A woman clad in coveralls made her way across the linoleum floor toward one of the rooms. She carried a limp cormorant—a large seabird common in Alaska—in her arms. That was where I needed to go. I hurried to catch her.

The dorm room was cleared of everything except a large, plain, Formica table. Down both sides two rows of Rubbermaid dishpans were lined up like miniature bathtubs. The tarred bodies of common murres and loons looked out of place in the warm, sudsy water.

Each bird had two human handlers. One gently, but firmly, cradled the bird's delicate neck to keep its eyes out of the soap, while a partner worked the diluted Dawn dishwashing soap through the stubborn residue of oil that clung to the creature's feathers with the tenacity of Super Glue. A third person waited on each team, ready to slide fresh pans of water onto the table upon command.

Quietly, I stood back and watched. It could take as many as thirty pans of water before a bird was clean. When the water was no longer a murky brown, it was time to take the bird to the designated rinse area. I remembered the hours I'd spent washing birds during the northern California spill. We'd had over two thousand birds come through the California Conservation Corps warehouse during the week I'd helped. It was awful, and I'd hoped I'd never see so many suffering and dying birds again. But it wasn't to be. It was time to get my hands dirty again.

I'd spotted Jay the moment I'd come into the room. He was gently lowering a heavily oiled loon into the cleansing suds when I walked over and nudged him with my shoulder. "Need some help here?"

He turned, his hands still immersed in the water. "Terri!"

"How's it going?"

"I fear we're on the losing side right now," Jay replied as he turned back to the volunteer next to him. "Keep her head up and be sure you use the Water Pik to work the oil out above her eyes."

He wrung his hands free of black suds and motioned for an anxious volunteer to come take his place. "I heard you were coming," Jay said, putting his arm around my shoulders. "It's good to have someone else here with some experience.

"Let me show you our setup. We sure don't have the room we had at the warehouse in California, but you take whatever you can get in Valdez."

For the next twenty minutes Jay walked me through the transformed dormitory. He was right, it was small, but Alice and Jay had done a great job of working with what they had.

There was a total of five rooms, plus a bathroom. He showed me the drying room first, which was across the hall from where the washing was being done. The birds were transferred into a third room after they were dry. They would remain here until they were ready to be released.

"How soon do you think you'll be able to let them go, Jay?"

"I have no idea. Right now we don't know of a safe place to release them. Sure would hate for them to have gone through all this, just to get back out in the oil again."

Jay showed me the bathroom where all the rinsing was done. A hose with a nozzle on the end had been adapted to fit the faucet and was at the moment being used on a large loon that didn't at all like its shower. The last room I saw was set up for rescue coordination. It, like all the other rooms, was full of people trying their hardest to help—even though more than half of them were inexperienced.

"Well, are you ready to get worn out?" Jay asked when our tour was over. "Because I've got plenty of birds to keep you busy for a very long time."

"You've got me for five days."

"I'll take whatever I can get."

I threw my parka onto a chair in the corner of the office and located my veteran coveralls in my backpack and pulled them on. All that was left to do was to roll up my sleeves and take off my watch. It was three-thirty in the afternoon when I stuffed my watch in my pocket and walked into the wash room to clean my first bird.

During the next twelve hours I passed into a trancelike state I recognized all too well. It seemed to happen every time my body needed to ignore aching muscles, the growling pains of hunger, and the need for sleep. A force of will kicked in that denied the passage of time. All I saw were the birds . . . hour after hour after hour.

"Where are the otters?" I asked Alice as we washed two more murres.

"The townspeople think they've gone off somewhere to die," Alice replied. "The press are going nuts waiting around." She yawned as we worked our bare fingers through the mass of black goop coating the birds. "They've got enough pictures of sick birds for the next ten oil spills. They're salivating for some otters to come in."

"What's going to happen if the rescue teams do find some?" I asked.

"They will bring them here. That's why we haven't been able to use the other end of the dorm. It's being saved for the otters."

"But who's going to take care of them?" I knew we certainly didn't have time to, and more important, I didn't know the first thing about taking care of oiled sea otters and I expected the rest of the people here didn't, either.

"Exxon's brought up Dr. Randy Davis, a biologist from the research unit of Sea World in San Diego. He did a study in 1985 on the effects of crude oil on sea otters." Alice continued to talk as she moved her murre into the next pan of water.

"I met him briefly yesterday. Nice guy, but very shy. I got the impression he'd be more comfortable studying sea mammals off some deserted coastline."

I got to make up my own mind about Randy Davis the next morning. I'd managed to get a brief three hours of sleep during the early morning hours, in a corner of the recovery room. I was still half asleep when I opened the door to the office. All I was thinking about was finding a cup of coffee so I could wake up before the next group of oil-covered birds arrived.

As I swung open the door, I ran into a man who looked as if he was carrying the weight of the world, or at least this small portion of the world, on his shoulders.

"I'm sorry. Are you okay?" I asked.

"Oh, I'm fine. I think the bump helped wake me up."

"Maybe I should try it," Extending my hand, I introduced myself, "I'm Terri and I'm helping Jay and Alice with the birds."

"Hi. I'm Randy Davis," he said, letting go of my hand. "The washing takes its toll on the hands, doesn't it?"

I nodded, looking at how red and swollen mine had become already.

"It's worse on the birds though."

Our conversation was interrupted when Randy was called away to the phone. So I got my cup of strong coffee and my second day of bird washing began.

"Someone just dropped off a box of sandwiches. Why don't you go grab one? I'll take over here." It was the volunteer who'd been supplying me with fresh pans of water during the morning rush of birds.

"Thanks." I pulled my watch out of my pocket. It was four o'clock in the afternoon. I'd been at it nine hours straight.

The sandwiches, under normal circumstances, would have looked anything but appetizing, but when you're hungry, you learn to eat just about anything. I grabbed two cheese sandwiches, a bag of Doritos, and a warm can of Coke. The only other thing I needed was some fresh air. The fumes from the oiled birds had caused a dull ache in my head.

There had been no time during the day to notice what was going on at the prospective otter center. I assumed that if some otters had arrived, I would have heard about it, but I hadn't heard anything. The only news I'd gotten was that more birds were being brought in—heavily oiled. Not the kind of news you want to hear when there are already birds backed up from the morning that you haven't been able to get to yet.

When I got outside, I discovered the news guys had not given up. They were still hanging around for the "big arrival," but in the meantime, they were hitting up Randy for as much information as he had. I found an empty airline crate to sit on while I ate my one meal of the day and watched a half dozen reporters bounce questions off Randy at the same time.

"Are the otters being left to die in the Sound?" a short, stocky man asked as he scribbled some notes on his pad.

"Is it true there are ten thousand otters in these waters?"

"If you get any otters, how long will you keep them?"

Randy just shook his head and looked from one face to the next. He obviously was not used to dealing with the pushy story gatherers of the world.

"I can answer some of those questions." It was a tanned, brown-haired woman in her early thirties that came to Randy's rescue.

"Who are you?" asked a reporter standing slightly in front of the rest of the group.

"I'm Terrie Williams. Randy's partner from Sea World."

That seemed to suit the members of the press, because they refocused their attention on Terrie.

For the next thirty minutes, Terrie patiently answered the questions thrown at her. The final question came from a tall guy with a thick brown beard. "How long will the otters stay here after they have been washed?"

I'll never forget Terrie's answer: "Probably no more than two weeks."

Those two weeks stretched out to almost six months.

13

Organizing

It was no use. My eyes opened and I stared at the ceiling. Every muscle in my body screamed, "Just one more hour!" But my mind kept me awake. When I closed my eyes, all I could see were crumpled bodies of oil-covered birds.

I'd fallen into bed without undressing sometime after three A.M. Removing even a sock would have required more energy than I had. The gray light of another March morning peered through a gap in the curtain as I tossed the covers back and sat up on the edge of my bed, trying to wake up. I felt as if I hadn't slept, changed clothes, or brushed my teeth for weeks.

I managed to reach my Sorrel boots, and one at a time, I jammed my feet into them and laced them, not missing too many of the holes. It was now time to stand up. I did a much better job of yawning. I shuffled to the bathroom, my boots clopping against the hard wood floor, and splashed some cold water on my face. It helped, but when I straightened up and stared into the mirror, I realized it was going to take a lot more than water to fix how I looked and felt.

Bundled up to keep out the bitter cold of another twenty-degree day, I trudged to the dormitory once again. I had been in Valdez for three days now. It seemed more like three weeks.

Exxon Valdez *Oil Spill*

Before I could even see the dormitory, I knew something was going on. There were cars parked everywhere, loud voices disturbed the normal quiet, a large truck sat noisily idling, but it was another sound that made my heart start to beat faster. The high-pitched squeal of a sea otter told me they'd finally arrived.

When I turned the corner, I saw a scene I could hardly believe. It looked as if the entire town of Valdez had descended on what used to be *just* the bird center. I think these otters would have upstaged even a Hollywood celebrity, though I knew all they wanted was to be left alone. A part of me wished to remain at the corner and not contribute to the mass confusion.

Standing off to one side of the crowd was a volunteer I'd worked with the day before. She, too, seemed as if she couldn't believe the transformation that had occurred overnight. I walked up behind her. "Obviously the otters have arrived." My comment made her turn around.

"Uh huh. Seven of them to be exact. They started arriving about an hour ago."

"How bad are they?" I asked, afraid of the answer.

"I don't know. I haven't seen them. They have them in airline crates inside."

I decided I couldn't avoid the crowd any longer. If otters had arrived, there probably were more birds too. I pushed my way through the throng of people that were hanging out at the door, hoping to catch a glimpse of the otters.

The main hall now looked like Grand Central Station at rush hour. The only thing different was the smell. It passed through the fine wool of my scarf and assaulted my nostrils with a pungency that reminded me of an open can of gasoline. The building was hot, which magnified the sickening odor.

I squeezed through the solid mass of bodies. The voices around me tore the air with hateful accusations. Faces were streaked with tears. Photographers captured the visible emotions while reporters wrote down the words.

I'd managed to get almost halfway down the hall when the bright glow of a television camera lit up the normally dim hall like a movie set. The lens was aimed at a row of airline carriers, pushed up against the wall. The world was about to get its first glimpse of an oil-covered sea otter.

Anger was what I felt at that moment. The otter they had on camera was almost comatose. It lay in a black pool of excrement mixed with toxic crude oil, and all anyone was doing was taking its picture. Instead of helping these poor creatures, they were only being made to suffer more.

At the end of the hall I spotted Alice, her hair covered with her trademark red bandanna, busy herding volunteers back into the bird rooms.

I pushed through the crowd until I could make myself heard

"Can you believe this!" I shouted to Alice when she glanced my way.

"It's pathetic," she yelled back, grabbing another stray volunteer before he could slip past her.

"Have you seen Randy or Terrie?" I asked.

"No. I haven't been down to that end of the hall. It's too dangerous." I knew what Alice meant.

"Can you spare me for a while? I want to see if I can find Randy."

"Go ahead. We've got things under control here. Haven't gotten any new birds in the last couple of hours."

I threw a quick wave of thanks and forced my way back into the melee. I scanned the faces around me, and I recognized no one. I asked a few people who looked as though they might be in charge if they'd seen Randy or Terrie. No one knew who they were. The situation was definitely out of control.

The more I saw, the angrier I got. These animals were sick, and if somebody didn't do something fast, they'd all be dead.

Jay had shown me their supplies in a broom closet in the office. I went to it and surveyed the shelves. What could I use? A roll of gray duct tape caught my eye. Close by was a red marker. Using the pen, I wrote in big letters lengthwise on the tape: VOLUNTEER COORDINATOR. I pulled the tape from the roll and slapped it across my oil-stained yellow overalls. A clipboard caught my attention next. They always make you look official. I slipped a couple pieces of blank paper under the clip and hugged it under my arm. A box of file folder labels would have to do for name tags. I closed the closet door behind me. I was ready.

I marched back into the mess and was immediately surrounded by people. Everyone talked at once. The more determined ones shoved their way to the front of the crowd, and I felt myself being pushed up against the wall.

I raised a hand. "Stop," I shouted. "We're not going to get anything accomplished this way."

A reporter took advantage of the brief lull, and asked, "Could I ask you a few questions? I've got to file my story in less than an hour."

I just glared at him. There were more important things that had to be done first. I needed to assess who all these people were and what they wanted.

I hoped some of them wanted to volunteer. When I'd worked the oil spill at home, we'd had hundreds of people show up to help take care of the birds. It had become my job to try and coordinate these untrained people. Somehow that had gotten done, but the first few days were absolutely crazy. Now, in Valdez, I was feeling a sense of déjà vu.

People were certainly going to be needed to take care of the otters. I assumed Randy and Terrie couldn't do it alone. Maybe Exxon was going to bring more people in to help? If so, where were they? All I knew for sure was that there were too many people in this building and they needed to be weeded out for the well-being of the otters. I particularly wanted to get rid of the curiosity seekers, who would only gawk and get in the way.

I addressed the crowd again, "Anyone interested in volunteering? If so, raise your hand." I counted thirty-seven people.

"I want those people to move down to the last room on the right side of the hall and wait for me there." I pointed in the direction of the dorm room I'd peeked into yesterday. It was empty except for some mattresses leaning up against the wall.

The crowd thinned by over half.

"How many of you are with the media?" I asked of those who remained. Another ten hands went up.

"I have a message here from one of our rescue boats. They radioed in about two hours ago to let us know they're bringing in a dozen heavily oiled otters. They estimate they'll be arriving at the harbor in about forty-five minutes. You may want to be there." I didn't have to say any more. They believed my lie. Before they got back, I'd find a way to keep them out of the building and away from the otters. There would be time for them to get their pictures and write their stories. This wasn't the time, though.

The remaining twenty-odd people included several fishermen who wanted to know if we needed any fish to feed the otters. I sent them to wait with the other volunteers. Then some guys wanted to know if we were going to be selling the pelts of the dead otters. I bit my tongue to keep from saying something I'd regret. They left after I told them the pelts would be too badly oiled to be used for anything. A nicely dressed woman wanted to know if she could bring her fourth grade class by to see the oiled otters. I told her maybe in a few days. What I then ended up with were the gawkers.

"I'm afraid I'll have to ask you people to leave." I spoke with authority that hadn't been given to me, but no one questioned my instructions. They sneaked one more peak at the otters and left.

I'd made some progress.

I heard some applause from behind me, followed by, "Bravo! Bravo!"

It was the volunteer I'd spoken with earlier that morning.

"I'm glad *somebody* finally did something."

"I haven't done much yet," I replied. I knew this was just a temporary lull in the storm.

When I walked into the room where the volunteers waited, I was looking for a particular type of person to fill my first two volunteer jobs. I spotted them immediately.

Within ten minutes, the only two entrances to the dormitory were guarded by a pair of the burliest fishermen Valdez had to offer. No one would get into the building, unless they were coming to help the otters.

Now, I had thirty-five more people to figure out what to do with.

I relied on common sense and my work with the birds to put together my volunteer job list. As I started to assign jobs, I'd give each volunteer a file-folder label to use as a name tag. Certainly we'd need to feed the otters, and I knew I already had several fishermen with fish. But I didn't know if they were giving the fish away or if they would have to be bought. With about twenty-five dollars in my back pocket, I knew I wouldn't be buying it.

Of course, it seemed only fair that Exxon feed the otters. I talked with the fishermen and they weren't in a charitable mood. Even I knew the prices they wanted were high, but it seemed everyone was trying to bleed Exxon for every cent they could get. I asked if the fishermen could hang around until Randy arrived. Expecting to make some big money, they weren't going anywhere I figured.

I knew from talking to Alice that the empty dorm rooms were being saved for the otter center. I had two volunteers check them out and report back to me. It seemed some of them were pretty dirty, so I assigned a team of six volunteers to start cleaning them up. In the office closet I'd seen a broom and mop, plus some assorted cleaning supplies that they could use.

In the bird area the floors were covered with heavy plastic to protect them from all the water that was getting spilled. I asked two guys to work along with the cleaning crew and lay down plastic once the floors were clean in the rooms where the otters would be taken.

I'd heard Terrie talking the day before about building wash stations for cleaning the otters. I assumed a carpenter or plumber might come in handy to work on these. It turned out I had three in the group. I explained we'd have to wait until Terrie or Randy returned, since they had the plans. Or at least I hoped they did.

The remaining volunteers were given miscellaneous jobs to do. The walkways into the dorm needed shoveling, there were a few extra airline crates that had been dropped off for us to use and they could use a scrubbing, and the kitchen area where we'd been eating was getting pretty disgusting.

I had everyone busy doing something when I spotted Randy coming through the door.

"Sorry, sir, but you can't come in unless you have a name tag on." It was one of the "doormen" doing his job, but it was Randy he was talking to.

"No. It's okay. This is Randy Davis. He's been hired to be in charge of the otter center," I explained as I came down the hall. The doorman apologized as Randy smiled.

There had been a meeting with Exxon officials that morning, and for the next half hour Randy told me as much as he knew about the otters and what the oil company planned to do to help them. He guessed we'd be in operation for two, maybe three weeks, and Exxon was covering all otter-related expenses. Volunteers would be needed, since the only other person Exxon had flown in so far was Judy McBain, a veterinarian, also from San Diego. Randy was working on getting more experienced help from some of the other Sea World parks too.

"I hope you don't mind what I did this morning," I said after Randy finished updating me.

He interrupted before I could say more. "No. I'm glad you were here to start getting the volunteers organized. Somebody had to do it, and I certainly wouldn't know where to begin."

I then explained to Randy what I'd assigned the volunteers to do. He gave me some other volunteer jobs to fill and asked to see the two carpenters and plumber. The otters were still lined up along the hall, in desperate need of a bath and some medical attention.

As I started to leave to look for the carpenters and plumber, Randy stopped me. "Just one more thing. How long are you here for?"

"I'm afraid only one more day." I'd promised Jennifer I'd be home in time for her birthday. I couldn't let her down.

"Too bad. We could use you a lot longer."

I'd already begun to realize that.

"Are you Terri?"

I turned to see who had tapped me on the shoulder. A man, nicely dressed in slacks and a freshly pressed shirt, stood behind me. I noticed he wasn't wearing rubber boots. Instead he had on shiny loafers, something I'd not seen since I'd arrived in Valdez.

"Can I talk with you?" the man asked. Then in a softer voice he said, "I'm with Exxon."

This was the first one of *them* I'd met.

"Can I finish with this otter first?"

"Sure. I'll be in the hall waiting." The nicely dressed man wasted no time leaving the wash room. I'm sure he felt he was in enemy territory.

There were five of us around the wash station. The carpenters and plumber had managed to rig together three stations that day. There were still some bugs that had to be worked out of the design, but we were at least able to get this first group of otters cleaned. As I helped rinse the large male otter we'd been working on for nearly an hour, I wondered what the man from Exxon wanted to talk with me about. After the otter was lifted from the table to be returned to a clean crate, I walked into the hall, massaging my lower back. Cleaning otters took its toll on the body too.

"You guys are doing a great job in there," the man said as I approached.

What a cleverly calculated thing to say, I thought to myself. It was too bad the job had to be done at all, though.

"What can I do for you?" I asked, leaning up against the wall.

"Randy says you've been doing a great job organizing the volunteers."

"Uh huh." It was a combination of being tired and not wanting to have this conversation that made me wish this man would just get to the point so I could get back to what I had to do. My time in Valdez was quickly running out.

"He also told me that you're leaving tomorrow."

I nodded, surprised at how quickly news spread in this small community.

"Is there any chance I could persuade you to stay longer?" he asked. "Exxon will pay you."

I didn't know what to say. I couldn't imagine working for Exxon, yet I knew that if I stayed, there was more that I could do to help the otters. But there was Jennifer to think about. I'd have to bring her back an extra special present to make up for missing her birthday.

"We would also provide you with a place to live, a vehicle, three meals a day, and then fly you home when this is over." I think he thought I was holding out for a better deal. Little did he know . . . I would have stayed for a lot less.

"How long do you think you'll need me?"

"No more than three weeks," he guessed.

Finally I shrugged and said, "Well, I guess I'll stay."

I ended up staying for six months.

14

Resting Place

I'd been up for two days straight and I was exhausted. Agreeing to stay in Valdez for several more weeks meant it would be a while before I could once again indulge in eight hours of uninterrupted sleep. With relief no longer just days away, my body began to let me know it refused to do another all-nighter.

It was a Friday evening, and there were three volunteers and myself on duty at the center. It had been another day of endless demands and more otters, and we'd been promised relief at midnight. It was now three A.M. None of us could leave until someone showed up to relieve us. We were running an intensive care unit for some very sick otters, and we never knew when new victims would arrive.

The four of us stayed busy, trying not to think about how tired we were. We'd learned you didn't stop, because you wouldn't be able to get yourself going again. So we dragged ourselves from cage to cage, monitoring the condition of the otters. We continued to offer food, but few of the otters ate. Chunks of ice were pushed through the cage doors in hopes the otters would chew on them and take in some fluid. The cages needed to be cleaned continually to prevent the otters from lying in their own excrement. There was lots to do, and we were doing it with dwindling energy.

I was tempted to find a quiet corner and at least rest my eyes for a few minutes, but I knew I'd fall asleep. Hopefully, our replacements would arrive soon. Until then, I'd check on the otters one more time.

If only I had a cup of coffee, I thought to myself. I decided to check to see if there might be something in the office that might suffice for caffeine before I started my next rounds.

I never made it to the office.

When I left the wash room, I heard a faint noise. The sound came from the room across the hall. I pushed the door open slowly, and in the darkest corner, stretched out on the cold linoleum floor, lay a large sea otter. I knew why he wasn't caged . . . he was dying.

In all the commotion of the day, someone must have stuck him in here and forgotten to tell us. I knew no one had checked on him all night. There wasn't much we could have done for him, but at least his existence deserved validation. Cautiously, I approached and stood looking down at another one of the victims of this oil spill. His breathing was labored and shallow. I knew he wouldn't last much longer.

It was in a quiet moment like this that I allowed myself to think about the unfairness of this oil spill. I couldn't afford to do this very often, because my anger would have gotten in the way of the work I was trying to do. I didn't attempt to hold back the anger now. It was hard to when the end result of a human mistake lay before you.

I wanted to scoop this animal up and take him to some isolated stretch of shoreline. It seemed only fair he be allowed to die in his world, not ours. But I couldn't. The otters were now evidence in the case against Exxon. The dead ones were being bagged and stacked in a heavily guarded refrigerated tractor trailer. When they were no longer needed, they'd be burned.

I decided to stay with the otter so at least he wouldn't die alone. I bent down next to him and lifted his shoulders off the cold linoleum. Still holding him in my hands I sat on the floor and eased my legs underneath his upper body. He didn't resist. In fact, I was pretty certain he didn't even know I was there. But I knew.

I touched his thick fur and marveled at how magnificent it was, even though it had been coated with oil. The team that washed him had done a good job of scrubbing away the deadly substance, but the efforts had come too late. I'd heard Randy doing an interview earlier in the day, and when asked what the otters were dying from, his response was, "Shock, hypothermia, emphysema, gastric erosion, and captive stress syndrome, usually in combination."

Diluted dishwashing soap couldn't get rid of these killers.

Out of Harm's Way

As I stroked the otter, oil continued to trickle out his anus. The black toxin spread on the floor and stained my yellow overalls. I leaned my head against the wall behind me and closed my eyes. The other otters, in the rooms across the hall, screeched loudly. I could see them in my head. they were in pain . . . and they were frightened.

I opened my eyes and pulled the otter higher, so I could rock the inert body in my arms. He wouldn't suffer much longer. I hummed to him, the way I would to a sick child, as I waited for that last breath.

"Terri." The voice came from the doorway.

When I opened my eyes, I saw the veterinarian who had been scheduled to relieve us at midnight.

"I've been looking for you," she explained as she stepped into the room. "Sorry I'm late." In her arms she carried a stack of medical notes that we'd started to keep on the otters.

"Do you know anything about this otter?" I asked.

She shuffled through her notes as she spoke. "Yeah, that's the one that came in late this afternoon. He was in real bad shape. We washed him but didn't expect he'd last long. Is he still alive?" the vet asked as she stepped closer.

"Barely," I replied in a hoarse voice. "Can't something be done? If nothing else, why can't he be euthanized?"

"I don't have the authority," was her response.

"Who does?" I could hear the anger in my voice.

"Otters are under Fish and Wildlife's jurisdiction," she said. "They have to make the decision to euthanize."

"Why aren't they here, then?" I knew I was tired, which made me lash out at the vet.

"I'm sorry," I said after a few moments when neither one of us said anything. "This just seems so unfair."

"I know." The vet nodded, and then she excused herself to start her rounds.

The otter died in my arms just before daybreak. I sat with him and continued to stroke his lifeless body as the toxic stream persisted. The otter's eyes were fixed open, staring up at me. His body was completely relaxed. The small front legs had slid to his side and his back flippers had relaxed into the large puddle of crude oil that stretched beyond us across the linoleum. The room smelled of excrement and death.

I eventually dozed off, the dead otter still draped across my outstretched legs. A volunteer woke me just as the first hints of daylight began to peek into the dark room. She helped me find a plastic bag to put the otter in. Before we lowered him inside, I said good-bye. We carried him outside and lifted the lid of one of the green garbage cans that were being used to store the dead otters. He was not the only one who had not survived the night.

"Tell Randy or Terrie, I'll be back in a bit," I said to the volunteer as I put the lid back on the can.

"Where are you going to be if they need you?"

I didn't answer.

The streets of Valdez were still deserted, except for an occasional passing car. I walked past the inn where I was now staying and crossed the main street of town. The stores were still closed, but the gas station was open. I kept walking until I got to the harbor.

When I could see the water . . . I cried. I wished I could have given the otter a proper burial.

15

Improvising

Every town has its one "character." The person that "normal" people can spend their time talking about. From the moment he rode into Valdez on his shiny black-and-chrome Harley, Manfred was a regular topic of discussion for the Valdez gossip circuit.

A towering six foot three, he cruised the muddy streets of Valdez decked out in full Harley-Davidson biker gear—black Levi's and T-shirt, steel-toed boots, and a heavy canvas duster coat with a large flying-eagle emblem stitched to the back.

He seemed to delight in flaunting his renegade image. His thick, jet-black hair was worn slicked back in a ponytail, making it easy to notice the small gold hoop that pierced one ear. He'd also cultivated a full beard that nearly reached the enormous oval belt buckle that caught your attention when the sun hit the polished silver just right.

His favorite hangout was Acres, a small bar on the outskirts of town. You could find him at a table in the back most nights. After he'd ordered a Bud, he'd remove his black coat, revealing muscular arms that displayed the talent of some tattoo artist. He'd play several games of pool, not saying much to anyone, then pay his tab and ride up the road to the small cabin he was renting in the woods.

No one, including me, knew much about this man they'd nick-named "Man."

He'd been one of the first to show up to help the otters. We desper-ately needed volunteers and would take just about anyone we could get. Manfred was definitely not your usual volunteer, but he came every day and sometimes put in as many as twelve hours ... most of which were between six P.M. and six A.M.

You get to know a person with whom you share repeated three A.M.'s During those early morning hours, I became friends with Manfred. Once, when we were pulling an otter out of a cage, he suddenly winced and held his lower back. I asked if he was all right. He told me he'd been shot in Vietnam, and since then he'd had to learn to live with pain. "I promise it won't stop me from helping the otters," he said as if he was afraid I might hold this against him.

Manfred was right, nothing got in his way when it came to the otters.

By the end of the first week, the otter center had already outgrown the dormitory. We'd been forced to use every bit of available space, and we were starting to encroach on the bird center. When I had a spare moment, I'd check to see how Alice and Jay were doing. I felt bad about abandoning them, but they knew I was needed with the otters. I could see that the birds were growing in numbers, too, and Alice and Jay had been forced to move the healthy birds into aviaries that had been built out back.

In addition to having a few of the otters outside, we were sticking the critically sick ones in bathtubs or corralling them in corners, with plywood on two sides to keep them from scooting away. The healthier ones, who constantly looked for any possible escape route, were still being kept in the airline crates. It bothered all of us to see them crammed into such a tiny space, with no water to swim in, but we had nothing else. When I walked into one of the dorm rooms late one evening and saw that the volunteers had been forced to stack the crated otters two high in the closet, I knew it was definitely time to move.

Randy had already begun talking with Exxon about the need for more space. They were willing to give us whatever we needed, but there was one problem—all the prespill empty buildings in Valdez were empty no longer. When we had begun to feel that we'd just have to make do with what we had, news came that a place had been found. So for the next two days, thirty plumbers and carpenters worked around the clock to transform the community college's gymnasium into the new otter center.

When I walked through the door of the gym for the first time, I couldn't believe what I saw. The carpenters had done an amazing job. A new, three-foot-high floor had been built that covered three quarters of the room. I could peek underneath the floor and see that the plumbers had created an intricate maze of pipes that connected to the pens on the floor above.

Each pen had a five-foot fence around it to prevent the otters from escaping, and inside there was a five-foot-square plastic box, or tote, as they were called in the fishing industry, that was tall enough to partially fill with water. The carpenters had also built benches, half the size of the tote, that had been lowered inside to give the otters someplace to go to get out of the water. What an improvement this was.

When I spotted Randy across the room talking to one of the foremen, I walked over and waited to talk with him.

"What a job! Am I ever impressed," I said to Randy when he had finished.

"Yeah. This is some otter center," Randy agreed.

"When can we start moving the otters over? I've got some volunteers who are pretty anxious to get them out of the dorm and into their new accommodations."

"The foreman told me they should be done here later this afternoon, so if we have enough volunteers available, we can start moving them this evening."

"There will be more than enough volunteers—" Before I could finish I was interrupted by an official-looking man who had just walked up.

"Are you Randy?" he asked.

"Yes. Can I help you?"

"I'm with the city, and I'm here to let you know that no otters will be moving into this gym until the sewage problem is resolved."

He told us that the city didn't like our plan to use the drain in the floor of the men's rest room to access the city sewer. If we wanted to dump oiled otter waste, we had to first filter out the feces, and shedded fur, which was considered a toxic substance after the spill. We should have been filtering the otter and bird wash water too, but until now, no one had thought to put this safeguard in place.

What followed this news was a meeting in the men's rest room. In attendance were Randy and myself, plus two representatives of the city of Valdez and an equal number of Exxon reps. The plumbing foreman joined us, too, to share his knowledge of filtering systems.

"Okay! Okay! I've said we'll put in a filter system. We'll comply with anything you want." Exxon's chief spokesperson for the otters, sounded ragged. "But you let us get those otters in here in the meantime."

"I'm afraid we can't allow that," said one of the city officials.

"It could take a week to get the filter we need here and installed. And more otters will die in that time." The Exxon executive's voice rose an octave as he spoke. He'd already loosened his tie. Now he struggled to yank it off his neck.

"You seem to have forgotten why they are dying in the first place," was the piercing response from a Valdez official.

For a few brief seconds the bathroom was absolutely quiet. I don't think anybody quite believed what they'd just heard. The Exxon guy took one step forward and was quickly restrained by his colleague.

Seeing this man's response made me realize he genuinely cared about these otters, even if he did work for Exxon. Suddenly the corporate monster that was hated by the world for what *they* had done to Prince William Sound became less of a monster to me. For the first time, I realized there were probably other individuals within Exxon who were equally concerned about what had happened, not only to the otters, but to the environment.

In the months that followed I got to know a lot of Exxon employees who were rotated through Valdez from their jobs in Texas, Oklahoma, Oregon, and California. They were under relentless pressure as they struggled to handle the repercussions of this ecological disaster. It took eighteen- and twenty-hour shifts seven days a week to keep up with all the demands. The sewage problem was just one of many difficulties this man from Exxon had to deal with.

"This isn't solving our problem," Randy said, hoping to get this situation resolved, so he could go back to helping otters.

In the next twenty minutes I learned more than I ever wanted to know about sewers and filtration systems. It seemed the filter we needed did not exist in Valdez, which didn't surprise me. The plumbing foreman thought there might be a place in Anchorage to buy one, if not, certainly Seattle would have one. I began to realize it would be days, possibly weeks, before anyone here saw this filter. There were so many supplies being driven and flown into Valdez that everything was backlogged, no matter how important it was.

What surprised me next was the price tag for the filter—at least one hundred thousand dollars. The Exxon representative would have to get authorization to spend that kind of money. I couldn't stand to listen anymore. Everything was getting too complicated, and the otters were paying the price. I walked out of the men's rest room, unnoticed by the six arguing men.

"I thought this was the men's room." It was Manfred, whom I bumped into when I came through the door.

"It is," I said tersely as I pushed him aside.

Manfred followed me into the main part of the gym, which was still crowded with plumbers and carpenters putting the finishing touches on the otter center.

"Easy, Terri," Manfred said with that little quizzical smile he had. "What's going on?"

I was too angry to talk, but Manfred didn't give up.

"Some of the volunteers were wondering how much longer it would be until we could start loading the otters up and bringing them over here, so they sent me over to check." Manfred wasn't prepared for my response.

"Don't ask me. Go check with those guys in the bathroom."

"Yeah. I saw those guys standing around that drain in the floor. I thought they were having a pissing contest." Manfred chuckled.

"It's not funny, Man." I knew my voice was sharp. "The city's got a problem with us dumping otter crap into their sewer, so we need a filter. The way it's going in there, it'll be weeks before one arrives." I shook my head in disgust. "And you know what? No otters will be moving in here until that filter is installed."

Now it was Manfred's turn to be angry.

Before I could say another word, he turned and marched into the men's room, his black coat trailing in the air behind him. I followed after him.

"Gentlemen," Manfred said, after clearing his throat. "Looks to me like we got a standoff at the OK Corral. I'm here to offer you a simple solution to your dilemma."

The six men were not in the mood for a joke.

"Do you mind! We're having a meeting here," said a city official. "If you need to use the bathroom, there's one in the cafeteria."

Manfred ignored the man. "Five dollars will solve your problem in fifteen minutes," he said directly to the Exxon spokesperson.

The looks on those six faces were almost comical.

"As I said. Five dollars and your problem is solved."

"If you need five dollars—here." The Valdez official dug into his pocket and held out the bill to Manfred. "This should buy you a couple drinks at Acres."

Manfred turned to me, and I could see the disgust in his eyes. This guy was trying to do something to help the otters—in what way I wasn't sure—and I thought he at least deserved to be heard. Heaven knows this group wasn't making much headway.

"This is Manfred, one of the otter center volunteers," I said quickly. "I think you should listen to his idea."

The stares from the six men told me they thought otherwise. Manfred brushed past me, and whispered, "Just keep them here. I'll be back in fifteen minutes." Then he left without giving me time to ask questions.

Manfred returned as promised, carrying a small brown grocery bag from Foodmart.

He walked back into the bathroom, into the center of the knot of frustrated men. They stepped back after he asked, "Would any of you like to see what I've got in here?" He waved the bag in the air in a teasing manner as he spoke.

All eyes were riveted to the swinging bag, including mine.

It was a challenge that none of the men wanted to answer, though, so I piped up, and said, "I want to see."

"Glad to see there's someone in this room who wants to get this show on the road."

"Is this a joke?" the city official asked, his patience worn thin.

Manfred's face hardened. "Dying otters are nothing to joke about."

All eyes watched as Manfred opened the bag and reached inside.

With all the finesse of a magician, he pulled out a pair of extra-long, queen size, honey beige, support stockings.

No one knew what to say, so Manfred continued.

He looked at the white plastic pipe that jutted out of the wall near the sinks, its end resting over the drain in the floor. It was the pipe that was going to be used to transport the dirty water from the otter totes in the gym to the drain in the men's bathroom. Two strides and Manfred was squatting in front of it. First he hung the panty hose waistband around the opening. Then he pulled a rubber band from his coat pocket and clumsily tried to maneuver it up over the dangling legs. The men were losing their patience.

"Let me help," I offered, and crouched beside Manfred.

In a few seconds the rubber band held the waistband in place over the end of the pipe. "A metal clamp would do the job better, but on such short notice, this was all I could find," my friend explained as we surveyed his handiwork.

Eight pairs of eyes stared at the limp nylons.

"Now, wait. This isn't all of it yet," Manfred said as he stepped out of the bathroom and returned a moment later with a child's hard plastic wading pool. "Friend of mine donated this. Said it was his contribution to helping the otters."

At that point I wanted to laugh. Actually a good, deep belly laugh probably would have done us all some good.

Manfred didn't waste any more time. He stepped back to the drain and dropped the plastic pool on the ground, covering the opening.

"Now, everyone come closer," he ordered. "Well, come on, it won't bite you," he demanded impatiently.

One by one the six men eased their tense bodies down into a viewing position around the swimming pool.

"First thing you do is cut a hole in the middle of the pool." Manfred's finger pointed to the spot. "You want it the size of the drain."

The six heads began to nod up and down. I tried not to laugh. They were all concentrating so hard.

"You seal the area around the cut so the water can't leak out. Then the waste water filters through the panty hose legs into the pool, catching the otter shit, before the water goes down the drain. When the panty hose fills up—you just slip on a new pair." Manfred stopped and looked from man to man. I wasn't sure if they approved or not, but I thought his plan was brilliant.

Finally, one of them was brave enough to admit, "It just might work."

"Of course it will work," Randy said. "And, we'll be able to start moving otters in here tonight as planned."

All eyes focused on one of the city officials. The decision was up to him. I could swear he was trying hard not to smile. "Yeah. I guess it could work." He paused as he assessed the makeshift solution further. "Let's give it a try . . . but we may still need that filter system." The plumbing foreman agreed to try and locate one just in case.

Everyone shook hands after that. The standoff was over. I patted Manfred on the back, and whispered so only he could hear, "I think they're pretty impressed, even if they won't admit it."

"I wasn't trying to prove anything. I just wanted the otters out of the dorm." I knew what Manfred's motives had been, and I respected him even more after that.

It was time to deal with other problems, so we left the plumbing foreman to get Manfred's filtration system hooked up. Manfred and I were on our way out the door to tell the volunteers we were moving when the Exxon executive stopped me.

"Terri, can I talk to you a moment?"

"Sure. Just a second." I told Manfred to go ahead back to the dorm and tell the volunteers the good news. He'd earned the privilege.

"I think it's about time we start to hire some of the volunteers. Otherwise, I think we're going to start losing our help." He had a point. Frequently in disasters, there is an initial outpouring of volunteers, but if a situation lasts longer than a few weeks even committed volunteers have to attend to the other responsibilities in their lives and have less time available to help out. We were already seeing it happen at the otter center.

"After you get the otters all settled into their new quarters tonight, why don't you come see me at Exxon headquarters tomorrow and we'll talk about positions and salaries." The Exxon executive was putting on his coat as he talked.

"Sure. How about eleven?" I asked.

"Is that A.M. or P.M.?" He laughed.

"I hope A.M.," I said as we walked out the door.

"Oh! And, Terri, I think the first person you should hire is Manfred."

When I got to the other side of the snow-filled parking lot, Manfred was waiting for me, seated on his shiny black-and-silver Harley.

"I know you walked over here, so I thought I'd wait and give you a ride," Manfred said as he patted the seat behind him.

I just smiled and hopped on.

And so we cruised to the dormitory . . . the newly hired "panty hose attendant" and I.

16

Number Twenty-seven

I'd just gotten off Manfred's Harley when I spotted a U-Haul truck turning the corner. A Fish and Wildlife agent was driving, and he yelled through his open window, as he pulled the truck to an abrupt halt at the curb alongside the dormitory, "Hey. I need some help over here. Quick."

Kurt and Lew, two of our most dedicated volunteers came running, followed by Manfred and me. We knew what was inside the truck, and there was no time to waste. Quickly, we removed six airline crates containing twenty-seven heavily oiled otters that had been captured that morning on Green Island. The Fish and Wildlife agent told us they were all in need of immediate medical care if they were to have any chance of surviving.

Terrie Williams and Judy McBain were waiting to triage the otters as they were brought in. We had only three wash stations, so when we got a group of more than three, the triage team would have to determine which otters had the greatest chance of surviving, and they would get washed first.

They wasted no time sight-checking these latest arrivals while we lined them up outside the wash room. As Manfred and I set the last carrier down on the floor, Terrie stooped in front of the cage and peered inside. She confirmed what we'd already expected when she stood up and said, "This one's in real bad shape. We'll wash it last."

The first three otters put up very little fight when they were removed from their crates—an indication of how sick they were. After sedating each one, a numbered tag was attached to its back flipper so we could identify it. Then it was moved to a wash station, where a team of five otter handlers began the job of removing the oil from its dense fur.

It took at least an hour to get an otter completely washed and rinsed. Diluted dishwashing soap was used to break down the oil, and continual rinsings eventually flushed their fur of the toxic substance. While this was going on, one of the veterinarians would hook up an IV to get some fluid into the dehydrated bodies, check the otter's temperature, and draw blood.

"How's this one doing?" asked the Fish and Wildlife agent as he stood next to me.

"We just finished," I replied. I ran my bare fingers through the clean fur to make sure we'd rinsed out all the soap.

"You ready for the last one?" Terrie asked as she walked back into the wash room from the hall.

"Is it still alive?" Kurt asked. He'd been certain that by the time we got to it, it would have died.

"Barely. In fact, I don't think we'll even need to sedate it," Terrie said. She moved out of the way so that we could place the otter we'd been washing in a crate. "I have to warn you that this last one could die before you get done with it."

Otter twenty-seven was a female, born the previous spring. She sagged like a waterlogged towel in Kurt's arms as he carried her into the wash room and laid her on the plastic grating that covered the washtubs. Our wash team was unusually silent as we worked the soap through the black fur. Five solemn faces watched as Terrie hooked up an IV, inserted a thermometer, and drew some blood from the lifeless body. This was not fair. She was too young to die.

She hung on for another hour, long enough for us to get her clean and put her somewhere to rest.

The arrival of these otters delayed our move to the gym until the next morning. When we did begin, it was amazing to see how much we'd collected in such a short period of time. The U-Haul truck made repeated runs back and forth between the dormitory and the gym all morning, hauling such things as medical supplies, hoses, fish, a freezer, buckets, mops, garbage cans, a washer, rolls of plastic . . . and otters. We transferred the most critical ones on the last trip.

I had been at the new facility since dawn, helping to direct where things should be placed, and had not been back to the dormitory since I'd left late the night before. The last thing I'd done before I walked out the door at 11:30 P.M. was to check on otter twenty-seven. She was still alive then, but barely.

"Where do the critical otters go?"

I looked up from my clipboard to see two volunteers standing before me with an airline crate between them.

"The critical care area is against that wall," I said, pointing across the room.

When the volunteers bent down to pick up the crate, I noticed the medical record on top. *It couldn't be,* I thought to myself. I looked inside the crate to be sure, and I immediately recognized otter twenty-seven. She was still hanging on.

When I saw Kurt an hour later, he, too, was surprised that otter twenty-seven had survived the night. She survived the following night too, and Mary, one of the otter handlers, had even gotten her to eat some fish during the day. It was too early to get our hopes up, but for the first time we actually thought otter twenty-seven *might* just make it.

"Terri," Kurt yelled to get my attention as I walked through the door of the gym the next day. I'd been in a meeting with Exxon all morning and had not had a chance to check on the status of otter twenty-seven. "I'm afraid I've got some bad news."

I immediately knew it was about that last otter.

"Otter twenty-seven took a turn for the worse last night."

"Did she die?" I asked, looking across the gym toward her pen.

"Not yet. But Judy said she doesn't expect her to last the day. She's with her now."

Kurt and I found Judy and Mary bent over otter twenty-seven's pen. Mary's eyes were red as she watched Judy scribbling some notes on the sick otter's medical record. We didn't say a word. We moved so we could see into the pen, expecting that otter twenty-seven would be lying there dead, but we were surprised. She was alive.

"I just gave her some Toxiban," Judy said as she continued to write. "I think it's our last hope of saving her."

The otter center had just started using Toxiban, which is a charcoal-based powder that farmers use when livestock accidently ingest pesticides. It had helped to save a lot of animals by absorbing the poison that had gotten into their system. When we tried it on the otters, it seemed to work.

Throughout the day, Kurt and I would check on otter twenty-seven. Mary continued to offer fish, but the food lay on the bottom of the pen, untouched. Judy hooked up another IV to get some fluids into the dehydrated body. Our otter was fading.

I caught Judy outside later that evening. There was something I had to ask.

"Are we trying too hard to save otter twenty-seven when the humane thing to do would be to euthanize her?" Judy was silent as she looked up toward the sky, now illuminated by a full moon. I knew it was a tough call, but I needed someone to put my mind at ease.

Finally, she looked at me and told me that if otter twenty-seven was no better by morning, she would talk with the Fish and Wildlife agent about euthanizing her.

I went back inside the softly lit gym and was surprised to find Mary. Her shift had ended hours earlier, but she'd come back. She was sitting on an upside-down bucket next to otter twenty-seven's pen. Her right arm hung inside the enclosure far enough to allow her to gently stroke the otter's fur with her hand. Her chin rested on her other arm, which rested on the rim of the pen. I could hear her humming softly.

I remembered the large male otter I'd cradled in my arms while he was dying. This was Mary's otter to comfort until the end.

I cried all the way back to my cottage.

The news the following morning was better than I'd expected. Our otter had survived another night. Judy gave her another dose of Toxi-ban when she got in, and by afternoon the fish were beginning to disappear from the bottom of the pen. Later that night a volunteer caught otter twenty-seven trying to crawl out of her pen, something we'd not had to worry about before.

Over the next few days I found myself spending more time with otter twenty-seven. She was hard to resist. It was great fun to watch her personality reveal itself as she regained her strength. She'd sit up, almost like a dog begging for its favorite treat, when someone stopped to check on her. And we'd learned not to try to give her something she didn't like. She'd take every piece of fish from your outstretched hand, and if some of it didn't suit her, she'd toss it back at you.

We were all getting attached to this otter with an incredible will to live, even though we knew we shouldn't. We'd refrained from naming the otters, because these were wild creatures, not pets. The survivors

of this oil spill would be returned to Prince William Sound, and we
wanted them to go home as untouched by this experience as possible.
But we hadn't planned on otter twenty-seven touching our hearts the
way she did.

This time we made an exception. This otter deserved a name and
not just a number. We named her Katie.

Katie now lives at Sea World in San Diego. She was one of just a
few otters chosen to be a part of an ongoing study to see what long-
term medical problems may develop from having ingested so much
oil in its most toxic state. Katie was a perfect choice, because she,
more than any of the other otters, seemed to like living with us
humans.

I visited her for the first time at Sea World in January of 1994, and
when I saw her swimming around in the new exhibit that was built
to educate the public about what happened to the otters during the
Exxon spill, it was like being with an old friend again . . . one that
you had almost lost.

17

The Towel Museum

I'd begun to suspect that we'd be taking care of otters a lot longer than two weeks when I picked up a copy of the *Anchorage Times* and noticed it was already April 16. I'd been in Valdez for three weeks.

Exxon confirmed my suspicion when they asked if I could stay at least another month and start hiring additional employees for the otter center. Our volunteer force was beginning to dwindle as people returned to lives that had initially been disrupted by the spill. The remaining volunteers had proved their dedication to the otters, so they were offered jobs first. For several weeks I hired otter handlers, fish preparers, radio dispatchers, secretaries, veterinarians, truck drivers, expediters, pathologists, and parking attendants. By the end of April, we topped out at one hundred thirty-nine full-time employees.

The only vacancy left was that of . . . daughter.

It had been almost a month since I'd left Jennifer with the promise I'd be home in five days. It was the longest we'd ever been separated, and neither one of us liked it. I decided it was time to fill the vacancy.

"Hey, kiddo," I said when the voice I missed so much answered the phone at my parent's house.

"Mama! I've been waiting for you to call."

"I've got a surprise for you."

"Are you coming home?" she asked with an excitement that confirmed how much she missed me.

"No—"

"Mama, why not?" Jennifer interrupted before I could continue. I could hear the disappointment in her voice.

"Because, you're coming here to see me instead."

"What? I am?" Her girlish giggles made me miss her more. "When?"

"As soon as I can get you on a plane."

The next day I made all the arrangements. I talked with the school principal in Valdez and to Jennifer's teacher at home. It would be no problem to transfer her records and have her finish fourth grade in Alaska. Then I called the airline and had her scheduled on a flight that would arrive the following afternoon.

When I saw Jennifer walk off the plane in Anchorage, I realized how much I'd missed my daughter. I actually stayed away from the otter center for an entire day, once we flew back to Valdez from Anchorage. It was great to hear Jennifer laugh and to listen to her tell me about everyone at home. She assured me that Henry and Tigger were doing great, thanks to my friend Pat, who'd volunteered to take care of them until we returned. I wished I could have had Jennifer bring them with her, because I really missed having a cat around.

After I got Jennifer settled into school the next day, I returned to my responsibilities at the otter center. One of my many jobs was to pick up the mail each day at the post office. We'd gotten a PO box, and most days it was crammed full of letters from people thanking us for helping the otters, individuals wanting to know if we needed more help, and out-of-town staff members' families wishing them well. But on this morning, there was something different.

Tucked inside the stack of letters was a yellow postcard that told me there was a box to pick up at the counter. I had to wait in line seemingly forever, but finally it was my turn.

"How are the otters today?" the mail clerk asked as I handed him the yellow card.

"Got another six this morning."

"It's really sad," he replied before disappearing around the corner to grab my box.

As he handed me my package, I noticed it was from Michigan and addressed to the otter center, but it had no one's name on it. When I got back to the center, I asked Randy what I should do with the box, and he said, "Open it. Maybe there is something inside that will tell us whom it belongs to."

I pulled off the wrapping and tore open the box. Inside were five big, fluffy white towels . . . and nothing else. There was no clue as to whom they were for or why they'd been sent. Since we didn't know whom to give them to, we put them to use immediately.

Exxon had been supplying us with whatever materials we needed for the otters. But there was one item we always seemed to run short of—towels. We used them to dry off otters since the washing took away their natural ability to stay warm when wet. The leftover towels were used to mop cages and floors, and for the otters to lie on in their cages for added cushioning.

In the wild, otters rarely come ashore, so they are not accustomed to lying on hard surfaces for very long. In the cages we had made for them, they were spending most of their time lying on hard plastic grates. This was causing sores and calluses on their bodies, so we covered the grates with towels.

As soon as we put the towels in the cages, the otters began cuddling the terry cloth between their front paws. Some would fall asleep with the towels still tucked up close under their chins. We began to wonder if, when it came time to release the otters, we'd have to send each one off with its own towel.

Any of the towels that came in contact with oil had to be disposed of in orange plastic bags. We could not wash them and reuse them because they were contaminated by a toxic substance. Therefore, our supply of towels was depleted quickly.

When the five white towels arrived, we were down to just a few stacks. It seemed as if someone knew we needed towels, but who?

When I made my usual run to the post office the next morning, I stopped to rummage through the garbage can in the post office lobby. I was looking for discarded catalogs, and there were usually plenty. The stores in Valdez didn't provide the selection I was accustomed to at home, so I'd been forced to catalog shop—something I'd always kidded my mom about. She must be on every catalog mailing list in the Western Hemisphere, and her dislike for shopping malls made her a dedicated mail-order customer.

When I finally got to the mailbox with my wide selection of catalogs, I discovered another yellow postcard on top of the stack. This time it had written on it in big red letters, "PICK UP AT LOADING DOCK." I didn't think much about it as I walked out the front door of the post office browsing through a Spiegel catalog.

Out of Harm's Way

I drove my rented green Chevy truck to the rear of the building and got out to ring the doorbell. When the door opened, a man peered at me over his square, wire-framed glasses.

I handed him my yellow card as I said, "Good morning."

He looked at the card I'd given him and then over my shoulder at the truck I'd left idling. On cold mornings I didn't dare turn it off once I got it running.

"Is that yours?" he asked.

"Well, yes. Kinda. It actually belongs to a man here in Valdez, but Exxon is renting it from him for me. You know, rental cars are not real plentiful around here."

He nodded, then crooked his index finger and signaled for me to follow him inside.

The receiving area was one large room stuffed with boxes. All I could see, from floor to ceiling, were big ones, medium-size ones, mammoth ones, brown ones, white ones, and one blue-striped one. I imagined this post office had never before seen so many boxes at one time. It was just another one of the many changes brought on by the spill.

While I looked around at all the boxes and rubbed my hands together to warm them, the postal clerk logged in the number off my yellow card on his clipboard.

"Sign here," he said as he pointed to the line where he wanted my signature.

"Which box is mine?" I asked as I handed him back his clipboard.

The man was silent, but a mischievous grin spread across his face.

"You're not going to believe this," he said. "But all of these boxes are yours."

"What?" I exclaimed, looking at the hundreds of boxes piled in front of me. "No way. You must be mistaken. They can't all be for the otter center."

"Look for yourself," the postal clerk said, pulling a box off one of the stacks. "What does it say?"

"Otter center," I read out loud.

"And all the others say the same thing."

I had to see it to believe it, because this was just too strange. He was right. Every box I looked at was addressed to the otter center.

"They're all from Michigan," I noted, remembering the box from yesterday.

"Exxon doesn't have offices there, do they?" the postal clerk asked.

"I don't think so," I said, half listening to him.

"You should open one and see what's inside," the curious clerk suggested.

"Okay."

I grabbed one of the bigger boxes. After I got the wrapping off, I used the postal clerk's box cutter and sliced through the cardboard. Inside, under a layer of tissue paper was a neat pile of towels.

"Towels," he said, obviously disappointed. "Why would anyone send you towels?"

"I really don't know."

We opened ten more boxes—and you guessed it—all towels.

"How am I going to get all these boxes back to the otter center?" I asked after opening the last of the ten boxes.

"That's why I asked you if the truck was yours. I'm afraid these boxes won't all fit. You'll have to make at least five trips to haul all of these out of here."

And that is what I did for the next hour.

The next day the yellow postcard read, "PICK UP AT LOADING DOCK," and in parentheses, "BRING U-HAUL TRUCK." This went on for almost a week before we solved the mystery of the towels.

A newspaper clipping came in one of the boxes that told the story of a Michigan woman who had taken it upon herself to launch a campaign to provide towels for the otters. She'd gone on TV and radio, and had stories in several newspapers, declaring the otter center in Valdez needed towels, and I think everyone in Michigan believed her.

I tracked down our "towel lady" through the *Detroit News.* "I do so love otters," she told me across three thousand miles of telephone cables. "I wanted to help, but I'm getting on in years, and I knew that if I came there, I'd just be underfoot."

She went on to tell me that she'd gone to a lecture given by a veterinarian who'd been at the otter center. "I gathered from what he said that you needed towels," she explained. "So I decided to help."

I thanked her for her help and assured her we now had plenty of towels. My next call was to the Michigan media, asking them to announce that the otter center no longer needed more towels. Eventually, the boxes stopped arriving, but it wasn't until after we had been forced to rent a warehouse in Valdez just to store all our towels.

It actually became a much-awaited daily event, finding out what kind of towels were in the boxes that arrived each day. You have to remember, Valdez was short on entertainment.

There were always a few boxes in each shipment that made us smile. One box contained twenty-four towels. They had come from an elementary school class. Each child had brought a towel from home, and before the towels were boxed up, the students each signed their name on their towel. One pair came with a gift card from Bonwit Teller that simply said, "For the Otters." They smelled of lilacs and were tied with a purple satin ribbon and had to have cost a fortune. Inside another box was a note with a picture attached. It was of a Doberman standing on a beach at the water's edge. The caption read, "This is Rocky standing guard against the next invasion of Exxon."

We were all having fun with the towels, but one staff member took it a step further.

It was another drizzly morning in May when I walked into the gymnasium and was greeted by a familiar face. The perfectly round, yellow face was on a towel, and below it were the words "HAVE A NICE DAY!"

On the wall next to the smiley face was a big Harley-Davidson emblem, adorning a beach-size towel. And beside that one was another towel with a pair of dolphins cresting out of the ocean. A ladder blocked my view of the next towel.

On the top step of the ladder was Bob, busy securing the final corner of a brightly colored piece of terry cloth. When he backed down the ladder, I could see a slender girl in a grass skirt, doing the hula against a background of palm trees. "VISIT BEAUTIFUL HAWAII," it enticed.

"Bob. What are you doing?" I said, half laughing.

"What do you think? Isn't this quite a collection." Bob looked at the wall as if he were a museum curator setting up a priceless art exhibit.

"Well . . ." All I could do was laugh.

Everyone monitored the progress of Bob's work that day, eager to hand over towels that they thought worthy of the collection. By the end of the day, the walls of the gym were a patchwork of colors. There was a section with the Rams, 49ers, and Steelers represented. A smooching Minnie and Mickey hung over the bathroom door. A towering Golden Gate Bridge made me homesick for California. The caricature of a quirky scuba diver boasted, "Divers Do It Deeper."

The finishing touch was a sign that Bob painted and hung over the main entrance of the gym: VALDEZ TOWEL MUSEUM. Our exhibit attracted quite a crowd and generated a lot of laughter.

Each time I looked at the towel-covered walls and thought of all the other towels we'd used in caring for the otters, it reminded me that other people cared ... especially some really special people in Michigan.

18

Ken

By June there was time for movies and popcorn. I'd stopped by Video Express and rented *Anne of Green Gables* on the way home from the otter center. Tonight Jennifer and I would have a *normal* evening at home—if I could remember what that was.

The Jiffy Pop dome expanded like a silver balloon on the stove top as I shook it back and forth. My daughter was perched on the countertop next to me, her legs kicking the cabinet door below in an annoying staccato.

"Jennifer, stop that," I said.

"Mama, I talked to Ken today."

She was starting again. Two weeks ago she'd announced that this guy who worked in the fish room would make a great new daddy. Jennifer had no recollection of her real father, but she did know that she wanted a daddy, and she thought I needed a husband. Therefore she was always on the lookout for the perfect candidate. It seemed Ken fit her description.

"Jennifer, quick, grab me a bowl."

She pulled a yellow one from the dish drainer as I pulled back the aluminum foil and filled the bowl with freshly popped popcorn.

"Mama, guess what I found out today?" Jennifer teased as she grabbed for a fistful of popcorn.

"What," I asked, hoping she was changing the subject. Maybe she'd tell me something about school instead.

"Ken's from San Diego. That's not far from where we live."

It was time for me to change the subject. "Jennifer, go start the movie while I pour us some Coke."

Reluctantly, she jumped down from the counter and stuck the movie in the VCR.

"Get your pajamas on too," I yelled over the TV. "And turn that thing down."

A few minutes later we were propped up on the couch with our popcorn and Coke, ready for the movie to begin. Before the previews were over, though, she started again.

"Mama, he likes dogs and cats." Jennifer looked at me sideways to see my reaction.

I had too much popcorn in my mouth to respond.

"He was in the navy nine years—on a submarine. Maybe he could take us for a ride on one?"

"*Shhhh,* Jennifer. The movie's starting."

"Mama . . ."

I had had enough. Before she could tell me one more thing about the guy from the fish room, I turned to her and said, "Jennifer, I'm not interested. Okay?" It was enough to hurt her feelings.

My daughter seemed to shrink into herself like a deflating balloon. I suddenly felt bad. Maybe there was more to this than I thought.

I reached out with my arm and pulled her closer to me. "Hey, kiddo, I appreciate what you're trying to do, but don't you know how happy I am just to have you in my life?"

"Yeah. But I want a daddy of my own," she mumbled under her breath. "Everyone else at school has a daddy but me."

"I wish I could get you a daddy, but I'm afraid it's not as easy as it seems," I explained as I wondered whether bringing her to Alaska had been the right thing to do. We didn't spend time together the way we did at home, but there were lots of people around who adored her. The office staff had even made up a name tag for her that read: "THE KID."

"Jennifer someday you'll have a new daddy, but until then we just have to be patient. All right?"

She nodded her head. I suspected I'd not heard the last of Ken, though.

The following evening, we decided we'd eat dinner at the otter center. Exxon provided the staff with three meals a day, and the food was usually very good. But what really made you look forward to mealtime was sitting around the large picnic tables the carpenters had made and eating with the rest of the staff. After spending several, very intense months with these folks we were like family—complete with laughter, teasing, debates, crying and an occasional food fight.

· As we were waiting our turn in line to get dinner, I tried to rub some of that day's dirt off of Jennifer's face. She moaned and groaned, just the way a kid is supposed to do. We moved along with the line, and when it was our turn, I looked at the first serving pan on the table . . . prime rib. I decided we'd eat somewhere else.

Too much of a good thing causes it to no longer be a treat. That was how I was beginning to feel about prime rib. It seemed we had an awful lot of it, and I finally figured out why. The chefs had come up with a way to remind us when it was Sunday, the end of another *long* week. None of us could keep track of time. When you're working twelve-hour shifts, seven days a week, and the sun only disappears from the sky overhead for a few brief hours, the days begin to blend together. It was nice of the chefs to try and get us back in sync, but why couldn't they use something like fresh raspberries on Sunday night to remind us, instead of prime rib.

Just as I was leaving the dining room, intending to take Jennifer into town for dinner, Ken walked through the door. There was no avoiding him. I had to say something, and Jennifer saw to it that I did.

"We're going to town for dinner. Do you want to go with us?" Jennifer asked.

I couldn't believe what my daughter had just done. Now what was I going to do?

Poor Ken just stood there, not sure what to say. There was an uncomfortably long pause before I spoke. 'They're serving prime rib again tonight. If you're as tired of it as we are, you're welcome to join us."

"Okay," he said simply. "Where are we going?"

"We hadn't thought that far," I replied. "But it shouldn't be too hard a decision, considering what we have to choose from in Valdez."

"How about Fu Kung's?" Ken suggested.

"Sounds great, and Jennifer loves Chinese food," I said, glaring at my daughter as she stood next to me with a mischievous grin on her face.

"Mama, I don't want Chinese food. I'm going to stay here and eat."

"No you aren't." I knew what she was up to. "You have to go because I'm not coming back here to pick you up later."

"I'll bring her home." It was Kym, the office secretary, who offered. She'd overheard our conversation, and I suspected she was in cahoots with Jennifer.

I was outnumbered.

Dinner, much to my surprise, was delightful. Ken was much different from the impression I'd pieced together in the brief moments I'd had occasion to talk with him. But what can you learn about a person when all you talk about is the price of clams and mussels?

Now I learned his roots were in Kansas, which explained his good-heartedness and genuine kindness. His father had been in the military, so they moved a lot when he was a kid. Somehow he'd avoided the pitfall of becoming a military brat. Right after high school he and a buddy joined the navy together, and he spent the next nine years cruising the world aboard a submarine.

The more Ken told me about himself, the more interested I became. All of a sudden I wished I'd listened to my daughter sooner.

Starting that night, Ken, Jennifer, and I spent a lot of time together. We'd spend our free time laughing, playing volleyball in the gym, eating lots of ice cream, hiking in the wilderness that surrounded Valdez, watching movies, and trying not to think about the future.

At the end of June, I flew home to California with Jennifer. Before the Exxon spill had occurred, we had made arrangements for her to go to camp, and we couldn't cancel now and get our money back. My parents had agreed to take care of her until I was finished in Alaska.

It felt good to be at home for those three days, but I also couldn't wait to get back to Valdez. Ken was one of the biggest reasons.

When I saw Ken waiting for me inside the terminal in Valdez, I realized I wanted this man to remain in my life, and for the next two months he did. Ken slid into my life like a hand into a soft glove. We were a perfect match, and I couldn't remember ever being happier.

The second week of July I called my mom.

"You want me to send you what?" I had to laugh at the disbelief in her voice.

"A G.I. Joe coloring book and a gray Porsche," I repeated.

"A real one?" My mom knew I had finally been able to save some money, but certainly I hadn't saved enough for a Porsche.

"No. A Matchbox car."

"Have you adopted a little boy, or something?" my mom asked.

I couldn't tease her any longer. "You might say that." I paused for a moment. "I've met someone I'm very fond of."

"Is his name Ken, by any chance?"

"Jennifer told," I said, disappointed she ruined my surprise.

"She's talked about him a lot since she got back, and she really seems to like him."

I was pleased. Jennifer and I were a package deal, and I didn't want anyone in our lives that couldn't accept that, nor could I bring someone into my life that Jennifer did not approve of. It seemed we had finally come up with a person suitable to be a new husband and daddy.

"So why do you need the coloring book and the Porsche?"

"It's Ken's birthday at the end of the month."

"Don't you think he's a little too old to be coloring and playing with toy cars?" I laughed and my mom joined in.

I stayed on the phone with my mom for another fifteen minutes, sharing my plans for Ken's birthday. Before we hung up, my mom promised she'd stop by Toys "R" Us.

When July 26 arrived, I'd managed to get all my shopping done, which was primarily accomplished through catalogs. While Ken went to take a shower, I dashed into the spare bedroom and pulled from the closet the gifts I'd managed to wrap and hide without getting caught. It took three trips to get them into the bedroom, where I spread them out on the bed. When he walked back into the bedroom, he was indeed surprised.

"Happy Birthday," I yelled as he lowered the towel he'd been using to rub his hair dry.

"How did you know?" he asked, still not believing the boxes spread across the bed.

"You forget who hired you," I said with a smile. "I know everything."

"There are so many of them. I don't think I've gotten this many birthday presents in my whole life."

"There are thirty of them. One for each birthday I've missed. And if you don't start opening them, we'll both be late for work," I said, clearing a place for him to sit down next to me.

Ken reached for the biggest one, and I grabbed it from him. "No! You have to open them in order. I'll hand them to you."

I gave him the package with the rattle tied into the light blue bow first. Inside was a baby's bib embroidered with a polar bear.

"This is for birthday number two," I said, handing him the one with green alligators on the paper.

He unwrapped the G.I. Joe coloring book and crayons for his third birthday.

For his fifth birthday, he got the gray Porsche. The former Cub Scout got a Swiss Army knife to celebrate becoming a teenager. I got more creative as the years went on. He loved the espresso maker I got to mark his twenty-ninth birthday. The thirtieth had to be really special. I decided upon a day-long raft trip to Shoup Bay so we could see a glacier up close and be near otters that hadn't been affected by the oil spill.

With each package came a card, signed *"Love, Terri."*

We sat on the bed in the middle of paper, ribbons, and the thirty years of presents, laughing. It had been a lot of work tearing open all the gifts, but Ken survived to tell me that no one had ever done anything like this for him. I was glad I'd made him happy.

I dropped Ken off at the computer lab at the community college, where he was tabulating the otters' food consumption. By then he thought his birthday celebration was over. But I had more surprises in store for him.

"Close your eyes," I said gently when he climbed into the car at six that evening.

"What?"

"Now, don't ask questions, just do as you're told," I ordered. From beneath the seat, I pulled out a scarf and placed it over his eyes.

While I secured the material in place, Ken kept trying to get me to tell him what was going on, but I remained silent.

My destination was the old town site, where Valdez had stood prior to the earthquake that had leveled it in 1973. It was only on the other side of the harbor, but I took thirty minutes to get us there. With Valdez being so small, I thought that if I drove directly there, Ken would be able to figure out where we were headed, and I wanted to keep it a surprise for as long as I could.

Therefore, I drove in circles, backed up, crisscrossed through downtown, and finally headed out of town, continually ordering Ken not to peek. When we reached the outskirts of the abandoned town, I told him he could take off the blindfold.

"What are we doing here?" he asked as his eyes readjusted to the light.

"You've told me you have a fascination with ghost towns, and this was as close as I could come to one around here. I thought it would be fun to rummage around and see what's out here."

Ken agreed. A big smile came over his face, followed by a kiss that said, "Thank you."

"Oh, and I brought dinner with us," I said, reaching into the back-seat to pull a picnic basket out from under some unfolded towels.

Before we ate, we wandered through the old town site. It was a landscape that had been reclaimed by nature. Grasses and vines had a strong roothold over the crumbled concrete and decaying wood. Clumps of Canadian thistles poked through crevices of the old foundations.

Ken grabbed a long stick and poked around in the dirt, looking for hidden treasures. He turned up smooth-edged pieces of blue-and-green glass and rusted trinkets that seemed to make him happier than finding something brand-new. A rusty bottle opener turned out to be his most prized discovery.

For over an hour, Ken rummaged to his heart's content, while I watched—pleased that such simple things could make this man happy.

We eventually returned for the picnic basket, walking back through a field of wildflowers. I gathered forget-me-nots, fireweed, and laven-der irises to fill the vase in the cottage we'd moved into in June. The transformation of Valdez over the last few weeks, from a world of solid white to one of endless wildflowers, had been absolutely amaz-ing. It must have been the promise of summer's brilliance that got people through the long, dark months of winter.

A fallen tree, close to the water's edge provided a perfect setting for our picnic. As we ate plump strawberries dipped in powdered sugar, smoked salmon, french bread, and brie cheese and drank a bottle of chardonnay, we absorbed the scenery around us. It was abso-lutely spectacular.

We took turns using the binoculars I'd brought to count the bears on Candy Kiss Mountain gorging themselves on blueberries. Across the harbor we could see the Octagon, the last holding facility for the otters before they would be released. It was those magnificent crea-tures that had brought us together, but for how much longer?

Ken had already told me he didn't want to go back to San Diego and that he was thinking of staying in Alaska. I had to go back home. Jennifer needed her mom.

We were very quiet as the wine took effect and the peacefulness of our surroundings eased us into a relaxed state. The evening would have been perfect if we hadn't both been thinking about the decision we'd soon have to make. Letting go would be a hard thing to do.

*　　*　　*

The first group of otters would be released in a week, came the announcement the next morning.

Ken was quiet all day, and I didn't say much. As we drove back to our cottage that night, he asked if I'd like to drive to Bridal Veil, the spectacular waterfall a couple of miles past the turnoff to our place. That sounded nice. Ken had taken me there on our first date.

For a while we sat on a boulder within hearing distance of the falling water. "I was thinking," he said finally. "It doesn't matter where I live . . . as long as I'm with you."

Before I could respond, he told me something else, "I want you to know how much I admire you. What you stand for. I'd like to be able to continue to be a part of your life . . . and Jennifer's."

I hadn't expected such a declaration.

"You mean it?" I whispered.

"Yes," he replied. "And I want to tell you something else. I'm glad my friend Mike insisted that I take a six-month leave from my job in San Diego to come to Alaska. I can't remember doing anything that's given me such a feeling of satisfaction as helping the otters has. And I think you will continue to give the same kind of meaning to my life."

I couldn't say anything . . . but the combination of tears and the smile on my face told Ken he'd made the right decision.

"I suggest," he continued, "that when it comes time to leave here, we leave together. You've always wanted to go to Victoria, so let's spend a week there and then decide what to do next."

I thought his plan was perfect.

There were only twenty of us left when the last group of otters was released at the end of August. It was a very emotional time. We crowded on the shore of Nelson Bay, near Cordova, Alaska, and forced ourselves to smile at each other, but tears accompanied the joy. We'd toiled so long for this victorious moment. We'd saved one hundred ninety-seven otters . . . and it was time to let the last of them go.

One by one we opened the airline crates and freed the otters. They sliced through the water like sleek, black comets across a shadowy sky. I think we expected them to turn and at least take one last look at us, but they never looked back. The empty crates were piled in the helicopter, and as we flew over Nelson Bay, we could see our otters below. They looked happy to be home.

It was now time for us to go home.

Ken and I spent the week in Victoria, British Columbia, catching up on our sleep, shopping in stores abundant with merchandise I'd been deprived of for months, indulging our taste buds with rich and fattening foods, drinking lots of English tea in the middle of the afternoon, and relaxing. It was over afternoon tea one day in the Empress Hotel that Ken proposed.

My immediate answer was, "Yes!"

We flew back to Santa Clara to announce our plans. I knew Jennifer would be delighted to be getting a new daddy—almost as happy as I was to be getting the husband I'd always dreamed of but had begun to expect would exist only in my dreams.

Ken and I were married on October 7.

My family now consisted of a husband I adored, a daughter who was proud of her new daddy, Henry and Tigger, plus two new cats, Wally and Slick, who'd adopted us in Valdez. We were all content with this part of what the Exxon spill had given us.

Ken went to work at Santa Clara University in November, shortly after we'd learned I was pregnant. Six months later, a job in the Anthropology/Sociology Department at the university became available, and I filled the vacancy. I took the position because I knew that it would give me the flexibility I needed to be able to respond to future disasters.

Fortunately, the disasters slowed down for a while, allowing me to enjoy motherhood a second and third time. Amy, our blue-eyed redhead arrived in May of 1990, and Megan was born just in time for Christmas in 1992. The holidays that year were wonderful—abundant with family and laughter. There was only one person who could have made it more complete . . . my dear friend Irene.

In Between Disasters

19

No Scared

The telephone had been ringing all day. News of my return from Alaska had spread quickly among my friends and family. Everyone was most anxious to hear of my adventures in Valdez—and to meet Ken.

My brother, Todd, and his fiancée, Deb, had come over to join us for lunch, and several times during the meal I'd had to jump up to take another call. My brother joked as I ran to the phone the last time, "Did you take out an ad to say you're back?"

I laughed. It was so good to see my brother again.

"Hello," I said into the receiver.

The only response was heavy, labored breathing, like the painful inhalations of a person with asthma.

"Who is this?" I asked.

"Te . . . rri?" The voice was a raw whisper. I could barely make it out.

"Yes," I answered quickly.

"Cats. Trap. Come." The words were pushed out slowly, one by one, in an English accent I started to recognize.

"Irene? Is that you?" I asked.

"Yesssss." It seemed to take every bit of her strength to respond.

"Irene, I'll be over in just a few minutes," I told her before hanging up the phone. It sounded as though she needed help with her cats again, but I was more concerned about her.

I'd known Irene for nearly two years. She'd been one of the first referrals from the Humane Society. I was told by the woman who called from the shelter, "Be prepared. This lady has lots of cats."

Irene lived in a small Victorian home in downtown San Jose, with her thirty-some felines. None of them were indoor cats. In fact, they were all wild, but she loved them just the same. Each one had a name and a story.

I'd been to Irene's many times. When a cat was sick, she'd ask me to come by and trap it. Irene couldn't afford to pay vet bills on her meager income from Social Security, so the cats would be taken to the Humane Society and euthanized. As each cat was loaded into my car, Irene would spend time with each one, saying good-bye. She would lean down close to the cage and whisper, "No scared. No scared." It was hard to see her friends leave, but she knew it had to be done.

To help ease the losses, I had trapped several of Irene's favorite female cats and had them spayed and vaccinated. They were all doing fine living in Irene's backyard. Several of them had even started to let her pick them up.

The time I spent with Irene was always special. Frequently, Jennifer and I would stop by to see how she was doing. She was in her seventies and she had no family, so sometimes I worried about her. She always told me her cats were great company, but I know she looked forward to our visits. When we arrived, there would always be a fresh pot of English tea and tiny homemade cookies waiting for us.

When I hung up the phone, I suspected this visit was going to be different.

After loading half a dozen traps and transfer cages into my car, I headed for downtown San Jose with Deb, who'd offered to come and help. It was good to spend some time with my future sister-in-law. Todd had met Deb just before I'd left for Alaska, so we hadn't had much of a chance so far to get to know each other. After I got to Irene's, I was especially glad Deb had come with me.

When we pulled up in front of the small Victorian, I was stunned at how much it had deteriorated in the months since I'd last been there. The usually green and beautifully manicured lawn was now just a sun-baked parcel of dirt, with weeds growing in a few places.

The flower beds—full and glorious when I'd seen them last—were barren.

Deb and I sat for a moment looking at the house. I tried to explain to her what it used to look like, but I knew it must be hard to imagine when it looked so bad now. I pulled the car into the driveway. It was time to find Irene.

Looking down the driveway into the backyard, we could now see some of the cats. It looked as if there were more than normal. We tried counting them, but so many looked alike and they kept moving about. Our guess was forty-two.

"I've never seen so many cats," Deb said as we got out of the car.

"Yeah. Irene can't turn away a hungry kitty." I suspected a lot of the cats had been intentionally dumped at her house because the word around the neighborhood was, you have a cat you don't want—take it to Irene.

When my car doors slammed shut, a handful of cats leaped from the porch and scooted around the side of the house. I noticed two of them were pregnant.

"Why don't you start unloading the traps, and I'll go see where Irene is," I said and headed toward the front door.

"I guess I should get them all out. Right?"

"Yep. I think we'll need all of them this time."

I stepped over a collection of throwaway newspapers as I made my way up the steps. The smell of cat urine was strong on the porch as I stood there looking around. Spread across its wooden floor was an assortment of dirty pie tins, plastic butter tubs, and aluminum containers used to feed the cats. They had all been licked clean some time ago. A large cooking pot had a small amount of slimy green water in the bottom of it.

This was not how Irene took care of her cats. I knew then that something was definitely wrong.

I went to the screen door and knocked. After five knocks I still had gotten no response, so I opened the screen door and used the brass door knocker. Still nothing.

"Irene. Are you home?" I yelled, with my face close to the door.

Still nothing.

By then Deb had come up on the porch. "Do you think she went somewhere?"

"I doubt it from the way she sounded on the phone," I said as I banged on the door.

I then tried the knob and it turned. The door opened when I pushed against it. It took a few moments for my eyes to adjust to the dark living room. Again I called out Irene's name but didn't get the response I wanted. The house was silent except for the ticktock of the clock on the mantel.

Deb followed as I stepped inside. It smelled like the convalescent home my great grandmother had been in when I was just a kid, not the flower-scented living room I'd sat in months before. The yellowed window shades were all pulled down, and the faded floral-print drapes were drawn. I pushed the door open a little further and stepped over mail that had come through the slot in the door.

I wasn't five feet past the door when I finally saw Irene. She was sitting, slouched down in her favorite overstuffed chair, like a flower that had been beaten down in a rainstorm. Her chin rested heavily on her chest. She wore a stained pink nightgown and her long, thin hair, which had always been neatly wrapped in a bun, hung down on both sides of her face. Her feet were uncovered, and I could see her toenails extending beyond the end of her toes.

"Is . . . she alive?" Deb whispered.

"Yeah. I can see her breathing."

Just then Irene moved slightly. She was trying to lift her head. I moved closer, and knelt down so she could see me.

"Te . . . rri?"

"Yes, Irene. It's me."

"Hel—p my cats." I could barely hear Irene as she spoke.

I reached for her hand and held it between mine. It was ice cold.

"Let me get you to bed first."

"Noooo. Hel—p cats . . . first."

For the next ten minutes Deb and I tried to convince Irene to let us help her. She kept insisting she wanted the cats taken care of instead. When she started to cry, I knew I had to fulfill her wish.

There was a crocheted blanket on the couch that I wrapped around Irene, as Deb went to the kitchen to fix a pot of tea. Irene had two sips of the hot liquid. I pulled back the drapes to allow some light into the room and opened the living room window a crack. We asked Irene if she wanted something to eat, but she shook her head no.

I pulled Irene's hair back from her face. The yellow light cast shadows into her tired, watery eyes. I took one of Irene's frail hands between my own. They were warmer than before.

"Won't you let me take you to the hospital?" I asked my friend gently.

"Hel—p cats"—there was a long pause before she finished—
"all-l-l of them."

For the next five hours, Deb and I trapped all of Irene's cats. Even
her favorite females. We found two litters of newborn kittens in the
potting shed and four dead cats in the garage. It looked as if they'd
gotten locked inside and starved to death. In total, we had found
forty-nine cats. It took five trips to get them all to the Humane Society.
When we were done, we went back to help Irene.

"Irene, they are all gone," I said, leaning down in front of her.

She said nothing. Instead, I heard her take in a long deep breath
and let it out slowly. I knew she was relieved.

Deb and I each took one of Irene's arms and helped her out of the
chair. This time she did not resist. We walked her into the bedroom
and laid her on the bed that Deb had made up with fresh sheets. In
one of the dresser drawers we found a clean nightgown, which we
managed to put on her. I brushed her hair and braided it into two
strands that I wound into one neat bun. Deb had gone back into the
kitchen to fix something for Irene to eat. She came back to tell me
the cupboards were all empty except for cat food.

While I ran to the store to get some food, Deb stayed to clean the
house. A thick layer of dust coated every surface and cobwebs hung
everywhere. By the time I got back, the house no longer smelled like
a convalescent home. The bouquet of fresh flowers I'd picked up at
a nearby florist helped.

I warmed the soup I'd bought and carried it in to Irene on a tray.
She finished less than half the bowl. A short while later she dozed off.

The room was quiet as I sat and watched Irene sleep. There was a
feeling of comfort and well-being in the room. A slight breeze waved
the delicate lace curtains. I could smell the flowers I'd arranged in a
vase and put on her nightstand. Irene's face looked relaxed. She slept
for almost an hour.

When she woke up, Irene looked at me for a long time before she
spoke.

"Stories," she whispered. "Alaska."

Irene was one of the last people I'd called before I'd left for Valdez.
She had been so excited that I was going. I'd promised her that when
I got home I'd tell her all about it. My mom had called Irene when
my stay was extended to six months, and again she told my mom she
couldn't wait to see me and hear the stories.

For two hours I told Irene the stories. She particularly liked hearing
about the otters. Irene had told me many times how much she loved

the ocean and all its fascinating creatures. Before she quit driving, she used to travel down to the coast in Monterey and sit for hours watching the sea otters frolicking in the water just offshore and the pelicans dive-bombing for their meals. "When I die, I want to be a part of that world," Irene had told me one evening when we were sitting on her porch talking.

I ended my stories by telling Irene about Ken. She smiled. I know she was happy for me.

It was a little after eleven when Deb and I finally left. We'd gotten Irene to eat a little more soup and then helped her into the bathroom. I'd finally gotten her to promise that she'd let me take her to see a doctor in the morning. Her breathing was better, and her body relaxed, but I knew she needed medical care. Deb and I had looked through the house for any prescribed medication and there was nothing. I did find a Medi-cal number, which I wrote down on a piece of paper. I'd call in the morning to find out where I could take Irene.

The last thing I did before I left was tuck Irene's blanket up under her chin, and as I softly kissed her cheek, I whispered, "Good night, Irene."

A short, stocky man in his early fifties pushed open the screen door when I pulled into Irene's driveway the next morning.

"Hi. I'm Terri," I said as I approached, not sure who this man was.

"Oh, yeah. I heard Irene talk about you," the man said as he came out on the porch.

"I'm Joe. The landlord. Came by to collect the rent—she was three months behind, and I found her dead in bed." The man's words did not surprise me. I'd suspected my good night to Irene just hours before might be the last one.

This woman, who so dearly loved her cats, had kept death waiting until she knew they were all taken care of. I was glad I'd gotten home from Alaska in time to help her.

"The coroner just left. I didn't know who else to call. It's sad when a person doesn't have any kin. But at least she had her cats." I smiled as he spoke of Irene's friends.

Jennifer and I drove in silence to Monterey. It was a spectacular day to be going to the ocean. The sky and water blended into an uninterrupted slate of blue along the horizon. A group of brown pelicans skimmed the water in search of food. The breeze that came through the window was warm. I knew Irene would have enjoyed the day.

When we got near the pier, we parked the car. It was a short walk to the boat docks. I carried my backpack and held Jennifer's hand. A man I'd spoken to on the phone three days earlier was waiting at his boat for us.

We passed the breakwater and headed a mile out to sea. The spray from the ocean mixed with the warmth of the September sun was like a child's lullaby. I closed me eyes and thought about Irene. When the boat stopped, I knew it was time.

I opened my backpack as Jennifer watched. I'd talked with her the night before about what we were going to do in Monterey, and I think she understood. This was the first person she'd known who had died. Before Jennifer fell asleep, she told me she would miss the little homemade cookies that Irene always made.

From the backpack, I pulled out the small brass urn. Jennifer followed as I moved to the railing. I held the urn with my left hand as I unscrewed the top. Before I removed the lid, I stood there for a moment and looked around. Irene was right—this was a wonderful resting place.

I removed the lid and slowly tipped the urn toward the water. As the ashes mixed with the sea, I whispered, "No scared. No scared."

20

Elvira

It was just before the Fourth of July weekend when the all too familiar phone call came. Another person asking me to trap a mother cat and her offspring. The woman said she could hear them in the ivy outside her kitchen window. "They sound so pathetic," she reported sadly. "Please can you come get them?"

I arranged to come by the following morning.

Since I knew where the kittens were, I decided to trap the mother cat first. As I watched the pitifully thin feline cross the backyard fence, it saddened me to think of how many cats there were living this way, each struggling to stay alive. Since the beginning of May I'd stayed busy trapping lots of cats that looked just like this one.

The brown-and-black-multicolored mother cat detoured off the fence when she got a whiff of the tuna in the trap set in the bushes below. She jumped down from the fence and moved toward it cautiously. After spending a good five minutes sniffing the wire trap, she then decided to venture inside. She crept forward slowly, eating the food trail that lured her to the flat metal trigger piece at the back. When she stepped on it, the door closed behind her. It startled her for only a second, but she quickly resumed eating. She was so hungry.

When she finished, I approached the trap and draped a towel over it. She hissed when I picked it up and carried it into the shade near my car. Before I went to look for the kittens, I dropped some more food through the metal bars for the mother cat. As soon as I walked away, she started eating again.

It took only a matter of minutes to locate the kittens. Gathering them was what took longer. The litter was about four weeks old, and they came in all colors. The kittens had already had their lesson on how to avoid being caught by people, but they hadn't had a chance to practice until then. With my gloves on, I managed to scoop up all four of them and put them in a cage next to their mother's.

"Are you sure this is all of them?" I asked the woman as I loaded the cats into my car.

"Four and the mom," she assured me as she nodded to verify the truth of what she was telling me.

Before going home I dropped the mother and her kittens off at the Humane Society and tried not to think about what would happen to them in three days.

The phone woke me the following morning.

"I must have miscounted," the voice said apologetically. "I could hear another kitten meowing all night."

"I'll be there within the hour," I said. As I drove to Los Gatos, I thought about the kitten. What a frightful night it must have had.

Loud, insistent meowing led me to the last kitten. I carefully eased my way through the ivy, knowing how much lizards like to hide in this stuff too. I finally caught sight of the last holdout wedged up against the gas meter. When it saw me approaching, it took off in the opposite direction, determined not to get caught. But its escape route dead-ended where the house and the fence met. There was no escape.

It turned to face me. The tiny ears were laid back, its back arched, the yellow eyes glowed meanness, and it hissed like a teapot letting off steam. I went to grab it, and it batted my glove valiantly. The mother had taught this one well.

"Oh, you're a feisty one," I said as I reached for the jet-black kitten again.

This time I grabbed it. With all its might it wiggled and twisted, trying to free itself from my grasp. It spat and clawed and fought me every inch of the way into the holding cage.

"Now, are you sure this is all of them?" I asked the bathrobe-clad woman.

"It has to be. She's never had more than five kittens at a time."

"You mean this cat didn't just show up with these kittens recently?" I asked, surprised.

"Oh, no. She's lived in the neighborhood a long time."

"What happened to all her other kittens?" I was afraid of what I might hear.

"Some get hit by cars or they get sick. Eventually they just all disappear. But not the mom. Somehow she always survives."

At least the vicious cycle of unwanted births and painful deaths had been stopped—until the next cat came along.

Before dropping the kitten off at the Humane Society, I stopped by Joelle's house to pick up one of my traps I'd loaned her several weeks earlier. Joelle had gotten good at trapping cats. She'd had the three she'd caught in the past six months altered and then released them on her property. A scrawny, pregnant cat had been the last one to show up. Joelle added one more feeding dish and plaid, circular pet bed to the growing number on her patio.

"What have you got in here?" Joelle asked as she placed the trap in the back of my car. She carefully lifted the towel covering the cage, then let out a cry of surprise as the kitten lunged forward. "He's a real little scrapper, isn't he?"

"Yeah, he's about as wild as they come."

"I don't suppose there's much hope of this one getting adopted?"

I shook my head. The Humane Society was full of adorable, sweet kittens right now that they couldn't find homes for. This one didn't have a chance.

"Pity," she mused.

I had gotten to know Joelle pretty well in the past few months, and I recognized the look on her face. She was planning something in that head of hers.

"Why don't you leave the kitten with me?" Joelle paused. "Maybe I can tame it and find it a home."

"You're kidding. Do you know how hard it is to tame a feral cat? Most of them never give in to being domesticated." I wished I were wrong, but I'd known too many people who'd tried and not succeeded.

"My husband is out of town on business for a month," she said. "Let me at least try to make it friendly." She reminded me of Jennifer when she was trying to persuade me to give in to something she wanted. I was just waiting for the, "Pretty please."

I couldn't say no.

As I handed Joelle the cage with its ornery occupant, I warned her to be careful. Even though the kitten was small, it had the fighting capabilities of a big cat.

"I'll call you in a week and give you an update," Joelle said as I pulled away.

Driving home I thought about the kitten and hoped Joelle would be successful. I was ready for a "happy ending" story for at least one cat.

Joelle phoned Sunday morning. "I got George's kennel from the garage and put it in the laundry room." I'd seen Joelle's laundry room. It was as large as the average living room.

"I put out enough food and water for a couple days in the room and left her alone. She stopped crying after the first day." Joelle sounded relieved.

"Then I brought all my daughter's stuffed animals out of storage and scattered them on the laundry room floor." Joelle's tactic was a new one. "Oh, and by the way, I think my little visitor is a girl."

Joelle told me that by day three she figured the kitten was ready for some "live" company, so she moved in and spent the morning with the kitten. It seemed the kitten decided to be nonsocial and stayed behind the washing machine the entire time Joelle was in the room.

"I go in every morning and give her fresh food now and spend about half an hour talking to her. And then I do the same thing again in the evening," I was told during the next update. I was beginning to admire Joelle's patience. Most people would have already given up on the kitten, but not Joelle.

At the end of two weeks Joelle could put food out and sit down nearby as the kitten ate it. "She's not running away from me any longer." I had never heard Joelle so excited. "In fact, I think she listens for me, because she's always waiting near the door when I come into the laundry room."

Day by day, Joelle reported progress. She was delighted when the kitten finally came up to her and sniffed her. One afternoon the kitten even fell asleep at Joelle's feet as she stood in the laundry room ironing. "I wanted so badly to pet her, but I knew it was too soon," she told me.

"Have you named her yet?" I asked one afternoon when Joelle called.

"No. I don't want to get too attached." I suspected it was already too late.

"How about Elvira, after the Halloween witch who steals hearts?" I teased. It seemed a perfect name.

"Not bad. I'll think about it," Joelle said before hanging up.

Two days later the phone rang and a jubilant Joelle was on the other end. "Guess what! Elvira crawled onto my lap last night, and it gets better . . . she let me pet her. What do you think of that?"

I was thinking that Elvira was one very lucky cat to have found a person like Joelle.

My next update was the one I'd been waiting to hear. The call came late in the evening. "Terri. I hope I didn't wake you," Joelle said. "But I had to call you. You know how I told you I'd been bringing Elvira into the living room at night while I watched TV."

"Uh hum."

"Well, this evening, Elvira decided she'd watch TV sitting on my lap, which she'd done a couple times already, but this time . . . she purred." Joelle was half laughing and half crying. "Terri . . . I think I won."

The following day I decided it was time to visit the new Elvira. The glossy, solid-bodied feline that walked with confidence across the plush living room carpet to check me out was not the same kitten I'd left at Joelle's three weeks earlier. She'd become a loving cat who craved attention. I knew Joelle had given her plenty.

I spent the next hour on the floor in Joelle's living room playing with Elvira. She had more toys than a spoiled child. I was just thinking that Elvira had found the perfect home when Joelle spoke. "It's time to find Elvira a new family."

"You're not going to keep her?" I blurted out.

"My husband is due back at the end of next week, and he doesn't want a cat in the house. I'm afraid if Elvira were put back outdoors, she'd revert to being wild," Joelle looked at Elvira as she batted around a felt mouse. "I couldn't do that to her. I want her to get a good home where she'll continue to be loved."

I knew Joelle was right, but I still thought this kitten belonged with her.

It was Elvira's second time riding in a cage in my car. I wondered if she remembered the first trip. Before we left, Joelle had hugged the ball of fur, kissed her on the nose, and said, "Now, be good, and remember everything I taught you." She then opened the cage door and put her in.

"Good-bye, my dear Elvira." Joelle took one last look in the cage and turned to go back in the house.

In Between Disasters

I decided to take Elvira home. It was to be a temporary living arrangement until I found her the perfect, permanent home to move into. We now had five cats—Tigger, Henry, Wally, Slick, and the newest Humane Society adoptee, Freddie. In addition, there was Spenard, our black Lab, whom we had adopted as a puppy three months earlier. There definitely was no room for any more four-legged creatures in our household.

But from the moment we let her out of her carrying case and she stepped daintily into our living room, she claimed her space. Spenard approached slowly to investigate the newcomer and was smacked on his nose for his trouble. Elvira had learned how to handle dogs, having lived with George. Spenard retreated to his favorite corner. The cats one by one came up and sniffed. There were a few hisses, but no flying fur, which was a good sign. By evening, everyone had decided Elvira could stay, temporarily.

It was when I went to check on Amy later that night and saw Elvira curled up and purring in the cluster of stuffed animals that outlined Amy's pillow that I knew.

My daughter opened one sleepy eye as I tugged the blankets up around her shoulders. "Where's my kitty?" She spotted Elvira and gently reached out to pet her. The contented cat purred even louder.

Elvira had found her new home.

Hurricane Andrew
Dade County, Florida . . .

Down South they call them "canes," those screaming winds that blow in from the ocean devastating everything in their path. On August 24, 1992, at five in the morning, a big one slammed ashore at Biscayne Bay, Florida. This one was named Andrew.

Nothing stood intact in the wake of this hurricane. It descended on the farm fields of Homestead like an out-of-control garbage disposal, churning every acre within a fifty-mile radius into a nature-made rubbish heap.

In the hours immediately following Andrew's demise, news about people began to trickle out of the devastated area in bits and pieces, but there was no mention about the effect this disaster had had upon animals. On August 26, 1992, I flew to southern Florida to find out what had become of the forgotten victims.

21

Only One Choice

There could be only one place hotter than southern Florida in August—hell. The wall of stupefying heat and humidity that greeted me when I dragged my luggage through the doors of the Fort Lauderdale terminal was so overwhelming, my body begged me to do an about-face and get back on a plane to California.

I'd never been in Florida. It wasn't high on the list of places I wanted to go after I'd learned the state was known for their really big bugs . . . and lizards. As I stood waiting in the late afternoon sun for the green National van to take me to my rental car, I wished Hurricane Andrew had picked a more hospitable place to come ashore.

Sitting in the comfort of my air-conditioned van, I studied the area map to get my bearings. Homestead was about as far south as you could go. I guessed it was about sixty miles from Fort Lauderdale, which would normally take about an hour to drive. From the news reports I'd heard at home, though, it might as well have been six hundred miles. The main artery into the devastated area was the Florida Turnpike, and it was a gridlock of official vehicles carrying people and emergency supplies. I'd never make it down there before dark.

Leaving the airport, I went in search of a phone booth. A good friend of mine lived in Fort Lauderdale. I'd met Kathy Henderson several years before at the Humane Society in Santa Clara. She was that shelter's education director up until her husband's job took them back to Florida. Kathy had been after me for a while to come visit, but she always said, "Don't come in August or September, or you will never come see us again."

I now knew why.

Kathy had offered to let me stay at her house; so after getting directions, I headed to her place with the assurance that her two sons, Scott and David, had shooed all the lizards out of the house.

When I'd talked with Kathy the day before, I'd asked her to listen for any local news about the animals. As we sat in her living room drinking tall glasses of iced tea, she brought me up-to-date on what she'd heard.

"I'm afraid there has been very little mention of animals," Kathy said, annoyed. "I did hear, though, that the Fort Lauderdale Kennel Club is collecting food and plans to take it down to Homestead and distribute it."

"Do you know how I can get in touch with them?" I asked, pleased that at least some efforts to help the animals were already underway.

Kathy gave me the phone number of Linda Gruskin, the club's president.

After trying for over an hour to get through to her, I was finally able to speak with Linda. She told me a group of volunteers from the Kennel Club were passing out dog and cat food on Dixie Highway in the parking lot next door to what used to be a Taco Bell. I told her I'd meet them there the next morning.

In the muggy darkness before the dawn, I said good-bye to Kathy.

"Be careful," she whispered as she gave me a hug. "I guess we'll see you when we see you?"

"It may be late," I warned.

"We'll leave the door unlocked and a light on."

Kathy stood in the driveway and waved until I turned the corner. The anticipation of what lay ahead made me dread the time I'd waste just trying to get to Homestead. If only I'd had a helicopter.

The Florida Turnpike heading south reminded me of the Los Angeles freeways at rush hour. But it was the Humvees and troop carriers, filled with solemn-faced soldiers cradling M-16s, that made me feel as if I were in a war zone. As I got closer to Homestead, never going faster than ten miles per hour, I began to see destruction that equaled what I'd seen in pictures shot in Vietnam during the seventies. Hurricane Andrew had spared nothing.

Hurricane Andrew

Both sides of the turnpike, for as far as I could see, looked like a battleground. The hurricane had definitely won. Whole subdivisions were destroyed. I passed one after another. Hardware stores, supermarkets, restaurants, gas stations, beauty shops, car dealerships, department stores, had been reduced to piles of rubble. Everything was gone, including the electricity, telephone service, and running water. Whole communities had ceased to exist in a matter of hours, and it would most likely take years to rebuild them.

I pulled off the turnpike below Kendall, about five miles north of the worst-hit area. All around me was confusion. Stop signs had been yanked from the concrete. A few streetlights dangled above the crowded intersections. Debris cluttered the roads. Street signs no longer existed to tell me where I was.

I had to stop a dozen times to ask directions to Dixie Highway. When I finally found it, I guessed and turned right. About a mile later I spotted the remnants of the Taco Bell—and the beginnings of the relief efforts for the four-legged victims of Hurricane Andrew. A makeshift sign, made from an odd-shaped sheet of plywood, was leaning against a broken bus bench at the corner. On it was spray-painted in big red letters, "FREE PET FOOD."

Past the sign was an assortment of vehicles, all loaded with just about every kind of dog and cat food. Spread out around the vehicles were volunteers who greeted the human victims, desperate to feed their pets. I pulled my van into the parking lot, detouring around more debris, careful not to run over any sharp objects that would puncture my tires. I'd already seen too many cars pulled off to the side of the road with flats. Stopping my van next to a large chunk of what used to be Taco Bell's roof, I turned the ignition off and sat for a second.

The reality of where I was hit me full force. This was *really* a disaster. The flood and fire at home seemed very small all of a sudden, and the Exxon spill was an entirely different kind of disaster. Man had created that one. This one nature created, and I was struck by her awesome ability to destroy. Was I ready for this? I'd have to be. I owed it to the animals in this disaster to use what I'd learned from my past experiences. I hoped it would make a difference for at least a few animals.

It was time to get busy.

I'd learned from watching John during the flood in Alviso that you don't just barge into a disaster. You go slowly and observe, piecing together the information you take in. I also knew I had to control my eagerness to help—or I'd get into trouble.

It took a few minutes to decide who was probably in charge. I looked for the person who had the most people standing around them, asking questions. It was a woman in her mid-thirties, whom I followed when she finally escaped the crowd to grab a bag of dog food out of a Dodge Caravan.

"Hi. I'm Terri," I said. "I spoke with Linda Gruskin yesterday, and she said you all might need some help?"

"Great," the woman said as she handed me the forty-pound bag of dog food she'd pulled from the van. "Why don't you give this to that lady sitting in that blue car over there. She's got three very hungry rottweilers at home."

It was the first of many bags of dog and cat food that I helped load into people's cars that day. I never stopped, nor did the flow of people. Late in the afternoon, when our supply of food was almost completely gone, I finally sat down on the tailgate of a pickup truck. The woman in charge came over and joined me.

"Well, what do you think? Is what we're doing helping?" she asked, wiping the sweat from her forehead with the sleeve of her T-shirt.

"Sure," I replied. "But I think we need to take some of this food and pass it out in the neighborhoods. There have got to be people without cars who can't get here, others who don't know we exist, and then there are the animals"—I paused for a second—"who no longer have somebody who cares if they eat or not. We've got to find them."

"Would you like to load up your van tomorrow and do that?" she asked. "We've already got a ton of food that needs to be given out, and there is a lot more on its way."

"Yeah. And I think we could use a few more people with vehicles. That way we can cover more area."

The woman agreed and went to try to recruit some of the volunteers for that job as I passed out more food. She came back a while later to tell me she'd had no luck. It seemed they were scared. They'd drawn their own boundaries, and this was as close as they were willing to get to the realities of what Hurricane Andrew had done. During the day we had heard horror stories of a landscape littered with dead and injured animals. These people weren't ready to witness the suffering up that close.

I'd go alone then. If I didn't, who else would?

The alarm went off at four A.M. It seemed as if I'd been in bed less than an hour, but in fact I'd managed to get five hours of sleep. Kathy met me in the kitchen with a thermos of coffee and another warning to be careful, as I tiptoed out the back door.

"Whoa," I exclaimed as I climbed into the van. The inside of my Lumina smelled like a feed store, and it looked as though I'd become a traveling salesman, peddling every existing brand of dog and cat food on the market. The night before I'd stopped by the warehouse in Fort Lauderdale where they were collecting food and crammed bags, cans, and jugs of drinking water into the van. I even had a ten-pound bag of Purina Puppy Chow on the floor in front of my seat. I'd left just enough space for me and some basic provisions.

In the duffel bag beside me I'd packed some granola bars, three bottles of Evian water, a first aid kit that included sunscreen and mosquito spray, a change of clothes, a pair of heavy gloves, a compass, a map, a Swiss Army knife, a flashlight complete with emergency flasher, and a letter from Belton Mouras, the president of United Animal Nations, outlining what the organization hoped I could do for the animals in the aftermath of Hurricane Andrew.

I'd already pulled from my bag two red-and-white magnetic signs that had printed on them in big letters "EMERGENCY ANIMAL RESCUE SERVICE." They were attached to each of the front doors. I was ready to head back into the war zone.

The ride down to Homestead didn't take quite as long as it had the day before, but it was still slow going. I watched in awe as the sky lightened all around me, and the moon and stars disappeared. I'm rarely up in time to watch the start of a new day. When I am, it makes me realize how amazing the universe is. It also amazed me how hot it could be before the sun even appeared on the eastern horizon.

I pulled off the turnpike shortly before seven o'clock. The intersection at the end of the off ramp had a barrier across it. It would be fifteen minutes before the curfew was lifted. I pulled to the side of the road and got in line behind other vehicles waiting to gain entry into the cordoned-off area. I watched camouflage-clad soldiers, with persuasive weapons slung over their shoulders, patrolling the checkpoint as I drank my third cup of coffee. I hoped to be able to convince them to let me in.

The beat-up dump truck ahead of me inched its way forward. Promptly at seven the barricade had come down, and one by one each vehicle was stopped and a soldier would inquire what business the occupants had in Homestead. The truck ahead of me now pulled up alongside the soldier. The driver rolled down his window and a muscular arm handed a paper to the uniformed guy, who looked as if he couldn't be much older than twenty. He read the paper for a brief moment and handed it back. The truck shifted into gear and turned the corner. It was now my turn.

I didn't wait for the interrogation. "Morning," I said in my official voice. "I'll be passing out dog and cat food to people who can't get to our distribution site on Dixie Highway."

The soldier was scanning the contents of my van as I continued. "I'll also be looking for dead and injured animals, noting their location, and passing the information on to Animal Control." I stretched the truth slightly, but I thought it would add an official importance to my mission.

"You do what you can for them, miss," he said finally, waving me forward. "And be careful. There are a lot of trigger-happy people just waiting to shoot what they think is a looter."

"I will, sir." I wondered if I should salute or something at that point. Instead I just smiled.

My smile quickly disappeared as I saw a dog lying dead in the road, not far from the checkpoint. It was a medium-size black dog, and the car that had hit him had been brutal. I knew what I had to do.

I pulled over to the curb and turned off the car. From my duffel bag I pulled out my gloves and put them on. I opened my door a crack and waited for a troop carrier to pass before I stepped from the car and approached the dog, trying not to look at the mangled body.

At home I called Animal Control when I saw a dead animal on the road, because I hated to see them continue to get run over, even after they had died. But now, there was no one to call. I'd have to remove the dead dog myself, something I'd never done.

I grabbed a back leg and dragged him off the road and into some nearby bushes. When I let go, I wanted to cry, but I didn't. If I allowed my emotions to take over, I'd never make it through the day. There would be time for tears later. Right now I needed to get back into my van and find some animals that were still alive, that needed to eat.

And I found plenty of them.

22

Sally

The stench of death validated my comparison of Homestead to a war zone. The nauseating odor was everywhere. Several times that morning it had gotten so bad, I'd been forced to tie my bandanna across my nose and mouth. That helped, but there was nothing I could do to block out the sight of lifeless animals. They were everywhere.

Front-end loaders were scooping up dead dogs, cats, horses, cows, pigs, goats, and sheep along with the furniture, blocks of concrete, twisted metal, and fragmented wood, to clear pathways through the debris-cluttered streets.

I was on my way back to Dixie Highway to refill my van, when I saw a dead dalmatian puppy, half buried, in the back of the dump truck stopped ahead of me. I covered my eyes, but I couldn't block out the pained expression on that tiny face. Nature was certainly testing my strength. By the time I pulled into the parking lot at Taco Bell, I felt as though I'd been to hell and back. This was a lot tougher than I'd expected, but I wasn't ready to give up.

Sally helped keep me going.

I saw her truck first. The half-ton brown beauty was parked next to what had been the fast-food restaurant's drive-up window. Two floodlights were attached to the top of the cab, like giant eyes with the ability to penetrate darkness. The front bumper had a large metal scoop attached to it that could easily push heavy debris out of its way. Mounted on the back was a winch powerful enough to pull a well-rooted tree out of the ground. The pencil-thin antennae no doubt belonged to a CB unit inside the cab.

It was magnificent! You could keep your shiny Porsches and Mercedeses. What I wouldn't give for a rig like this one.

A magnetic sign attached to the driver's door read, "C.A.P.O." I had no idea what it stood for, but I was about to find out. Just then the truck door opened and a tall, model-slim blonde eased her long legs to the ground. Before she could get away, I walked up to her.

"You've got quite a truck there." I tried to restrain my childlike fascination with the big toy.

"Thanks. My husband put it together for me. Wait till you see what's back here." She moved toward the rear of the truck. Around its perimeter were a series of metal cabinets that held first aid supplies, feeding dishes, collapsible cages, a shovel, tools, leashes, a stretcher, food, and water. It was amazing how complete this mobile rescue unit was.

"It's incredible," I said.

"By the way. I'm Sally Matluk," she said, extending her tanned hand.

"Terri Crisp," I replied.

"You aren't from around here, are you?"

"No, I'm from California—"

Sally interrupted, "California? I can't even get people from Fort Lauderdale to come down here and help the animals."

I then explained to Sally that I was from United Animal Nations, and I'd been sent to see what needed to be done to help the animals.

"Plenty," was her reply. "This is the worst place on earth for animals to live, even when there hasn't been a hurricane. The people who are *supposed* to be helping the animals don't give a damn if they live or die. It's disgusting."

Sally then told me about her organization, C.A.P.O. "It stands for Citizens Against Pet Overpopulation," she explained. As I listened to her, I began to realize the animals had a real ally in this woman. Sally preached spay and neuter to everyone, whether they listened or not.

"So what have you been doing since you got here?" Sally asked.

"I've been distributing food throughout the neighborhoods."

"Oh," she exclaimed. "You're the one. I was just in an area to do the same thing, and the people told me someone had already been by. You going back out?"

"Yeah. As soon as I load up my van with more food."

"I know a place where there are a lot of animals. If you wait for me to load up too, we could both head out that way and work together."

"Sure. It would help to work with someone who knows the area."

Sally and I covered a lot of territory that afternoon. We gave out hundreds of bags of dog and cat food to people who couldn't thank us enough. With each bag went a jug of drinking water too.

Whenever we saw a stray dog, we'd stop. Very few came to us. They were so frightened, and most of them would take off running as soon as we opened our doors. Others circled at a safe distance while we tore open a bag of dry food and laid it on the ground next to a pie tin we'd filled with fresh water. Only when we got back into our vehicles would they come close enough to eat. We'd watch them practically inhale the food, wishing we could do more.

There were no animal shelters in Homestead. Dade County had an Animal Control facility in Miami, but it was too far away, especially in the heavy traffic. We could easily spend a good portion of one day making the trip up there and back, and our vehicles would have held only a small number of strays. There were rumors circulating, too, that animals were not being held longer than the normal three days. That did not give people time to come and claim them.

So all we could do was hope that the dogs would find their way home and that someone would still be there to take care of them.

We saw very few cats that day. Cats find a safe spot within their territory and stay put, especially during the hottest part of the day. We wouldn't be able to find the cats until after dark, which would be impossible with a seven P.M. curfew still in effect.

Once in a while, we would hear a cat crying, usually from a pile of debris that was too thick to penetrate. We could only leave food and water and hope the cat could crawl out of the debris to reach it.

There were also fish, birds, hamsters, rabbits, guinea pigs, turtles, monkeys, and pet lizards that we learned needed food too. There wasn't a grocery store, feed store, or pet store open for at least a thirty-mile radius, which made it difficult for people to get supplies for their pets. I wrote down the addresses and promised the owners I'd bring back what they needed the next day.

Out of Harm's Way

Sally and I got quieter as the afternoon passed. The frustration of not being able to do enough and the debilitating heat were taking their toll. When we arrived back at the Taco Bell an hour before curfew, we found a rare spot of shade and sat in complete silence.

My new friend and I had seen an awful lot in one day . . . and it wasn't over yet.

23

An Angel

It wasn't until my van was parallel with her that I spotted the dog, sitting in the weeds alongside the road. If I'd blinked, I would have missed her.

I pulled off onto the dirt and watched her for a few seconds through the side mirror, expecting at any moment that the large Afghan mix would take off running, as all the others had. But she didn't move.

Her head hung low to the ground, motionless. The long white tail was pulled in between her back legs. A gash had stained the white fur around her shoulder red. She was steadily panting as she stared at nothing. This dog had given up. I'm sure she'd decided death couldn't be any worse than what she had been through. When the next car came by, I wondered if she'd step out in front of it.

I had to get her.

I waited until there were no cars coming in either direction on the two-lane road, and then I squeezed out my door. I moved slowly so I wouldn't scare her. When I opened the back of the van to get her something to eat and drink, she neither looked at me nor moved. All I had left was canned food, so I fumbled around in the mess I'd created in the back of the van for the can opener. Just as I finished opening the Pedigree and was about to dump the beef-and-liver mix

1 5 7

into an aluminum pie plate, I felt something nudge my elbow . . . it was her.

After letting me know she was there, she obediently sat down on the dirt next to me, waiting for her dinner to be served.

"Well," I said as I carefully reached out to stroke the top of her head. "Did you decide you were hungry?"

She just sat there panting.

I set the food down in front of her, and she stood up. With all the manners of a lady, she began to eat. I filled another pie plate with some water and set it down beside the food. She took a long drink and returned to the plate of food.

While she ate, I attempted to straighten up the back end of the van while I had some daylight left. It was almost time for the barricades to go back up. I'd left Sally over an hour ago so she could get back to Fort Lauderdale to feed her own dogs. I had decided to make one last food delivery in a subdivision near the turnpike. Sally had been sorry she couldn't come with me, and before she left, she handed me her business card.

"I don't know when I'll be down here again," she said. "We suffered a lot of tree damage on our property, and I may have someone coming out tomorrow to give me an estimate."

"Well, I hope to see you again before I leave."

"When do you go home?" she asked, with a hint in her voice that she'd wish I'd hang around for a while.

"I don't know . . . Maybe a week?" It all depended on how much more time I could stay away from my job at the university.

"Whatever happens, give me a call when you get home. Maybe we can work to get this place better prepared to take care of the animals *when* this happens again."

With that, Sally gave me a big hug, jumped into her truck, and drove off.

As the Afghan mix started on her second plate of food, I sat down in the back of the van with my legs dangling over the edge, thinking— something I'd tried not to do all day. The only way to survive the enormity of this disaster was to switch the mind to autopilot. But I couldn't do it any longer.

I tilted my head back and closed my eyes. Tears stung my sunburned face. I couldn't escape the haunting images of the scared dogs I'd seen all day. Why couldn't they understand that I wanted to help them? But what would I have done with them all? This wasn't fair. Why was this happening to the animals again?

I felt a tongue gently lick my hand. The Afghan mix stood before me with a full belly. For the first time since I'd seen her, her tail wagged. I grabbed her around the neck and hugged her. "Thank you," I cried, "for letting me help you."

I held on to her for a long time. It was exactly what I needed.

Suddenly I realized it was getting late. The barricades were probably already in place, and I'd heard they were hauling curfew violators to jail—and that wasn't where I wanted to spend the night. It was time to get moving.

I gently grabbed the dog by her ears and directed her eyes toward mine. "Well, girl, I guess you better come with me. Somehow I suspect you wouldn't last for long on your own." Her white tail wagged in agreement.

She jumped in the car when I opened the passenger door, and before I'd gotten to the next corner, she was curled up on the seat, sound asleep. We passed through the checkpoint without a bit of trouble. When I saw the traffic on the turnpike, I knew I'd have at least two hours to figure out what to do with my hitchhiker once I got back to Fort Lauderdale.

I knew I couldn't take the dog to Kathy's house, because the boys had allergies and their yard wasn't set up to confine a dog of this size. When I saw the turnoff for Miami Airport, I momentarily thought of flying her to California, but this dog undoubtedly belonged to someone, who I hoped wanted her back. If only Animal Control were able to hold dogs longer. I was quickly running out of options.

Suddenly I spotted Sally's business card sticking out of the ashtray. *Sally* . . .

I'd driven far enough away from Homestead to be able to find phones that worked. I got off at the next exit and didn't have to go far before I found a phone booth at a Shell station. When I turned the car off, the dog lifted her head and looked around as if to say, "Are we there yet?"

I dialed the number. As I listened to the phone ringing, I looked at my watch. It was almost eleven o'clock.

After four rings I heard Sally's voice. "Hello."

"Sally?"

"Yeah?" I knew she hadn't recognized my voice yet.

"It's Terri. I have a big favor to ask." I thought the best approach was to just come right out and say it. "Do you have a place to keep a big dog tonight?"

"Of course." Sally hadn't hesitated for an instant.

My problem was solved, at least for tonight.

Sally gave me directions to her house, and it took me about forty-five minutes to finally pull up in front of the driveway gate. A flashlight approached from the other side. Sally waved and then unhooked the gate. I drove into a gravel parking area and stopped the car.

After Sally closed the gate, she came over to my side of the car. The dog was already halfway in my lap with her head hanging out my window by then.

"You weren't exaggerating," Sally said. "This is a *big* dog."

We got her out of the car, and she followed us to a picnic table, where Sally had made a bed from a couple of old blankets. "I thought she'd be okay here tonight. I have a chain, and we can hook her to one of the table legs."

"She'll need a collar too. Do you have an extra one that's big enough?"

Thank goodness Sally had big dogs, because she returned in no time with a collar that fit perfectly.

The dog decided it was definitely way past her bedtime, so she made several turns on the blanket and plopped down. It wasn't long before she was snoring. Sally and I watched her, silently wondering how this dog had survived. She'd been one of the lucky ones.

"Out of all the dogs we saw today, there is only one that we know is safe tonight." My voice trailed off.

"I'm glad you stopped and picked her up. I think we needed to bring at least one animal out of that hellhole today to maintain some of our sanity." Sally stood up, and her voice softened. "But what about all the rest?"

The animals certainly needed help, but what more could we do? We were only two people, and we had limited resources, not to mention no place to properly shelter animals. I had had a hard enough time finding a place to keep one dog. What could we do with all the others? There were hundreds of them.

"We need some kind of shelter, right in Homestead. A place we can take the animals where they'll be safe," I said, half speaking to myself.

"You know ..." Sally started slowly, "Joe Torregrosa from the SPCA is starting to keep stray horses in a pasture at Krome Avenue, near ... oh, I think it was 224th Street. I passed there today, and he wasn't using the five-acre pasture closest to the road. I wonder if whoever owns it would let us use it as a temporary collection site for dogs and cats? The perimeter fence is still standing, so it would be perfect."

I thought about the possibility. It would definitely make it easier for people to find their animals if they were confined to one location. We'd only be able to house dogs in the open field, and there'd be no way to separate them. But I knew that even this makeshift solution would be better than having the dogs running loose on the streets.

"In a large pasture you could set up some tents to put the animals in. We could get plenty of donated food. I'm sure we could find some water," Sally continued.

"I haven't told you about my husband's movie production company here in Lauderdale—it's called Production Central. John has all kinds of things that we could use, like a generator, tarps, floodlights, walkie-talkies, and we have a motor home that sleeps six." Sally's excitement was contagious.

Now I couldn't sit down.

"Terri, I know we can make this work. In fact, we *have* to make it work."

Sally was right.

"Tomorrow, I'll call Joe and see what he thinks. If he thinks it might be okay with the owner, I'll go down there and find him . . . and convince him to give it to us," Sally said with a determination in her voice that I suspected would get us what we needed.

"Why don't you plan on meeting me at Krome and 224th between one and one-thirty tomorrow, prepared to create a MASH unit for dogs and cats?" Sally said, grinning.

I would be there.

Before Sally headed to Homestead the next morning, she went to check on the Afghan mix. The dog was gone. We could never figure out how she got loose. The chain was still attached to the leg of the picnic table, but the collar and dog were gone. We never saw her again, even though we did everything we could to find her.

I've thought about that white dog often and wondered, *What if I'd blinked, and not seen her sitting in the weeds alongside the road?*

I'm just grateful I found her. Because of that dog, a lot of other animals were saved in the following weeks.

She was, indeed, our angel.

24

Help

The darkness of night was a welcome respite. Temperatures would eventually drop to the lower nineties, and a timid breeze from the Atlantic would stir after the sun disappeared in the west. It was the illusion the darkness provided that we looked forward to the most. At night, Hurricane Andrew's destruction disappeared in the blackness. You'd look toward the dark canopy above, scattered with twinkling stars, and almost believe all was well with the world. But when the merciless sun returned, you stopped pretending.

When my alarm went off the next day, I opened my eyes and was startled by the brightness of the sun coming through the bedroom window. I thought at first I had set the alarm wrong . . . that it had to be late. Then I realized my mistake and remembered my promise to buy food for the pets that didn't eat dog or cat food. I'd found a store in Fort Lauderdale that opened at nine o'clock so that I could stock up and still meet Sally by one.

There was time to call home before I went shopping. It was good to hear Ken's voice after three days. The girls were still asleep, so I couldn't talk to them, but Ken filled me in on all that they were doing. Megan was just starting to sit up without falling over—an amazing feat with her rounded bottom. The evening before, Amy had displayed her artistic talent by coloring on the side of our dining room hutch. Jennifer was complaining about having no life—a common gripe among big sisters who get "stuck" watching their little sisters all the time. She kept telling Ken she couldn't wait until school started. It would take only a day or two of being back in school for that to change.

After I hung up, I walked into the kitchen. Kathy was already sitting at the dining room table, reading the morning paper, which was full of news on the aftermath of Hurricane Andrew.

"Good morning," Kathy said, looking up from the paper. "There's juice in the fridge, and I just made a fresh pot of coffee."

I nodded, still thinking about Ken and the girls.

"You call home yet?" she asked.

"I just did," I said as I opened the refrigerator and grabbed the orange juice.

"They all alive and well?"

"Ken said they are doing okay. I didn't get to talk with the girls, though," I replied, and took a drink of the cold juice.

"It must be hard to leave them, especially Megan, when she is still so young," Kathy said.

"It's terrible. But thank goodness the girls have Ken."

I, too, was very fortunate.

The pet store opened promptly at nine o'clock, and I was their first customer. When I explained what I needed the food for, the manager was eager to donate most of it, and he even threw in some extra leashes and collars, something I knew would come in handy. With my van once again full of provisions, I headed south. I estimated I had just enough time to reach Sally. Hopefully, she'd have good news.

After two and a half hours of bumper-to-bumper traffic, I was glad to be off the turnpike. But the streets in Homestead were not much better. Intersections were blocked with cars and trucks, fighting for their turn to cross. Horns voiced people's frustration. Patient military personnel tried to direct the chaos, but they were outnumbered. I detoured through a subdivision, hoping to escape some of the congestion of the main streets, and I was glad that I did.

Spray-painted in large letters on the side of a ramshackle gray house was "QUIET! FILMING MOVIE—GONE WITH THE WIND." Somebody had salvaged their sense of humor. Several blocks away there was another house decorated with some more badly needed comic relief: "ANDREW. JUST LIKE A MAN. CAME TOO FAST AND TOOK

EVERYTHING." But it was a third house that really made me laugh: "MY HOUSE HAS FALLEN, AND IT CAN'T GET UP!"

When I pulled out of the subdivision onto Krome Avenue, I felt better. Laughter has an amazing ability to relieve what ails you.

According to my map and a lot of guesswork, I had to be pretty close to 224th Street. A few miles later, I finally spotted Sally frantically waving her arms. She was standing in the middle of a horse pasture that looked like heaven on earth.

As I got out of my van, Sally ran toward me, shouting, "We got it! We got it!"

"Thank God!" I said, giving Sally a big hug.

Sally, still trying to catch her breath, explained that the pasture belonged to a man named Robbie Addison, who owned one of the local feed stores. After Sally tracked him down, he was more than willing to let us use the property for as long as we needed it—for free.

"And wait until I tell you what else happened." Sally could barely contain her excitement as she began to tell me about Colonel McCorcle.

"I'd just pulled into the driveway that runs along the back side of the pasture and was sitting in my truck trying to spot Joe. The back pasture and barn area were an absolute zoo, with people and horses everywhere." As Sally spoke, I could see the area, and it didn't look much different now.

"I was about to get out of the truck to look for Joe when I spotted in my rearview mirror six soldiers wearing fatigues, red berets, and carrying rifles over their shoulders. They were checking out my truck very suspiciously. That was when I decided I better stay put," Sally said as she brushed a strand of blond hair away from her face.

"I rolled down my window and, in a very innocent voice, said hello as they approached. The officer in front was polite and returned my hello. Then he wanted to know what I was doing." Sally chuckled.

By the time she had finished talking with the colonel, Sally had explained to him the need for a small-animal MASH unit for dogs and cats, outlined what supplies would be needed to run the place, and gotten his telephone number.

The officer turned out to be a Colonel Thelton "Mac" McCorcle, a veterinarian from Alabama, and he was certain he could get permission from his superiors to help us. In addition, he thought he could get us some military tents and some of the other supplies on Sally's long list.

"When you know you have the pasture, give me a call," the colonel said. "Meanwhile, I'll check with the chain of command."

"Then he left," Sally said. "I just sat in the truck, dumbfounded. It's like this man came out of the middle of nowhere. He was the answer to my prayers."

I didn't know whether to laugh or cry, but there wasn't time for either. There were animals that needed saving, and some of them were no doubt running out of time.

"So have you called the colonel yet?" I asked.

"I tried, but the phone lines are too busy to get a call out. I'll wait and try tonight when they're apt to be less busy."

"In the meantime, where do we begin?" I said, looking around at the empty field.

"I must have seen thirty dogs running loose on my way down here this morning. I suppose we could go try and find them," Sally suggested.

I'd seen almost as many dogs since I'd gotten off the turnpike. Between the two of us, it wasn't going to take long to fill up this field. I wished we had cages to separate the dogs and tents to provide the animals with shade, but we had neither. I kept telling myself at least they'd be safe and we'd be able to keep them fed.

I tried not to think about the injured animals. We wouldn't be able to do much for them unless the colonel joined us. Sally had heard the day before that there were sixteen veterinary practices in the area that had been totally destroyed. That meant the closest medical care for injured animals would be in Miami. It would be an all-day trip to travel up there and back. There were so many animals that had already died, some of them slow and agonizing deaths. Unfortunately there would be more.

It was time to focus on what we could do. Our rescue team of two stayed busy that afternoon collecting stray dogs, and we didn't have to go far to find them. Within several blocks of the horse pasture, we were finding more dogs than we knew what to do with. It was becoming apparent that our forces would have to increase before too long. I couldn't return to Kathy's that night, which meant I'd seen my last decent night's sleep for a while. These animals were our responsibility now, so we couldn't very well abandon them after dark. The horse pasture had become our new home away from home.

Sally, in all her earlier excitement, had forgotten to tell me that reinforcements were on their way. When we returned from one of our runs with four more stray dogs, she told me her husband, John, and one of his employees, a guy named David, were coming to help. Sally and I had been collecting animals for less than three hours, and already four people were not going to be enough to take care of them. We could have used at least triple that number.

By the time John and David arrived, we had over thirty dogs running loose in the field. It was an interesting assortment of canines that scattered as John drove the motor home into the field. We had big dogs, little dogs, fat dogs, skinny dogs, friendly dogs, standoffish dogs, and . . . six rottweilers. We had no choice but to mix the males in with the females, and as a result we spent a good portion of our time being chaperones. A few litters were conceived during that first day, but we couldn't do much to prevent it.

Most of the dogs, thank goodness, were too exhausted to think about doing anything but sleeping. We created some shade using tarps that I had bought in Fort Lauderdale, and the precious space filled up quickly with panting dogs. While they slept, Sally and I tried to figure out what to do next, juggling equally important lists of priorities. John and David wasted no time joining us.

John held out his hand as he stepped from the motor home. "Hello, I'm John Boisseau."

"No. You're a saint," I said, shaking his hand.

"I've been called a lot of things in my days, but never a saint," John replied with a grin on his tanned face. I immediately liked this man.

"I'm Terri, by the way. Just a crazy person who loves animals." I was beginning to believe the part about being crazy more than ever.

Sally joined us about then, having just broken up a disagreement between two dogs over who would have more shade.

"I see you two have met," Sally said, putting her arm around her husband as she spoke. "So what do you think? Isn't it wonderful."

John's eyes narrowed as he took in the six acres of uneven pastureland surrounding us. It required quite an imagination to see ahead to what *could* be considered a shelter for animals. But John, as I would soon learn, had an incredible ability to create with minimal resources. He would turn out to be one of our most valuable assets.

"You did good, Sal," he said finally. "I just want to know where the swimming pool is, though?" John's humor was what would keep us alive in the coming weeks.

"Yeah. Me too," said David.

With our team up to four, it was time to get busy, though a swim in a pool was what we all would have preferred.

The thirty-two-foot Fleetwood motor home was the centerpiece of the pasture. It would become our office, sleeping quarters, chow hall, only bathroom, and escape from the heat and the torrential downpour that arrived every afternoon about four-thirty.

John had brought dozens of blue-and-orange tarps that he and David started attaching to the perimeter fence, facing Krome Avenue. The makeshift lean-tos, became shelters for the dogs. He'd also brought chains, so we could start to hook the dogs to the fence in their own designated spaces.

Sally and I unloaded bags of dog and cat food and stacked them on some wooden pallets John had scavenged. Then there was the forty-four thousand pounds of donated pet food from IAMS. When John heard that the pet food company was looking for a warehouse to store their contribution to the pet relief efforts, he offered space at Production Central. Sam Yates, a representative from IAMS, gave us permission to distribute it in Homestead.

John and David had been able to haul only five thousand pounds of it down to the pasture, even with it stacked to the ceiling in the motor home and filling the back of the jeep. The load was so heavy it caused a tire to blow on the turnpike. We unloaded the IAMS bags and covered our growing inventory of food with a large tarp as the clouds appeared in the east, promising rain.

The next thing on our list was to get the awning up on the side of the motor home, in case we needed an isolation area for sick dogs. This was what really worried us. The last thing we needed was a dog with some contagious disease infecting the rest of the population.

With only a few more hours of daylight left, John decided it was time to get the generator cranked up. I'd never seen such a large generator. It was on wheels, and David had brought it from Production Central, pulling it behind John's jeep. I think we could have lit up half of Homestead with it.

John attached spotlights to our power source so we'd be able to see what we were doing after dark.

It was nearly eleven o'clock when the four of us finally collapsed in the air-conditioned motor home—one luxury the generator allowed us. We'd gotten a lot done in one day, but we knew there was still plenty more to do. We were incredibly tired and sunburned, but we felt good. At last we were really doing something that would make a big difference for some of the animals.

John, David, and I sat watching Sally, who was rummaging through the cupboards looking for something edible. None of us had eaten since early that morning.

"We're going to need some help," John said. "Sal, you have to go back home tomorrow and start making some calls. Surely there are people who would want to help."

"I wouldn't be too sure of that," Sally said as she unscrewed a jar of extra crunchy peanut butter. She had found our dinner. "It's always been hard to get people to do much of anything to help the animals down here."

"But, Sally, people are usually more willing to help during a disaster," I said, hoping I wouldn't be disappointed. "Don't forget the colonel's offer."

"I hope you're right, because we sure as hell are going to need some help," Sally said as she spread peanut butter on saltine crackers.

It was time to eat and go to bed.

During the night two more dogs arrived. A small terrier mix showed up on his own. We found him stretched out under the motor home when we got up in the morning. He'd just made himself right at home. The other one was brought to us by national guardsmen. The Labrador mix had wandered into their camp, worn out and hungry.

We'd been discovered—by the people and the animals.

When Sally pulled out of the horse pasture before dawn, there was an urgency to her mission. She'd call the colonel first, then make some more calls. Help had to come. Otherwise, more animals would die.

25

Outsmarting Death

The small-animal MASH unit officially opened the day after we were given the horse pasture on Krome Avenue. It was August 29, 1992, five days after Hurricane Andrew hit. We already had thirty-six dogs, but no cats.

That would soon change, though.

Just before noon a Humvee pulled off the road in front of our pasture. Two uniformed gentlemen wearing burgundy-colored berets got out and walked over to the fence where I was trying to untangle a springer spaniel that had gotten his foot tangled in his chain.

"Excuse me, ma'am." The deep voice made the dog bark.

"Hi, what can I do for you?" I asked, standing up, as the untangled dog started to jump on me, begging for more attention.

"Y'all are helping animals, aren't you?"

"We're trying to."

"We were patrolling a trailer park last night and saw lots of cats. They sure looked hungry. Thought y'all might be able to help them," said the guy closest to the fence as he leaned over the wire and started to pet the spaniel, who now was begging for attention from whomever he could get it.

"How many would you say there were?" I asked, knowing we still had no place to confine cats.

"At least fifty," the other guy said.

"Shoot," I exclaimed. Maybe I could have found a place to keep a few cats, but certainly not fifty.

I told the guardsmen that we weren't equipped to take in cats, though we hoped to be able to later. For now, all I could do was take them some food and water.

"If you need some more water, we got lots of it. Next time we come by here, we'll drop some off."

"Thanks. We sure could use some," I replied. The gallon jugs of water that I had gotten from the Kennel Club were going quickly.

"We have to get going, but the name of the trailer park is Quail Roost. You head that way three blocks and turn right," the guardsmen said, pointing north. "You can't miss it. What's left of it is on the left side of the road."

I later found out they were right. Quail Roost had been hit hard.

I'd waited as long as I could for Sally to return from Fort Lauderdale, but by midafternoon I decided I'd better go ahead and feed the cats. John and David said they'd be able to keep an eye on the dogs while I was gone. Sally was due back at any time, with a crew of energized volunteers, I hoped.

When I pulled into the driveway of the former gatehouse at the entrance to Quail Roost Mobile Home Park, two armed national guardsmen met me. I was surprised when they approached and announced, "You must be the lady coming to feed the cats."

"Right," I said, sounding puzzled.

"Two guys came by a bit ago and told us about you. Hope you brought lots of food, cause there's a whole hell of a lot of cats roaming round this place."

"I think I've got plenty," I assured them. I'd also stocked up on dog food, in case I came across more dogs that were too frightened to be caught. Sally and I had seen plenty of them the day before. Thank goodness some were now starting to get so hungry and thirsty that they gave in and allowed us to help them.

"Have you seen any dogs?" I asked.

"We saw one pass on the other side of the road about an hour ago, but that's been the only one we've seen around here. If they had any sense, they'd all head to the hills. There are too many absentminded drivers around here now, and dogs and cars sure don't mix well."

I agreed. This was certainly no place to be a lost dog.

"Have you seen any injured cats?" I wanted to know what to expect as I drove through Quail Roost.

"No, but most of them are so scared they won't let you get too close," said the guy with glasses as he swatted a mosquito that had landed on his freckled arm.

"Well, I'd better get busy. I'll only be able to stay a little while. I don't know if the guys who stopped by earlier told you, but we're setting up a small-animal MASH unit down on Krome."

"Good for you. It's about time somebody did something for these poor animals. I have to warn you, we have four men patrolling the park. I'll radio them and let 'em know what you'll be doing, though."

"Thanks," I said as I put up my window to savor what little air-conditioning I could before I had to get back out into the late afternoon heat.

Quail Roost looked like a landfill. Piled five, six, seven feet high, on both sides of the road, were the remnants of people's lives, scrambled together in bent, splintered, waterlogged and shattered pieces. Very little had survived.

Entire mobile homes had been picked up and flipped onto their roofs. Steel beams were twisted as if they were made out of pipe cleaners. Some of the homes had not a single standing wall, leaving bathrooms and kitchens exposed, with refrigerators and toilets as markers of what had been.

Quail Roost was a harsh reminder of how fragile our existence is.

I was searching for cats well hidden from the late afternoon sun when I found something I hadn't expected. As I turned a corner, I saw a middle-aged woman, swathed in white gauze, standing in the middle of the street.

My foot slammed on the brakes, and the car stopped a few feet from her. As if she hadn't even noticed me, she remained in the same spot, staring directly at me, her arms hanging by her sides. This was too creepy. I really think if I had not stopped, this lady would not have gotten out of my way. The prospect of having nearly hit someone made my heart beat faster.

I put the van in park, shoved my door open, and stood behind it, in case I had to jump back in the van in a hurry. There had been stories in the newspaper about the effects the hurricane was having on people. Tempers, aggravated by stress, were explosive. Men, women, and children were reacting violently, sometimes to things that would normally not even have upset them. I wasn't going to take any chances.

"Are you all right? Do you need help?" I asked.

The woman remained still, except for her eyes.

"I have some water. Would you like some?" I raised my voice some, thinking maybe she hadn't heard me.

Still no response.

I wasn't quite sure what to say or do next, so I asked her if she'd seen any cats.

The woman swayed a bit, but didn't say a word.

"Do you have any pets?"

Suddenly, in a slow, timid voice, she said, *"Doooog."*

"Do you have a dog?"

The woman barely nodded her head up and down, and then held up two fingers in front of her chest.

"Where are they?" I asked, hoping she wasn't about to tell me they had died as a result of the hurricane.

She didn't respond to this question but continued to stand still, holding up her two fingers.

I hesitated before I asked the next question. I was afraid what a no answer might cause her to do, but I had to know.

"Are your dogs . . ." I paused a moment. ". . . alive?"

"Yes," she said quietly as tears started to streak her dirty cheeks.

"Do you need some food for them?" I asked, not at all expecting the response I got.

"Where? Where?" she nearly screamed. "Food. Where is the food?" she continued to shout as she came toward me.

"It's, ah, in the back, ah, of my van," I said in a startled voice.

Before I could even move, the woman had limped to the back of my van and was fumbling with the latch, trying to open the door. I held back my hands for a second, but when she yelled, *"Please! Help,"* I knew the woman would not hurt me.

I squeezed the release mechanism, and the door popped up. Before I could let it go, this woman, who was probably no more than five foot three, and couldn't have weighed more than a hundred pounds, had leaned into the back of the van and grabbed two twenty-pound bags of dog food.

She pulled them toward her, hoisted them under her arms, and took off running, in what looked like record time. I grabbed some jugs of water, slammed the door shut, and kept an eye on her until she rounded a corner. When I found her, she was standing next to a blue Chevy Nova ripping the bags open with her bare hands. Beside her, two very hungry dogs hovered.

Hurricane Andrew

I stood back, with the water jugs still clutched in my arms, waiting for the right moment to approach. The dogs had started to eat right out of the bags as the woman stood between them. In a soft voice she kept repeating to them, "I'm sorry. I'm sorry."

Not far from the dogs were two cooking pots that looked as if they were being used to give the dogs water. Both were completely empty. It wouldn't be long before the dogs wanted water to wash down all the food they were gobbling, so I slowly moved toward the pots and filled each one. The dogs just wagged their tails and continued eating. As I backed away from the bowls, the woman reached for my arm and said in a soft voice, "Thank you."

For the next hour, I sat on the ground with the woman as she explained to me what had happened to her and the dogs during the hurricane. It was a miracle they were alive.

"The military was taking those of us who didn't have transportation to the Red Cross shelter on Sunday afternoon," the woman began. "I was standing on my front porch, my suitcase in one hand and the dogs on leashes in the other, when the truck pulled up in front of my place. I stepped off the porch to get aboard—" The woman stopped suddenly. When she began again, she was crying. "They told me . . . I couldn't bring the dogs."

I was learning that a lot of people were not aware that the Red Cross can not allow animals to stay at the shelters that have been set up for people. It's the health department that makes the rule. Shelters serve food during disasters, so they come under the same regulations as restaurants. In addition, Red Cross shelters are where people go to feel safe. If you have people in a shelter who are afraid of dogs or are allergic to some animals, it would just add to their already high stress level.

An alternate shelter for people with pets has to exist during disasters. This woman was a perfect example of why.

"After arguing with the officer for a few minutes, I finally had no choice but to stay behind with my dogs. They're my only family." She petted the black-and-white shepherd mix, which had come and lain down beside her, as she continued. "That truck pulled away while the three of us sat on the porch. I was so worried, but what else could I do?"

There should have been another choice. Subjecting people and animals to this kind of terror is unacceptable. She'd managed to survive one of the worst hurricanes to ever hit the United States, but with a slight twist of fate she and her dogs could easily have been killed. I listened as she continued, unable to imagine what they must have gone through.

After the truck full of evacuees left, Quail Roost had been empty—except for this woman and her two dogs. She had gone back into the mobile home and turned on the radio as she put masking tape on the windows. As it started to get dark, and anything that wasn't tied down outside started to scatter with the wind, she got scared. When the electricity went out, she decided to take refuge in her bedroom. Eventually she fell asleep on her bed, with the dogs curled up next to her.

"It was the noise that woke me," she began again. "A loud roar like an airplane taking off. And it wouldn't stop. The trailer was rocking. Things were falling on the roof with such force, I thought for sure they'd tear open my ceiling. Flying debris was bumping and scraping up against the metal siding. The rain hitting the aluminum awning was deafening. It sounded like the world was being torn apart—piece by piece."

As the hurricane worsened, she decided the bedroom was no longer a safe place to be. The dogs were still at her side, and she had grabbed both of them by their collars, hoping to move into the bathroom with them. Before she could, the roof of the mobile home finally collapsed on her. Everything went black as she fell to the floor.

When she came to, she could feel the rain on her face. It was still dark outside, and the wind was vicious. In a semiconscious state, she realized all the walls of her bedroom were gone, leaving her completely exposed to the storm. As she lay on the floor, on top of pieces of paneling, splintered two-by-fours, and soggy carpeting and ceiling insulation, she tried moving her legs and arms. They hurt, but it didn't feel as if anything was broken.

"My car, which hasn't worked for months, was still in the driveway. I figured that would be a safer place . . . if I could get there." The woman stopped and stared into space. "It was awful, really awful."

She then described how she crawled through her bedroom, squeezed past the debris that had collected in the hall, and pushed broken furniture out of her way in order to get into the kitchen. If she could get to the doorway, she thought, maybe the stairs would still be in place. She had to crawl over her refrigerator, lying on its side on the linoleum, littered with broken bowls, plates, and glasses.

The stairs had been forced away from the house, but she could reach them. When her foot touched the landing, it slid out from underneath her and she fell to the concrete slab below.

"That was when I cried out loud and asked God to help me. I knew without his help . . . I was going to die." The memory brought more tears to her eyes and mine. I reached out and held her bandaged hand.

Eventually she had pulled herself up on her knees and crawled the rest of the way to her car. It took the last of her energy to reach up for the handle and fight with the wind to get the car door open. Grabbing on to the steering wheel, she pulled herself inside.

It was an exhausted and terrified woman, with scratches, scrapes, cuts, bruises, and gouges over most of her body, who lay in a fetal position on the front seat of her Chevy Nova, shaking, as the wind lifted one side of the vehicle up off the ground and dropped it repeatedly.

"I remember lying there thinking it was the devil himself outside that car, and he was furious that I had outsmarted death." She brought her hands to her mouth and held them together as if she were about to pray. "It was God that saved me."

"Where were the dogs this whole time?" I asked.

"After I had been in the front seat of the car for a while, I suddenly sat straight up, realizing I hadn't seen the dogs since I'd blacked out. It was a horrifying feeling. I thought for sure they were lying buried in the rubble, severely injured or maybe even dead." She began petting both dogs, as they rested contentedly beside her. "I knew I had to go back outside and face the devil again. I *had* to find the dogs."

Before she had opened the door, she was startled by a thud on the hood of the car. Standing inches from the windshield were the two dogs, staring in at her. Somehow she managed to ease the door open again, and both dogs jumped off the hood and scurried inside the car. It was a happy reunion, complete with kisses, hugs, and lots of wet fur.

Until daybreak, the three survivors sat huddled together on the floorboard of the car. The devil had finally given up.

On Wednesday, two days after Hurricane Andrew had come and gone, the Red Cross found this woman and her dogs, sitting on the hood of her Nova. She was in bad shape. They provided some emergency first aid, but they knew she needed more extensive care for some of the deeper cuts that she had, particularly the ones on her feet. It looked as though she'd walked miles across broken glass. Actually, it had just been across her kitchen.

It finally took the police to get her to leave her dogs so she could be taken to the hospital. She protested the entire time she was in the patrol car. Once at the hospital her wounds were cleaned. Some required stitches before bandages were applied. By the time the nurses finished, she looked like a gauze-wrapped mummy. She continued to protest as she ate the first meal she'd had in three days.

"I woke up in the middle of the night in that hospital, and I was scared someone might take my dogs, so I got dressed and sneaked downstairs." She seemed pleased as she told me of her escape. "It was easy to go unnoticed. Even at that late hour, the place was full of people. I found a truck driver on the highway, who gave me a ride. I ended up having to walk only about a mile. When I got back, the dogs were still sitting on the hood of the car . . . waiting for me."

This woman's love for her dogs was incredible.

In the time that we had been sitting there talking, I'd caught glimpses of cats darting in and out of the debris around us. A large brown tabby, meowing from the top of a battered piano, reminded me why I'd come to Quail Roost. It was time to feed the cats and get back to the MASH unit. Certainly Sally had returned by now, and I was anxious to find out if she'd found us any help.

"Listen, I've got to feed all the cats around here. When I get done, why don't you let me take you and your dogs back to the small-animal MASH unit we've set up. If you feel good about the place, we can take care of your dogs while you take care of yourself. I think all three of you need to get out of here."

The woman didn't say anything for a while. She just kept petting the dogs in long, slow motions. I could see she was tired.

Finally, she looked me in the eyes, and spoke, "You promise they'll be okay?"

"I promise."

It took several days in the hospital for Sheila to recover. Rusty and Boscoe stayed at the MASH unit until the Red Cross helped Sheila find a duplex where she and the dogs could live. When she came to pick up the dogs, I walked with her to the car that was waiting for her. Two happy dogs jumped into the backseat, and Sheila closed the door behind them. Before she got into the car, she gave me a big hug.

"Thank you for saving us," she said as she squeezed me tighter. "I don't know what I would have done if you hadn't come along."

"You would have survived," I said as my voice broke. "You loved your dogs too much to give up."

"I guess you're right."

Sheila got in the car after that and left. As I walked back toward the motor home, I thanked God for bringing me to Florida.

26

Pulling It Together

Quail Roost Mobile Home Park had confirmed my worst fear. There were as many cats as dogs in Homestead needing our help. Maybe even more. As I walked Sheila's dogs, Rusty and Boscoe, that evening, I kept a watchful eye toward Krome Avenue. Sally had not returned since leaving that morning, so we still didn't know whether she'd recruited any volunteers. If she'd been unsuccessful in getting us help, we were looking at even longer days ahead of us.

It was after ten when Sally finally returned. As she passed me on my way back from walking a sheltie, she yelled out her open window, "Volunteers will be here tomorrow. And we got our vet."

The news couldn't have been any better. The four of us celebrated that night with sandwiches that Sally had picked up from Subway on her way back from Fort Lauderdale and a bottle of chilled wine.

It was nearly noon the next day when the military jeep slowed to turn the corner onto 224th Street. I was repairing a torn tarp as I watched the jeep drive through the opening we'd made in the fence and come to a stop alongside the motor home. The uniformed gentleman who sat in the passenger seat puffed on a pipe as he took his time surveying our makeshift camp. It certainly lacked the systematic efficiency of a military field post, but what we lacked in organization, we made up for in dedication.

Sally had just stepped out of the motor home carrying a small black puppy that had been dropped off by a truck driver who'd found him on the side of the road. When she spotted the jeep, she smiled and headed toward it. Then it dawned on me—this must be our vet.

I continued to work on the torn tarp as the man stepped from the jeep and pulled his sweat-soaked shirt away from his back. He reminded me of Dave Thomas in the Wendy's hamburger commercials—you just needed to cover the camouflage green uniform with a grease-splattered apron. I liked him almost immediately. I felt as if I could talk to him as easily as to a longtime neighbor. The image I had of the unapproachable military officer disappeared. As Sally walked up, his full-faced smile confirmed my first impression.

He petted the puppy in Sally's arms as they talked and laughed. I continued working on the tarp, with the assistance of a playful dalmatian who had decided to play tug-of-war with the torn plastic.

I had just taped the last tear in the tarp and moved the dalmatian out of reach of it when Sally walked up, with the officer following a few feet behind her. "Terri. I'd like you to meet Colonel Thelton McCorcle, the officer I told you about—our veterinarian."

"Colonel McCorcle. Glad to meet you sir," I said, wiping my dirty hands on my jeans. "Am I'm ever glad that you found us."

"Glad to be of service," he replied, shaking my hand. "But do me a favor . . . just call me Mac."

"How long can you stay?" I asked, hoping this wasn't a short-term assignment.

"We've got him for as long as we need him." Sally was glowing. "Can you believe our luck!"

"It just seems to follow us, doesn't it?" I said to Sally, thankful that luck or whatever you want to call it, had been on our side so far.

Mac unbuttoned his shirt pocket and pulled out a small spiral pad. "Now, I need you ladies to give me a list of the supplies you need," he said, pulling a stubby pencil out of another pocket.

The list was long, and at the top was tents. It had rained both afternoons since we'd been in the field, and it had been a mad scramble trying to get everything covered with tarps. Tents would give us dry space to keep more food on the property and save daily trips to Production Central to load up more bags. In addition, we could utilize part of the space to set up cages so we could start to take in cats. All day I'd thought about the cats I'd seen the night before in Quail Roost. After dark I planned to go back to feed them.

After Sally and I finished rattling off our two-page list of wishes, Mac held the pad at a distance and looked at it. "You two don't want much do you?" he said as Sally and I looked at each other and grinned.

"There should be no problem getting you the tents." Mac paused. "And probably most of these other supplies."

Sally looked at me and I stared back, in disbelief. In two days, we'd gone from having nowhere to keep all the stray dogs to acquiring a field, tents, and a veterinarian who had the makings of a Santa Claus. It had all happened faster than we'd ever expected.

"Well, it looks like we're in business," Sally said as she reached out to shake Mac's hand. "Thank you," I said as I shook the colonel's hand too. "We couldn't have done this without you."

Mac in his shy manner replied, "Well, I haven't gotten the stuff yet . . . but if one of you'd like to drive, we'll go shopping."

It was my first time chauffeuring a colonel, and I was on my best behavior. Our destination was an army supply warehouse on the outskirts of Miami. When we arrived and walked through a doorway large enough to drive a semitrailer, though, I was amazed at what I saw. The warehouse was a drop-off site for items being donated for the hurricane victims, and people had been extremely generous.

"Why don't you stay here and pick out anything that you can use at the MASH unit," Mac said as we passed open boxes full of kitchen utensils, clothing, toys, toiletry items, canned food, and first aid supplies. "I have to go upstairs to talk with the brass about the tents."

The power of the man who'd joined our effort earlier that day was demonstrated when he returned less than ten minutes later with the required signatures on the bottom of an official military requisition form. We'd gotten three tents and a lot more. Colonel McCorcle had commandeered a camouflage-green army truck, with twelve soldiers seated in the back. They'd been assigned to help put up our newly acquired tents. It was a detail Sally and I had not thought about. If the job had been left to us, we'd probably still be in Homestead trying to erect tents.

When we returned to the field, we were greeted by Sally and five new volunteers, eager to do whatever we asked, and another twelve dogs. Sally and I decided where the tents should go as the military detachment unloaded the tents from the back of the truck. It seemed best to line them up along the fence, running parallel to Krome. Mac agreed. With that decided, the volunteers pitched in alongside the soldiers, laying the tents out flat on top of the knee-high grass.

What happened in the next hour was amazing. Support poles were put in place, stakes were hammered into the cement-hard ground, ropes were pulled tight and attached to the stakes; then four people got on each side and pulled on other ropes. The green canvas looked like a hot-air balloon being inflated for flight. By dark, two of the tents were up and filled with supplies . . . and more dogs.

While the tents were being put up, Mac had gotten a ride to the barracks to collect his gear and his camper, which he'd driven from Alabama. It would become his sleeping quarters and storage for the medical supplies he'd brought with him. Mac must have realized, as he was packing, that his veterinary skills would somehow be utilized in Florida.

The following day, the third military tent was transformed into a triage area for injured and sick animals. We improvised and made two exam tables using a couple of extra-large airline crates to support doors that had been salvaged from a neighboring pile of debris. In the days that followed, more donated medical supplies began to arrive, in addition to veterinarians and veterinary technicians who wanted to donate their time to help.

When Mac saw his first patient, it had been eight days since Hurricane Andrew had struck. Veterinary services had been needed in Homestead from the first day, and because they had not been available, animals suffered and died. Daily, we saw the results of people having been unprepared to take care of animals, and we struggled with our anger. It was not fair. Once again, it was the animals who were paying the ultimate price for human indifference.

27

The Holdout

By the first week in September, news of the MASH unit finally began to reach concerned people outside of southern Florida. Desperately needed supplies and volunteers began to trickle in as a result. Two of the people who showed up to help made a big difference for the cats in Homestead.

Shirley Minshew, the director of an animal shelter in Warner Robins, Georgia, was one of the first to arrive. In the days following Hurricane Andrew, Shirley began to collect pet food and medical supplies that she thought would be needed in the worst-hit areas. Her red truck looked like Santa's sleigh on Christmas Eve when she pulled into our pasture the day after the last military tent was in place.

When Shirley finally determined that Sally and I were the ones in charge of what was finally starting to resemble a refuge for animals, she cornered us and asked what needed to be done. At that moment we could have given her at least a dozen different jobs and still had some left over. So we told her an abbreviated version of what had happened in those first hectic days, concluding with the instructions, "If you see something that needs to be done . . . go for it."

And Shirley did just that for six weeks.

The next good Samaritan to walk through our gate was Sue

McCloud. She brought with her two hundred large airline crates that had been donated to help animals in the aftermath of Hurricane Hugo. As the relief efforts wound down in South Carolina, the crates were put into storage to await the next disaster, which turned out to be Hurricane Andrew. The crates enabled us to start adding cats to our growing population of animals, which by then had grown to over a hundred dogs, and one obnoxious potbellied pig we named Sir Andrew.

Each night, after we'd walked the dogs one last time, I'd load up my van with bags of cat food and go in search of hungry felines. I only had to go as far as the nearby mobile home parks. Left behind were hundreds of cats that no one seemed to care about. Quail Roost had the most.

I had set up four feeding locations in Quail Roost, which had spaces for five hundred mobile homes. At one of the feeding sites I fed from twenty-five to fifty cats each night . . . in addition to one very fat toad who was especially fond of Meow Mix.

The cats instinctively stayed close to what had been their home or territory before the hurricane. Some of the abandoned cats would be sitting and waiting for me when I arrived, but others would appear only after I'd put food down and moved a safe distance away. There were always a few new cats each night, relieved to finally find some food, fresh water, and someone who had the time to pick them up and comfort them.

It was so hard, during those first days, to get back into my van and drive off, leaving the cats behind. Especially the ones who craved attention even more than the food I left them. There was one cat I particularly hated to leave. She looked just like my Elvira.

Each night she sat on the same, upside-down brown-and-orange La-Z-Boy recliner, waiting for my arrival. While I filled salvaged kitchen drawers, hub caps, and plastic containers with dry food, she'd brush up against my legs, meowing the entire time. Once all my make-shift feeding dishes were full, I'd lean down and pick her up. She'd drape her front legs over my shoulder and nudge my cheek with the top of her head. She purred so loudly, she nearly drowned out the chatter of the nighttime bugs.

How I wished I could take her back to the MASH unit. To know that at least one of these cats was safe would have eased the frustration I felt in not being able to do more for them. Until I found a cage to put her in, she could have stayed in the motor home with me. But I had no choice. I had to leave her. She had stashed somewhere in all the rubble a litter of kittens. Until I found the kittens, the mother cat had to remain, or her babies would starve to death.

I discovered she was a mother the first night I fed her. When I picked her up, I noticed the fur around three of her nipples was still damp, so I knew she'd nursed kittens recently. For over an hour, I tried to persuade her to go back to her babies, so that I could follow her to their hiding place, but she wouldn't leave my side, and I had no idea where to start looking for them. There were endless possible hiding spots.

The debris was also too dangerous to dig through. Busted furniture, snapped tree limbs, jagged sheets of aluminum siding, and heavy sections of paneled walls lay on top of one another, sometimes precariously. If I moved the wrong thing, something could come tumbling down on the kittens and kill them. I tried shining my flashlight into the piles of rubble, hoping to get a reflection off the kittens' eyes, but I only saw lizards scurrying through the debris—another real good reason not to go digging around in that stuff.

Each night I'd try again to locate the kittens, but I was having no luck. If only there were some way to make the mother realize I wanted to help her and her family. My growing fear was that when the bulldozers arrived to clear the debris from the park, the kittens would be too small to scurry out of the way and they'd be buried alive.

Time was running out for all the cats. I knew they needed to be moved to the MASH unit. Living in the debris was becoming deadly. When I first discovered these forgotten victims, I was relieved to find that most of them had survived the hurricane without any noticeable injuries, unlike the other animals in the area. But as they lived in the piles of rubble, with sharp metal and shards of glass, they began to sustain eye injuries, sliced paws, and even severed legs.

With the arrival of the cages and Shirley, we were finally able to start gathering up the cats and save them from further suffering and death.

Shirley and I would load up her truck and my van with cages, humane traps, and lots of cans of smelly tuna and begin collecting cats after dark. The frightened felines would cautiously make their way through the unstable piles of debris to reach the food and water that we put out for them. As we'd stand back and watch them eat, we could hear other cats crying. The pitiful wailing came from the dense wreckage—still too dangerous for us to penetrate. Not being able to reach these cats, even to get food and water to them, was heartbreaking. We tried to ignore their cries for help, but nothing could block them out.

So one by one, we picked up the cats that we could help. The ones still too frightened to let us get near them, we set traps for. It sometimes took several nights, but eventually we would capture them. Some of the cats were wild, but not all of them. Once we got the ones that were just frightened back to the MASH unit, we found that a little tender loving care from our growing number of volunteers transformed them back into huggable animals. Mac tended to the ones with injuries, cleaning wounds, stitching up cuts, and removing shards of glass.

It did my heart good to walk through the cat tent and finally see it full. By the second week in September, we had more cats than dogs on the property. Thank goodness for volunteers like Grace Sugar, Karen Hull, and Carol Marren who made sure all the animals gots lots of love and attention. They gave enough to make up for all the days the dogs and cats had gone without. But there was still one cat that was missing, my Elvira look-alike.

I continued to take food and water to her every night, hoping that one of the evenings I'd arrive to see her and the kittens sitting on the upside-down brown-and-orange La-Z-Boy recliner waiting for me. But she was always alone.

"Why won't you let me help you and your kittens?" I yelled at her one night while she sat curled up on my lap, purring. My patience with this cat was wearing thin. I would be returning home soon, and I knew I'd have to make a tough decision before I left.

"Do you know what's going to happen if you don't start cooperating?" I said as I picked her up and held her face inches from mine. "Do you want your kittens to die?"

That afternoon I'd heard from a police officer that the bulldozers were starting to shovel up the debris from the mobile home parks. It wouldn't be long until they reached Quail Roost.

"Please, show me where your kittens are." My eyes filled with tears as I hugged her against my chest. "Please."

The cat only looked up at me with her golden eyes and purred louder.

On the day of my departure, before leaving for the airport in Miami to catch my flight home, I was to pay one last visit to Quail Roost Mobile Home Park. I'd spent a lot of long nights in that park with Shirley, me braving the lizards and Shirley the spiders, in order to save the cats. It was a true test of our love for these animals. And we succeeded in putting our fears aside long enough to save over two hundred cats.

When I stopped my van in the customary spot that one last time, the upside-down brown-and-orange La-Z-Boy recliner was unoccupied. I slowly got out of the van and walked toward the recliner that was beginning to show the wear of sitting outdoors for weeks. I sat down on the sagging piece of furniture and looked out across the remnants of the park—and nowhere did I see a cat. They were all gone, safe at the MASH unit, waiting to be reclaimed or adopted.

Suddenly, I heard a familiar meow. My eyes quickly scanned the debris. My heart beat faster. I got up from the recliner and moved to where I could see better. Tears filled my eyes, blurring my vision. But I could still see my Elvira look-alike walking toward me . . . with four kittens behind her.

"Well, it's about time," I declared as I walked toward the stubborn cat. "Nothing like waiting until the last minute."

I had just enough time to gather up the family of five and drop them off at the MASH unit. Before jumping back into my car to head to the airport, I held the mother cat in my arms one last time, and whispered, "Thank you. Thank you for letting me save you *and* your kittens."

28

Pepsi

Shopping in Homestead was still not easy by the middle of September. With no stores open for miles in any direction, we had to be creative to locate the things that were needed to take care of the animals at the MASH unit. At the top of my shopping list on this particular morning were bathtubs. We were receiving dogs with severe skin irritations, and a bath would help to relieve some of their scratching, at least for a while. I was on my way to scout a nearby subdivision, certain I'd find a tub in the growing piles of debris that lined both sides of every street.

Leaning my head out the car window to see what had brought early morning traffic to a halt, all I could see were the cars ahead of me leading up to the intersection. The absence of a streetlight left it up to the drivers who'd managed to reach the crosswalk to decide who went first. And each driver thought it should be him. Blaring horns, curses, and furious finger gestures confirmed that people were losing their patience with one another.

"Lady, move your damn jeep." It was the guy in the black convertible behind me. I pressed my foot on the gas pedal and the jeep moved two feet closer to the intersection.

It took me ten more minutes to move four car lengths closer to the congested intersection. The driver in the dented Toyota ahead of me suddenly decided he'd had enough. He made a U-turn and headed back in the direction we'd come from. This put me one car closer to the dangerous crossing ahead and close enough to finally see what had caused this traffic jam.

Hurricane Andrew

In the middle of the intersection was a dog.

It was a medium-size Doberman that stood on the hot asphalt, shaking, as cars came at her from four directions. Her eyes frantically searched for a way to escape. But there was no place to go.

This was not the time to patiently wait to be first in line. Grabbing the steering wheel with both hands, I yanked it to the right and aimed for the nearest driveway. An obstacle course of damaged furniture, slabs of stucco-covered walls, twisted window frames, and broken terra-cotta roof tiles littered people's lawns, but I just drove around them. I didn't look at the people still in the backup to my left, who angrily voiced their disapproval at me for cutting the line. But I had no choice. If someone didn't come to this dog's rescue soon, there was no question she'd end up getting hit. I wasn't going to let the animal die, if I could prevent it.

I swerved to miss an anxious driver in a Mercedes that came at me from the right. My next obstacle was a dump truck approaching from the opposite side of the intersection. The Doberman would have no chance of surviving if this driver decided he didn't have time to detour around a dog. I had to position my jeep between the truck and the helpless dog.

I shifted the jeep into first and steered straight for him, hoping somehow it knew I intended to help it and not run it over. The dog did not move, but the dump truck did—straight forward toward the frightened dog. I gave the jeep some more gas, and as I got even with the dog, I turned the wheels to the left and stopped. I'd succeeded in positioning myself between the dump truck and the dog. Brakes screeched and a horn screamed in anger. But I stood my ground.

Now was when the dog should have jumped into the car for our fast getaway, the way you see in the movies, but when I looked out my window, the dog had disappeared. The jerk in the dump truck still had his hand pressed against his horn, and by now he'd been joined by other drivers around us. It must have become too much for the dog, who it seemed had finally decided to find a way to get itself out of this predicament.

I had to move, or I would end up being the one flattened on the pavement. But before I went anywhere, I had to know that the dog hadn't crawled under my jeep. As I was fumbling to get my seat belt undone so I could look under the jeep, I cracked the door open with my other hand, and I was startled when it continued to open further on its own.

The door was now open far enough, to allow an eighty-five-pound Doberman to squeeze through. It was the black nose that I saw first, then the head, the shoulders, the body, and finally the tail. Every part of the large dog jumped into the jeep and landed on my lap . . . determined not to move.

"I hope you're friendly," I whispered, afraid for my face if I further alarmed the dog.

The panting dog just stared at me and shook.

"Well, if it's okay with you, I think it's time I move this jeep," I said, noticing that the guy in the dump truck had opened his door and most likely was headed in my direction.

Driving with an eighty-five-pound dog sitting on your lap is no easy thing to do. My left foot was searching for the clutch, and I already had the other foot waiting on the gas pedal. With all parts finally synchronized, I ground the gears into first and pushed my foot to the floor.

Luck was indeed still on my side.

I drove like a true daredevil, swerving to miss each car in my path, as the dog tried to balance on my lap. Its toenails dug into my legs as it tried to hold on.

When I was clear of the intersection and could see that the dump truck had continued on in the other direction, I pulled the jeep over to the curb. I put the jeep in park and began to talk quietly to the dog.

"So. How did you get yourself into that mess?"

The dog just continued to stare, its hot breath warming my face.

"It's a good thing I came along when I did, because I think that dump truck driver had you in his sights," I said as my hand slowly reached up to pet the dog on the forehead.

The dog's eyes slowly closed in response to my touch. She had to be tired, and her growling stomach confirmed she was hungry. I looked the dog over and did not find any cuts or injuries, and what I did find pleased me. A collar and a current rabies tag hung around the Doberman's neck. This was one of the few dogs that we had found with any form of identification.

"Well, it looks like we're going to be able to get you back home," I said, giving the dog a hug. She responded with a kiss right up the middle of my face.

"Okay. It's time you moved."

I placed my hands against her chest and gently pushed her toward the passenger seat. She followed my instructions and sat straight up in the seat, looking out the front window. I think she knew I was taking her home, and she was ready.

When we arrived back at the MASH unit, I got the dog out of the jeep and tied her to the bumper of the motor home. I could hardly wait to feed her and get her some water. Then I could use the cellular phone in the motor home to call Dade County Animal Control. Since I had the dog's rabies license number, Animal Control would be able to give me the owner's name and address. It took two hours of constantly hitting the redial button before I got through to Animal Control. After another ten minutes on hold, the officer at the other end was able to give me the information I needed.

Before I hung up, he said, "Oh, and if you want to know the dog's name . . . it's Pepsi."

I grabbed the piece of paper I'd scribbled the owner's name and address on, and went to tell Pepsi the good news.

This was definitely the right dog, because when I rounded the corner of the motor home and said, "Pepsi, you want to go home?" a very excited dog jumped up and down, and her tail wagged for the first time.

I knew that finding Pepsi's house wasn't going to be easy. The street maintenance department had not even begun to replace all the street signs that had been blown away. Fortunately, the insurance companies had instructed their policyholders to spray-paint their street name and number on the front of their homes, so that the companies' claim representatives could locate them. I read the fronts of the houses to direct me toward Pepsi's neighborhood, which, according to my map, was not far from the Miami Zoo.

After backtracking several times and asking for directions from an elderly man sitting on the front porch of his roofless house, I found the correct street. As I drove around the debris that still littered the street, I read the numbers on garage doors and the fronts of toppled houses. I knew we were getting close when Pepsi stood up in her seat and started knocking her tail against the van door.

The numbers 2364 were scribbled in large red letters on a scrap of plywood leaning against the twisted remains of a yellow VW Bug. We had found Pepsi's home.

The house was in bad shape. The roof had caved in, allowing the rain to drench the inside of the house. Shreds of drapery material hung in each window, no longer protected from the elements by glass panes. A large palm tree had fallen across the front corner of the house, exposing the living room. Torn pieces of pink insulation hung from the rafters. Broken sheets of drywall looked like playing cards that had been thrown in the air to settle upon upside-down furniture.

In spite of its condition, Pepsi still recognized her home.

I grabbed Pepsi's leash, and she followed me out my door. As we approached the front door, I called out, "Anyone at home?"

But I got no response.

Pepsi was pulling at the leash, not understanding why we couldn't go inside the house, when I heard a noise from the house next door. A man appeared in the doorway.

"Can I help you?" he asked as he stepped over the pieces of clay pots spread across his porch.

"Yes," I said, walking toward him. "I'm trying to find the family that lives here. I believe this is their dog."

The man crossed the yard and removed his glasses from his shirt pocket. "Yeah," he said, positioning his glasses on the bridge of his nose. "That looks like Pepsi."

When Pepsi heard her name, her black tail wagged even faster.

"Do you know where her owners are?" I asked.

"They were here this morning talking with some insurance guy, but they left about ten minutes ago," he told me as he patted Pepsi on the head. "They are living with family in Fort Lauderdale, but they've been coming back every day to salvage what they can from the house. They got hit real bad."

"I think what I'll do then is leave them a note and let them know I have Pepsi," I said. "I'm sure they will be glad to hear she is okay."

"I reckon so," the man replied.

I found a sheet of bright pink paper in my van and wrote the following:

> I FOUND YOUR DOG PEPSI. SHE IS FINE. I'VE
> TAKEN HER TO THE SMALL ANIMAL MASH
> UNIT AT 224TH AND KROME AVE. SHE
> WILL BE SAFE THERE UNTIL YOU CAN
> RECLAIM HER. PEPSI IS MOST ANXIOUS
> TO SEE YOU.—TERRI CRISP

I left Pepsi in the car while I hung the paper on a sharp fragment of the mostly intact doorframe. The owners couldn't miss my note when they returned. I was sure they'd find it and my business card that I had left and come to reclaim Pepsi the next day.

Three days passed . . . and Pepsi waited.

On Saturday morning, I had to head over toward the Miami Zoo again, and I decided to take Pepsi with me. I was hoping I'd catch her owners at home, since it was a weekend.

In the few days that Pepsi had been at the MASH unit, she had become very attached to me. So much so that she'd bark nonstop if she couldn't see me. Therefore, she followed me around the compound, slept close by at night, and rode with me whenever I had an animal to rescue or some cats to feed.

Whenever she saw me going to the van, she'd run ahead and wait for me to open the door. She'd jump into the van and position herself in the passenger seat so all the other dogs could see her. As we'd pass the dogs, panting in the hot sun, she'd sit in her air-conditioned seat as cool as could be.

Pepsi wasn't the only one getting attached.

As Pepsi and I drove together that Saturday morning, I felt a mixture of excitement and sadness. Pepsi had obviously been loved and well cared for, so I knew she belonged back with her owners, but I was beginning to realize how much I was going to miss her. Several times Pepsi tried to crawl into my lap as we got closer to her neighborhood, something she hadn't done since I'd found her. I think she was having mixed feelings too.

When we pulled up in front of the house, I immediately spotted the bright pink note in the same place I'd left it. They hadn't been back, which explained why I hadn't heard from them. I wasn't sure whether to be relieved or disappointed. I decided I'd update my note and let them know Pepsi was being well cared for; in fact, I could rightfully be accused of spoiling her.

Pepsi stayed in the van while I went to write the note. I noticed my business card was gone when I pulled the paper from the slice of the doorframe. As I held the paper I spotted some new writing in the lower right corner. It read, "OVER." I slowly turned to the back side.

In neat handwriting was a note to me:

WE DON'T WANT THE DOG.
DO WITH HER AS YOU PLEASE.

I couldn't believe what I was reading. Using my pen, I started to write an angry note back to them, but then I stopped and wadded up the piece of paper. If they cared so little about Pepsi . . . they didn't deserve her back.

From the porch I could see Pepsi through the smeared window. Her tail was going, and she was anxious to be let out of the car and returned to her owners. How would she understand that this was no longer her home?

I returned to the van, and had to hold Pepsi back as I slid into the driver's seat. She finally retreated to her own seat, and her tail stopped wagging. This was twice I'd brought her home, only to take her back to the MASH unit with me. She had to be confused.

I reached for Pepsi and put my arms around her neck. The Doberman's head rested on my shoulder as I told her, "Peps. They don't want ya."

Out of Harm's Way

*   *   *

When it came time to return to California, I couldn't leave Pepsi. We were finding good homes for the unclaimed dogs and cats that had arrived at the MASH unit, but I wanted to make sure Pepsi found an extra-special one . . . and I knew of just the place.

When Ken had dropped me at the airport several weeks earlier, his instructions had been very clear: "You are *not* to bring home anything with four legs."

I had assured Ken that I wouldn't get attached . . . but it was a promise I could not keep.

Two days after I arrived home with Pepsi, I caught Ken curled up on our bed with her sound asleep beside him. She immediately became a part of our family, but I thought we were going to lose her in December.

It was a Thursday evening and I was fixing dinner when the call came. Jennifer answered the phone, and I could hear her say, "Yes. I'll get her."

My heart stopped when I picked up the phone, and the woman on the other end asked, "Are you the lady who has Pepsi?"

Instantly I thought . . . her owners want her back.

I could barely speak. "Yes."

"My sons wanted me to call," she said.

I could guess what she was going to say next. The kids wanted their dog back. What was I going to do? There was no way I could give her up. She'd been a part of our family for only three months, but in that time my daughters had become attached to her too.

"When you found Pepsi, our lives were in utter turmoil. We didn't know where we were going to be living or how we could afford to take care of our family. Both my husband and I lost our jobs as a result of Hurricane Andrew. Having a dog to care for was just another responsibility we couldn't handle."

I listened to the woman as my eyes filled with tears.

"And I didn't think it was fair to Pepsi. She deserved someone who could take better care of her than we could." The woman paused. "My sons miss Pepsi, but I've explained that a really nice lady has her."

Suddenly I felt different about this woman. I began to understand what it was that they had gone through. They had lost so much. How could I keep their dog? I'd have to give Pepsi back.

"If you want Pepsi back, I can put her on a plane." I couldn't believe I'd said it, but I knew I had to.

"Oh. No," she said. "My sons just wanted to know if you could send us a picture of Pepsi once in a while. She's your dog now."

29

Letter
to a Husband

September 12, 1992

Dearest Ken:

I've tried to call you, but the cellular phone lines are so clogged it's impossible to get through. Being unable to speak with you and the girls makes me feel so far away. I'm hoping I can find someone who is headed north to give this letter to. The chances of mailing it myself are pretty slim. All the mailboxes around here got blown away. I saw one yesterday perched in the top of a palm tree.

It's 4:23 A.M. Sally and John went to bed about an hour ago. Shirley, my cat-trapping buddy, is sprawled out on the floor of her tent. I hope she's resting. She was bitten by a cat today and her arm is really bothering her, but it hasn't slowed her down. She's incredible, as is everyone else. I've never met such a dedicated group of people, who will do whatever it takes to help animals.

Out of Harm's Way

I should be asleep too, but I had to get this letter written before another day passed. I'm sure you've been worried about me, but don't be. I'm okay. I'm tired, but that'll be easily cured once I get home. What I worry about is how I'll adjust to being back in the "normal" world again. I think it's going to be tough.

Right now I'm sitting under one of the military tents that was loaned to us by the National Guard. My desk is the top of a shattered air-conditioner unit. How wonderful it would be if it worked. The heat here is unbearable, even at this hour. I'm using an upside-down metal bucket as a chair. We've all learned to improvise with whatever we can find.

There must be a million bugs swarming around my lantern right now. It's amazing how tolerant you can become of things when your energy is gone. I can't quite get used to the ever-present lizards, though. You would not believe how many there are. It's been a real test of my love for animals. If they didn't mean so much, I would have packed my bags and headed home a long time ago.

A delicate rain has started to fall. It tempts me to sleep, but I can't close my eyes. When I do, all I see are the animals we couldn't help. There have been so many. I know I can't save them all, but it seems there should be enough caring people in this world to be able to save more. There are so few of us here. Sometimes we feel incapable of making even a dent.

The camouflage-green tent I'm under has a bottle-cap-size hole near the support pole. Droplets of rain are sneaking in to dampen my writing tablet. The words on this page will be a little blurred when they reach you. It's raindrops, though—not tears—that are smearing the ink. I'm too tired right now to cry. There have been a lot of tears shed since I got down here. My mind feels like the rain clouds overheard. Burdened. Always needing to lighten its load. Sometimes the only way to do it is to have a good cry.

We keep the tent flaps rolled up at night to allow what little breeze there is to cool the animals inside. With the breeze comes the smell of death. It's a smell I can't escape. Hurricane Andrew was a killer. I've touched many of the victims. This afternoon it was a rottweiler. I just hope he died instantly. I wanted to bury him, but I couldn't find anything strong enough to penetrate the rock-hard soil.

I don't know how long I have been here. It must be about two weeks now. I'm not sure when I'm coming home. Leaving is going to be hard, in spite of how much I miss you. There is so much to do. Maybe tomorrow I'll find a shovel and go back and find some soft ground and bury the rottweiler. The rumor of the day was that the army is going to burn the dead animals. There are so many of them. Horses, cows, goats, pigs, sheep, dogs, and cats.

I just had to go check on a dog in the vet tent. Mac, our veterinarian, was bent down petting the dog when I came around the corner. It was the chocolate Lab I found today. He was pulling at the bandages on his injured leg. Mac said he'd keep an eye on him and told me to go back to bed.

Mac is amazing. If it weren't for him, we would have lost a lot more animals. It doesn't matter how late it gets, he's first out of bed to take care of an animal. I think he's had less sleep than all of us, but he never complains. Mac knows how to take care of himself. He escapes the sadness by drawing whimsical cartoons of the animals and us. They have been a great source of laughter for everyone. He relaxes by puffing on his pipe. I can smell the smoke from his pipe now. It is such a comforting smell. I hope the dog will be okay. He's fortunate to be alive. I found him under a collapsed roof. It was the reflection of the sun off his ID tag that caught my eye. If I had blinked, I probably would have missed it. The endless mounds of debris make finding the animals difficult. I try not to think about all those that are buried too deep for us to save.

I guess we have close to one hundred dogs chained to the perimeter fence and almost seventy-five cats in cages tonight. It's hard to keep an accurate count, because there are so many new ones arriving all day long. They are so scared. I am too. I'm afraid many of them are now ownerless. What will become of them is still unknown. I tell myself I can't bring them all home, but I want them to be safe and never suffer again. And don't worry . . . I remember the rule, "No more animals."

I hear a vehicle approaching from the north. When I glanced toward the road just now, I saw a rabbit dart across and disappear into the avocado orchard. Another survivor. It must be nearly five. My watchband broke while I was pulling a dead horse off the road. I'll never forget the look on that creature's face.

A shower stall and an endless supply of hot water is what I

1 9 5

want more than anything right now. If I'm lucky, I'll find a jug of spare water to splash over me. You should see me—I would advise from a distance, though. My clothes haven't seen the inside of a washer since I got here. We've been joking about going to the Red Cross to get a new wardrobe. My clothes may have to be buried when I get home. I don't think Tide could even penetrate the dirt. I vaguely remember brushing my teeth the day before yesterday. My arms are like an old piece of furniture that has been painted multiple times. You can scrape off the layers of mosquito spray, sunscreen, blood, dirt, and sweat. My hair could stay pulled back in a ponytail without a rubber band I think.

It's hard to imagine that there are people, right now, in other places, beginning their day in a house, able to take a shower, wearing clean clothes, seated at a breakfast table eating hot, fresh, and nutritious food. Those things that I always took for granted now are the focus of my dreams.

We awaken here to one hundred alarm clocks that bark until we struggle out of bed each morning, usually before the sun gets up. Breakfast, if you can call it that, is usually a stale donut and a cold cup of instant coffee that was never hot. It's a brutal diet plan, but it works. I really need a pair of suspenders for the jeans. I'm lucky if I find five minutes to brush my teeth and hair each day. I try to get some deodorant on too, but it's pretty much a wasted effort—and we try not to waste anything around here.

A military jeep is sloshing through the mud puddles on our gravel road, so I may have to interrupt this letter again. The military are ever-present. It makes you feel as if you are in a war zone. Armed soldiers stop periodically during the night to check on us. We occasionally hear gun fire after dark. I heard they shot a looter the other night. We really are out in the middle of nowhere. Flashlights are a constant companion after the sun goes down.

The jeep has stopped near the semitrailer where we store the dog and cat food. Two uniformed gentlemen have exited the jeep with rifles slung over their shoulders. The dogs are now awake and barking. A few cats are meowing in the cat tent. The rain has started to fall harder.

The men are pulling something from the back of the jeep. One of them has spotted Mac and is yelling to get his attention. There is a knot in my stomach. I'm afraid what we have is another four-legged victim. I must go. I may be needed . . .

I never finished this letter or mailed it. Ken went fourteen days straight without hearing from me. When I was unpacking all the junk and dirty cloths I hauled back from Florida with me, I found this letter crumpled up in the bottom of my backpack. I gave it to Ken then, and I'm glad I did. It helped him to understand what I'd been through. This is probably one of the most honest glimpses of the emotional turmoil I endured during the time I was in Homestead.

On September 12, my day began the moment I put down my pen and ran to see if my help was needed with our newest victim. Virtually every moment of my next twenty-one hours was spent helping animals.

In the back of the jeep was a six-month-old black Lab that had been found in the road. The officers thought he had been hit by a car—an all too common sight in the midst of the chaos. Their initial intent was to remove and dispose of the body, but when they got closer, they saw he was still breathing. A two inch-wide piece of aluminum, protruding from his right shoulder, had taken its toll, though. Fortunately the officers knew where to bring him.

When I saw him, he was wrapped in a blood-soaked army jacket. His chances of surviving didn't look good. For nearly two hours Mac worked to repair the small body. All the while the concerned officers stood by watching, the looters forgotten.

I stood across from Mac as he worked to save the puppy, stroking the blood-caked fur in hopes I could will the puppy to live. Glancing over Mac's shoulder, I remember staring at the sun as it appeared above the avocado trees across the road. It was going to be another hot day in southern Florida. The rain had stopped at some point. The only pleasure at that moment was the smell of the wet grass.

It was my job to brush away the flies that repeatedly tried to land on the puppy's wound, as Mac sewed up the puppy's damaged shoulder. He had done everything he could. The officers retrieved their bloody jacket and left with the promise they'd come back and check on the Lab later.

The puppy did survive . . . and we named him Will.

30

Lazarus

Hurricane Andrew taught me the true meaning of being tired. After three weeks at the MASH unit I was exhausted, both mentally and physically. At the end of the day, which usually arrived around three A.M., I would collapse on one of the bunks in the motor home, thinking, *I'll never be able to get up at five.*

But I did.

The dogs were our alarm clock. All it took was for one of the early birds to begin stirring, then the rest of them would start in with their relentless barking. Any attempt to drown out their pleas to be walked failed.

Half awake, I'd roll out of bed, still wearing the clothes I'd fallen asleep in just a few hours before. I'd yank on my knee-high rubber boots as I stumbled out the door. I always considered it quite an accomplishment when I managed to get the correct foot in the correct boot. There were a couple times, though, that I'd gone through half a day before I realized I'd gotten my shoes on the wrong feet. It was easy not to notice the discomfort. When your entire body aches, you lose the ability to pinpoint pain.

On the first walk of the day, the dogs were in charge. They'd pull me wherever *they* wanted to go, taking advantage of my sleepy inability to take charge and deliver the command, "heel." As they did their business, I'd stand with the leash in my hand and close my eyes in hopes of gaining just a few more moments of sleep. A sharp tug of the leash would always cut my snooze short.

While I finished walking my charges, I'd reflect on what Sally and I, plus the team of dedicated volunteers, had assembled. Sometimes it seemed quite amazing that we had been able to accomplish so much in such a short time. On this particular September morning we had close to six hundred survivors on the property. One of them was a dog named Lazarus.

A few days earlier I was sorting through a box of dog collars that had just been donated by a kennel club when Shirley ran up. "You seen Mac?" she asked, out of breath.

"The last I saw him he was headed toward the tractor trailer. But that was about an hour ago," I replied, looking toward the trailer we used to store our fluctuating inventory of pet food.

"Great. I'll check over there," Shirley said as she took off running.

A moment later I saw Shirley and Mac heading for the vet tent. The looks on their faces told me that whatever they were talking about was serious. I decided the dog collars could wait.

When I got to the vet tent, the two exam tables were occupied. A sedated rabbit lay on one. He'd been brought in about an hour before, crawling with maggots. A vet, who'd volunteered just for the day, was painstakingly removing each maggot, one at a time with a pair of tweezers, from the open wounds on the rabbit's stomach. I had been relieved to hear there was a chance the rabbit would survive.

It was hard to see what was on the other makeshift exam table. Peeking through the group of people that surrounded the table, I could just make out that it was a large black dog. I guessed a rottweiler or Doberman. When I got close enough to peek over Shirley's shoulder, I saw it was a Doberman with a gaping hole in its shoulder. A blood-soaked towel lay across the dog's upper body. Mac was responding quickly to stop the bleeding.

"Shirley," I whispered. "What happened to the dog?"

"Some fool shot him," she replied with anger in her voice.

"How'd he get here?" I asked as I winced in response to the yelp the dog let out when Mac touched its injured shoulder.

Shirley beckoned with her head for me to follow her. When we were far enough away from the vet tent for anyone to hear, she told me what she knew.

"The dog belongs to a family that lives near Homestead Air Force

Base. When they evacuated, they tied the dog to a tree in their back-yard and left."

"How can people be so stupid?" I interrupted. "Are those the own-ers?" I asked, looking toward the vet tent. I was about ready to march over and tell them what I thought of them when Shirley told me that they were not the dog's owners. They lived next door.

It took the owners two days to return to their home after the storm, the neighbors had told Shirley. Their house was in really bad shape, and it didn't take them long to rummage through their belongings and load what could be salvaged into their aging station wagon. The last thing the man did before the family drove off was walk into the backyard.

"When the lady told me what happened next, I wanted to track that man down and kill him," Shirley told me, holding back tears.

"What did he do?" I asked, afraid of what Shirley was going to tell me.

"He shot the dog. Just . . . shot him."

I put my arms around Shirley, and we both cried, neither one of us able to say a word. It had become increasingly difficult to keep our emotions under control by the third week. We'd seen so much suffering in such a short period of time, and it was a strain, both physically and mentally, that made it harder for us to fight off tears.

"I guess we should go back and see if Mac needs any help," Shirley finally said as she wiped her eyes.

"Do you think the dog will make it?" I asked as we walked toward the tent.

"It doesn't look good."

Mac was still cleaning the wound when we returned. Sweat was streaming down his temples as he worked. The dog was now sedated, and an IV hung from one of the tent supports, dripping fluids into the motionless body. The couple who had brought the dog in stood in the same place, staring at the dog with tears in their eyes.

I stood beside the woman and put my arm around her shoulders. "Thank you for bringing him in," I whispered. "He's really lucky you found him."

"Do you think the doctor can save him?" the woman asked.

"I know he'll try."

Mac had already performed some miracles, and I hoped this dog would be yet another one.

It took another hour for Mac to finish. He'd done everything that was medically possible. The man who'd brought in the Doberman helped Mac move the dog to the recovery tent, where they placed him on a gray army blanket spread out on the grass.

"In a way I hope the dog dies," the woman said to me as we waited for her husband to return. "Those people have never treated that dog right. They shouldn't be allowed to have a pet."

The woman went on to tell me how she would frequently slip into her neighbors' backyard to feed the friendly Doberman after the owners left for work. "I really think the dog would have starved to death if I hadn't have kept it fed," she said, shaking her head.

"Did you ever call to report the owners for abuse?" I asked her.

"Sure. But no one ever came out and did anything," she said disgustedly. "I was tempted to just steal the dog and find it a new home, but I figured I would be the one that would end up getting in trouble."

Just then Mac and the woman's husband walked up.

"Well, what do you think, Mac?" I asked.

"I'll be real surprised if he makes it to morning," he said as he pulled a handkerchief from his back pocket to wipe away the sweat on his forehead. "It's an old dog, and the bullet did some pretty severe damage."

"I knew I should have stole him," the woman said, crying. "Why didn't I just go with my gut feeling and do it?"

"Can we check back with you tomorrow to see how the dog is doing?" the husband asked as he put his arm around his wife's shoulders.

"Sure, but don't get your hopes up," Mac replied.

The couple thanked Mac for his efforts, and they walked slowly back to their car. It made my heart feel good to see how much they cared.

Mac was the first up the next morning. He was on his way to the recovery tent to check on the Doberman when Sally leaned out the motor home door and asked Mac if he wanted a hot cup of coffee. The offer was too good to resist.

Mac, Sally, John, and I indulged ourselves and spent twenty minutes having breakfast, which consisted of the first hot coffee we'd had in weeks and a box of stale miniature powdered donuts. Amazingly, the dogs had decided to sleep in, which allowed us this luxury.

We were on our second cup of coffee when the door to the motor home opened. Robin Hanson, one of the most dependable volunteers, stuck her head in the door. "Good morning, you-all," she said in a cheerful voice. "Hate to interrupt, but Mac, do you want me to walk that Doberman in the recovery tent?"

I looked at Mac, knowing which dog Robin was asking about.

"No, it won't be necessary," Mac said before gulping down the last of his coffee. "I expect the dog is dead."

"You might want to check, but I think the dog is still alive," Robin said. "When I walked into the tent, the dog lifted his head."

It didn't take Mac and I any time to reach the recovery tent, with Robin two steps behind us. Mac knelt beside the dog and laid his hand across the dog's neck as Robin and I watched, hoping for the best.

"Well, I'll be damned," Mac declared. "The ol' guy is still alive."

The Doberman opened his eyes as Mac spoke. "Did you ever fool me," Mac said as he patted the dog between his ears.

Mac had pulled off another miracle, one that a lot of people had been praying for.

We named the dog Lazarus. The couple who brought him to us stopped by often to check on him. They told us that the dog's owners had been back to their house several times to collect more of their belongings, but there was never any mention of the dog in the few times they'd spoken to them.

Lazarus continued to get better under Mac's care. The wound was healing nicely, and each day the dog was able to walk a little further. Our patient regained his appetite in no time, and his bulging sides proved it. They were quickly filling out, thanks in part to the chicken that two of the national guardsmen would make disappear from their military mess tent each evening.

This dog, who'd only known what it was like to be abused before he came to the MASH unit, was eager for the attention everyone was giving him. When someone walked toward him, he'd stand up and his stump of a tail would start wagging. Once you were close enough, he'd lean against you, waiting to have his ears rubbed. Lazarus absorbed all the attention he could. I think he feared that one day it would all end, and he'd be returned to his owners. We all hoped not.

Sally and I were taking inventory of the pet food in the semitrailer one morning when a soft voice interrupted our counting.

"Excuse me."

A woman wearing a blue-checked cotton dress, with the face of a Norman Rockwell grandmother, stood at the back door of the semi.

"I'm sorry to disturb you," she said. "But are one of you Sally or Terri?"

"I'm Sally. What can I do for you?"

"I would like to adopt one of your dogs," the woman replied as she swatted at an annoying fly.

"Great," Sally said, looking at me with a smile on her face.

We didn't have a lot of people coming to us to adopt an animal. Most were just bringing us more to take care of.

"What kind of dog did you have in mind?" I asked, hoping we'd be able to give her exactly what she was looking for. There was a good chance of it, because we had one of just about everything. Many of the animals on the property had been with us for at least a week with no identification; legally we could make them available for adoption after seventy-two hours. It was our ongoing hope that the animals would be reclaimed by their owners, but all of us at the MASH unit were struggling with the growing certainty that very few people were searching for lost pets.

Sally and I jumped down from the trailer as the woman told us she didn't have any specific type of dog in mind. "I just want a nice companion," she said as the three of us walked toward the fence where the dogs were tethered.

"I drove down from Palm Beach when I heard about this place. These poor animals must be so scared. . . . I just lost my German shepherd two weeks ago. Duke was with me for twelve years. My grandkids gave him to me when my husband died. Thought he'd be good company for me. And he was." She pulled an embroidered handkerchief from her dress pocket and dabbed the corner of her eye.

Suddenly, it occurred to me that we might just have the perfect match.

"Ma'am. Would you be interested in a very gentle Doberman?" I asked as I looked at Sally. She knew immediately which dog I was referring to.

"Well, I suppose. Can I meet the dog?" The woman asked as she folded her handkerchief and put it back in her pocket.

"Just follow us," Sally said, taking the lead.

The dog was asleep when we entered the vet tent, but when he heard Sally call his name, he opened his eyes and stood up—the short stump of a tail wagging in anticipation of more attention.

"This is Lazarus," Sally said, as she patted the top of the excited dog's head. "He's a very special dog in need of someone who has lots of time to scratch his ears."

The woman listened intently as Sally went on to tell her what had happened to Lazarus. She gasped and moved close enough to pet the dog when Sally told her he'd been shot by his owner and left to die. Lazarus leaned against the woman and looked up at her with contented eyes as she continued to stroke the black fur.

Sally didn't have to say any more. Lazarus took over from there, and it was an easy sell.

31

Expectations

The small-animal MASH unit had become quite an attraction in Homestead. Cars, with curious faces staring out the windows, would slow down all day as they passed on Krome Avenue, their occupants probably wondering if the circus had come to town. "When the elephants arrive, it's definitely time to go home," John joked one evening as we sat around eating more of Sally's famous peanut butter sandwiches. It was as good a gauge as any as to how much longer we'd keep the MASH unit open.

There were a lot of people who didn't just drive by our horse pasture, though. Many days it seemed as though *everyone* stopped. Most of the people who came through our gate needed help, and it wasn't always with animals. We frequently provided directions. So when the 480 Mercedes convertible cruised to a stop alongside our fence, we thought for sure we were about to help another lost person get his bearings.

Sally and I watched curiously as the driver uncoiled his lean, gym-worked body out of the front seat. He stood by the side of his car for a moment, which allowed us to get a better view of this man who looked as if he'd stepped from the cover of *Gentlemen's Quarterly*. A dark summer-weight suit, without a single wrinkle, covered a light-blue-and-white-striped shirt. His tie and shoes were expertly matched. Gold circled his wrist and fingers. His blond hair framed an evenly tanned complexion.

Sally and I couldn't help staring. Neither of us had seen anyone this clean in days.

Bet he's an insurance man looking for one of his policyholders," Sally guessed.

"I bet you're right," I said as we continued to survey this man who looked so out of place.

We were surprised when the stranger then turned his car alarm on. Neither Sally nor I could figure out any reason he'd have for staying more than five minutes.

"Maybe he's not an insurance person," Sally said.

"He sure does look official," I added. "Maybe we're in violation of some zoning code, and this guy has been sent to break the news to us."

The man took off his sunglasses and scanned the chaos of animals and people in the field. He'd definitely come with a purpose. . . . I hoped it was a good one.

"I'll see what he wants," I offered as he headed toward the gate.

"Please do. If he is the bearer of bad news, I'm not in the mood for it," Sally said as she turned to blend in with the surrounding chaos.

"Hi. Can I help you?" I asked, getting a closer look at this meticulous man.

"I sure hope so. My name's Grady Parks, and I've come to volunteer," he said as he reached out his perfectly manicured hand for mine.

I was almost too shocked to respond. If I had heard this man correctly, he wanted to . . . *volunteer?*

I finally managed to ask, "Are you hoping to do this today?"

"Yes, if you can use me," he replied with an astonishing amount of eagerness.

"Well," I said, barely able to conceal my disbelief, "did you have anything in mind that you would like to do?"

"Anything's fine. I love animals and I want to do something to help."

I didn't think this man fully realized what we were doing. He was tailored to be sitting in a corporate boardroom, not some dirty

An oiled sea otter arriving in an airline carrier at the Otter Rehabilitation Center in Valdez, Alaska.

The holding area for once-oiled sea otters outside of the gymnasium in Valdez, Alaska.

A recuperating sea otter asleep in some of the towels that arrived from Michigan.

A recovered sea otter asleep, while awaiting his release.

An orphaned sea otter pup that arrived at the Otter Rehabilitation Center.

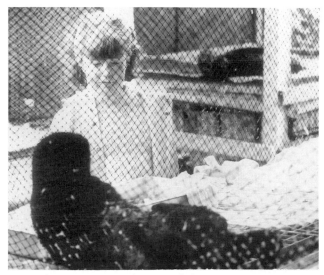

Jennifer visiting with one of the rescued sca otters.

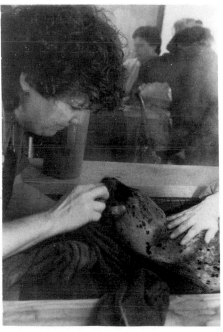

Me cleaning oil off one of the seal pups that arrived at the Otter Rehabilitation Center.

Me holding one of the seal pups after it was cleaned.

Ken's 30th birthday raft trip to Shoup Bay.

Recovered sea otters ready to go home.

Distributing pet food from my van in one of the mobile home parks devastated by Hurricane Andrew.

The MASH unit where I worked in the weeks following Hurricane Andrew.

The mobile home belonging to the woman who refused to evacuate during Hurricane Andrew, choosing to stay behind with her dogs instead. This is how the mobile home looked immediately following the storm. The mattress in the center of the picture was where she was lying when the roof blew in on her.

One of the two dogs belonging to the woman who refused to evacuate.

One of the feeding locations for cats set up in a mobile home park in the aftermath of Hurricane Andrew.

Me luring a cat from under a debris-covered mobile home.

A Hurricane
Andrew survivor
just waiting to
be rescued.

A dog standing in what remains of his owners' kitchen, waiting for help.

Lazarus, the dog shot by his owners.

Grady Parks, the cellular man.

Colonel "Mac" McCorcle, dressed in military fatigues, assisting with an injured dog.

Volunteers at the MASH unit comforting a rescued dog.

A German shepherd puppy cooling his feet at the MASH unit.

The warehouse in St. Charles, Missouri, that became the Animal
Disaster Relief Center during the Midwest floods.

Four of the thirty-two cats rescued in West Alton, Missouri, safe at
the warehouse in St. Charles.

Volunteer Nathaniel Miller holding a rescued puppy that he adopted.

Me rescuing one of Farmer Dwyer's hogs in Harvester, Missouri.

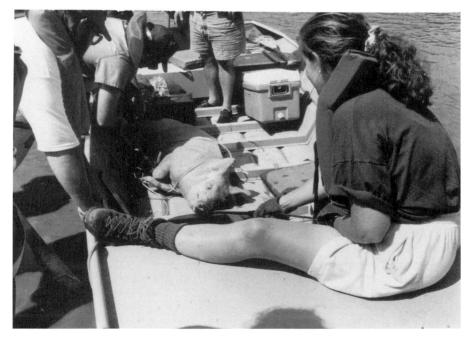

Farmer Dwyer's cattle and hogs, stranded in water behind his barn.

Two stranded deer being steered by volunteers in boats toward an opening in a fence that separates them from dry land. *Lauren Duffy, EARS volunteer*.

Volunteer Ed Bruemmer and Monique, the goat that lived indoors.

Bainbridge, Georgia, flood: Albert the once-nameless dog, being comforted by his friend Amy Chappel.

Bainbridge, Georgia, flood: Albert with an EARS volunteer, after he learned how to be a dog.

The Crisp Family: *Two-legged members* (left to right): Ken, Amy, Jennifer, me, and Megan. *Four-legged members* (left to right): Spenard (black Lab), Snuggles and Skittles (bunnies in Jennifer's lap), Pepsi (Doberman from Hurricane Andrew), Henry (cat from Alviso flood), and Tigger (cat).

More rescues since 1993.

horse pasture in the middle of a disaster area. I was sure once I explained to him the types of jobs volunteers did, he'd apologize for misunderstanding, write us a check, get back in his Mercedes and leave.

"You don't look like a typical volunteer, I must say." I hoped this man had a sense of humor.

He looked down at his clothing for a brief second and then at me. "I came straight from the office. I guess I'm a little over-dressed, huh?"

I started to laugh. I just couldn't help it. This had to be a joke.

A whimsical expression appeared on the man's face. "Does this mean I'm fired?"

"No, no. I'm sure we can find something for you to do. I just have to warn you, you may get dirty."

"It wouldn't be the first time," he assured me. I found that hard to believe.

"Well, let's find you something to do before you change your mind. Heaven knows we need all the help we can get," I said as I turned in the direction of the supply tent.

The man followed with a grin on his face. I was beginning to believe he really wanted to help, but what was I going to find for him to do?

All the volunteer jobs I thought of were sure to do some damage to this man's clothing and possibly his body. Bathing dogs was out of the question. Everyone walked away from that job soaked. There was another rescue team about ready to leave, but the dog they were going after was hiding out under a house. It would probably require some crawling around in the dirt to get him out. Not quite the thing you want to do in an expensive suit. The animal-intake area was well staffed, and it wasn't a job that could be quickly learned. John had mentioned earlier that the National Guard had twenty gallons of gasoline to give us for our generator if someone could pick it up. I couldn't see hauling cans of gasoline in a Mercedes.

I thought about a few other possibilities, but none of them were right for my neatest volunteer either. When I was just about to the bottom of the list, I thought of a job that might suit him.

"Would you mind walking the dogs?"

He responded with a definite yes.

"You know, you also have to pick up after them," I informed

him, thinking this piece of information would result in the definite "no."

"Fine. Just show me where the pooper-scooper is."

I couldn't believe it. He was really willing to do it.

"Okay, then, follow me, and I'll show you the routine."

We stopped in the supply tent and grabbed a long leash, and then walked over to our assortment of dozing canines chained along the fence. It only took one dog to get all the rest barking. Each dog begged to go first.

"None of these dogs will hurt you," I assured Grady. "We've been lucky not to have even one vicious dog so far. But that could change with the next dog that comes through the gate."

Grady watched as I walked over to a gentle golden retriever. "Sit," I commanded. The dog eventually obeyed, allowing me to hook the leash onto his collar.

"Come on, boy." I didn't have to encourage the dog to follow. He pulled me across the field to the area designated for walking dogs. Yellow police tape outlined the spot at the far end of the pasture. Leaning up against the fence was a pooper-scooper, and in an adjacent barrel was an ample supply of plastic bags, courtesy of Kmart.

"It's pretty simple. You just wait for the dog to do his thing, then use the scooper to pick up after him and dump it in one of the plastic bags. There's a garbage can over by the driveway gate," I said, pointing across the field. "Just throw the bags in there when you're done."

It was time for Grady to go to work. "Are you ready for this?" I asked, holding out the leash.

"Can you give me a minute?" he asked. "I have to get something out of my car first."

"Sure. I'll finish with this one and put him back, and you can start with the dog next to him. We try to walk all the dogs at least once every couple of hours. They may not have to go, but I think it's good just to give them the exercise."

"Good," Grady said. "I'll be right back."

The dog walker moved purposefully across the field. When he reached the car, he turned the alarm off and got inside. For a split second, I thought, *He's chickening out,* but once again he fooled me. The car did not move; only the top did, as it slowly unfolded to enclose the inside of the car.

Hurricane Andrew

Standing by the open door, Grady removed his jacket and carefully draped it over the back of the driver's seat. The tie came off next and disappeared into the car while Grady undid the top two buttons of his starched shirt. With even precision, he then rolled up the sleeves of his shirt, just below the elbow. The last thing he did was lean into his car and grab something that got stuffed in his pocket.

Grady slammed the car door shut and reset the alarm. He looked as if he was ready to do business—and that was no exaggeration.

From a distance I watched as Grady walked an elderly boxer and a really sweet chow. He looked as though he knew what he was doing, and he seemed to care about these dogs. The whole time he had a dog on the leash, I could see him talking with it, and the dog's tail would be wagging—so excited was it that someone was paying attention to it. When he ordered a rambunctious, one-hundred-twenty-pound rottweiler to sit and, after only two attempts, got him to mind, I knew Grady would do just fine.

After he had settled into his routine, a woman and a young teenage girl had come running through the gate, carrying a cardboard box. The look on the woman's face could only mean one thing—there was an animal in the box that needed help.

As I approached them, the woman, cried out, "Please help us. Our kitten is hurt . . ." She couldn't say any more.

I peered inside the towel-draped box. A small gray kitten lay in the bottom, covered with blood. "Follow me," I directed as the woman and the girl whom I guessed to be her daughter, followed. Both were crying when the woman set the box down on our makeshift exam table. Mac was there in an instant to take over.

The woman was able to tell Mac what had happened as he worked. Their next-door neighbor's fences had all come down during the hurricane, and they had no secure way to confine their Doberman. The dog had broken loose from his chain that morning and found the kitten asleep on the front porch. The kitten didn't have a chance. It took three men to get the dog to drop it. When the kitten fell to the ground, they thought for sure it was dead.

Mac did everything he could to save the kitten, but the dog had done major damage. Finally, it was Mac's recommendation to euthanize the kitten. The mother agreed it was the humane thing to do, but it was a tough thing for a fourteen-year-old to understand, especially for the first time.

We had seen so many parents who were struggling to remain strong for their kids, but it was hard, so I sat with the daughter for over an hour and tried to comfort her. This was just one too many heartbreaks for the mother to handle. Hurricane Andrew had been cruel to this family, and both of these victims needed someone just to be with them while they cried.

Mac had wrapped the dead kitten in a towel and handed it to the girl. She decided she didn't want us to dispose of her kitten. As I walked them to their car, she cradled the tiny feline in her arms. They were going home to bury Snowball, alongside their dog that had died during the hurricane.

As I was watching the car bump along our dirt road, I spotted Grady. And I was glad I had. I was ready for a distraction. The last hour had not been easy.

At the far end of the field our dog walker was continuing to walk dogs, but he had something black wedged in between his shoulder and right ear. It took me a while to figure out what it was . . . a cellular phone. This man had brought his business to our horse pasture. We'd certainly attracted an interesting collection of people.

It was a little after six when Grady came to say good-bye.

"I want to thank you for letting me be a part of this effort. It's done my heart good," he said as he looked over toward the dogs. "They're a great bunch of animals. I hope they all get reclaimed, or find terrific new homes. They deserve it."

"Will we see you again?" I asked as I noticed the large, muddy paw print that decorated the pocket of Grady's once spotless shirt.

"I'm really busy." He paused for a second and then shook his head. "Well, you saw. There's no escaping the constant phone calls. They can even find me in a horse pasture in the middle of a disaster zone." We both laughed.

"In answer to your questions, I'm afraid I won't be able to come down again. But I'm really glad I made it today. I wanted to do *something* to help the animals, and you allowed me that. I'll never forget this."

I was really glad this man had shared his time with us, even if it was so short. If more people had given just an afternoon of their time, we could have done so much more to help the animals.

Grady reached his hand out, but I held mine back as I said, "No . . . volunteers get hugs." When we stepped apart, I could

2 1 0

see the tears forming in his brilliant blue eyes. This man really cared.

"Oh, I almost forgot," Grady said as he reached into his back pocket. "This is for the animals." He handed me a check for five hundred dollars. "Maybe you can use it to hire a professional dog walker." He chuckled.

I would have hired Grady Parks in a minute.

32

Normalcy

It took only a few hours for Hurricane Andrew to erase people's normal routines in southern Florida. By the end of the fourth week, we at the MASH unit had fallen into a newly created routine of living from one moment to the next. We never knew who, or what, would come through our gate to direct the course of our day. As a result, we did an awful lot of prioritizing as we responded to each new crisis. We had evolved into a true MASH unit. The only difference was our casualties were animals, not humans.

As the days passed, more animals needed our help, especially ones that were sick or injured. Dogs who had been hit by cars were a frequent emergency. With fences blown down, owners no longer had a secure way to confine their dogs; so they got loose, and the streets of Homestead were deadly.

One of the dogs that Mac pieced back together was a German shepherd puppy. He was not wandering the streets when he got hit. The woman who found the six-month-old dog discovered him lying in his own driveway. It was the owner who had run him over, and witnesses later told us it was no accident. In fact, the owner ran the dog over twice before he disappeared down the street, leaving the dog behind to die.

Hurricane Andrew

News of another injured dog came to us from a woman who showed up at the MASH unit close to midnight one night. Her arrival was announced by her screeching brakes, a good clue that another crisis had found us.

With her engine still running, she got out of the car and came through the gate of our dimly lit pasture. "Can someone help me?" she yelled frantically. "There's a dog that's been hit on the road."

It didn't take long to wake up Mac, load some equipment into the van, get directions from the woman, and head south, praying we'd get to the dog before it died.

Sally was the first to spot the animal. The van's headlights confirmed that the black, motionless form lying on the white divider line was a rottweiler. The volunteer from the Jacksonville Humane Society pulled the van off to the side of the road after Mac and Sally jumped out.

Everyone stood back as Mac slowly approached the dog, which showed no signs of being alive. Using his flashlight, Mac scanned the dog's body for obvious injuries before he bent down and placed two fingers on the dog's neck. Everyone held his or her breath as we waited for the prognosis.

"Well, she's still alive," Mac said, "And I don't think she's been hit."

"Then why is she lying in the middle of the road?" Sally asked, puzzled.

"I think her paws can explain that," Mac said, directing his flashlight to one of the dog's front legs as the rest of the rescue team moved closer.

"This dog has covered a lot of ground. Look at her pads." Mac held the leg in his hand so the others could see how badly the pads had been worn down.

"Her feet hurt, and she is completely exhausted," was Mac's conclusion. "We'll have to carry her into the van, because this dog can't take another step in her condition."

"We've got a stretcher in the van," said one of the volunteers from Jacksonville.

"Good. Let's use it," Mac said as he stood up.

Just then the squeak of a screen door caught the attention of the group. A woman approached from the direction of the noise.

"Where you taking that dog?" she asked as she got closer.

"To the animal MASH unit so she can get some medical attention," Sally informed her. "Do you know who the dog belongs to?"

"No. It's been around here all day," the woman said, eyeing the dog cautiously as it was carried past her on the stretcher. "It looked so lost and worn out, but I'm afraid of big dogs."

As the dog was lifted into the van, Sally gave the woman the location of the MASH unit, should she hear of anyone in the area missing a female rottweiler.

The rottweiler's feet mended nicely, but her heart was slower to heal. Day after day she stared at the pasture gate, searching each face for her owner, but they never came to claim her.

A lot of the animals that ended up at the MASH unit had been abandoned by their owners. One of those dogs was a red Irish setter. Bob Lange was a rescue volunteer who'd come down from Jupiter, Florida, to help. He had recognized the urgency of a field report that an Irish setter had been left in a barn with no food or water. When Bob located the dog, he was appalled at what he found. She was too weak to stand, and her hip bones were protruding. Bob scooped up the malnourished dog in his arms and carefully placed her in an airline crate in the back of his vehicle.

After a week of hearty meals and lots of TLC, the dog was up and running around with all the abundant energy of a healthy Irish setter.

When Bob returned to Jupiter, the dog went with him. When you ask him about his companion, he will tell you, "She was my reward for coming down to help."

All the volunteers who came to feed, walk, bathe, medicate, comfort, rescue, and love the animals were rewarded. Money, applause, or a shiny trophy could not replace the inner fulfillment the volunteers felt when they saw an injured dog slowly regain its strength, or when they handed an animal over to an owner who had been frantically searching for it, or when they heard a frightened cat purr for the first time. It was moments such as these that kept them going, in spite of how difficult the work was.

We didn't keep track of how many people came to help during the six weeks that the MASH unit was open or how many hours they spent volunteering, but it was a lot. I remember one afternoon crawling up on top of the motor home to shoot some video footage of the compound. As I captured the activity on tape, I was amazed at the number of people scattered throughout the field. I counted thirty-three volunteers that afternoon.

By the middle of September our volunteer force began to dwindle, though. People had the demands of their own lives to contend with—jobs, families, school, fatigue, or emotional burnout. As fewer people showed up to help, it meant those of us who remained had more jobs to do each day.

I remembered how tired we'd been in the beginning, but it was worse after four weeks of twenty-hour days, seven days a week. Plus, we had a lot more animals to take care of. The strain was becoming evident. Tempers flared often, the tears came easier, our patience wore thin, and it took longer to get moving in the morning. We wanted to quit, but we couldn't.

Laughter helped keep us going.

It was another late night when Sally and I finally dragged ourselves into the motor home. John was outside tinkering with the generator, and Shirley and Mac were attending to another injured animal. Sally and I contemplated eating, which pleased our growling stomachs, but the thought of another meal of peanut butter and crackers was not what we craved. Besides, the kitchen was a mess.

There were at least two days worth of dirty plates, glasses, and silverware scattered everywhere in the tiny kitchen, so we decided to wash the dishes, in spite of being so completely worn out. A mindless task was really what we wanted to do at that moment, just because it was simple and normal, something we'd been deprived of for weeks.

"We've got a problem," Sally said as she shuffled things around under the sink. "We have no dishwashing soap."

"Are you sure?" I asked, remembering having seen an almost full container of Dawn the day before.

"Yeah," Sally said, standing up. "And I know where it disappeared to. I remember telling some volunteers they could use it to bathe some dogs today."

"Well, then, let's go to the store," I said, getting up from my seat.

"Terri, have you forgotten where we are?" Sally said, half laughing. "There isn't a store open within fifty miles of here, and I don't wish to use up my few precious sleeping hours driving all the way to Miami just to buy some soap."

"We don't have to go that far," I said as I headed toward the door. "In fact, it'll take us less then ten minutes to get our soap and come back."

Sally's curiosity won out.

"Okay. Where are you taking me?" Sally asked as I started the jeep, which immediately caused half the dogs to start barking.

"You'll see," I said, grinning—something I'd not done much of that day.

Out of Harm's Way

Mac, Shirley, and John thought for sure the pressures had gotten to us when we pulled up alongside Mac's camper and told them we were headed to the store to buy dishwashing soap. They became convinced of our mental instability when we told them we'd be back in ten minutes.

When I pulled out onto Krome Avenue, Sally pushed my only tape—Kenny G—into the cassette player. It was the potency of the saxophone that made me push the pedal to the floor as we headed north. The rush of hot night air blowing through the jeep mingled with the music, making me think of home—and Ken.

Sally and I were quiet as we drove. The silence was a rare treat. Three blocks later I turned off Krome onto a side street lined with military vehicles. Set up at the corner was an enormous collection of green tents, much larger versions of what we had. Near the entrance to one of the tents a group of soldiers clustered in a group, smoking cigarettes.

"What is this place?" Sally asked as she took in the sight.

"It's where we get the soap," I replied as I pulled up alongside the group of soldiers, who immediately put out their cigarettes and jumped to attention.

"Are you sure we're in the right place?" Sally said in a whisper. "You know, I believe there is still a curfew in effect, and it's these guys that haul you off for violating it."

"Don't worry," I said as I turned off the ignition.

By then, one of the soldiers had approached my side of the jeep. Slung over his shoulder was a rifle like all the other ones I'd seen for weeks.

"Terri, what are you doing here?" the soldier asked. "You round up all those cats at Quail Roost yet?"

"Nope. Still working on it," I replied, stepping from the jeep.

"What can I do for you?" the soldier asked as a few more of his buddies came over to join us.

"We need some dishwashing soap."

"What? Dishwashing soap?" the soldier asked, laughing.

"Yeah. You got some?"

The other soldiers joined in laughing, as Sally sat in the jeep, not quite sure what to think of this unusual way of shopping.

"You mean you two are out this late, all by yourselves, looking for soap?" the soldier asked. "I thought you all spent your nights looking for cats."

"Well, tonight we had housekeeping chores to do instead. Our dirty dishes have kind of piled up, and unless we want to eat our dinner out of dog food bowls, we need to find some soap."

"Well, then, ladies, let me show you to the cleaning-product aisle of our store," the soldier said as he headed for the nearest tent.

"Come on, Sally," I said. "Wait until you see what's in this tent."

"I can hardly wait," Sally said, laughing, as she stepped out of the jeep and followed behind me.

The solider was holding the tent flap up for us to enter. I watched Sally's face as she surveyed the inside of the circus-size tent. Lined up were rows of pallets with boxes and boxes of stuff on top of them that had been donated for the disaster victims. Inside the boxes were the kinds of things that Hurricane Andrew had stolen when it blew through Dade County—diapers, coffee, Band-Aids, canned goods, toilet paper, bread, toothpaste, and dishwashing soap.

"I can't believe this," Sally exclaimed. "It's almost like shopping at Kmart."

"Yeah. But the two differences are: you don't have to pay and they don't have shopping carts," I said as I reached for a container of Dawn.

"You guys need anything else?" the solider asked. "If so, grab it. You all have earned it."

For the next half hour, Sally and I pretended we were at Kmart doing something very normal, shopping. We filled up empty boxes with cans of tuna, chocolate pudding, Oreo cookies, fruit juice, deodorant, individual boxes of Froot Loops, sunscreen, and oranges—skipping the peanut butter and crackers. Each box, once it was full, was carried out to our jeep by one of the soldiers, eager to have something to do.

When we climbed back into our well-stocked jeep, the soldier who had greeted us walked up to my side of the vehicle. "If you-all need anything else, come back," he said with a grin. "We're open twenty-four hours a day for the convenience of our customers."

Sally and I both laughed.

As we pulled away, the soldier yelled, "You make sure you get all those cats at Quail Roost."

"We will," I said as I waved good-bye.

When we pulled back into the horse pasture, Shirley, Mac, and John were still up. The familiar smell of Mac's pipe conjured up images of comfort and peace. It was good to be back at the MASH unit. Even though we'd been gone less than an hour, it was all the break we had needed.

Out of Harm's Way

"Where have you two been?" John asked as we stepped into Mac's camper. "We were about ready to call out the troops to look for you."

"We went to Kmart to get dishwashing soap," Sally replied. "And now we're going to do the dishes."

Shirley, Mac, and John just shook their heads.

For the next hour we scrubbed dishes, ate Oreo cookies dunked in fruit juice, and laughed. It felt good to be normal again.

33

Teamwork

Sally's trademark expression was, "If we build it, they will come." And boy . . . was she right. For six weeks the MASH unit did attract animals and people. Mac swore that in those early days we had our own Star of Bethlehem that led people to us bearing sick, injured, lost, and abandoned animals. Their numbers ended up totaling over 2,600.

Every animal that was logged into our record system was either reclaimed by its owner or adopted, with the exception of the animals that died from the injuries they sustained as a result of Hurricane Andrew.

There were only three animals we had to euthanize. The poodle mix who never recovered from the emotional trauma of being left on her own in a bathroom that the hurricane demolished. She suffered no physical injury, but we learned this was not the only type of injury that can kill.

Claudio, another of the rescue volunteers, managed to trap a sharpei that had been on the loose before the hurricane ever hit. Months of trying to survive on his own resulted in a severe case of diarrhea and a prolapsed rectum. When he was brought back to the MASH unit in a trap for Mac to look at, the recommendation was to euthanize the dog.

Then there was Snowball, the white kitten that had been attacked by the Doberman.

There were a lot of other animals that would have been euthanized if they'd shown up in any other shelter in the United States on any given day. These were the dogs and cats that weren't cute, young, or well behaved. But they were disaster animals, which made them special. We had people fighting to adopt our dogs and cats, animals whose descriptions matched those of the hundreds of thousands of animals across the country that are destroyed every day because no one wants them. But it seemed everyone wanted ours.

When we evacuated seventy-five dogs from a ramshackle kennel belonging to a woman who for some time had been collecting strays, I thought for sure the majority of the animals would have to be euthanized.

The dogs were not your best adoption candidates. There was not a one in the bunch that resembled a breed that we could identify. In addition to not being *cute,* it became apparent right away, most of the dogs were not accustomed to people being nice to them. When we passed the pieced-together wire-and-wood cages, the dogs would cower as if they expected us to kick or beat them. Some had more than likely been abused by a previous owner, but it also didn't help that most of the dogs had been confined in their cages for months with minimal human contact. The woman was a "collector" who was trying to do the right thing, but she simply lacked the resources to properly provide for so many animals, and Hurricane Andrew had made it even more difficult.

Fortunately, the woman realized she needed help, which is why she came to the MASH unit. Once we saw her dogs and the conditions they were living in, it became clear that they would have to be removed. The owner gave us permission to do just that. But where was I going to put the seventy-five mongrels? Finding room for them at the MASH unit was definitely not going to be easy, but there was no way we could leave them in the hellhole where we found them, even if it meant they would all end up being destroyed.

The kennel had been inadequate before the hurricane destroyed most of the cages, leaving the dogs to be crowded together in spaces barely large enough for one dog. These conditions increased the risk of the animals spreading diseases to one another, including kennel cough, distemper, or parvovirus, since most of them had not been vaccinated. Another concern we had was the lack of running water to clean the cages. Already, most of the animals were forced to stand in their own excrement.

As if all this weren't bad enough, most of these dogs had mange. For this reason they would have to be isolated from each other and the rest of the population of the MASH unit—and our five acres were full. We should have hung out the No Vacancy sign days before, but we couldn't turn an animal away. There was no other place for these animals to go.

When it came time to decide where to keep the dogs, a solution arrived in the form of volunteers from a Humane Society in Georgia. Their timing couldn't have been more perfect. They'd driven down to help and ended up going back home that same day with their three vans full of the seventy-five dogs.

The last report we got was that all but five had been adopted.

It seemed everyone wanted our rottweilers too. One afternoon two big, burly guys showed up at the MASH unit wanting to know if they could buy all our rotties. We had no intention of selling them, but we played along with them long enough to find out why they wanted to buy the twenty-five rottweilers we had that day.

They were frightfully honest, telling us they intended to take them all down to one of the busiest corners in Homestead and sell them to people who needed guard dogs to protect what little remained of their homes or businesses. These men expected to make some "big bucks."

When we informed the two entrepreneurs that the dogs were not for sale because they all had owners, they didn't believe us and became quite angry. They were still cussing us out as they got back into their beat-up Chevy half-ton and took off down the road, leaving a cloud of dust. Our greatest fear was that they would come back later that night and try to steal the dogs.

Since we had no way to lock up our facility and no alarm system, we once again had to improvise—something we were becoming experts at. Before we went to bed that night, we took all the little yippy dogs and tied them to the perimeter fence so that they could warn us of any intruders. The rottweilers got tied to the motor home.

We didn't sleep much that night, and it wasn't just because we were listening for dognappers. With twenty-five rottweilers tied to the motor home, it felt as though we were on top of a very active earthquake fault. By morning we were sure the dogs had dragged the motor home a good six inches.

Fortunately, we never saw the two burly guys again.

Another precaution we had to take involved black cats. Because it was legal at the time to sacrifice animals for religious purposes in Florida, we restricted the adoption of black cats to people we knew or animal-welfare organizations outside the state. And because black cats are the most common, there were a lot of them that earned some frequent-flyer mileage, compliments of USAir.

There were lots of other companies that helped us out during those six weeks. In addition to IAMS, Friskies, Kal Kan, and Alpo also donated food to help us feed the animals at the MASH unit and those out in the community. Jonny Cat brought us cat litter and disposable litter boxes, which were welcome gifts. Until then, we'd been using the cardboard boxes that the cans of cat food came in, lined with the plastic wrap from the box. In the beginning the cats were lucky if they got much more than a teaspoon of litter to dig in.

Several pharmaceutical companies donated medical supplies that enabled us to respond to the injured animals and to prevent the healthy ones from getting sick. Many of the veterinarians who so graciously donated their time also brought medical supplies from their own practices.

Animal organizations, both small and large, were another appreciated resource. Some sent supplies, others people. The Humane Society of the United States rotated Laura Bevan, Ken Johnson, Steve Kritzech, and Nicholas Gilman through the Krome facility. Martha Lentz, from the Orlando Humane Society, loaned us a fifth-wheel camping trailer and the forty-foot long semitrailer for storing the food. Having the fifth wheel allowed most of the volunteers to sleep indoors, and not on the ground in tents—along with the lizards and fire ants.

Nora, Maria, and Angie were three volunteers who lived close enough to go home everyday. If the dogs didn't wake us in the morning, they did. Like clockwork, they returned each day to walk and feed the animals, and do whatever else needed to be done.

John Hanson, our youngest volunteer, arrived almost every day with his mom and dad to help pass out animal food to the public. Tons of it was distributed in the six weeks we were there. Robin and Glen were glad their son was learning at a young age the rewards of helping others. Rafael Magruda was another young volunteer who will grow up understanding why animals need help in a disaster.

Candyce Paincot came almost every day to help out with paperwork, the job most people prefer not to do. It would have been impossible to keep track of all the animals without the forms I'd brought with me, but, then, keeping track of the paper itself was no easy job either. We rewarded Candyce by giving her Mash, our mascot. Mash was just five weeks old when she was found wandering in traffic. The tiny black puppy stole everyone's heart.

Trying to complete paperwork outdoors is no easy feat, especially in an open field in Florida. Whenever the wind picked up, someone always had to run after wayward sheets of paper. The afternoon rains usually smeared ink and stuck important sheets of paper together. The dogs didn't help, either. Some decided to leave their mark on stacks of unused forms, while others saw the sheets of paper as something that needed to be shredded. This necessitated trying to piece scraps back together with transparent tape, which wouldn't stick because of the humidity. We had to make do with the altered forms, though, because our supplies were limited and there was no Kinko's copy center close by.

Things really got backlogged when our on-site copier broke. Sally had brought a small portable one down with her, and it had the reputation of being ornery at the worst times. One afternoon it finally decided it had suffered enough abuse and just quit working in protest. After numerous attempts we were able to reach Able Business Machines in Fort Lauderdale. At eleven that night, the repairman showed up to resurrect our machine. It turned out he made the trip on his own time because he loved animals.

There was another man who volunteered with us who loved not only animals, but plants. Bill Lynch, a veteran of Hurricane Hugo, came down with Sue McCloud from South Carolina to help. Many nights he'd accompany Shirley and me when we went into the mobile home parks in search of cats.

In one of the parks there was one last female tabby that we were especially desperate to catch. She was pregnant and due to have her kittens any day. If we didn't get her before the kittens arrived, there was little chance of the litter surviving the front-end loaders that were being used to clear away debris.

We set a trap for a week straight, but the cautious feline wouldn't come anywhere near it. In desperation, we decided to leave it set overnight and come back and check it first thing in the morning. Bill and I took the jeep to check the trap the next day. Hitched to the jeep was a flatbed trailer, loaded with twenty airline crates, that we hadn't taken time to unhitch.

When we stopped at the National Guard checkpoint at the entrance to the mobile home park, the soldier was surprised to see us. "Hey, what are you guys doing out in the daylight," he said, laughing. "We thought you all only worked after dark."

"We're running out of time," I replied.

"With all these cages, you must be expecting to catch yourself a load full," the soldier said as he eyed the airline crates.

"We'd be happy just to catch one," I said as I started to pull away, anxious to get to the trap. It was already starting to get hot, and it wasn't even seven yet. I didn't want the cat sitting in the sun. That is, if we'd even caught her.

As we drove toward the cul-de-sac where we'd left the trap, Bill started to see what we'd been missing at night. It was not cats . . . but houseplants. It seemed no one had retrieved their spider plants, violets, ferns, or ivies. They were scattered everywhere.

Some had died when their pots had been broken and the soil had been scattered by the wind, but others had managed to survive with the help of the afternoon rainstorms. Bill decided the plants needed rescuing too. So he collected the plants and lined them up in the airline crates, eventually filling all twenty of them, while I went off on foot to check the trap.

It was my loud scream that brought Bill running a few minutes later, certain I'd been attacked by lizards. But what he found was me, holding the trap, with one very pregnant cat in it. We had gotten her in time.

When we drove back past the checkpoint, the soldier who had greeted us earlier approached. "Can I see how many cats you caught?" he asked as he walked toward the airline crates.

The puzzled expression on the unsuspecting soldier's face when he surveyed our catch provided us with a good laugh.

The National Guard, for the entire time we were set up in Homestead, remained our most constant ally. In addition to the tents, they supplied us with those hard-to-find items in a disaster, such as water, gasoline, tarps, batteries, and a Porta Potti.

In addition to the supplies, they shared their time. One of the units had gone two weeks without a break. When they finally got a day's leave, all they could talk about the evening before was going to Miami for some much deserved R and R. That was why we were so surprised when they showed up the next day in the middle of the afternoon.

"What are you guys doing here?" I asked as the five of them came through the gate. "You're crazy to be standing out here in this hot sun when you could be in an air-conditioned bar, sipping something nice and cold."

"We could," one of the soldiers replied. "But that can wait."

"When we were here yesterday, we noticed you were running out of room on the fence line to tether the dogs," said another one of the soldiers. "So we came to build the dogs some shelters so you can use the areas away from the fence for more dogs."

I didn't know what to say . . . so a hug seemed an appropriate way to say thanks.

For the next five hours, the soldiers worked in the ninety-five-degree heat, digging postholes in the hard ground. Before inserting a two by four in each hole, they laid a Hula Hoop–size metal ring on the ground circling the hole. When the post was in place, a flat piece of plywood was then nailed to it to provide some shade. The ingenious part was that when the dogs' chains were hooked to the metal rings, the dogs couldn't tangle the chains and themselves around the two by four.

When the soldiers were done, they had built twenty-five new shelters for the dogs. All the supplies had either been bought with their own money or salvaged from the mounds of debris.

The MASH unit was built by people who saw a problem and did what they could to solve it. I remember something Sally said in an interview months after the MASH unit had finally closed. She was having a hard time completing the interview, because it triggered powerful emotions that had not faded with time. "There are a lot of good people in this world who really love animals . . . and I will never forget them."

Sally could say no more . . . her tears said the rest.

We may not recall all the names of the people who worked with us in that horse pasture on Krome Avenue, but we will always remember the faces of the individuals who made a difference for the animals—at a time when they needed us the most.

34

Letting Go

By the end of September I was numb, physically and emotionally. All I wanted to do was sit alone in a corner of the pasture and stare at nothing, but I couldn't. There were so many things that had to be done before I flew home, and the thing I dreaded the most was saying good-bye to Sally.

This woman, who'd entered my life so unexpectedly, had in a few short weeks become a different kind of friend, the kind I've learned you can acquire during disasters. Our friendship grew in spite of hard times, cemented by tears, losses, anger, successes, frustration, laughter, and mutual respect. It was our total commitment to animals that kept us from walking away from the demands of working at the MASH unit.

Our physical and emotional endurance was tested continually, and there were hundreds of times we wanted to say, "The hell with it," yet we didn't. Our reward for not giving up was a genuine friendship that we didn't expect, but were grateful to have found.

Fortunately, things were as hectic as usual my last morning there, so I could put leaving the MASH unit out of my mind. As I continued to respond to that day's crises, it amazed me that the pace of activity had not slowed down. We were aware, though, that a growing number of the animals brought to us were not hurricane victims.

Hurricane Andrew

It was the man from West Palm Beach, a community unaffected by Andrew, that made us realize it was almost time to start taking down the tents. He arrived with a litter of five purebred German shepherd puppies in the back of his Volvo station wagon. The story we heard is one that is repeated thousands of times a day in shelters all across the country, "I can't find homes for the puppies. Can you take them?"

We were becoming a shelter, something that was desperately needed in Homestead, but we weren't in a financial position to create a permanent facility. The MASH unit was set up to deal with a crisis, and the one created by Hurricane Andrew was just about over for us.

Sally, John, Mac, and Shirley would keep the MASH unit open another two weeks after I left. It was my job at Santa Clara University that determined when I had to leave. If I could have, I would have quit my job and stayed longer, but I had my own life to consider.

One of the things I had to do that last morning was make a decision about my Elvira look-alike. If I hadn't been able to find her kittens when I made my final trip to Quail Roost, I had decided to take her back to the MASH unit without them. She and her family of four ended up being my final rescue, and it was one of the greatest successes I had when I was in Florida, especially because it came so close to being a tragedy instead.

I was getting the family of five cats resettled in a cage under the cat tent when I looked at my watch and realized, it was time. My flight left from Miami in less than three hours, and Pepsi and I had to be on it.

Suddenly I wished there were a way that I could delay my departure. In spite of the turbulent ups and downs, I didn't want the experience to end. If only I could have had just one more day or even one more hour, but I couldn't. No matter when I left, it was going to be hard; so it was best to just do it and get it over with. Besides, I knew it was time to go home.

Ken had been incredibly patient, in spite of the never-ending demands he faced being "Mr. Mom" for the weeks that I had been gone. During the few times I'd been able to talk with him on the phone, we'd compared disasters—mine in Florida and his at home. Sometimes it was difficult to say whose was worse.

It was going to be wonderful to see him and the girls again, especially Megan, who had arrived only eight months before. I needed to spend time with my child whom I'd known for such a short time. There were *my* animals too, the cats—Henry, Tigger, Wally, Gar, and

Slick—and Spenard, our black Lab. I felt a desperate longing to hug them all as my time to return to them drew closer.

Sally and I said good-bye underneath the first tent that had gone up in the pasture, a most appropriate place, though neither of us planned it. But that was how it had been from the beginning. The MASH unit seemed to evolve through a chain of events that were meant to be.

"We did it," I whispered as I gave Sally a last hug. Sally could only nod as she squeezed me tighter.

"I'm going to miss you," she said as I stepped away.

"I'm going to miss you, too."

It was then time to go. Pepsi was in the front seat of my van, and I'd already said good-bye to John, Mac, and Shirley. I'd miss them all terribly.

I was almost to my van when I heard Sally yell, "Terri, what if I run out of dishwashing soap?"

"Call me, and we'll go to Kmart."

It was my last image of the MASH unit, and it was a great one.

I got through those final good-byes knowing that my family would be waiting for me when Pepsi and I arrived in San Francisco. Their hugs, licks, laughter, purrs, smiles, and Megan's toothless grin sustained me through those first few days at home.

It was a difficult transition . . . but I survived.

Midwest Flood

St. Charles, Missouri . . .

If you live close to a river, you know floods are a potential danger. If you live ten miles from a river, you consider yourself beyond the reach of floodwaters. During the summer of 1993, people in the Midwest learned that rivers know no boundaries.

The flood began in April, but it didn't make the news then. The people affected, accustomed to spring flooding, gathered up their belongings once again and carried them to higher ground, then waited for the water to recede. But it didn't happen.

A combination of rain and the winter snowmelt from up north caused floodwaters to continue to spread farther and farther beyond their shores. Eventually the Mississippi and Missouri rivers merged into one river, causing entire communities to disappear under the muddy water.

By early July, the "Flood of the Century" still showed no signs of receding. The flood had now made its way to the front pages of the newspapers, and it was the lead story on the evening news. We learned that each day more people were being evacuated out of the path of the floodwaters. It was an interview with the director of the St. Charles Humane Society that confirmed my fear—animals were being left behind again.

I left for the Midwest on July 14.

35

S.O.S.

I pressed my nose against the cold window as the plane began its descent into St. Louis. We had to be getting close now. Suddenly, a break in the cloud cover revealed what I'd been searching for. Beneath me were miles and miles of brown, muddy water, in places it didn't belong.

The Midwest flood was worse than I had imagined.

My map showed that St. Charles was about eight miles from the airport, near the normal junction of the Missouri and Mississippi rivers, not a good place to be in this disaster. Fortunately, the community's Humane Society was in a commercial district beyond the greed of the rivers.

When I pulled into the strip mall where it was located, I saw what Lisa Thess, the executive director had meant when she'd said the facility was small and had not been designed to be an animal shelter. The space was more suitable for an insurance office or gift shop, but the Humane Society had learned to make do.

The shelter consisted of two adjoining rooms, each measuring about thirty square feet. In one they had set up an office, and the other one had become a temporary home for a number of animals, which were currently in cages lining three of the four walls. Lisa had explained on the phone that they only had space for cats and a few puppies, and since they had no dog runs, large dogs were turned away unless they could find a foster home for them.

When I walked through the door, I realized there wasn't much space for people either. The shelter was crammed full of men and women bumping into one another as they stacked bags of pet food, cleaned cages, and answered phones.

Much of the activity on that hot July morning revolved around a dark-haired woman who sat at a card table in the center of the room lined with cages. I assumed she was Lisa Thess. Her cluttered "desk" wobbled as scraps of paper with hastily scribbled names and phone numbers were dropped on its oilcloth covering, unnoticed by the woman who was trying to direct the chaos.

I didn't introduce myself right away. Instead, I stood near the doorway, dodging people as they scurried about, while I tried to get some sense of what was going on. I listened as people bombarded the dark-haired woman with questions from all sides, causing her head to pivot as if she were watching a tennis match.

"Somebody's got fifty bags of dog food outside. Where do you want me to put them?" yelled a young fellow from across the room.

"There are three dogs on a roof in West Alton. Can we go get them?" asked a woman as she held a telephone receiver against her chest. I assumed the reporting party was still on the other end.

"Where do you keep the toilet paper?" came an inquiry from another woman, whose head was poking out of the half-open bathroom door.

Lots of questions, but no answers.

The poor woman to whom all these people were looking for answers looked as if she wanted to crawl under the card table and hide, but even that space was taken by a pink airline crate, the temporary residence of a boisterous Siamese.

It was time to offer my help.

"Lisa?" I asked as I reached my hand out. "I'm Terri Crisp. We spoke on the phone yesterday."

"Oh, thank God. The cavalry has arrived," were the first words out of Lisa's mouth as she grabbed my outstretched hand and held it as if she were afraid to let go.

"Well, I don't know if I'd call myself that, but I do know I'm here to do what I can to help you—so fill me in."

"Where do I begin?" She eyed the table in front of her and shook her head.

"Do you know what all these pieces of paper are about?" I asked as I picked up what had been a corner of a desk calendar. I could almost make out the name Mike with a local phone number scribbled below it.

"I have no idea," she said, reading a few of the notes on top of the mess. "Some of these people probably need help, and I hope some want to help, but you can see for yourself—it's hard to tell who's who."

As we talked, three more slips of paper were dropped on the table by one of the women answering the phone. I thought one of them might have information on it about the dogs on the roof in West Alton. That was one piece of paper I didn't want to see get buried in the mess, but, then, these were probably not the only animals in need of help whose plight had been called in.

If the chaos continued to escalate at this pace, the card table wouldn't hold up until evening and neither would Lisa.

I'd seen enough. It was time to get busy.

"Lisa. What have you heard about the animals?" I asked.

"I was out for a while last night, and there were a lot of dogs running loose in areas which I'm sure have flooded by now," she told me as tears welled up in her eyes. "How can we help them all?"

I remembered those first days after Hurricane Andrew. I, too, had been overwhelmed when I drove through the neighborhoods in Homestead and saw how many animals there were that needed help. It would have been insane to think I could save them all, so I did what I could, one animal at a time. That was what we'd have to do with the mounds of paper that had already found their way to Lisa's makeshift desk, and if we didn't get busy, we'd get so far behind, it would be difficult to get caught up.

"Lisa," I said, looking her straight in the eye, "you need to tell me what you are willing to let me do."

I knew Lisa had to be cautious. We'd talked for the first time only the day before, and all of a sudden here was this stranger sitting in her shelter, asking to help do her job. We needed to be real clear from the beginning what my boundaries were, because the last thing I wanted to do was step on Lisa's toes.

It took a few moments for her to respond. "You told me you helped set up a place after Hurricane Andrew for the animals," Lisa said as she used a piece of cardboard to fan herself. "I think we need something like that here."

I agreed.

233

"I've never done anything like this before, so what do you have to do to make this work."

"What we need, in order for this to work, is cooperation and lots of dedicated volunteers," I said, remembering back to what had been accomplished at the MASH unit. "And, I warn you . . . it's still not going to be easy." Hurricane Andrew had taught me that.

No one had interrupted us while we'd been talking. The people who'd already showed up to help seemed to sense the importance of our conversation. But the tall man couldn't wait.

"Excuse me. Can I get past?" the man said as he squeezed through the room toward us. In his arms he carried a small brown-and-white dog, whose wide eyes took in the clamor of activity around him.

"Are you the one in charge?" The question was directed to Lisa.

"Sort of, but this lady can help you," Lisa said as she looked at me and smiled.

"I have to evacuate and I have no place to take my dog," the man explained. "Could you please take care of him until I can get back into my house?"

I don't know whose eyes were sadder, the man's or the dog's, but they were a persuasive duo, and I had no choice but to say, "Sure. We'll keep your dog."

Where exactly we would put him, I wasn't sure, but we'd find a place. I remembered the seventy-five mangy dogs we'd had at the MASH unit; we'd found shelter for them. So how difficult could it be to find a place to keep just one dog?

The man was finding it hard not to cry as he told his dog, "You'll be fine. These people will take good care of you." He hugged the dog tightly. "I'll be back real soon to get you. I promise."

Then he handed the dog to Lisa and turned to leave.

"Wait. We're not done yet," I said, reaching for my briefcase. "There's some information we need to get from you."

I attached an animal-intake form to a clipboard I'd spotted sitting on a corner of the card table. "You need to fill this out," I told the man. "It'll ensure that you get your dog back when you're ready to take him home."

The man seemed even more relieved and thanked us repeatedly before he gave the dog one last hug and left to evacuate whatever else he could from his home before the floodwaters rose any higher.

Meanwhile, Lisa found a crate in the back room to put the dog in. It didn't take him long to settle down, and when I passed his cage later, he seemed happy to be somewhere safe and dry. I was wondering how many more dogs were in need of a safe refuge when someone asked, "Can I do something to help?"

I turned to see a young woman standing behind me who seemed perfect for the job I needed done. "Sure," I said as I put my arm around her shoulder. "How would you like to go around and collect every piece of paper you can find with a name and/or phone number written on it? I don't care how insignificant it may look, I want to see it."

"Okay," she said, slightly puzzled. I'm sure she was expecting me to tell her to clean a litter box or walk a dog, but my first recruit seemed willing to do whatever needed to be done.

"Once you have them all rounded up, let me know," I said.

After a few more instructions, the volunteer began her task.

Using a cleaning bucket, she picked up and read every piece of paper she could find. She even dug through the garbage cans, in case any important messages had accidently gotten tossed. An hour later she handed me the bucket, filled nearly to the top with what appeared to be trash, but was actually the beginning of weeks of work.

Her next job was to divide the messages into categories. Papers with just a name on it went in one pile. Another pile was started for pieces of paper that had a name and a phone number. If the word rescue was written anywhere on a scrap of paper, it went into a third pile. Illegible messages were put aside in case the person who wrote the information down could be found to decipher it.

While she worked on this project, I went back to the area where the phones were being answered. This was another part of the operation that had to be tightly organized. The phones were our link to the community, and it was vital that the information given to the public be correct and consistent. Otherwise, we'd be adding to the already existing confusion.

Before I interrupted the three women answering phones, I found a large piece of cardboard wedged behind a file cabinet and, in big letters, wrote on it the ten most frequently asked questions, followed by their answers. When I was done, I hung it on the wall above the phones so that all three women could read it. Their smiles confirmed they were glad that someone had finally given them some answers.

One of the woman then answered *my* question in between calls. "How many lines do we have?" I asked the one wearing short overalls.

"A single line and four phones," she replied. "Thanks to my husband, Dave, who works for the phone company."

"Your husband's an angel," I replied.

"And who are you?" she asked, smiling.

"I'm sorry. My name's Terri Crisp, and I travel around the country setting up disaster relief efforts for animals," I told her. "I'm here to do what I can to help."

"Thank God someone knows what they're doing," she said.

"It's going to take more than one person to make this work, and you and your husband have already made a significant contribution."

The volunteer in overalls was Tracy Thornton, and though she'd never been through a disaster before, she learned quickly and ended up helping many of the animals affected by the Midwest flood, as did all the other recruits that joined our team.

36

Falling Into Place

"Well, are we making progress?" Lisa asked as she caught me waiting my turn for the bathroom, something I finally decided I had to find time to do.

"Right now yes, but it could change in an instant," I said. "You'll learn that in a disaster; you take a lot of steps forward, and sometimes just as many backward."

Since arriving at the Humane Society that morning, I'd determined that our greatest asset was the volunteers. The people who'd already arrived were incredible, and there were so many of them. This was quite a switch from Hurricane Andrew, but, then, these were two completely different kinds of disasters and had impacted the two communities differently. A lot of the people who lived around St. Charles had not been affected by the flood, so they were able to help, and I was sure glad that they were.

One of those people was a broad-shouldered man in his late twenties, with a full, bushy beard and red hair tucked under a well-worn baseball cap. He planted himself in front of me that first afternoon, and said in a deep voice, "I learned search and rescue in the navy and I'm here to help."

"What's your name?" I asked.

"Mark. Mark Veverka. I'm from Illinois—farm country."

"How long can you stay, Mark?"

"For as long as you need me," he replied. "I've got no other commitments at the moment."

As I listened to Mark, I knew how I could use him right then. He would be perfect.

"Are you ready to start now?" I asked, hoping he'd say yes.

"You bet. What do you want me to do?" Mark replied.

I led him to the front door of the shelter and told him to stay put while I went to grab an armchair, which looked as though it had been used repeatedly as a cat-scratching post.

"I want you to direct traffic," I told Mark as he sat in the chair I offered him. "There needs to be some control over who comes in and out of this building."

Mark seemed quite pleased with his new assignment as I went on to explain who should be allowed in our cramped quarters.

"If someone wants to donate food, have them leave it outside under the overhang. If a disaster victim needs pet food, tell them to take enough to feed their dog or cat or whatever for a week, and when they run out, they can come back for more."

My other instructions included what to do with people who wished to volunteer, requests to rescue animals, and how to handle displaced individuals needing a place to house their pet. Mark listened intently. He'd do fine as our bouncer, just like my two fishermen had in Valdez.

The last thing to do was provide Mark with volunteer applications to pass out to inquiring individuals. As I was handing a stack to him, a woman with short auburn hair stood waiting her turn to talk with me. Without even having spoken to her, I could already tell this lady was a powerhouse, and Sharon Polster was.

Sharon stepped right in front of me the moment I finished with Mark. Her eyes seemed to bore into my face, reminding me of a deaf person trying to read lips—except I hadn't said anything yet. Sharon Polster led the conversation.

"Let me tell you what you need," Sharon began. "We need more space. This place is a claustrophobic person's worst nightmare."

She followed my glance around the room as I said, "Yes. We're getting a bit cramped. You don't know any realtors, do you?"

"Well, it just so happens I'm a realtor, and I think I might be able to find you something larger," Sharon said.

"I'm not good at eye-balling room measurements, but I guess we

need something in the range of three to four thousand square feet—
a warehouse would be perfect," I determined as we talked.

"I'll go home and make some calls so I don't tie up the phones
here. You'll hear from me as soon as I find something," Sharon said.
She patted me on the shoulder and headed for the door.

I had no doubt I'd be hearing from Sharon. Until then, I had a lot
more to do to get the St. Charles flood relief center fully up and
operating. I'd heard from several people who'd hastily dropped their
cats off for us to take care of that the swollen rivers were rising
quickly, which meant we were going to get a lot busier. It was time
to assess our ability to respond to rescue requests.

I had the volunteer who'd collected and sorted all the scraps of
paper now making phone calls. Using the rescue-request forms I'd
brought with me, she and another volunteer were starting to collect
information on rescues that needed to be done. When I checked with
them an hour after they'd started on the project, they had already
completed a sizable stack of forms. As I flipped through them, I was
relieved to read that none of the animals were in immediate danger,
so we had a little time, but not much.

Experience had taught me that in order to rescue animals, you need
two things—equipment and people. I'd already inventoried the shelter's rescue equipment, and it was almost nonexistent. Three cat traps
were about the extent of it, and one of them looked as if it had seen
the underside of a truck.

It was time to call Bill Brothers at Animal Care Equipment and
Service in southern California. I'd met Bill at a workshop in Sacramento a few months after I'd returned from Florida. I'd explained to
him how unprepared we had been to rescue animals in the aftermath
of Hurricane Andrew.

Our biggest problem had been that we lacked proper equipment,
which made attempting rescues unsafe for the animals and the volunteers. It would have been too dangerous, for example, to try to capture
a feral cat without a trap and protective gloves or to approach an
aggressive dog without a catch pole. There were many instances
where we couldn't do anything for an animal because we didn't have
the equipment to do the job properly.

Bill had told me to call him in the next disaster and he'd make it
a priority to get us the equipment we needed, no matter where we
were. With the ACES catalog in hand, I went down the order form
and checked off what we needed: cat and dog traps, transfer cages,
catch poles, grasper poles, throw nets, pole nets, cat gloves, Evac-

sacks, squeeze cages, and snake-grasper poles—a *very* important piece of equipment.

When I learned that water moccasins like to drop out of the trees into passing boats, I almost considered *not* going to the Midwest, but I had to trust the grasper to do its job and remove any snake that fell into a rescue boat before it could sink its fangs into some human flesh.

The order was called in, and UPS delivered nearly ten thousand dollars worth of rescue equipment the next morning, paid for with donations. We were equipped to do the job of rescuing animals. Now all we needed were the right people, because Lisa and I certainly couldn't tackle this disaster by ourselves.

I'd already asked Lisa if she had any humane officers on her staff, and I learned that she and one part-time person, who cleaned cages, were the only paid employees.

"Are there any other animal welfare agencies in this community?" I asked as the value of the volunteers became more apparent.

"St. Charles Animal Control has two officers and a shelter," Lisa explained. "But the shelter is already under water, and the two officers have their hands full right now just keeping up with the ongoing day-to-day demands."

The same applied to the Humane Society. Not all of St. Charles was affected by the flood, and a lot of the normal animal situations that the Humane Society and Animal Control responded to still existed. The two organizations needed to be able to operate, separate from the flood-relief efforts, which further justified moving the relief operations into another facility.

The other thing I asked the two volunteers to do as they returned phone calls was to recruit *rescue* volunteers. If someone was interested in helping, the person was asked if he or she wanted specifically to rescue animals from flooded areas. It seemed that most volunteers did, even though very few of them had any experience. It was going to be necessary to do a crash course in Rescue Work 101.

Classes were scheduled for that Thursday and Saturday night. It was *mandatory* that anyone who wished to do rescue work take one of the four-hour classes. The sign-up lists got longer as new calls came in and the two volunteers returned more phone calls. One hundred and ten people showed up for the training, and they were exactly what we needed to fully implement the rescue program.

One of the volunteers who showed up for the class was Dara Hoffman.

I spotted her as she came through the door of the Humane Society.

Midwest Flood

She reminded me of Grady Parks, our dog walker at the MASH unit. This lady didn't match the physical description of your typical volunteer, either, so I guessed she had stopped by to make a donation. Once again, I was wrong.

The young woman stood in the doorway with a puzzled expression on her face, so I walked over to her and asked, "Can I help you?"

"Yes. I'm here for the rescue training class that starts at six," she said in a quiet voice.

I couldn't help but wonder, as I glanced at her professionally manicured nails, which would change her mind first, a broken fingernail or a water moccasin. But I had learned from Grady Parks not to be too quick to judge a book by its cover.

"Fine," I said, trying not to show my skepticism. "We'll be starting in about ten minutes. You may want to grab a chair in the other room before they're all gone."

I couldn't picture this woman, who was wearing a tailored peach-colored suit with perfectly matched pumps and purse, sitting on the floor, nor could I imagine her wearing waders and a life jacket.

There were forty-five people in the first class, including Dara, who sat on an airline crate at the back of the crowded room. I launched into my opening remarks and then got to the important items, the first being safety.

"Your well-being is my primary concern," I said as I scanned the faces in the room. "If any of you are seriously hurt or, God forbid, killed, none of us will be rescuing any more animals. So, don't take any foolish risks."

Then I detailed what they needed to know to safely rescue animals and, at the same time, protect themselves. Each volunteer got a chance to practice using the traps, catch pole, grasper pole, and nets as the evening went on. I was pleased at how quickly they learned—but, then, they knew that if they didn't do it right, animals could die.

"Now that you all know how to use the equipment," I said as the last person finished setting one of the cat traps. "I want you to understand something else. No matter how many people we send out into flooded areas, and no matter how much equipment we take . . . *we will not be able to save all the animals.*"

The volunteers suddenly got very serious. This is not what they wanted to hear, but they had to realize there would be losses—animals that were in places too risky to reach, animals that wouldn't let us help them, and animals that we would not know about in time.

Out of Harm's Way

"Well . . . we'll just make sure we get all the rest." It was Dara who spoke first. "So, when can we start?"

The first rescue team was in the field that Saturday morning, and over the next four weeks hundreds of dogs, cats, birds, rabbits, chickens, horses, cows, hogs, goats, and one iguana were saved. Each and every one of the rescue volunteers was incredible. They became experts in a very short time, and their hard work resulted in animals living and not dying.

37

A New Home

The Flood of the Century was certainly a tragedy, but combined with the losses was the comforting realization that people are still capable of being *good* to one another, especially during a disaster. That old American practice of helping your neighbors, whether you know them or not, was what sustained the relief efforts in the Midwest for weeks.

Volunteers were willing to fill sandbags, distribute hot meals, store victims' belongings, lend a sympathetic ear, and take care of displaced animals. By that first Saturday, the Humane Society was crowded with lots of these caring people and plenty of animals.

My number-one priority that morning was finding larger accommodations. We'd been receiving animals for three days, and the shelter was ready to explode. Each report of another failing levee meant there would be more people and animals in need of temporary shelter. The Red Cross and the Salvation Army were there immediately to help the evacuated people, and we wanted to do the same for the animals. But we knew that if we were going to be able to provide the services they needed, we would have to move our operation.

Sharon Polster, a realtor as well as a volunteer, was still working on locating a vacant warehouse, but what we were looking for didn't seem to exist in St. Charles or the surrounding areas. If we didn't find something quickly, my plan was to start looking for another horse pasture. It had worked in Florida, so why not again?

My other concern was time: how long were lives going to be disrupted by this disaster? With the rivers still rising and unlikely to recede anytime soon, it could be weeks, maybe months, before people would be able to reclaim their pets. Long-term solutions were going to be needed. It looked as if it would be necessary to start a foster program so people wouldn't be forced to give up their pets simply because they didn't have a place to keep them.

I instructed the people manning the phones to ask prospective volunteers if they would be interested in fostering a displaced animal. We especially needed homes for big dogs, which were showing up with increasing frequency and requiring us to do some creative juggling of animals and cages.

If someone was interested, they were instructed to come to the Humane Society and complete one of the foster applications I had brought with me. This was about the only way we had of reducing the chances of an animal being placed in an unsuitable home. Those who showed up at the shelter had been told on the phone there was no guarantee they would be asked to foster an animal.

The foster program was organized and started that first week. Wendy Borowsky, Kim Misciagna, Marty Ferguson, Sharon Maag, and Tracy Thornton shared the coordination of the animal intake area and, with the help of other volunteers, made sure that every animal that arrived at our facility was placed in a good home, whether it was a temporary or a permanent one.

The foster home binders ended up containing more than seven hundred and fifty approved homes, which is where almost all the animals that we received were kept, some for as long as a year. A few aggressive dogs and some feral cats, unsuitable for fostering in private homes, were taken to Kennelwood, a boarding facility in the area. The people who were willing to open up their homes or kennels to the hundreds of dogs and cats that needed a temporary place to live were our unseen volunteer force. Without them, we never could have helped as many animals as we did.

The foster program did not eliminate our need for a larger facility, though. We still needed space to store all the donated food and pet supplies, plus the rescue equipment. Until the animals could be moved into foster homes, we needed space to set up enough cages and portable runs. The animal intake area, which started out on Lisa's wobbly card table, needed room to expand as they received more and more animals.

When Sharon returned to the shelter later that morning, I hoped she had good news, because as she arrived, a female beagle mix with eight puppies heaped in a laundry basket came through the door too. They had been found under a mobile home, huddled together on a woodpile. The man who heard the mother frantically barking said the rising water didn't have far to go before the wood and the dogs would have disappeared.

"Well, do we have a new home?" I asked Sharon as she approached.

"I'm afraid not," she said, shaking her head. "But I did find a Xerox machine we can use. It'll be here this afternoon."

A photocopier was one of the items on our wish list, but as I looked around the shelter I thought to myself, *Where are we going to put it?* It added one more bit of pressure on us to move.

"We've gotten a lot more animals since I left here this morning," Sharon noted as she watched two volunteers putting the beagle and her puppies in an airline crate located in the bathroom.

"Yeah. And it's only going to get worse," I responded. "We may have to take up residence in a horse pasture if we don't find something quick."

"Maybe I can help you find a place?" asked a woman I'd seen earlier in the day. I'd noticed her because of the red roller-skate earrings dangling from her earlobes, not quite what you'd expect a woman in her early fifties to be wearing.

"Do you have a warehouse?" I was quick to ask.

A broad smile spread across the woman's face as she spoke, "No, but I think my husband, Harlan, can find you one. Just tell me what you need."

I told her what we'd been looking for, a three-thousand-square-foot warehouse whose owner would not object to having dogs and cats occupy it.

"I'll go make some calls and get back to you," the woman said as she turned and headed toward the door. "Oh, by the way, I'm Anne Pals."

Anne and Harlan got us our warehouse that afternoon. A former bread bakery that belonged to Magna Bank had been sitting vacant for some time. Harlan was on the bank's board of directors, and all it took was one call to Kent McNeil, the president, and the deal was made. The warehouse was ours for as long as we needed it, rent free. We started moving in that day.

Men and women, mostly friends of the Pals's, were armed with brooms, mops, rags, and buckets and cleaning the warehouse for its new occupants when I saw the building late Saturday afternoon. Ann introduced me to our plumber, Bill Hicks, when he stuck his head out of the bathroom to report he had fixed the toilet. The man with the bulging carpenter's belt slung around his waist was Dennis Ottolini. He was busy wiring some additional electrical outlets so we could plug in a refrigerator and two industrial-size fans that would help cool the place. It was an impressive crew of volunteers and a perfect place to set up the St. Charles animal relief center.

When I returned to the shelter, anxious to announce we were moving, one of the phone volunteers caught me as I came in the door.

"Terri, the Coast Guard is on the phone," she said with an urgency in her voice. "They want to know if we can get some cats off a roof in West Alton."

As I followed her to the phone, I thought to myself, *West Alton?* I'd seen pictures of it on the news the night before, and it had looked bad. This rural community, located between the Mississippi and Missouri rivers, was quickly disappearing as the two rivers merged.

"Hi, this is Terri," I said as I covered my other ear to block out the noise in the shelter. "I hear you found some cats that need help."

"Yeah. We were out on patrol, and we could hear cats meowing," the gentleman on the phone told me. "We would have tried to get them ourselves, but we didn't have anything to put them in."

"Do you know how many there are?" I asked, writing his answers on a rescue form.

"Lots."

It took me five minutes to get the rest of the information I needed and another ten to pull together a rescue team and the equipment we would need to rescue *a lot* of cats.

The Coast Guard was waiting for us when we arrived at the Salvation Army's mobile feeding site on Highway 94. The gentleman I'd spoken to on the phone offered to take us in their boats, since they were already in the water and it would save time. We didn't have much daylight left, so we gathered our gear and climbed into the two Coast Guard boats. Tagging along behind us was a television crew from CNN who had been looking for a story. The idea of the rescue of a lot of cats had caught their attention.

CNN got their story, giving their viewers another glimpse of the Midwest flood. This time the victims were animals. Within ten minutes of arriving at the house we had rescued seven cats. They had found refuge from the rising waters, but there was no shade, food, or fresh water for them on the roof. Thank goodness the men from the Coast Guard had heard the cats when they did, because their time had been running out.

In addition to the cats on the roof, there were more in the attic. We could hear their hoarse meows, but getting to them was not going to be easy. Gaining access to the attic through the house would be difficult because the rooms were flooded almost to the ceiling. With less then an hour of daylight left, we decided we'd have to come back in the morning. Trying to attempt a rescue after dark would have been too dangerous.

When we got back to the shelter with the seven cats, the place was more crowded than ever. Additional animals had arrived while we were gone, along with more volunteers who had been put to work packing for the move to the warehouse.

It was just after midnight when I shooed the last volunteer out of the warehouse. Before I locked the door that night, I took one more peak at the space that had been transformed into the St. Charles animal relief center.

Already in place was a row of tables right inside the door, where volunteers would greet the public and answer their questions. Behind the tables was the animal intake area, the nerve center of our operation. The wobbly card table had been replaced with several tables and a desk.

In a back corner we had four telephones set up, waiting to receive the multitude of calls that had been keeping the phone volunteers busy from seven A.M. until ten P.M. Thousands of pounds of dog food and cat food were lined up against one wall, along with shelves loaded with donated pet supplies, all waiting to be handed out. And then there were cages and portable runs for the dogs and cats, whom we'd move over in the morning. By tomorrow we'd be completely moved and ready to do business, with space to spare.

38

A Crowder of Cats

The locals nicknamed it "Nature's Still," the vast expanse of water that had swallowed the fields of West Alton. Beneath the surface of the floodwaters, acres and acres of corn lay fermenting in the relentless summer heat. The smell was nauseating, but the rescue team ignored it. We had cats to save, and as our four boats crossed the cornfields of West Alton, all our senses were focused on doing just that.

The team was made up of eager graduates from the Saturday night training class. They had shown up at the Humane Society before most people had even poured their first cup of coffee or had a chance to read the Sunday comics, which did not surprise me. These people wanted to help animals, and this was their chance to do that.

Ed Coplan had been the first to arrive, with his boat. I learned later that, in spite of being displaced by the flood himself, he made time for the animals.

It wasn't long after Ed arrived that John Misciagna pulled into the parking lot with his boat in tow too. He would chauffeur many animals to safety over the next four weeks in his sixteen-foot *Noah's Ark.*

Alonzo Roberts was the third member of this rescue team. The gentle, sixty-eight-year-old man never showed his age, keeping up with the youngest of the rescuers. "This is the reason I get up in the morning," he told me several weeks after he started volunteering. "I don't know what I'll find to do after this ends."

The fourth member of our team was Steve Prince. The lean, blue-eyed man in his mid-twenties had shown up at the Humane Society the day before and stopped me as I was heading out the door to pick up some Polaroid film.

"I heard you need some boats," Steve had said

"We sure do," I replied. "Do you have one?"

"Well, I sail a twenty-four-foot Pace, but I figured my flat-bottomed one would be what you'd want for the job."

"Sounds perfect. When are you available?" I asked, hoping he could be generous with his time.

"I'm always available for an animal in trouble."

And Steve Prince was.

With our team assembled, we loaded up the boats with transfer cages, cans of tuna, Evacsacks, nets, grasper poles, cat gloves, flashlights, and gasoline for the boats.

Steve knew where we could launch, so he led us out of the parking lot. We traveled east on Interstate 70 that Sunday morning, each of the four trucks bearing a red-and-white magnetic sign that read, "EMERGENCY ANIMAL RESCUE SERVICE."

Everyone was quiet once we got the boats in the water and started passing one house after another with only their roofs still visible. Reality had set in. Some of these new volunteers were seeing a disaster up close for the first time, and I remembered what that felt like. The Alviso flood had been nowhere near as devastating or widespread as this one, but it had left me silent too.

"Damn." Steve's voice interrupted my thoughts.

"What is it?" I asked, watching his face.

"Something's caught in my propeller," Steve replied, as he cut the engine and lifted his motor out of the water.

The other boats pulled up alongside us just as Steve discovered the problem. Twisted around the propeller blades were rotting cornstalks.

"You guys better check yours too," Steve yelled above the motors as he began to pull the mess off each blade.

It turned out the other boats had collected their share of the stuff too.

"A unique way to harvest crops," Steve said as he untangled the

249

last of what looked like lettuce that had been left in the refrigerator for months.

With all the propellers cleaned, we once again headed toward our rescue site. This time, though, we used the power lines which hung just inches above the surface of the water, to guide us down what would have been the road. We hoped that if we didn't cross over the cornfields, we wouldn't have to stop as often to clean propellers.

But we had to stop again. This time it wasn't because of rotting cornstalks.

Ed was the one that spotted them. Perched in the upper branches of a sycamore tree was a group of cats, their refuge completely surrounded by water and not a building close enough to swim to. From a distance it looked as if it would be an easy rescue. All we would have to do was use the grasper poles to reach up through the branches and grab the cats, but our plan had to be rethought when we got a closer look.

Between the eight cats and the surface of the water, where we were floating quietly in our boats, was a swarm of very agitated bees. There was no way that we could get to the cats without further upsetting the bees and suffering the consequences.

"Well, boss, what do we do?" Steve asked as I wondered how long the cats had been in the tree. My guess was maybe a week.

"We find a beekeeper and come back," I said, remembering what I'd told the volunteers in the training class, *"Your well-being is my primary concern."*

Without disturbing the bees, we left some open cans of tuna wedged in the lower branches of the tree and continued on our way. Thanks to the Humane Society of Missouri the eight "tree-bound" cats were later rescued.

When we finally reached our destination, I could tell the water had risen nearly a foot just overnight. In another day or two the water would be in the attic, flooding the cats' last refuge. The rescue took on a greater urgency now that we realized this was probably going to be our last chance to save these cats.

"What do you want us to do?" John asked as he cut his engine and eased up alongside Steve's boat. Ed and Alonzo held back waiting for their instructions too.

"Let's just sit here a minute and see if we can hear the cats meowing," I suggested. "Hopefully, they'll cooperate and give away their hiding place."

At first, all we heard were frogs, one of the few creatures quite pleased that nature had decided to flood the Midwest. Their repeated rivits made one think of summer and the way life used to be in this rural community. On Sunday morning there should have been the sounds of lawn mowers, children playing, people returning from church, and dogs barking. Instead, there was an eerie silence and no meowing cats.

"Steve, why don't we go around to the back and see if we can hear anything there. The rest of you stay put and keep your ears open," I instructed as Steve reached for the edge of the roof and started pulling our boat toward the corner of the house.

As we made our way down the driveway side of the house, I sat in the front of the boat so I could push floating debris out of the way with a paddle. Red velvet cushions, a Barbie Doll, cookbooks, a Styrofoam ice chest, winter coats, a Monopoly game, all littered our path.

When we reached the back, we once again sat silently, listening. It was then that we heard the muffled meows. We pulled the boat closer to the sound as the meows continued.

"Looks like I can pry this vent cover off," Steve said as he searched for an entry point under the eaves. "Can you get me the crowbar out of my toolbox?"

I handed Steve what he asked for, and he forced it under one corner of the metal vent. After a couple of tugs, the cover popped off and disappeared into the water. He'd created a space big enough for cats to escape, but there was no way any one of us would fit through the opening. He handed back the crowbar and then grabbed a yellow flashlight from under one of the seats.

In a kneeling position, Steve situated himself under the vent and slowly raised his head through the rectangular-shaped hole. With the flashlight, he scanned the interior. He could not see into the attic because a wall of plywood was in the way, but it didn't matter, he'd found what he was looking for. What he discovered was a narrow corridor that ran the length of the house. It was barely the width of a cat's shoulders, he said, and not even high enough for a large tom to stand up, but it was enough space for cats to hide.

"How many would you say there are?" I asked anxiously.

"I can't tell. But there's a lot," Steve replied as he lowered his head out of the opening. "And we have to get them out of there—it's suffocatingly hot."

Steve brushed some cobwebs from his hair and looked at me with a surprised expression. "I don't know how they've survived."

"They must have someone higher up than them keeping an eye on 'em," I said, remembering all the other animals I'd rescued before death nabbed them.

"Well, let's get them out of there."

While Steve opened cans of tuna and lined up cages, I yelled for the rest of our rescue team, "Guys, come on back. We found them."

I showed Ed, John, and Alonzo where to position their boats so that we could quickly hand them cats as we pulled them out of the attic. They had cages opened and waiting for the rescued felines.

"Okay. Ready?" I asked as I looked around at our setup. All heads nodded yes.

The plan was that Steve would lure the cats out of the opening, one at a time, using an open can of tuna as an enticement. Then I would put them in a cage and hand them to the waiting boats. We were relieved when it didn't take much encouragement to get the cats to go along with our plan. They were indeed starved and ready to be rescued.

The first one through the opening was a pitiful little creature with a bad eye. The smell of the tuna was all it took to lure him from his hiding place and into the boat below. The poor thing didn't lift his head once as he stood on the seat desperately attacking the food. When I reached for the can, he let out a warning growl but didn't stop eating. I slowly moved the food toward the opened cage, while the cat continued to eat. When I slid the can into the cage, the ravenous feline followed. I don't think he even noticed when I closed the door and handed the cage to Ed.

One by one, like beads on a string of pearls, the cats escaped from the attic. But there are always a few stubborn ones in every group, and this time was no different. We could hear more meows, but no matter how good the tuna smelled, they were not ready to venture out of their hiding spot. Eventually, a few more poked their noses out of the opening and jumped cautiously into the boat, but we couldn't get the rest of them to follow suit.

It was time for plan B, which I hadn't thought up yet, but I had some time. We had no more empty cages, so we needed to take the captured cats back to the Humane Society to free up more space. Rather than pull all the boats out of the water, I asked Ed and John to transport the cats. I used my cellular phone to call the Humane Society and warn them that twenty-four cats were moving in with us. It was a good thing we had moved into the warehouse the day before, otherwise, we'd have had cats stacked to the ceiling.

"Twenty-four?" Sharon Polster yelled when she heard the number.

"That's right," I assured her. "And that's not even all of them."

Now it was time to start putting together plan B.

"Sharon, didn't you tell me that someone called in and said they were a diver," I asked, wondering if I was just hoping I'd heard that.

"Yeah. His name is Frank, and he's with search and rescue," Sharon told me.

"Is he available to help?"

"I can call him and find out," Sharon offered. "If he is, what do you want me to tell him?"

"Find out if he can come back out with Ed and John, because we need him to swim into this house and gain access to the attic," I explained. "I think that's the only way we're going to get these last holdouts."

The hot afternoon sun made the waiting seem longer. There was no place to go to escape the heat, considering we didn't want to sit under a tree and risk a snake paying us an unfriendly visit. So we drank water and listened to the frogs.

It was almost two o'clock when Ed and John returned with empty cages—and the diver. They were a most welcome sight. I introduced myself to Frank when Ed's boat pulled up alongside ours.

"Boy, are we glad to see you," I said, shaking Frank's hand. "You ready to go swimming?"

"You bet. Just tell me what you want me to do."

"We know there are still a few more cats in the attic and possibly some small kittens that can't get to the opening we created. What I'd like you to do is get up in the attic and look for kittens first, then grab any cats that are willing to be caught," I explained. "The unwilling ones we'll set traps for."

"Gotcha," Frank said as he put his mouthpiece in and lowered his mask over his face.

"And, Frank—be careful."

In reply, Frank gave me a thumbs-up, then tucked himself into a fetal position and rolled backward into the water.

Frank resurfaced by the front door a minute later and removed his mouthpiece. "I tried the handle, and the door's locked."

"I can remedy that," Steve said as he grabbed one of his oars and used it to move his boat within reach of the front door. "Do I have your permission to break the glass?" Steve looked at me and asked.

"Why not. Everything else is already damaged," I replied.

Frank moved out of the way as Steve turned his back to the door.

With one swift thrust with his oar, he hit the door's panel of glass that was still above water. Using the oar, Steve broke away the rest of the glass and then reached through the opening and unlocked the door. With some help from Frank, he pushed the front door open.

"Okay. I'm going in," Frank said before replacing his mouthpiece and disappearing under the water. We all stared at the house as we listened to Frank's air bubbles from inside.

"Terri," Frank yelled, "there's still some space between the water's surface and the ceiling, so I can stay above water and let you know what I see."

"Good," I replied in relief. This would make it easier for Frank to find the access to the attic.

Those of us outside waited impatiently. It was hard not being in the house helping. We listened as Frank moved things out of his way and gave us updates on where he was in the house.

"I've got company in here."

"What?" I yelled. Frank was in a back part of the house, so it was hard to hear him.

It was taking a long time for Frank to respond, and I became concerned. "Frank. Are you okay?"

Still there was no answer.

"We may have to go swimming in a minute, guys," I announced, hoping otherwise.

"It's gone," we finally heard Frank yell.

"What's gone?" I asked.

"The water moccasin. It slithered out a broken window," Frank replied, seemingly with little concern.

I felt like an overprotective mother as I expelled my breath in relief.

It was quiet again except for the sound of Frank swimming from room to room in search of the attic access. It seemed like forever before we heard his excited cry, "I found it, and we're in luck. There's a ladder set up below it."

So that's how the cats got in there, I thought to myself.

It didn't take long for Frank to climb into the attic, where he continued to keep us informed of what he saw.

"Boy, it's hot up here. And God it stinks," was Frank's first report.

Then we heard the words that we'd been waiting for, "I found one! And here's another."

I raised my fists to the sky and screamed, "Hallelujah!"

The first one out was not a kitten, but an old black tom who was not fond of water. Frank had the wet cat by the scruff of the neck when he came through the door. I think the only reason the cat was willing to cooperate was that he was more frightened of being dropped and forced to swim.

With my gloves on I grabbed the cat, just below Frank's hand, and he let go. As I reached for the tom's hind legs, his front paws latched on to the gutter and he hung on. He thought he'd found an escape, but I was more determined than he was.

I'd barely gotten the tom into a cage before Frank was handing me a marmalade kitten. She had the most woebegone look, but seemed quite pleased to be out of the attic. As I was putting her in a cage, I noticed she had an extra toe on each of her front paws.

Two tiny kittens followed, their eyes barely open. "I think they're reproducing up there faster than we're pulling 'em out," I heard Alonzo say. We all laughed.

For the next half hour, furry body after furry body was silhouetted against the house's dim interior as Frank handed them to us.

"She's the last one," Frank said as he deposited in my lap a four-month-old brown tabby. It shook itself and blinked, unaccustomed to the brightness of the daylight, then looked up at me and meowed.

"I know, you're hungry," I said, lifting the kitten in front of my face, so I could kiss her on her nose.

"Let's get these guys back to the Humane Society," I announced as I opened a can of sardines for our last evacuee. I figured she deserved a treat, and she agreed. Within minutes she polished off four of the small fish with no manners at all.

It had been a long, hot day, but as we caravaned back to the shelter, each member of the rescue team felt great. We'd accomplished what we set out to do that morning, only the rewards were greater than we had expected—there were thirty-two of them to be exact.

39

The Right Decision

The thirty-two cats from West Alton were not the only animals to be rescued that first weekend. There was another rescue late Sunday afternoon that wouldn't have happened if the volunteers on the rescue team had listened to me during the training class, but thank goodness they didn't.

I'd just gotten off the phone with a woman offering free boarding for displaced horses when I heard my name. I assumed it was another volunteer wanting to know what else needed to be moved to the warehouse, but instead, when I turned to identify the soft voice, I spotted a thin, delicate-featured woman with long blond hair standing a couple steps behind me.

"I don't know if you remember me, but I'm Dawn Clanton," the woman said when she knew she had my attention. "I went through the second training class."

"Sure. I remember you," I said, recognizing her face.

"We just got back from our first rescue," Dawn said with some hesitancy in her voice.

"How'd it go?" I asked, expecting to get an enthusiastic report.

Dawn paused and looked at the floor nervously, reminding me of a child who had to tell her parents something that she knew was going to get her in trouble.

Midwest Flood

"I think you're going to be mad at us," Dawn finally said, unable to look me in the eye.

"Why would I be mad at you?" I asked as I moved aside to allow a volunteer, his arms loaded with bags of dog food, to pass.

"Let me show you."

Dawn turned as if she were anxious to escape and headed for the outside door. I followed her through the crowd of people that filled the shelter, wondering why she thought I might be mad. As we crossed the parking lot toward a red van, I still had not come up with a reason. I expected that the three men who silently watched us approach were part of Dawn's rescue team. Maybe they were going to tell me?

Standing at the rear of the van was Dawn's husband, Rod, and two other volunteers, Nat and Ed. Their solemn looks matched the expression of their female team member

"Okay, you guys, what's going on?" I asked with a smile on my face. "You all look way too serious."

Dawn was the one who spoke. It seemed that she had been appointed to give me what I was expecting might be bad news.

"Remember in the training class you told us that we were not to rescue wildlife?" Dawn said quickly.

"Yes," I said, remembering the reason why as well. I had explained in both classes that wild animals were not our primary concern. It wasn't that I didn't care what happened to them, because I did, but our job during this disaster was to rescue dogs and cats, and possibly some farm animals. There were wildlife experts in the area, and they were prepared to intervene should a wild animal need help.

I'd learned in other disasters that wild animals usually know how to take care of themselves during fires, floods, or hurricanes. With some notable exceptions, like the oil spill in Valdez, Alaska, disasters are a natural occurrence in the environment and nature's way of regulating animal and bird populations. Most of the animals that die during a disaster are either old or sick.

The volunteers were told to report any sightings of injured wild animals to Missouri Wildlife Rescue. If a volunteer found what looked like an orphaned bird or animal, they were told to keep their distance and wait to see if the parents returned. Often the parents were close by, intending to return to their young. Only after waiting a half hour were they allowed to capture and transport an orphaned bird or infant wild animal, which would then be turned over to the wildlife experts. If a volunteer encountered a wild animal trapped by floodwaters, they had been instructed to keep a safe distance while trying to help usher it in the direction of dry land if they could.

When another team of volunteers found two panicked adult deer swimming back and forth in front of a tall chain-link fence, unable to find a way to reach the dry land on the other side, they used their boats to herd them toward an open section in the fence. They made the right decision, because it wouldn't have made sense to try and chase the deer down, rope them, drag them into a boat, and then confine them in a cage in order to transport them to a safe area. It would have been extremely dangerous for the volunteers and so frightening for the deer that it might have killed them.

The open doors on the back of the red van, plus Dawn's reference to wild animals, made me suspect that the reason these volunteers were acting so funny was inside the van . . . and I was right.

Confined in a large airline crate was a fawn with big black eyes that stared back at us, too frightened to even blink.

"Oh, my goodness. Where did you come from?" I lowered my voice, so as not to frighten her more.

"We found her on Highway 367," Dawn whispered.

"Is she hurt?" I asked as I slowly moved closer to the confined animal.

"Uh huh. She's got a gouge in her left hind leg," Rod explained. "It looks like she might have gotten tangled up in some barbed wire."

"Can she stand on it?" I asked as I stepped back.

"Yeah. But she limps pretty bad."

Just then I heard what sounded like the chirp of a baby bird, and the sound was coming from inside the van.

"What else have you guys got in there?" I asked.

Nat was the first to respond. "Some lady gave us a baby bird she found. Don't know what kind it is, though."

"Yeah. The woman was hugely pregnant and she waddled up to us with this bird inside a cat carrier," Dawn explained. "She said she was going to take it to a vet, but when she saw us, she asked if we would take it instead."

By then Ed had gotten the cat carrier from the middle seat, and I peered inside the cardboard container. Looking up at me was a noisy fledgling with a long outstretched neck and a wide open mouth. I'm sure he was hoping I was his mother returning with a tasty morsel of food.

"Well, you guys got anything else alive aboard this ark?" I asked, laughing.

Midwest Flood

"As a matter of fact, we do," Dawn said, producing another carrier, containing one very pregnant cat. "She's actually the reason we were on Highway 367 in the first place."

"Well, you better tell me the story," I said, making myself comfortable on the bumper of the van, while the fawn lay quietly in her crate. By now the mood around the van had relaxed as the four rescue volunteers took turns telling me about their first rescue.

Earlier in the day, Rod and Dawn had been distributing flyers to the local Red Cross shelters. The bright yellow papers explained the services we were providing at the St. Charles Humane Society. One of the Red Cross volunteers told Rod and Dawn of a cat named Tasha that belonged to a woman staying at the shelter. She hadn't known what to do with her cat when she evacuated, so she left it behind. Her home was in West Alton.

Rod and Dawn knew they couldn't reach the house by car, so they returned to the shelter to recruit a boat and some more help. That was when Nat and Ed joined their team.

The four volunteers piled into Ed's red van and headed toward Highway 367 with Ed's boat in tow, to rescue the cat who'd been living on its own for two weeks. When they got to the place where they could launch their boat, they talked with two water patrol officers who also had access to a boat and offered to take them to the house. So, Ed and Nat grabbed an Evacsack, a grasper pole, and a pair of cat gloves, and went with the officers.

Meanwhile, Dawn went to use the Porta Potti next to the Salvation Army mobile feeding trailer. As she came out of the bathroom, she was spotted by a woman she used to work with who knew of Dawn's involvement with animals.

"Dawn," she exclaimed. "I can't believe I ran into you. I need your help."

The friend told her about the fawn she'd seen earlier that day standing on the shoulder along 367.

"It looked like it was hurt," the friend explained. "If you want to go with me, I can show you where I saw it."

The two women wasted no time climbing into the friend's pickup. The highway had been narrowed down to two lanes by the floodwaters where it passed through West Alton, and the traffic barely moved. The Sunday drivers who stopped to take pictures of the floodwaters that had spread to both sides of the highway made things worse. Both women were silent as the truck creeped along, praying they'd find the fawn before it wandered onto the road and got hit.

When they finally got to the location where the friend had last seen the fawn, they spotted her standing on the ten-foot-wide shoulder, munching on some mulberry leaves. As Dawn and her friend approached slowly on foot, the fawn moved into the bushes and lay down, hoping to blend in with the underbrush and disappear.

"Well, what do we do?" the friend asked, looking at Dawn.

"We need to make a circle around her, so she doesn't get out on the road," Dawn responded. "Then we grab her."

"Yeah, right," the friend exclaimed. "We're going to need some more people in order to catch this fawn, 'cause we certainly can't do it ourselves."

Dawn knew that Ed and Nat would probably not be back for a while, and even if they went back to the Salvation Army's feeding location to get Rod, they still wouldn't have enough people

Luckily, some passersby, who noticed the fawn and figured out what the two women were trying to do, stopped to see if they could help, and in no time, Dawn had a large enough group.

When the fawn realized her hiding spot had been discovered, she stood up suddenly and started limping along the shoulder away from the audience she'd attracted. She stayed close to the bushes, which is what the group wanted her to do. Under Dawn's direction, the impromptu volunteers positioned themselves between the fawn and the road, while trying to shorten the distance she could travel. Gradually the circle of people got tighter around the frightened animal. One of the guys, finally got close enough to grab the fawn around its midsection.

"Now what do you want me to do?" he asked as he stood with the fawn in his arms, all four of her legs dangling.

"Do you mind riding back with us to where our van is?" Dawn asked. "It's not far, and I have an airline crate we can put her in."

The guy didn't have to be asked twice.

When Dawn got back to the van, she found Rod, Nat, and Ed waiting for her. She could see an Evacsack in the back of the van, with a mound in the middle. It looked as if their rescue mission must have been a success.

"Well, what did *you* find?" Rod asked as he walked toward the truck. The guy was still sitting in the back, cradling the fawn in his arms.

"An injured fawn," Dawn replied with a triumphant grin, which faded quickly when she remembered my words, *"We don't rescue wildlife."* "Do you think Terri will be mad at me?"

"Nope. She'll understand," Ed assured her.

"I hope you're right, or I will be the first volunteer in this disaster to be fired."

Dawn then explained how her plan to rescue the fawn had worked, while she helped the guys get the fawn in the empty airline crate. "You know, all those years growing up on a farm and rounding up hogs finally paid off," Dawn said as she stood back and looked at the fawn, whose life she had probably saved.

"What you got in there?" It was one of the water patrol officers, who walked up behind the group and was peering into the large airline crate.

"A fawn that we found alongside the road," Dawn explained. "She's got an injured leg that needs to be looked at."

"She'd be better off if we just shot her now," the officer suggested. "Leg injuries are hard to mend."

"No," Dawn was quick to respond. "It's not that bad, and I know that Missouri Wildlife can help her."

"Have it your way, but I think she should be shot," he said, directing his attention to the cat.

"How's the cat doing?" he asked as he moved closer to the van.

"She'll be fine after we get her something to eat and have a vet look at her," Rod said with some annoyance in his voice.

"Where did you find Tasha?" Dawn asked.

Ed and Nat told of finding the pregnant tortie on the screened porch, perched on a beam less than an inch from the surface of the water. "It wouldn't have been long before she was forced to swim," Nat explained. "And there was no place for her to go. The screened porch was closed up tight, with no possible escape routes. She was fortunate to have survived this long."

"With no more animals to rescue, we returned to the shelter to tell you what we'd done," Dawn said.

After pausing a moment, she asked, "Are you mad at us?"

The four volunteers stared at me, not quite sure what I was going to say or what punishment I might inflict for their behavior.

"You guys are terrific," I said, looking at each one of them. "And, you did exactly what I would have done in the situation."

You could see the relief on all of their faces, especially Dawn's.

"Now let's get these guys inside," I said, as I stood up. "I haven't a clue what to feed the fawn and the bird, so we'd better call the wildlife experts. They'll know."

*　　*　　*

Out of Harm's Way

The fawn was taken to the Missouri Wildlife Rescue Center and eventually released in a wildlife preserve in the southern part of the state. When Dawn talked to Susie Sutton, the director at the wildlife facility, several weeks after the rescue, she was told that the fawn was too young to have been able to survive on her own. She was just starting to eat on her own, but she still needed her mother's milk.

Dawn had definitely made the right decision.

The fledgling turned out to be a grebe, which is a bird not found in Missouri. The bird experts were puzzled how it had made it to West Alton, when its normal habitat is the Great Lakes area. They wondered if it could possibly have floated that far south on one of the flooded rivers. The bird was eventually released back up north, making that trip by plane.

Tasha gave birth to a single long-haired gray kitten, named Flow. Her owner never came to reclaim her, so both cats now live with Dawn and Rod.

During the month that the warehouse was open, we didn't have any more wild animals or birds to rescue. If the occasion had arisen, I'm certain the volunteers would have known what to do. They were all learning that when you're not sure what to do in a rescue situation, good old common sense is the best decision maker.

40

Effective Allies

Flat-bottom boats were at the top of our wish list the first Monday we were in the warehouse. With more and more of the surrounding landscape being swallowed up by water, it was obvious that without more boats we'd be unable to respond to the rescue requests we were receiving. I knew there had to be boat owners willing to lend themselves and their boats to our rescue efforts, but how was I going to find them? It was time to call Ben Sherman.

Ben lived in Keene, New Hampshire. Boats were definitely in high demand throughout the flooded Midwest, but they had not become so scarce that I had to extend my search to New England. Ben was employed by Gehrung Associates, the public relations firm that represented Santa Clara University. I had met Ben at a meeting on campus, several months after I'd returned from Florida. At that time we set up a plan to help animals in future disasters. This was going to be the test to see if that plan worked.

"Ben. It's Terri Crisp," I said when he answered the phone.

"Don't tell me." He paused. "You're in the Midwest."

"Good guess . . . and I need your help."

I spent the next twenty minutes explaining to Ben what we had set up in the warehouse.

"Okay. Let me see if I've got this right," Ben said when I finished. "You need johnboats or similar flat-bottom boats to be able to get into flooded areas to rescue animals that owners left behind. Most of the animals you have helped so far have been dogs and cats, but you expect to get some calls to help with cows and horses too."

"Right," I responded. "And be sure to let people know that if they have a boat to offer, they have to accompany the boat on the rescue," I explained. "And, they are responsible for any damage done to their boats."

"That might make it harder to find boats," Ben commented.

"Yes. But I'm sure there will still be people willing to help us out," I said, hoping I was right.

"Okay. I think I have everything I need," Ben said. "I'll write this up and call you back within the hour."

By the end of the day, Ben had written and sent out forty-one press releases to news agencies he thought could help us with what we needed. The media within the St. Louis area got the press releases specifically asking for boats. We saw the first results of that effort when a tall, skinny individual walked through the door at the warehouse. I immediately knew he was with the press. Who else would walk around with a microphone in his hand and a cameraman shadowing him?

"That's John Pertzborn," Sharon Polster whispered as we watched the two men approach the information table. "He's one of the local NBC reporters."

"Well, I better go see what he wants," I said. "Hopefully, he's here to do a story that'll get us the boats we need."

One of the volunteers was already talking with the reporter, and I could hear her say to him as I got closer to the table, "You need to talk with Terri Crisp about that."

That was my cue.

"Hi. I'm Terri," I said as I stepped up beside the volunteer, who was nervously blushing. "What can I do to help you?" I asked, extending my hand.

"We got your press release this afternoon, and I understand you need some boats. We're here to see what we can do to help you get them," John explained as he shook my hand.

While we were making our introductions, John had been surveying the activity in the warehouse. "You have quite an operation set up here," John said. "It reminds me of a Red Cross shelter, but you're helping the animals, instead."

"Right. But we're also helping people," I explained. "A lot of the animals we've taken in belong to people who were frantic to find a place to keep their pets until they could return home. If we weren't here, some of these animals might still be treading water."

"This is a great service you all are offering," John said as he turned to his cameraman. "Why don't you get some shots of the animals in the cages first, especially that kitten in the cage over there that keeps sticking his paw out between the wire." He pointed to one of the youngest kittens that we had pulled from the attic in West Alton.

I followed John and the cameraman around the warehouse as they got more footage of what we did. They captured volunteers cleaning litter boxes, stacking bags of dog food, sorting collars, answering phones, filling out paperwork on animals that were just arriving, and grabbing cages to head out on another rescue. While the two men were deciding where they wanted me to stand while John asked me some questions, Sharon sneaked up behind me.

"You're going to tell them we need at least fifteen boats, aren't you?" she whispered. "And make sure they know we need flat-bottomed boats."

"Terri, are your ready?" John asked. "If so, we'd like you to stand in front of this row of cages so we can get some cats in the picture too."

I moved to the spot he was pointing to, and he stood in front of me with his microphone ready.

"Ms. Crisp," he began, "tell me what has been set up here."

"The volunteers have worked together to establish a relief center for animals displaced by the flood," I began. "So far, we have received over one hundred dogs and cats, and we expect to see a lot more before this is over."

"What can the community do to help?" John asked.

"The person who can best answer that question is standing right here," I said, directing John's attention to Sharon.

"Sharon Polster is in charge of scheduling rescues," I explained as I looked at the camera. "And she'll tell you what our greatest need is right now."

Sharon was ready. Her hands found her hips, her jaw jutted forward, and there was no hesitation as she began. "We need boats," she declared. "See these animals in this warehouse?" she said as the camera followed her lead. "They arrived this morning, because we had boats that could get to where they were stranded. But we will need more boats if we are going to be able to rescue all the animals that are still out there in flooded areas."

"What kind of boats do you need?" John asked.

"We need at least fifteen johnboats, flat-bottomed boats that can make it through shallow water and yet still handle some current," she explained as she stared into the camera.

"How can people get ahold of you?"

"They can call us," she said, pointing to the phone area. "See those ladies back there? Give them a call now."

I had to laugh as I watched. Sharon was a natural.

John turned and stared at the camera. "You heard the lady. If you have a johnboat, and the time to operate it, these people need your help *now*. Call them at the number you see on your screen, and do something that will not only help animals, but people too."

"Thank you, Terri," John said as he lowered the microphone. "I applaud you and the volunteers for doing a job that certainly needed to be done."

After the microphone and camera were turned off, John shook my hand and then handed me his business card. "If there is anything else we can do to help, let us know. My number is on the card."

"Thanks," I said as I put the card in my pocket. "I really appreciate the offer."

That was the first of many interviews that followed in the next couple of weeks. It accomplished exactly what I'd wanted it to: we got our boats, enabling us to respond to all the rescue requests that we received during the time we were in the warehouse.

Ben's press releases also caught the attention of CNN, *The Washington Post,* the *Today* show, *The Los Angeles Times,* National Public Radio, Nickelodeon, and *The Wall Street Journal,* and ABC picked me as their Person of the Week. It was an amazing response that even surprised Ben.

Our plan had worked.

I only wished we'd had the same plan in place during the weeks we had had the MASH unit set up in Florida. What a difference it would have made, not only for the animals, but for a lot of their owners too. During those six weeks, we could not get the attention of the media. There were a few reporters who stopped by, who thought what we were doing was great, but they couldn't get their assignment editors to agree. They were told to report on stories that would help people, not animals.

If the television and radio stations and the newspapers had understood how interrelated people and animals are, they would have realized that by including information about animals in their stories, they would have been doing a lot to help people too. The exclusion of animals resulted in people not knowing that we had free pet food to give out, so animals starved. Injured animals were killed because owners didn't know they could get free medical care at the MASH unit. People reluctantly gave up pets because they didn't have a temporary place to keep their animals, not knowing we could have taken care of them. If the media had used their incredible resources to communicate for us, a lot more animals would not have suffered or died.

Eventually, there were a couple of articles that appeared in some of the newspapers, but they came too late to help the animals who had so desperately needed medical care, food, and shelter in the beginning, when it was impossible for us, alone, to communicate with the people in Dade County.

That was why, when I returned from Florida, I made an appointment with Tom Black, who was news bureau manager at Santa Clara University. I had never dealt with the media, and I didn't have a clue about how to grab their attention, conduct an effective interview, or how to get past being nervous in front of a camera. That was when Tom put me in touch with Ben Sherman.

As Ben said during our first meeting, "I'll get the reporters to your door. Then it's up to you to tell them what *they* need to know."

And that's what I did during the flood of 1993.

The stories that appeared in newspapers and magazines, plus the countless radio and television interviews that reached readers, listeners, and viewers across the States, and in some other countries, made it possible for us to do *everything* we needed to do to help the animals affected by the immediate crisis. But the media attention did something else too.

Because the media gave such a significant amount of coverage to the plight of animals during the flood, for the first time many people realized that animals can be victims during disasters too. The phone calls and letters that poured in from all over the country were from people supporting what we were doing, and they were also apologizing. Many of them admitted that they had never thought about what happened to animals during fires, earthquakes, floods, or hurricanes.

"I just thought the animals knew how to take care of themselves," wrote one woman from Portland, Oregon.

"It was always my impression that the Red Cross took care of the animals too," a man from New York City told me on the phone one afternoon. "Now I understand why they can't."

Out of Harm's Way

A young woman, who cried the entire time she was on the phone with one of our volunteers, couldn't apologize enough for being so ignorant. "Because I never heard animals mentioned on the news during previous disasters, I just figured they didn't need help," she said. "I now know how wrong I was, and it kills me to think of how many animals have died."

The flood of 1993 was a blessing in disguise for animals. It's unfortunate that not all the animals in the Midwest could be saved, but in future disasters more animals *will* survive because of what happened during those few weeks that the media helped us capture Americans' attention. We were able to educate a lot of people, and it'll be the animals in future disasters that benefit.

My thanks go out to the representatives of the press and to Ben Sherman for raising the public's level of awareness much more quickly than we could ever have done on our own. You were indeed effective allies.

41

The Unexpected

At the end of our first week in the warehouse, we had more than enough boats for the nonstop requests we were getting to rescue animals. It was a good thing too; because we needed every boat we could get when we got the call from farmer Dwyer.

"Terri," Sharon Polster shouted from across the packed warehouse. "I need you for a second."

I pushed my way through the crowd that was typical of a Saturday. All the volunteers who had full-time jobs during the week showed up to help on the weekends.

Sharon was standing with the phone pressed against her chest when I finally made it back to the phone area. "I think we're going to need some cowhands for this rescue," she said, grinning. "This farmer needs help herding his cows to higher ground. Apparently a levee broke near Harvester this morning, and the water is spreading across his property."

"Okay. Let me talk to him," I said as I reached for the phone.

I could immediately tell the situation was serious by the urgency in the farmer's voice. He said his cows were already standing in several inches of water, and at the rate the water was rising, they'd be swimming real quick.

Out of Harm's Way

"I'll get a team together, and we'll be there within the hour," I said after getting more information and directions.

As soon as I hung up, I raised my hands to my mouth and shouted, "Steve. Lauren. Mark. John. Alonzo."

As soon as they heard their names they stopped what they were doing and gathered in the rescue staging area. They'd been hanging around since early that morning, waiting to respond to a rescue, and I suspected this was going to be one that would keep all of us busy for most of the morning.

Two other men also joined the group when they heard me gathering the rescue teams. Frank Johnston and Ed Walsh, a photographer and a reporter, respectively, for *The Washington Post,* had been hanging around the warehouse, waiting for a story. Their news sense told them this just might be the story they'd been hoping for.

"Okay. Listen up," I said as the group gathered in closer. "There's a farmer out in Harvester, which is about twenty minutes southwest from here, who needs help herding his cattle to dry ground. They aren't swimming yet, but it won't be much longer before they are."

"How many cows are there?" Mark asked.

"He's got thirty head," I replied. "And one of them, he's particularly concerned about. Her name is Jeannie, and apparently his grandson shows her at the fair each year."

"Well, let's go get them then," Mark said with all the enthusiasm of a cowboy.

"I'm ready to lasso a few myself," John said. "We got any ropes?"

The team grabbed some ropes and other equipment they thought they might need before we filed out of the warehouse and jumped into the trucks with boats attached. These guys were getting good. Their response time was getting quicker with each rescue, which improved the chances of getting to the animals that needed help before they drowned.

We were supposed to meet farmer Dwyer on the Katy Trail, which was the closest we could get to his farm by vehicle. From that point on, we'd have to go by boat. An hour after the initial phone call came in, we were parked along the trail looking for our farmer.

We'd just gotten out of the trucks when we spotted a man in worn coveralls waving his arms. The man approached with an urgent stride.

"I'm sure glad to see you-all. Ken Dwyer and his friend waited as long as they could, but the water was getting so high. They've gone ahead to do what they can, so they asked me to stay here and take you to where they are."

Midwest Flood

I didn't have to tell the rest of the team what to do. They were already backing their trucks toward the water so that we could get our three boats launched—a job they did in record time.

"Which direction are we headed?" I asked the coverall-clad man as I scanned the vast expanse of water spread before us.

"They should be on the other side of that tree line," the man said, pointing to the row of old sycamore trees that were already half submerged in water.

"Okay. We'll be ready as soon as they get the last boat in the water," I said as I watched John and Steve sliding the boat off the trailer.

The ride was bumpy—and dangerous. Enormous tree trunks rushed by like uncontrolled submarines armed to destroy. We swerved to miss several while still keeping an eye out for whirlpools and water moccasins. I could see from the intense expressions on the faces of the guys steering the boats that this was no Disneyland ride.

Everyone was quiet, absorbed in their own thoughts, as we followed close behind one another. This area had flooded so quickly that I wondered if the wildlife had had time to escape the raging water. Animals that could climb were quickly running out of upper tree limbs to find refuge on as the trees disappeared out of view.

"Oh, Christ." Lauren's sudden yell startled me.

Her gaze directed my eyes toward the faded green cab of a John Deere tractor, barely breaking the surface of the water. A soaking wet fox had taken refuge on the only thing he'd been able to reach that was still above water. We assumed the tractor was sitting on high ground, or maybe it had been driven up onto the back of some kind of flatbed trailer, otherwise, there was no way the tractor would still be partially visible.

Before we could even think of what to do to help the fox, it jumped into the water and was swept away by the current.

Lauren summed up all of our feelings with one word, "Damn."

But there was no time to mourn the loss. We were approaching the tree line, where menacing branches, some as thick as a weight lifter's arm, hung low as if waiting to bat us out of the boats. We crouched low and kept our eyes pointed forward as we slowly passed through the tree line. *The Washington Post* guys, new to rescue work, followed our example.

Once we cleared the trees, we were not surprised to discover more water, spread out in all directions as far as we could see. We were beginning to wonder if all of Missouri was going to be swallowed up by water before the flood was over. On a knoll about a mile ahead of us was a barn that was still above water, though. We assumed it was where farmer Dwyer intended to take his cows, since some of the ground surrounding the red building was still dry. But for how much longer?

"There they are," our guide shouted.

About half a mile to our right was a single boat following behind a herd of slow-swimming cows. I immediately thought of the cattle drives I'd seen in old western movies; only this time it wasn't the Rio Grande or the Colorado River that the cows were being herded across. Instead, these cattle were crossing a cornfield hidden beneath at least ten feet of Missouri River water pouring in through an opening in a collapsed levee, and we could tell these *cowboys* needed help.

As we approached the boat, I guess that farmer Dwyer and his friend were both in their late sixties. They both wore wrinkled tan work shirts with rolled-up sleeves, under wide, faded brown suspenders, which held up soggy green work pants. The only difference in their dress was the light blue fisherman's hat, its circular brim turned up, that the farmer wore over his gray hair.

"Mr. Dwyer," I yelled over the sound of the motors. "I'm Terri."

"Glad to see you-all," farmer Dwyer said. An accompanying smile spread across his creased face, weathered by years of laboring in the sun.

"Is that one hurt?" I asked, referring to the large brown-and-white cow with the rope around its neck being pulled alongside the farmer's boat.

"No. She's fine," he explained. "This here's my Jeannie."

"Okay. What do you want us to do?" I asked, since this was my first cattle drive.

"Why don't you divide up," farmer Dwyer said as our boats hovered near his. "We'll stay behind the herd, where we are now, and two of you get on the left side of the cows and the other on the right with my friend, and that should help keep them in line."

The rescue team got their instructions and before they took their places, farmer Dwyer had one more word of caution, "Keep an eye on the six calves. They seem to be doing okay now, but they'll be the first ones to tire."

The boats eased into place, and the crews on board each of them kept a watchful eye on the cows as they continued their swim toward the distant barn. Since they were cooperating so well, we had to assume they, too, wanted to get back onto dry land as quickly as possible. Occasionally the lead cow would let out a loud *mooooo* as if to reassure the rest of the herd it wasn't much further.

Our journey was going well, but it was about to take an unexpected detour.

John was the first to spot them. His keen eyes had focused on something unusual. About three hundred yards to our left was what looked like a string of giant pink fishing floaters, bobbing up and down in the water.

"What's that over there?" John asked when the boat I was in got up close alongside his.

I shaded my eyes from the glare off the water and looked in the direction he was pointing.

"I can't tell," I replied. "It doesn't look like logs."

Farmer Dwyer then noticed John and I, staring off in the distance. After a quick glance in that direction, he told us what the mysterious objects in the water were.

"Those must be my hogs," shouted the farmer as he brought his boat up closer.

He had not mentioned any hogs when I talked with him on the phone earlier that morning.

"How many do you have?" I asked.

"Nine," he replied, matter-of-factly.

I estimated they must have been swimming for at least an hour, and I guessed they wouldn't last much longer.

"Can you take the cows the rest of the way now that your friend is here with his boat?" I asked farmer Dwyer.

"I think so," was his response as he judged the distance to the barn. "We don't have much farther to go, and the cows seem to be holding up okay."

"Good. Then we'll go see if we can get your hogs," I said, figuring we had enough people aboard each of the three boats to be able to grab all nine of them.

We reached the exhausted hogs just in time. They were already starting to sink, and I suspected they wouldn't have lasted another five minutes. There was not a moment to waste, so we had to do some pretty quick thinking. It took just a split second to rule out dragging the hogs into the boats. The water was too deep for us to be able to touch the bottom, so we would have had to stay in the boats and pull the hogs in over the sides. We realized that this would have ensured all of us going for a swim, something we preferred not to do.

Thank goodness Mark was with us. I learned, for the first time, that he'd grown up around hogs, and it was his knowledge of these animals that made me realize he was the best person to direct this rescue. He did a superb job of taking control of the situation.

"Everyone grab a hog and hang on to them by their ears," Mark yelled. "We've got to keep their noses above water."

Each boat was responsible for three hogs. It took some tricky maneuvering by John, Alonzo, and Steve to round up the scattered hogs, but eventually we'd collected them all. My fingers were clamped around the ears of a huge male, and I was pulling back on them to keep his head above water as I wondered what came next.

"Now what do we do, Mark?" I shouted, straining at the same time to hang on to the ears of the three-hundred-pound animal. The rest of the rescue team were eager for instructions too. We were already beginning to realize we had a big problem on our hands.

"Get a rope tied behind their shoulders," Mark instructed. "And keep your fingers away from their mouths, or they'll bite them off."

Thank goodness we had four people in every boat, including Frank and Ed from *The Washington Post.* I'd noticed in all the confusion that they had immediately laid down their camera and reporter's pad and pitched in to help. I was impressed with their genuine concern.

The fourth person making up each of the teams was the person steering. It was his or her job to assist with getting the ropes around each animal, while the rest of us hung on to the hogs, which already seemed to have doubled in weight.

It seemed an eternity before I heard the crews of the other two boats yell, "We did it," as the last rope got tied around a hog's shoulders and the excess rope draped across the inside of the boat. If we lost hold of a hog's ears, we could use the rope to reel the animal back.

"Now what, Mark?" I asked as my arm began to shake from the strain of the hog's weight. I could only be grateful that the hog was not putting up a fight yet. If he did decide he'd had enough of this, I wondered if I'd be able to hold on to him. I suspected I wouldn't. For the first time, I began to realize, we might have to let these guys go.

"We'll drag 'em along the side of the boat and head back toward the barn," Mark replied. "And try and keep the boats under five knots, so the wake doesn't spray up in the hogs' faces." The guys behind the wheel of the boats could only promise Mark they'd try.

Everyone repositioned themselves, trying to get as comfortable as possible for the ride back to the barn. We had a distance of about a half a mile to go, which under normal circumstances wouldn't have been far, but this, obviously, was not your normal situation. Not only did we have nine hundred pounds of drag slowing us down, but we were also going against the current.

Within too short a time, I was feeling the strain of towing the hog. The muscles in my back and shoulders ached, and my arms, from the elbow down, shuddered. The back of my forearms were forced to rest against the edge of the boat, and I could feel the hot metal cutting into my skin. My legs were cramping from being wedged awkwardly between the boat seat and a metal toolbox. Filthy floodwater sprayed into my eyes and nostrils, and I had no free hand to wipe it away. The sun was burning every spot of my exposed skin, and I could hear the buzz of relentless mosquitoes as they took advantage of my inability to swat them away.

The faces in the other boats mirrored my pain. I wanted to cry and so did everyone else, but we couldn't. We were not willing to give up yet, because if we did, the hogs would certainly drown.

"Alonzo, can you give it more gas?" I screamed.

"I've got it full throttle." I could hear the frustration in his voice.

I closed my eyes, gritted my teeth, and hung on, as did everyone else.

It took over an hour, but we saved all nine hogs.

Farmer Dwyer was at the barn waiting for us when we hauled the last one ashore. The worn-out hogs hightailed it to the back side of the barn, where they joined the cows, who by then were dry and busy munching on some feed.

"I can't thank you-all enough for what you've done," farmer Dwyer said as the rescue team collapsed on the ground, unaware of the frogs scrambling to keep from getting squashed.

I mustered up enough energy to speak for the group, "We were happy to help out."

I only wished farmer Dwyer had not believed the Army Corps of Engineers when they told him days earlier that the levee that bordered his property was secure and he didn't have to worry, it wouldn't give out from the force of the rising river. As a precaution, he could have moved his livestock before the animals were forced to swim.

Satisfied, that the cows and hogs were safe, we left farmer Dwyer that afternoon, never expecting to see him again, but he called us two days later.

"The waters come up higher than I expected," he explained. "The hogs are already chest deep in water. I need help getting them to the Katy Trail."

Out of Harm's Way

We responded with six boats, a large-animal veterinarian, and some hefty volunteer muscle power. This time we were going to be prepared.

Farmer Dwyer was waiting for us on the trail when our caravan of vehicles and boats arrived. The trucks each had a yellow flashing light on top, and on the doors were those red-and-white magnetic signs that read, "EMERGENCY ANIMAL RESCUE SERVICE."

"You really brought the troops," farmer Dwyer said as I approached him and his two friends that I recognized from our first rescue. "If you-all follow me out there, I'll show you where to wait while I go up to the barn and see where the animals are. I'm afraid if too many boats approach at once, it might spook them and scatter them into deeper water."

It sounded like a good plan.

The swift current we'd experienced on our first rescue had nearly disappeared. The surface of the water was almost still as our fleet of rescue boats followed behind farmer Dwyer's boat. The familiar smell of fermenting corn now blended with the stench of raw sewage, dead fish, gasoline, motor oil, pesticides, and, worst of all, the smell of death, making me think of the fox.

At the designated spot, farmer Dwyer instructed us to drop anchor. Our bows bumped up against one another as we floated silently in the sun waiting for the farmer to return. It was too hot to even talk.

On the distant horizon I stared at the towering skyscrapers of downtown Clayton, seemingly peeking over the treetops to get a look at the destruction caused by this flood that they had managed to escape. I'd heard on the radio that morning that forty percent of St. Charles County was now underwater, and I was sitting at that moment with twenty volunteers, in six boats, on a very small percentage of it.

"I think while we're waiting," Mark announced to the quiet group, "I should give you a crash course in hog calling."

"You're kidding?" John laughed.

"No. I think we need to know how to properly call hogs in case the ones we're about to rescue start to scatter," Mark replied with all the seriousness of someone who knew what he was talking about. "And I think there are a few more things you should know about hogs."

"Okay, Mark," Lauren piped up. "How do you call a hog?"

"By their name of course," Steve offered.

The group found the energy to laugh at that one as Mark continued his Hog 101 course.

2 7 6

"First of all, you need to know you never pull a hog. They're ornery creatures, and if you try pulling them, they will not budge," Mark said, scanning the faces of his pupils. "They can be backed up against a pitchfork and if you try pulling, they will continue to back up into the sharp points."

"So what do you do?" Dara asked.

"You push 'em," Mark replied. "You slap 'em on their butts, put your shoulder to their rears, even bite them on their hindquarters." Mark paused for the expected laugh. "Anything will work, just as long as you don't pull 'em."

"So when do we call them?" Steve inquired.

"I bet you didn't know that calling scares them," Mark responded. "They run away when they hear you yell *SOO-EEEY.* You just have to make sure you have them headed in the right direction when you start calling."

"How'd you do that again?" I asked Mark.

Our expert cupped his sun-browned hands around his mouth, and in a voice I'm sure they could hear clear over in Clayton, he yelled, *"SOO-EEEY. SOO-EEEY. SOO-EEEY. SOO-EEEY."*

As each of the volunteers, one-by-one, placed hands around his or her mouth, Mark gave us one more bit of explanation. "You say it real long and drawn out, then you yell *HAA—HAA.* And that's how it's done."

"Do it one more time, Mark—all together," Ed asked.

"SOO-EEEY. SOO-EEEY. SOO-EEEY. SOO-EEEY. HAA—HAA!" Mark sang out like a soprano performing to an audience of attentive listeners.

When farmer Dwyer returned, he must have thought we'd been in the sun too long. Sitting in a cluster in the middle of the lake that covered what used to be his cornfield were twenty adults in boats, screaming at the top of their lungs, *"SOO-EEY. SOO-EEEY. SOO-EEEY. SOO-EEEY. HAA—HAA!"* and there wasn't a hog in sight.

We quickly quieted down when we realized the farmer had returned. After all, this man had just lost his home, his personal belongings, his crops, his barn, and all his farming equipment. This disaster had destroyed almost everything he owned. It was now our job to make sure he didn't lose his animals too.

Farmer Dwyer told us his plan as we tried to imagine what it must be like to have your life turned upside down, practically overnight.

277

"The way I see it, we have no choice but to swim the cows to shore, which is a distance of about a mile and a half," farmer Dwyer began. "The calves and the hogs we'll have to put in the boats."

"Are all the animals we left at the barn two days ago still there?" I asked.

"Yeah. There are thirty-nine in total, and they are getting pretty skittish," farmer Dwyer said as he pulled a crumpled handkerchief out of his back pocket and wiped the sweat from his forehead.

"They have only two easy escape routes from the island they are on behind the barn. The barn and my silo block the two other directions," he explained, using his hands to show us the position of the natural barricades. "We need people and boats to spread out across the openings to the right and to the left of the barn, so that the animals don't scatter in those directions. If they do, and they get out into the deeper water, I'm afraid we've lost them."

"How are we going to get to the barn without spooking the animals with our motors?" Steve asked.

"I thought we'd just use the trolling motors to reach the front of the barn, then once we're in water shallow enough to wade through, we'll cut the motors and pull the boats into place," farmer Dwyer explained. "The water that the animals are standing in now is about two-feet deep."

"Then I guess we need to divide into two groups to cover the two escape routes," I concluded. "Three boats can go around the right side of the barn, and three boats can go around the left side."

"Right. And I'll wade back first and then give the order for you to start moving toward the animals, at the same time, from both directions, so that we can grab the six calves, the nine hogs, and Jeannie first," farmer Dwyer said, looking at the group to make sure we understood the plan. "Once we get those animals moved out of there, then we'll start swimming the cows."

"Well, let's go get them," Mark yelled, tired of all the talking.

Anchors were pulled up, and the electric trolling motors were switched on. All seven boats moved as quietly as possible toward the barn as the occupants of each one prayed we'd be able to pull this rescue off with no losses.

Farmer Dwyer did an excellent job of orchestrating the rescue. Boats and volunteers quickly cut off the animals' escape routes and eventually reduced their refuge to a manageable area. One by one the calves were cornered, roped, lifted by four men into a boat, and laid on their sides while their legs were tied together. Blindfolds were made from bandannas and then placed over the calves' eyes. On the trip back to shore, two volunteers sat on the calves, hoping they wouldn't decide halfway through the ride to try and stand up.

It took almost two hours to transport and load all six calves into a waiting horse trailer so that they could be taken to the fairgrounds where they were to be kept until farmer Dwyer found a more permanent location.

Now it was time for the hogs. The majority of the volunteers had kept them and the cows confined while the calves were being transported, two at a time, back to shore. As we attempted to corner the first hog, we learned something that Mark had failed to tell us in Hog 101—these creatures can be *very* noisy. The scream of a frightened hog measures at the same decibel level as a roaring jet engine.

In spite of the noise, we were able to capture all but one of the hogs, which we loaded into the boats, hog-tied and transported back to the shore. The loss of the ninth hog was unexpected.

Mark and Steve were trying to get this last one cornered, when all of a sudden it fell over on its side. Instantly, both men dropped to their knees and, in the waist-deep, filthy water, lifted the hog's head and chest above the water. Steve began pumping the hog's chest while Mark blew into its mouth. They repeated their efforts time, after time, but it was no use; the hog was dead. By the time the vet was able to reach Mark and Steve, there was nothing he could do.

We pushed the dead hog far enough into the water to be picked up by the current, and we all stood and watched as he floated downstream. The carcass would probably wash up on shore on some island of refuge, so other animals stranded by the flood could eat and stay alive. Once again, nature took one to save another.

A call from farmer Dwyer a few days later was to report that all the cows which we'd successfully swam to shore, had been moved from the fairgrounds to a pasture where they could stay until he decided what he was going to do—a decision complicated by the fact that he had no flood insurance

Jeannie was going to be entered in the fair as planned, and she was expected to earn another blue ribbon. Farmer Dwyer's grandson thought every one of his grandfather's cows deserved a gold medal, like the Olympic swimmers.

The nine hogs were taken to slaughter the day after we rescued them. It was difficult news to accept, especially when we'd risked our lives and worked so hard to save them from drowning. But there was nothing we could do. They were Farmer Dwyer's hogs.

42

Monique

"Well, it looks like my husband has a new lady in his life," Valerie said as she stood beside me with her arms crossed against her chest.

I had to agree when I followed her gaze to the far end of the crowded warehouse. A tall, brown-haired man was involved in earnest conversation with a blond female. The object of their discussion appeared to be an almond-eyed nanny goat that stood between them contentedly munching on a green apple.

Valerie was one of our veteran volunteers, having attended my first training class and arriving almost every day after that to help out. She was a quiet woman in her early forties who was always thinking of ways she could do more to help the animals. One of those ideas included her husband.

I remembered when I first met Ed. Valerie had put her arm around her husband's shoulders and pushed him forward as she'd introduced him. "This is my better half," she explained with a mischievous grin on her tanned face. "He wants to help us this weekend."

I looked at Ed and asked, "Is that right?"

"Yeah, I guess so. I made the mistake of asking my wife what she wanted for her birthday," Ed said with an easygoing smile. "And I should have known she wouldn't ask for something like jewelry or fine perfume."

All three of us laughed as Ed went on to describe what he'd been coerced into giving his wife.

"Val said you-all need boats, and I've got one. So, I'm here to offer my services."

"Good," I said. "We sure can use you *and* your boat."

"Mine is a V bottom, which rides better in swift current," Ed offered. "So use me for the tougher rescues."

I promised him I would.

From that day on, Ed came every weekend and on the occasional evening when he could get away early from his sign business. Valerie's gift grew to much more than she had expected, and the animals benefited at the same time.

One of the animals that Ed helped rescue that first weekend was a goat with persuasive eyelashes.

"We've got to get out of here," the woman on the phone screamed. "Our house is going under. Someone's got to come and get our goat." The frantic woman paused for a moment to holler at some noisy kids in the background before giving one of our telephone volunteers the rest of the information.

"She's an indoor nanny, and we've got nowhere to take her."

"Did you say an *indoor goat?*" the volunteer asked, certain she'd misunderstood the woman.

"Yes," she replied as if having a goat indoors was as normal as bringing a dog or cat inside.

"Okay," the volunteer responded with skepticism in her voice. "Where do you live?" The volunteer took down the rest of the information and hung up, still shaking her head.

"Ed," the volunteer yelled. "Have I got a rescue for you."

Ed gathered his rescue team, which included the blond woman, and they set out to find the nanny that lived in the house, half expecting that this was some kind of joke.

An hour later the rescue team returned to the warehouse with a brown-and-tan goat in tow. "We found her tied to the mailbox at the end of the road," Ed explained as he stood in front of the crowded intake area with the goat at his side. "I swear she reminded me of Claudette Colbert in that movie *It Happened One Night,*" Ed mused. "You know, that part where Claudette stood by the side of the road and lifted her skirt to try and hitch a ride with Clark Gable. Except Monique—"

"Monique!" the intake volunteer exclaimed. "Who's Monique?"

"The goat, of course," Ed said, eager to continue his story. "Monique just lifted her hoof and batted her eyelashes to get our attention. Have you seen how long her lashes are?"

The goat became the object of everyone's attention as Ed pointed to Monique's eyes.

"Looks like what you should be paying attention to are those udders," Mark, our farm-animal expert, suggested. "This goat needs to be milked . . . and soon."

"How do you milk a goat?" Dara asked.

"It can't be much different then milking a cow," Lois, the blond woman, concluded. "I'll give it a try."

Lois scouted the warehouse and found a plastic crate to use as a stool and an empty litter box to catch the milk, which she positioned underneath Monique. With udders in hand, Lois pulled, then squeezed. It took only two more tugs before a stream of goat milk hit the litter box and splattered Ed, who was standing real close to make sure Lois didn't tug too hard.

"Won't need to buy milk for dinner tonight," one of the onlookers laughed. We all decided a tall glass of ice-cold tea sounded a whole lot more appealing than warm goat's milk, especially out of a litter box.

"Ed, try this," Lois said as she glanced over her shoulder.

Ed was quick to take Lois's place on the stool. He seemed to have a real knack for milking, because the litter pan filled up quickly, in spite of his stopping after every few tugs to ask Monique if she was okay. She seemed to have no complaints.

The next morning, I was surprised to find Ed waiting outside the warehouse door. When I got out of my van, I asked him where Valerie was.

"I couldn't wait for her," he said with a hint of urgency in his voice. "She'll be here in a bit though."

I couldn't imagine what Ed had to do that was so important. As I was unlocking the door, I asked him how his goat was doing.

"Fine, I expect. That's why I'm here," Ed said as he moved closer to the door. "I'm sure she needs to go for a walk."

I wondered if this fifteen-year-old indoor nanny goat was accustomed to going for morning walks, especially on the end of a leash. I'd soon find out.

Ed was through the door before me, and it took him no time to hook a leash onto Monique's collar and head outside. I stood in the doorway watching as the two of them trotted off down the block—Monique behaving as though she'd recently graduated from obedience school.

"She won't eat grass," was Ed's conclusion upon their return. "But she loves elm tree leaves."

The indoor goat had other definite likes and dislikes we learned. Apples and cold pizza were at the top of her list of favorite foods. Our goat definitely didn't want to be kept in a pen, either, but rather preferred to mingle with the people in the warehouse. When Ed was around, she followed him like a lovesick fiancée temporarily ignoring everyone else. But once he left, she expected to be petted by everyone who passed. If you ignored her, she'd nudge up against your hand to remind you of what you should be doing. And I swear that goat really did bat her eyelashes when she thought it would get her something she wanted.

As Valerie and I stood watching the trio across the room, she shared with me something else she'd observed about Ed. "You know, this experience has changed things for Ed and me."

I waited to hear how.

"The real reason I asked Ed to bring his boat out of dry dock and come help us was that I wanted him to understand how important this experience has been for me," Valerie said as she looked across the room at her husband. "But I got so much more. Ed and I have learned new things about one another, and it's brought us closer. We have a good marriage, but I feel that this experience has made it even stronger."

The look on Valerie's face was full of admiration for her husband, who now was kneeling beside the almond-eyed nanny goat offering her another green apple.

"As I said earlier, my husband has a new lady in his life . . . and I couldn't be happier."

43

Reacting

"Boy, did you ever miss some excitement," Steve Prince teased as I sat down next to him on a stack of dog food bags and aimed my sweaty face toward the industrial fan that bellowed like a jet engine. "You'll be sorry you went home when you hear about the rescue we responded to on Thursday."

It had been a difficult decision to return to California for three days. The level of activity in the warehouse had not shown the slightest decline, but I knew I had to go home to be with my mom. August 4 had been the first anniversary of my uncle Kenny's death, and I wanted to spend the day with my family, remembering the uncle who'd been like a father to me.

I left feeling confident the volunteers could handle things while I was gone, and I was about to learn what a good job they'd done in my absence.

"Okay," I replied as I pulled my hair up off my neck so the air from the fan could reach it. "What did I miss?"

"You were probably flying over Colorado when the phone call came in," Steve guessed. "Sharon Polster knew immediately we had a big problem—so she called me at home."

Steve had been feeling pretty beat after putting in four sixteen-hour days of volunteer work, so he'd gone home earlier that morning to take a nap, promising he'd be back by two. His nap ended up being a short one.

"Steve, I need you back down here real fast," she's said with an urgency in her voice that made Steve sit up on the bed and reach for his jeans as Sharon began to explain what was going on.

"A guy called just a few minutes ago, and he was madder than hell." Sharon's voice was shaking as she spoke. "Apparently there are six stray goats, four horses, and a donkey who have taken refuge in a front yard on Lake Weber Road, and the animals are tearing up the grass. This guy said if we didn't get out there and get them, he'd get rid of them with his gun."

"What!" Steve yelled. "Did he kill any?"

"He didn't say that he had, but I wouldn't be surprised if you guys find some dead animals when you get out there."

"I'll be right over."

Steve arrived at the warehouse twenty minutes later to find Dara, John, and Kim, a recent veterinarian-school graduate, waiting for him. They had already gathered equipment for the rescue, and now they were just waiting for further instructions from Sharon. It had already been decided that they would go out to Lake Weber Road and do their best to defuse the situation, and then determine what would be needed to get the animals safely out of there.

"What's the latest?" Steve asked the group.

"Sharon is on the phone talking to one of the guy's neighbors right now," Dara said, looking up for a second before she returned to studying the map of St. Charles County that she had spread out on top of an airline crate. "Does anyone know where Lake Weber Road is?" she asked. "I can't find it anywhere on this map."

"It's spitting distance from Hideaway Harbor, where I keep my sailboat," Steve said as he pointed it out. "I was out there three days ago to check on my boat, and the water was getting pretty deep."

"How long will it take us to get there once we're in the boats?" John asked.

"Maybe ten minutes," Steve estimated. "It'll depend on how strong the currents are."

"Sharon just got off the phone," Dara interrupted.

The group watched as she hurried across the warehouse toward them, anxious to go before the trigger-happy guy hurt any of the animals.

"Okay. This is what I know," Sharon said when she joined the group. "I was on the phone with a woman who lives next door to the man with the gun, and she said, the guy, along with some of the other neighbors, are now shooing the animals back into the water."

"I don't believe it," Steve said in disgust.

"It seems these people are now upset because the goats are climbing up on the roofs of their partially submerged cars."

"As if the cars aren't already totaled from the water," Kim interjected as she smeared sunscreen on her arm.

"What's wrong with these people that they don't want to help those poor animals?" Dara asked, shaking her head.

"I don't know," Sharon replied. "But the good part is, Peggy just talked to the guy who owns the animals. What a strange coincidence that he'd call when he did. He said the water had swept the animals downstream before he'd had a chance to evacuate them, and he was calling to ask if we could help him find them."

Sharon had kept Peggy updated on what was happening on Lake Weber Road, so when Peggy learned where the owner lived and what he was missing, she put two and two together. The goats, horses, and donkey had to be his.

"The owner, a man named Ron, is going to meet you at Orchard Park. He's on his way there now," Sharon said, handing the completed rescue form to Dara. "You guys better get going."

"We're out of here," Steve said.

"You guys be safe out there," Sharon yelled as the four rescuers grabbed their gear and headed out the door.

When the team arrived at the rendezvous point, they spotted a man in his mid-thirties standing alongside the road, nervously smoking a cigarette. His graying hair was pulled back in a ponytail, exposing a forehead etched with deep frown lines. He dropped the butt on the ground and snuffed it out with the toe of his boot as the rescue team pulled up.

There was no time for introductions. Ron jumped into the back of John's truck, and the two rescue vehicles pulled back into traffic and headed for a spot where Steve knew they could launch both his and John's boats.

While the guys backed their boat trailers toward the water with Kim's help, Dara told Ron what she knew about the animals. As he listened he lit up another Camel.

"The goats are my daughter's 4-H project," he said, releasing the smoke he'd just inhaled. "I was trying to get my buddy's truck to haul them in, but the water rose too quickly," Ron said as the lines on his forehead deepened. He took another drag off his cigarette and watched the guys unhooking John's boat from the trailer.

"If that bastard kills any of my animals, he'll be looking at the end of a gun," Ron said grimly.

With both boats in the water, the team took their seats and headed toward Lake Weber Road, uncertain as to whether the animals they were speeding to rescue were still alive.

The sound of people yelling directed the rescue team to the location.

"*Shoo.* Get out of here."

"Hey, you dumb goat, move."

"You better not come back up here if you know what's good for you."

Then they heard a loud *smack,* followed by a shrill neigh, and they guessed someone was hitting one of the horses.

Steve and John, gave the boats more gas, while the group hoped that the next sound they heard wouldn't be that of gunfire. When the boats turned onto Lake Weber Road, Dara was the first to holler. "There they are!"

Immediately, the group started counting animals that were spread out in every direction. One, two, three, four, five, six. The goats were all still alive, and the horses and the donkey were standing too.

"Thank God," Ron said as he used the back of his hand to rub under his eyes. "They're mine."

The sound of the approaching boats caught the attention of the neighbors who had ganged up on the defenseless animals to protect their yards. They stopped what they were doing as the animals continued to thrash through the knee-deep water.

Dara moaned as her eyes began to fill with tears. "Those poor animals are absolutely terrified."

"Yeah. And see that young goat over there," Kim said, pointing toward the tiny creature. "It's having a hard time keeping its head above water. We better grab it first."

By now the boats were scraping bottom. Ron didn't wait for Steve to shut off the engine and tie up. He jumped out of the boat and splashed through the water, desperate to retrieve his animals. Meanwhile Kim and Dara tied the two boats to a mailbox, while the crowd of angry neighbors approached.

"Well, it's about time you people got here," said a man with a beer belly and red face.

"You should see what these animals have done to our yards," another man, wearing a St. Louis Cardinals T-shirt, added.

Steve bit his tongue to keep from telling the man what he thought of him and his damn yard. These people were already agitated enough, and at that point, all that mattered was getting those animals out of there alive.

"Folks, we'll take care of the animals," Steve said to the group. "Just give us a few minutes."

"Well, make it fast," the red-faced guy said. "Or else those goats will be back up here on our cars again."

"Okay. Okay," Steve said. "Let me go see what the plan is."

Steve joined the rest of the rescue team, who were gathered around the animals, trying to calm them down. Ron had managed to grab the small goat, and he stood cradling her in his arms. Kim was eyeing one of the horses who had an ugly, bleeding gash on its flank, probably inflicted by the earlier swat they'd heard. Every time she tried to approach it though, the horse would wade further into the water. She left it alone, hoping that when it calmed down, she'd be able to attend to the wound.

"All right," Dara said, "We'd better do something quick, because these people don't look like they have much patience left."

"Well, it's obvious we aren't going to get all these animals out of here by ourselves," Steve concluded. "I think we can take the goats now, and we'll have to come back for the rest."

"But, Steve, those horses and the donkey won't fit in our boats even after we unload the goats," Dara said. "We're going to need a barge or something to get them out of here."

"I know," said Steve, wiping the sweat from his sunburned forehead. "Once we get back to the warehouse, we'll have Sharon, our 'Boat Lady,' see what she can find for us."

Because the goats were so tired from being chased through the water by the neighbors, they had very little fight left in them. It took about twenty minutes to round up the other five and get ropes around their necks. While the rest of the rescue team led them to the boats, Steve returned to the group of neighbors.

"We're going to take the goats now and then come back with a larger boat and get the horses and the donkey. Until we return, *please do not torment those animals anymore.*"

"But what if they come back into our yards?" the Cardinals fan asked.

"Sir," Steve replied in a calm voice. "If I were you I wouldn't be worried about the horses destroying the yard. From the looks of things around here, I'm afraid your yard is going to be underwater before too long."

The neighbors were silent.

The ride back to shore was uneventful. The goats seemed to sense that these people had saved their lives, and they showed their appreciation by cooperating. Ron kept his herd of goats together while the boats were pulled out of the water and loaded onto their trailers once more. While Steve and John drove, Kim, Dara, and Ron rode in the back of the pickups with six goats that were grateful to be alive.

"Well, did you get them all?" Sharon asked as she met the trucks in the parking lot.

"We have the goats, but the horses and the donkey are still out there," Steve said, stepping down from the truck.

"Are they okay?" Sharon asked, hoping Steve wouldn't tell her they'd been shot.

"They're frightened, and one of the horses has a gash on its back end, but I think they'll be all right."

"Do you have someplace where we can keep these goats, since Ron doesn't have a barn or a pasture right now to keep them in?" Dara asked, still sitting in the truck with a rope in each hand, attached to two goats who were ready to eat and sleep.

"I have a farmer who has room for them," Sharon replied. "Let me get the address for you, and then I'll give him a call if you want to take them over there now."

"Sounds like a winner," John said, leaning against the side of the truck, with an ice-cold can of Coke pressed against his forehead.

"Before you go anywhere. I need to get their pictures," Wendy said as she joined the group with a Polaroid camera dangling from her arm. "And when you get back, we can complete the paperwork on this menagerie."

While the rescue team transported the goats to their temporary home, Sharon got on the phone to see if she could locate someone with a boat big enough to haul horses. Steve had suggested she call the Coast Guard, because he knew they had a floating ferry that would work.

"Okay, Boat Lady, did you dig us up an ark?" Steve asked when he returned from dropping off the goats.

Sharon looked up from the piece of paper she held in her hand, which had the list of names and phone numbers of the people who had offered their boats. "I'm afraid not. No one has anything big enough."

"Did you call the Coast Guard?"

"Called them first, but they said they couldn't help. Their ferry is being used for other things," Sharon said, anxiously tapping her pen on the top of the desk.

"Let me call them," Steve said, reaching for the phone. "I'm in the Coast Guard auxiliary, so maybe I can convince them to help us out."

Steve worked his way up through the chain of command, but the answer was still no.

"Now what are we going to do?" Steve asked as he hung up the phone. "It's getting late, and if we don't find something fast, those animals are going to have to stay out there another night—and by tomorrow there's probably not going to be any more dry land for them to stand on."

"I'll call the news people," Sharon blurted out. "Terri got them here when we needed boats before, so let's try it again."

While Sharon relayed the story to a reporter over the phone, Steve was on another line giving the news helicopter pilot directions to Lake Weber Road that he could follow from the air. They wanted to get some pictures of the stranded animals standing in the water, which everyone knew would greatly increase the chances of getting a big enough boat.

The story aired that evening, and once again people responded.

The fourth call was from a man offering his twenty-four-foot Carolina skiff, a boat Steve was familiar with. They're about ten feet wide, flat-bottomed, with very low sides and a square front. Steve and Joel, a volunteer familiar with horses, drove out to see the boat, and after they saw it, they knew they had their boat. It would be perfect for the job.

On their way back from looking at the boat, Steve detoured past a feed store to buy a couple bales of hay. With not more than an hour of daylight left, the guys realized it would be best to postpone the rescue until morning. There was still enough time left, though, to check on the animals, drop off the hay for them, and make sure the neighbors were leaving them alone.

The horses and the donkey were standing in ankle-deep water when Steve and Joel got back to Lake Weber Road. It was quiet, except for the hum of summer bugs and the sound of frogs. Steve thought the boat's motor would bring the neighbors back out of the houses that were surrounded by three-foot-high walls of sandbags, but no one appeared. It looked as though these people had finally given up and left.

Steve and Joel slowly approached the horses, and this time they didn't move. "These guys are in sorry shape," Joel said as he stood petting one of the females. "This is really a shame."

"Yeah. I just wish every horse owner could see these horses. It might make them realize why it's so important to have an evacuation plan for their own animals."

"I've known a lot of horse owners in my life, and I'm afraid most of them have this attitude of, it'll never happen to me," Joel said as he continued to stroke the horse. "Maybe this will make some of them realize it can."

The guys carried the bales of hay from the boat to what little dry ground still remained. Joel, who had recently moved to St. Charles from Wyoming, was a genuine cowboy, and he used the rope he'd tossed in the boat to lead each of the horses and the donkey to the dry patch of ground, where they immediately started to feed on the hay.

While the animals were eating, Joel squatted down and lifted one of the horses hoofs. "Steve, look at this," he said as he pressed his thumb against the hoof. "These horses have been standing in water so long their hooves are starting to get soft, and that can be crippling for a horse."

"Is it too late to do something to correct the problem?" Steve asked as he examined the hooves of the other animals and found that they were all in the same condition.

"No, I don't think so," Joel replied as he carefully lowered the horse's foot. "But if we can't get these horses out of here tomorrow, someone may be making the decision whether to euthanize them."

"Damn."

The guys stayed with the animals for as long as they could, and before they left, Steve patted each of them on the forehead as he told them to stay put. In a reassuring voice, he whispered, "I promise, we'll be back in the morning to get you out of here."

And Steve kept his promise.

The rescue team assembled at dawn. Steve, John, Ron, Dara, and Kim had been joined by Joel, Lauren, and a horse trainer who Ron thought might come in handy. The ninth member of the team was Sharon Polster.

"Sharon!" I said with real shock in my voice. "She went on the rescue!"

"Yes," Steve replied. "I was surprised too. When I got to the ware-

Midwest Flood

house that morning, she told me she had to go with us, because she thought the rescue might need some additional coordination from the field, and since you were in California, she felt it was her job to fill in for you."

"I can't believe it," I said, remembering Sharon's words the first day I met her, "I will do *anything* to help the animals, but I will not go out on a boat."

At first I had suspected Sharon did not know how to swim, but I later learned I was wrong.

A year earlier, Sharon's daughter and the family dog drowned in a boating accident, and Sharon had said then that she would never set foot in a boat again—but she did.

Sharon was indeed willing to do *anything* for the animals.

The rescue team sipped coffee as Steve ran through the plan. Sharon informed the group there would be five boats on the rescue, which included the two from the day before, plus the Carolina skiff and two Coast Guard escort vessels. The Guard had decided to help out after watching CBS's news broadcast.

By seven A.M. the team was ready to go. In the back of Steve's truck were several sheets of thick plywood for the horses and the donkey to use as a ramp to get into the skiff. Kim had grabbed some medical supplies so she could treat the horse with the gash. Joel brought his ropes and wore his cowboy hat. The *Marlboro Man* look-alike was ready to round up some horses.

"It was great. We looked like an armada," Steve said, his passion for boats obvious. "But I was concerned about Sharon."

"Why?" I asked.

"She was so quiet." He tried unsuccessfully to swat a fly that kept landing on his pant leg. "She just stared across the water with tears in her eyes. I knew she was worried about the horses and the donkey, but it seemed to be hitting her harder than I expected."

I wanted to tell Steve about Sharon's daughter, but I wasn't sure if she wanted anyone else to know.

"But I loosened Sharon up once we got to where the animals were." Steve chuckled.

"What did you do?"

"I stood up in my boat and pulled off my T-shirt," Steve explained. "Then I told Sharon she better get ready."

"For what?" Sharon had asked, puzzled.

"Didn't anyone tell you?" Steve asked with a serious look on his face.

"Tell me what?" Sharon said as she looked around at the other volunteers.

"To keep our clothes from getting drenched—we rescue naked." It took all his self-control, Steve told me, to keep from laughing.

"What!" Sharon shrieked. "Are you crazy?"

"We've been rescuing naked since the beginning," Lauren said, an innocent look on her face. "It's no big deal."

"Oh, my God," Sharon exclaimed as her face turned red. "You guys have to be kidding."

John, who had been listening to the conversation, finally had to turn his back to Sharon so she wouldn't see him trying to contain his laughter, but it was no use. He started laughing, and a second later Steve and Lauren joined in.

"I knew it," Sharon said as she started to laugh. "You guys are awful."

"Okay, let's go get those horses," Steve said. He pulled his T-shirt back on, stepped into the waist-deep water, and dragged the boat to a tree where he could tie it up.

The horses were still standing on their tiny patch of dry ground, but the noise from the larger boats made them scatter back into the water. Ron and Joel took off after the donkey. The plan was to transport the animals aboard the skiff one at a time, and the donkey got the first ride. Ron had made arrangements to borrow a truck and a horse trailer, which he used to transport the donkey to a friend's farm. Then he'd come back and wait to do the same with the horses.

While they waited for the skiff to return, Joel lassoed the injured horse, and Kim was able to do some preliminary cleaning of the wound on its flank. He was the next one to be ferried to shore.

It was just after noon when the third horse walked up the ramp into the skiff. So far the rescue had gone off without a hitch. The fact that the current was running slowly helped, not to mention having a team of people who knew what they were doing.

At last, there was just one horse left. With all the animals rounded up, it was time for everyone to return to shore.

The fleet of rescue boats had made it about halfway back when all of a sudden something must have spooked the last horse, and before anyone knew what was happening, the horse was over the side of the boat, along with Ron's horse-trainer friend, whose hand was caught in the horse's reins.

Joel was the first one in the water. "Ron's friend couldn't free his hand, so he was being dragged by the horse, who was snorting and swimming in circles because she was still wearing the blindfold we'd put on her when we loaded her aboard the skiff. In her panic she accidentally kicked Ron's friend in the shoulder, and the guy went under."

Joel dived under the water and managed to free the horse trainer's wrist from the reins, grab him under the armpits, and return to the surface, so that the Coast Guard could pull him aboard their boat.

"Was Ron's friend hurt?" I asked.

"He's a little sore but fine," Steve assured me.

Once Joel had felt it was safe, he'd inched his way back toward the swimming horse and eventually grasped her mane to help pull her head further out of the water, all the while talking to her in a soft, comforting voice.

At first the horse fought Joel as he slid onto her back, but she was unsuccessful in her attempts to buck him back into the water. He wrapped his arms around her neck and waited for the right moment to yank the blindfold away from the horse's eyes. As the blindfold came off the horse shook her head, but in a short time stopped trying to throw her rider. The onlookers applauded from their boats at Joel's amazing ability to control the horse.

"Okay, we'll have to swim it the rest of the way," Joel said as he leaned forward and slapped the horse lightly on her neck. "There's no way we'll ever get you back in that skiff again."

With no more fight from the horse, Joel successfully swam her the rest of the distance to shore. The rescue of the six goats, four horses, and one donkey was finally complete.

"See," Steve said as he got up from his seat atop the dog food bags, "I told you, you missed out. It was great, and I was mighty proud of my team."

I could see why.

44

Two Kinds of Stories

By the first week in August, the rescue volunteers had proven they no longer needed my supervision. They were now well-coordinated teams of talented individuals who knew how to safely rescue animals.

When I look back on the four weeks that I spent in St. Charles, I realize I don't have as many of my own rescue stories to tell, but the volunteers supplied me with plenty. In earlier disasters I had participated in nearly every rescue, because there were so few volunteers. It seemed funny to be hearing the stories secondhand in Missouri. There were two hundred and fifty people who came forward to help, and out of that number, seventy-five volunteers rescued animals. It was an impressive reply to our call for help, and it resulted in hundreds of animals being saved.

Missi was one of the best success stories.

We received a call from a deputy sheriff warning us that another mobile home park was about to be swallowed up by the river. The residents had been evacuated, but he suspected that some animals had been left behind.

While scouting the park, the team assigned to the rescue passed a man in a johnboat returning to his home for one last load of his personal belongings. They stopped and asked him if he'd seen any animals in the park.

"I know of one," he replied as he spit a wad of chewing tobacco into the already-filthy water. "My neighbors left their dog in the house. Said they didn't have room for her. If you want, you can follow me back to my place. I reckon they wouldn't mind you taking the dog."

"You would not believe how filthy the mobile home was," Dara said to me later, wrinkling her noise. "I don't think even cockroaches would want to live in it."

As I looked at the Yorkshire terrier that Dara cradled in her arms, the dog squirmed and struggled to scratch herself as fleas crisscrossed what little fur she hadn't yet scratched or chewed off. Bloody sores, from her constantly gnawing at her skin, were proof that the dog had probably never received any treatment for her flea problem.

"When we found her, she was sitting huddled in a corner of the living room, shaking," Dara explained. "She was the *only* thing the owners had left behind when they evacuated. They took all the furniture, the appliances, the drapes, the carpets, even the switch plates for the lights—but they left their dog."

This was Dara's first encounter with people who valued their belongings more than a pet. I remembered how tough it had been for me to accept this harsh reality during the flood in Alviso, and it hasn't gotten any easier as I've seen the same kind of indifference repeated in every disaster since.

"The guys were afraid she'd bite, but I knew she was just scared," Dara said, gently running her hand through the dirty fur. "I just started talking to her as I approached, and it didn't take long for her tail to start wagging. When I picked her up, I could hear her stomach growling. The only food the owners had left behind was a sealed package of hot dogs. Oh, and there was also a bowl of water," Dara said, "but it had been left on the counter out of the dog's reach."

"How about giving this dog a bath?" I suggested as the Yorkie continued to squirm. I was beginning to itch just from watching her.

Dara rubbed flea shampoo into the dog's fur, while I lathered and rinsed. You could see the immediate relief on the Yorkie's face as she stood perfectly still, loving all the attention.

"I think you need to see an orthodontist," I said to the dog as I was washing around her muzzle.

Dara pulled the face of the drenched dog close to hers and kissed the top of its soapy head. "I don't care if you have an overbite. I think you're cute just the way you are."

We didn't expect the dog's owners to come looking for her, and we were right. The rescue team had left removal notices inside and on the outside door of the mobile home, letting the owners know we had their dog, but they never called, and we were not the least bit disappointed. Dara agreed to foster the dog, whom she had named Missi, until a permanent home could be found for the Yorkie.

Missi still lives with Dara and her husband Randy.

Missi was just one of the many ownerless dogs that the volunteers adopted. Mark Veverka rescued a three-week-old yellow-and-white puppy that unexpectedly came swimming through an opening in a crumbled levee. There was barely time to grab the tiny dog as it frantically paddled past the rescue boat Mark was in.

The little yellow-and-white dog was half starved to death, but a diet of puppy formula remedied that problem. We kept him in the warehouse so we could take turns bottle-feeding him, but it was Mark who was adopted by the puppy. He was never claimed, so Levee now lives with Mark.

I didn't adopt any of the animals from the Midwest flood, remembering my husband Ken's words before I left for Missouri, "I will leave you at the airport if I come to pick you up and see you standing at the curb with any more animals."

But I brought some home for other people to adopt. The last tiny kitten to be pulled from the attic in West Alton was one of six cats that I took home with me to California. Millie, as the youngest one came to be called, was adopted by Dick and Sjoukje Zimmerman. The Zimmermans won the California lottery, and they had been generous in sharing their good fortune with animals and making room for homeless critters. When the Zimmerman family recently moved from the San Francisco Bay area to New Mexico, Dick chartered a Learjet to transport his four-legged family members. "I couldn't have them riding with the baggage," Dick told me after they got resettled in their new home. "Animals deserve better."

Millie's has become a true rags-to-riches story.

Another one of the West Alton cats was adopted by Sharon Young, a producer for the Fox Television Network. When her crew was following our story during the floods, she saw some footage of the West Alton rescue and decided she had to have one of those cats.

Moya now lives in Hollywood.

The four "rooftop" dogs that appeared on the front page of the *St.*

Midwest Flood

Louis Post Dispatch, standing on the roof of a house that was flooded clear up to the eves, generated a morning of phone calls from people concerned about their welfare.

Dr. Alice O'Dell, a doctor from St. Charles, fostered the four dogs, two of which were puppies. The two adult dogs turned out to have heartworms, but because one of them was pregnant, treatment on her could not begin until after she delivered the puppies. In addition, all of the dogs were extremely underweight and full of tapeworms. When I saw the dogs two weeks after Alice had taken them home, they looked so happy and healthy I couldn't believe they were the same ones.

The two adult dogs were both successfully treated for the heart-worms and have remained with Alice. She says she still considers them her foster "kids" and if the right home came along, she'd give them up, but I suspect Alice has already found the perfect home for them.

I brought the two puppies home with me, and they were adopted by a husband and wife who live in Santa Cruz, California. The wife is a veterinarian, so the dogs will have nothing but the best of care in addition to receiving a great deal of love. The family lives on the beach, so the two Labrador-rottweiler mixes have lots of room to run.

There were so many wonderful stories, but unfortunately there were also the stories we wished we didn't have to tell.

When I returned to the warehouse from a meeting at the emergency operation center, I parked alongside a silver Oldsmobile Ciera. Inside, Sharon Maag, a volunteer, sat alone, crying.

"Sharon. What's wrong?" I asked.

"I can't go back in the warehouse," she said between sobs. "I just can't face Lauren."

"Why?"

"I have to tell her about Miracle."

Lauren had found the tiny black kitten on the way back from a late-evening rescue, stranded in the upper branches of a tree that was surrounded by water. Her persistent meows caught Lauren's attention as they passed near the tree with a boatload of other animals they had rescued.

"Guys, hold on," Lauren ordered. "There's a cat somewhere close by crying."

It didn't take the rescue team long to spot the kitten. Her big yellow eyes stared down at the people below as they tried to figure out how they were going to get her out of the tree. The upper branches were too thin to support any of the volunteers' weight.

There was less than an hour of daylight left, which meant the team had to do something fast. It would have been nice to have had a ladder, but there wasn't enough time to locate one before darkness fell. They decided to look for something long enough to lightly bat the kitten out of the tree, otherwise she'd have to spend another night there.

Gary located a long-handled garden tool just long enough to reach the cat.

"Lauren, you're the softball player," Gary said, handing the tool to her. "So why don't you do the honors."

John positioned the boat right below the kitten, while Lauren carefully worked the handle of the tool up through the branches, hoping the kitten wouldn't climb to a higher branch.

"Okay, kitten," Lauren warned when the end of the handle was right behind the tiny feline. "Just know we're trying to save you and not hurt you."

It took only one gentle nudge with the handle to knock the kitten off the branch, and Gary was waiting with the pole net to retrieve the kitten once it landed in the water. The plan worked perfectly, and within a matter of seconds the cat was scooped out of the water, retrieved from the net, and stuffed in an Evacsack.

"Good going, guys," Lauren said as she peered into the sack at the hissing kitten. "We saved another one, and this one is a bit feisty."

"I don't blame it. I'd be upset, too, if someone had just pushed me out of a tree into the water," John commented.

When the team returned to the warehouse, Sharon Maag was working in the animal intake area. "What you got there?" she asked as Lauren set the Evacsack down on the desk.

"A small black kitten." Lauren reached her gloved hand into the Evacsack and pulled out the spitting ball of fur. "I named her Miracle, because I never expected we'd get her out of the tree she was perched in."

"You're not very old," Sharon said, examining the kitten as Lauren continued to hold it. "I'd guess maybe five weeks."

Sharon Maag is a real softy for kittens, so she decided she'd foster Miracle. Besides, she was concerned about the kitten's low weight. She hoped that after a few good meals and some TLC the kitten would be feeling better. But Miracle didn't respond to either.

A trip to the veterinarian confirmed what Sharon feared. Miracle tested positive for FIP, a disease that is fatal for cats. The decision was made to euthanize the kitten.

Sharon's daughter Cassie was with her at the vet, and just before handing the kitten over to the doctor, she held Miracle close to her chest and said, "Mom, how can I let her go when she is still purring?"

Sharon later took Miracle home and buried the kitten in her backyard.

"Terri, how am I going to tell Lauren that I had to have Miracle put to sleep?" Sharon stared out the window of the Oldsmobile. "Every day she's asked how the kitten was doing, and I've been telling her that she was coming along—even though I'd begun to suspect there was something really wrong with her."

I reached in the window and placed my hand on Sharon's shoulder. Neither one of us said anything for a minute.

"The doctor said that Miracle was actually ten weeks old, and I thought she was only five weeks. That's how sick she was," Sharon said as the tears started to slide down her cheek again. "This is so hard."

"Sharon," I said with tears in my own eyes, "Miracle was loved during the last few days of her life. If Lauren hadn't found her, she would probably have died alone in the top of that tree. Both you and Lauren made a difference for this kitten, and I'm sure Miracle is grateful for what you did to help her."

Lauren and Sharon got a big dose of a hard reality that day, but they didn't let it get them down. They both continued to do their best to save as many animals as they could, and there were a lot more victories for both of them in the days that the warehouse remained open.

Sharon Maag told me recently that the Midwest flood had changed her life. "I was a true 'Suzy Homemaker' until I saw you on the news and decided I wanted to do something to help the animals too," Sharon said. "I'd never done anything like this before, and I am now very glad that I did. I finally put my interest in animals into motion, and I haven't stopped since."

The day after Miracle died, Dara shared some more disappointing news with me.

Her team had been assigned a rescue in an area that they knew, from looking at the map, was dangerously close to the Mississippi River. The owners had left their three hunting dogs on the roof of their house, thinking they would be safe, but they now realized they hadn't put out enough food or fresh water for the dogs.

Out of Harm's Way

"They don't have a boat, so they have no way to reach the house," Dara said, reading from the rescue form.

"I just hope we can get out there," Alonzo said with a worried look on his face. "My boat can handle some pretty strong currents, but once you start getting near the river itself, those currents can be deadly."

"Well," Mark said, "let's go have a look."

"It was one of the most strenuous rescues I went on," Dara explained later. "Halfway out there, we came across an elevated railroad track still above water. Of course, where we needed to go was on the other side, so we got out of the boat, picked it up, and carried it over the tracks so we could set it back down in the water and continue on our way."

As I listened to Dara, I remembered my first impression of her when she came through the door of the Humane Society, impeccably dressed down to the smallest detail. This woman shattered my initial assessment of her time and time again, proving all that mattered to her were the animals.

"We hadn't gotten far when the engine on Alonzo's boat suddenly died. We knew we couldn't be out of gas, because we'd filled up before we left."

A green garden hose that had been floating unnoticed in the water had gotten tangled in the engine. It took a while, but Alonzo, with Mark's help, was able to dislodge the hose using his pocketknife. Fortunately it had caused no damage, and the team was able to resume their course, but again, they didn't go far.

"This is getting too strong," Alonzo yelled. "If we get swept up by the current and pulled out to the river, we'll be a bunch of goners."

The team sat in silence for a few minutes, faced with the reality that they were not going to be able to reach the dogs.

"It was horrible when we turned the boat around. In the direction we had been heading, we heard a dog barking," Dara said with tears in her eyes. "But there was nothing we could do."

There was something we could do when three cats arrived at the warehouse later that sweltering Sunday afternoon.

Marty and Paula were working in the animal intake area when a very nicely dressed woman in her late thirties approached their desk and asked, "Do you take cats that people find?"

"Yes," Marty responded, looking up from the paperwork she held in her hand.

"I found three cats in a garage, and I've got them with me," the woman explained. "Can I leave them with you now?"

"Sure," Marty said. "Do you need help with them?"

The woman said the cats were already confined and that she would have no trouble getting them herself.

When the woman returned, Marty and Paula could not believe what they saw. In the woman's arm was an enclosed cardboard box, with yards of package tape wrapped around it, and there was not a single breathing hole punched in the box.

"Are the cats in there?" Marty asked, half screaming.

"One is," the woman replied. "The other two are still in boxes in my trunk."

Marty quickly grabbed the box from the woman and set it down on top a stack of papers. Then she looked at the woman and said in a stern voice, "You get those other cats in here *now!*"

As the lady returned to her car, Marty and Paula tore into the box. There was so much tape attached to the box it could have survived three trips around the world and still remained intact. Even with scissors, it took what seemed like forever to free the cat. Once they got the top untaped, Marty cautiously lifted the lid flaps one at a time. Inside was a tortoiseshell cat, dangerously close to collapsing from heat exhaustion.

Carefully Marty reached for the cat, but it surprised both her and Paula when it suddenly lunged toward them, slipping past both women before they could get their hands on it. The cat spotted the open door and ran toward it just as the woman came walking through the doorway with two more boxes identical to the one she'd already brought in.

It was at that point that I realized something was going on that might need my attention, so I quickly ended my phone conversation and headed over.

"Quick. Someone grab a cage," Marty yelled. "We have an escaped cat."

One of the rescue teams had just returned from the field, so they grabbed what they needed and headed out the door for the AWOL cat.

"Ma'am," Marty yelled, "what's wrong with you? Don't you realize you could have killed these cats by putting them in a box without air and then transporting them in your trunk. What were you thinking?"

I had never seen Marty lose her cool.

"What's going on, Marty?" I asked as I stepped between her and the woman.

Out of Harm's Way

"This lady just brought us three cats in sealed boxes," Marty fumed. "And two of them are still in these boxes."

"Let's get them out of there," I instructed. I spotted several of the kennel volunteers standing nearby, watching what was going on, and I told them urgently, "Debbie, John, get two cages ready, and someone grab some ice from the freezer and put it in several Ziploc bags."

Marty and I worked on the bigger box, while Paula tore into the smaller one, exposing two more Torties. They were both soaking wet and listless.

While all this was going on, the nicely dressed woman stood and watched, making no effort to help us free the cats she'd brought us. We were finally reminded she was there when she said, "Why don't I drive my car around and see if I can find the cat that escaped."

"Before you leave," I said to her, "I want you to know that what you did was really stupid. If these cats had died, I would have made sure you were arrested for animal abuse."

I, too, could no longer control my anger. I'd seen too many irresponsible people in the last few days.

The woman was amazingly quiet and showed absolutely no emotion or remorse for what she'd done. She told us that if she found the cat, she'd bring it back to the warehouse, and then she left.

We recaptured the wayward tortoiseshell by setting a trap full of very smelly tuna. It turned out she was particularly hungry; she was pregnant.

The woman returned the next day, surprising us all. She had a basket full of young kittens. "I think these belong to one of the cats I brought in yesterday," she said. "I know they must be hungry."

The three cats had completely recovered from their ordeal and had been placed in foster homes, so a volunteer transported the kittens to each of the houses, looking for a mother that would accept them; otherwise we'd have another batch of babies to bottle-feed.

Fortunately, the cat that was fostered in O'Fallon, Missouri, took the kittens.

Before the woman left, she asked if she could talk to me. I learned that the three cats actually belonged to a friend of hers that lived in a neighborhood that had been evacuated.

"After my friend cleared out her house, she headed down to Texas, where some of her family lives. She asked if I'd take care of the cats until she got back," the woman said. "I was going over to feed them every day, but the water was starting to get closer, and I decided I'd better get the cats out of there before I could no longer get to the house to feed them."

I felt myself softening a bit toward this woman, but I still could not forgive what she'd done.

"I'm not used to cats, so I was afraid to put them in the car with me. I thought they might get loose and either bite or scratch me, so that is why I put them in the boxes in the trunk," the woman said as she looked me straight in the eyes.

"I now know that what I did was stupid, but at the time, I didn't know what else to do."

The owner never returned from Texas to reclaim her cats, so the three Torties and the two litters of kittens were put up for adoption, and all of them were placed in terrific homes, with instructions: *Never take the cats for a ride in a sealed cardboard box on a day when it's one hundred degrees outside.*

We all learned a lot during those weeks in the warehouse, not only about animals, but also about ourselves. Many of the volunteers, people who had never realized their potential to help animals, became addicted to doing something that made a difference, and as a result dogs, cats, birds, goats, rabbits, pigs, cows, donkeys, and horses, affected by the flood benefited immeasurably. However, when the floodwaters receded, the volunteers did not disappear. They realized the impact their effort could make, and they have continued to work in different ways to save animals.

45

Making a Difference

As August drew to a close, the Flood of the Century had finally exhausted itself, and it was time for me to go home to Ken and the girls who'd once again been so patient with my absence. It was difficult to hold back my tears as the volunteers whom I'd worked alongside of to save animals gathered one last time so we could say good-bye. As I stood at the back of the auditorium in the senior center where we'd gathered for a potluck dinner, I listened to Virginia Keim, the president of the Humane Society board, thank the volunteers for all their hard work—recognition they so rightfully deserved. I looked around at the faces of the people I had laughed and cried with since I'd arrived in St. Charles, and I knew then what an enormous impact they had had upon my life.

I have wonderful memories of each one of them that could easily fill several books. As time passes I know I will often think back to that time in my life and the people who made it so special. Every time I see a Hardee's Restaurant, I'll remember Kim Misciagna, who worked the night shift at St. Joseph's Hospital and volunteered with us during the day, still finding time to be a mom to her two sons, Bobby and "J."

What gave her the energy to put in her eight-hour shift and then show up at the warehouse to help me open up every morning? Besides her uncompromising commitment to animals, it had to have been all the Hardee's cinnamon biscuits, accompanied by orange juice and coffee, that we shared each day before the warehouse filled up with people and animals. It was a precious few moments of quiet that we both enjoyed.

Kim would often stay until the middle of the afternoon helping to oversee the animal-intake area before heading home to grab a few hours of sleep before her next shift at the hospital. She was incredible, and I will always be grateful to her for the support and laughter she so generously gave.

The expression "I don't do mornings" will always remind me of Wendy Borowsky. This former nurse is one of those people who thinks alarm clocks shouldn't be allowed to go off before ten A.M., so it was midafternoon when Wendy arrived at the St. Charles Humane Society for the first time and stopped me to ask, "Is there something I can do to help?"

At that moment, I desperately needed someone to set up the animal-intake area, something I'd not had time to do since I'd arrived the day before. People were starting to bring us dogs and cats and I needed a volunteer who could catch them at the door, get the appropriate paperwork completed, take Polaroid pictures of the animals, and get a temporary collar and tag around each of their necks. Wendy offered to do the job, and thank goodness she did.

In the weeks that followed I got to know Wendy well. I learned that she didn't do mornings when, at the end of her first day volunteering, she told me, "I can come back for as long as you need me, but you'll never see me here before noon."

Wendy was right. I rarely saw her in the morning, but I could count on seeing her until late at night.

As I'd collapse in a chair at the end of another *long* day, Wendy would still be going strong. I'd watch as she busied herself for at least another hour past the time the last volunteer had gone home.

During that last hour, when the warehouse was finally empty, she'd tidy up the animal-intake desk, which had remained her work area. I'd watch with half-closed eyes as she'd dust off the wooden desk, gather all the stray paper clips, straighten the animal-intake binders on an adjacent table, file completed paperwork, leave messages on yellow Post-it notes for Kim to read in the morning, and line up clipboards for the next day's rush of activity.

It was almost always well after eleven P.M. when Wendy would finally announce the place met her specifications for clean, and she was ready to go.

Just recently I learned that Wendy's need to be organized was not the only reason she kept me up so late.

"When I was in the warehouse, I stayed busy, concentrating on the survivors. When I got home, it was too quiet—and I couldn't help but think about the animals that hadn't survived." She told me what it had been like for her when she'd go home after being in the warehouse.

It would start on the way home. During the twenty-minute drive, when she was alone in her car with no distractions, she would remember the animals that had already died.

When she got home, she never failed to first remove her jeans, T-shirt, and shoes in the laundry room. I had told the volunteers it was important not to have contact with their own animals until they had removed the clothing they had been wearing when working around the flood animals. Contagious diseases can be carried on clothing, and I didn't want anyone's animals getting sick. This really stuck in Wendy's mind since she had two cats, which she'd suddenly had a stronger urge to hold and protect.

Then she'd tiptoe upstairs and through the bedroom, careful not to wake her husband, Les, who was beginning to realize just how much animals mattered to his wife of twelve years. Once in her bathroom, Wendy would sit on the cold tile floor and cry.

"There were several nights that my cat Latke would quietly push open the partially open bathroom door and crawl onto my lap," Wendy told me as the memory of this time once again made her pause in her story and take a deep breath. "I'd hug her so tight, grateful that I was not one of the people who'd lost their pet during the flood, which caused me to cry even harder."

Tears filled my own eyes as I listened to Wendy.

"One of the nights I was having a really hard time dealing with everything that had gone on during the day. It had been an especially difficult one, and I was even beginning to wonder if I had the strength to return to the warehouse," Wendy said as her voice softened. "Tears were streaming down my cheeks, and I was trying to muffle my sobs so I wouldn't wake Les, when suddenly Latke, who'd been sitting on my lap, stood up and very gently began to lick my tears."

Wendy didn't say anything for a moment.

"I wonder . . . if Latke knew what I was doing for the other animals?" Wendy said finally. "And if that was her way of saying don't stop, the animals need you."

Latke was right. Wendy was needed, and she did go back, staying until the very end.

Dorma Overbey is a quiet woman in her mid-sixties who regularly punctuates her sentences with "God bless you." She showed up almost every day to help answer the phones, and her quiet nature was a calming influence on everyone who dealt with the phones, which rang practically nonstop.

I'll never forget how she got her Gores mixed up one afternoon. When a call of support came from Vice President Al Gore's office, she thought it was Dr. Gore, the gynecologist in town, calling to speak to me. It was the only time I ever saw Dorma blush.

Every time I see a picnic basket, I will think of Peggy Schopp and the four farm wives. In the month that the warehouse was open, in addition to coordinating the phone area, Peggy had made it her job to keep the volunteers fed. With the Yellow Pages in front of her, each morning she'd go down the listings looking for local restaurants that might be willing to donate a lunch or a dinner. She was successful in getting such restaurants as the Red Lobster, Kentucky Fried Chicken, Captain D's, the Olive Garden, McDonald's, and some of the local pizza chains to donate meals.

Toward the end of the month, people were becoming a little less generous, but Peggy persisted. When a call came in one afternoon from a woman in her seventies who wanted to know what she could do to help, Peggy had the perfect job for her.

"Can you cook?" Peggy asked the eager woman.

"Well, yeah," she replied with some surprise in her voice.

"Good. Maybe there is a way you can help."

The woman came through the door of the warehouse the following evening with three of her lady friends. They looked as if they had stepped from a Norman Rockwell painting. The farm wives were dressed in cotton gingham dresses, protected by starched aprons. On their arms they carried picnic baskets laden with home cooking. We all watched ravenously as they removed from the baskets fried chicken, *real* mashed potatoes, garden-fresh green beans, yeast rolls, jars of homemade strawberry jam, and scrumptious blueberry and peach pies. It was a feast that remedied several days of eating cold pizza.

This disaster was the exception—we all gained weight.

I don't think there was anyone who loved the cats in our warehouse more than Julia Mathes. This quiet, petite nurse would commandeer Mark, and the two of them would wade through knee-deep water in mobile home parks, with bags of cat food perched on their shoulders. They were searching for cats reluctant to be caught but still needing to be fed. They'd return to the warehouse for more food, smelling like the inside of a garbage can, but they never took the time to get cleaned up. They stayed only long enough to grab what they needed and then returned to feed more cats. Julia's patient nature eventually persuaded a lot of the cats that she could be trusted, and they gave in to being rescued.

There was another volunteer who also had a special way with cats. Her name was Marty Ferguson. As I got to know this hairdresser in her early forties, she began to remind me of Dr. Doolittle. It was her uncanny ability to calm down and handle nasty cats that made her special. She became an integral member of the warehouse crew and a savior to the unsocialized cats.

When everyone else would back away from a spitting, hissing, angry feline, Marty would approach the cage with the attitude of "Okay, cat. I'm not going to put up with your shenanigans, so you'd better just cooperate." And the cats did.

Marty's husband and three sons had always demanded to be first. But during the month that she volunteered, she came every day to help the cats, often surprising the family that had come to expect her to stay at home and take care of them.

"The Midwest flood saved my life," Marty told me when I was interviewing her for this book. "I've never done anything that meant so much to me."

Marty now works part-time for the St. Charles Humane Society, and she continues to make a difference for the cats that arrive at the shelter.

Nathaniel Miller was always a welcome sight in the warehouse, because we knew how precious his time was. I'd met him when he was evacuating his *very* pregnant wife and two children from their soon-to-be flooded home.

We'd gotten a call about a dog and a puppy seen wandering in the empty mobile home park where Nat lived, and we were searching for them when we spotted him and his family, which also included two dogs that were safely tucked in the back of the packed station wagon.

"Hi," I said, approaching the tall man, just as he finished securing the tarp draped over the bulging luggage rack on top of his car. "We're looking for a small dog and a puppy that are supposedly wandering around here somewhere. Any chance you've seen them?"

"Yeah. I saw them earlier today, but I thought their owners were still around," the man replied as he stepped away from his car. "I'll show you where they were."

Nat led us right to the dogs, whose owner had gone off and left them sitting on the porch. Both the mother and her puppy were more than grateful to be taken back to the warehouse, where it was dry and there was plenty of food.

The following morning, I was talking with some people who'd lost their ten-year-old Sheltie when I spotted Nat coming through the warehouse door. My first thought was that he had changed his mind and was taking me up on my offer to foster his two dogs, but I'd guessed wrong.

"I thought you-all might need some more help," Nat said after I greeted him.

"Sure," I replied, wondering how he would find the time.

Nat found time to become a regular volunteer, in spite of being displaced by the flood, having two small children to keep up with, a pregnant wife due to deliver at any time, and a full-time job. As he said, when we were out on a rescue together, "I'd do anything for an animal."

He proved that time and time again. It amazed me what some people were willing to do for the animals.

Among those that helped were three little girls. They arrived in the warehouse on another one of those hot August afternoons, escorted by their mothers. The tallest of the three ten-year-olds carried a large brown wicker basket with a huge pink ribbon tied to the top of the handle, which she set down on the information table.

"We brought this for the animals," she said in a shy voice to the volunteer behind the table.

"What have you brought them?" the volunteer asked as she peered into the basket.

"Money, so that you can buy toys for the flood animals," replied the girl with a pink bow in her hair that matched the one on the basket. "My dog really likes to play with red balls."

By now I'd walked up to the table, unable to resist getting involved in the conversation. "Hi. I'm Terri," I said. "And who might you be?"

The girls told me their names one at a time, and then one of the mothers explained where the money had come from.

"They saw on TV what you were doing to help the animals, and they decided on their own that they wanted to collect money to replace the toys that the dogs and cats lost during the flood," the mother said with obvious pride. "So they went door-to-door and collected two hundred and sixty-one dollars and seventy-three cents."

Before the girls left, they went around and scratched the ears of every cat and patted each dog on the head, and they were rewarded with purrs and wagging tails.

The three girls were not the only kids to help out the animals. A Boy Scout troop stood outside a grocery store for an entire day and received enough donations to buy the materials to build us two dog runs for the warehouse, which came in handy when we needed a place to put one of our unruly guests—a potbellied pig named Princess. Children from the Harvester Ridge School proudly made a donation of fifteen hundred dollars too, which was matched by Petsmart, who joined in the efforts to help flood animals by offering to make matching donations up to ten thousand dollars.

My job was made easier because of the support from the board of the St. Charles Humane Society, especially two of its members, Teddy Norris and Theresa Didion, who welcomed me from the beginning. I appreciated their willingness to keep an open mind and to see beyond the current moment. They were frequently my sounding boards, and I thank them both for listening and for making suggestions that contributed to the success of our joint effort.

There were companies who came to our assistance too. The Manna Pro Pet Food Company, based in St. Louis, provided us with fresh bags of dog, cat, puppy, and kitten food to help feed the animals. Jonny Cat, in cooperation with Nancy Abbott and the Cat Fanciers Association, supplied us with kitty litter, scoops, and pans. Southwestern Bell and Cybertel provided cellular phones and pagers, which aided in our communicating.

The veterinarians who cared for the sick and injured animals we located, included Dr. Jay King, who loves chocolate almost as much as he loves animals, Dr. Kim Frasier, Dr. Daniel Lange, and Dr. Mike Crecelius. The Animal Emergency Clinic in Bridgeton pitched in at night and on weekends.

As is usual in disasters, there wasn't time to get everyone's name. Every person, whether they spent ten minutes or ten days helping, made a difference. Thanks to Ed Packer—an elementary school principal who kept a camera to his eye almost constantly, capturing the activity in the warehouse and during rescues—we have visual images of the animals and the people. They will help us to always remember the faces of those who did so much and the animals we became so attached to.

The volunteers were amazing, and I am awed by what they were able to accomplish during the month we were in full operation. I commend them for their dedication, hard work, compassion for animals, and their willingness to give so much of themselves so that animals would not have to suffer. Anyone who doubts the effectiveness of volunteers cannot help but be impressed by what these people did. They went beyond doing what was easy and confirmed over and over again their commitment to animals.

What's Next?

46

Meant to Be

When I showed up at the Humane Society of Santa Clara County twelve years ago to help animals during the Alviso flood, I had no idea the experience would forever change my life. As our small rescue boat maneuvered the flooded streets that first day, I had all the enthusiasm of a novice volunteer who wants nothing more than to save drowning animals.

I stumbled into that first disaster blindly, but I left Alviso with my eyes wide open. Four days of plucking dogs and cats out of rising floodwaters caused me to realize three things that continue to affect what I do today.

The fact that the Humane Society did not know how to effectively respond during a disaster was a startling realization. My expectation was that they would be the animals' Red Cross, but I learned afterward that the daily demands of helping animals had left them no time to create a disaster plan for our community. I realized that if something happened to me during a disaster that prevented me from taking care of my own animals, I could not count on my local Humane Society to step in and provide them with temporary care. It was a scary thought.

It was an even harsher jolt to my naive view of the world when I found out, the hard way, that not everyone cares about the animals they call their pets. I was appalled when I learned that some people in Alviso had intentionally chosen to save their television and not the family dog. Those first glimpses of drowned animals imprinted themselves on my mind, and in spite of wishing those images would fade away, I'm glad they haven't—they are what motivates me.

The third thing I uncovered in Alviso was my passion for animals. It had always been there, but it took a disaster for me to realize how deeply entwined it was with who I am. If this passion had not surfaced during the Alviso flood, that would have been my first and my last disaster effort.

These three things have directed the role I've played in disaster response-and-recovery efforts since 1983. I have participated in twenty disasters now, each one fueling my determination to do something to change the fact that animals have been victimized by nature *and* people for too long.

Natural disasters are inevitable. They are guaranteed disturbances that will continue to strike in the form of earthquakes, tornadoes, volcanic eruptions, wildfires, hurricanes, and floods. There is *nothing* anyone can do to prevent them from happening, which proves nature is in control and we need to be prepared to fight back.

Humans do have the power to curtail the losses by being prepared and ready to respond to the needs of those people affected by nature's rage. The American Red Cross is the agency most often associated with minimizing the pain and suffering of the people caught in the aftermath of a disaster, by providing shelter, food, medical care, and emotional comfort to them. But who routinely takes care of the animals that are victimized in a disaster? Until recently no one did.

The delayed reaction of the Humane Society of Santa Clara Valley to the Alviso flood was not unusual. Relief efforts for animals have traditionally been sporadic, disorganized, ineffective, slow in coming, and oftentimes nonexistent, even though it's known that animals are affected in every disaster. I believe animals deserve better, especially domesticated ones, since we have made them so dependent on us by meddling with their ability to escape injury and death during disasters. When an animal is confined in a cage, run, pen, pasture, house, or barn, they need a person to save them from an approaching fire or rising floodwaters, or to free them from fallen debris in an earthquake. If people are not there to help, animals die.

It's hard to imagine, but there was a time when the people in the United States were not guaranteed assistance during disasters either.

What's Next?

Clara Barton is the person we have to credit for recognizing the need for a national disaster-relief program for people and working so hard to fill the void. Years of perseverance resulted in the establishment of the American Red Cross in 1881.

Since its beginning in June of 1987, United Animal Nations (UAN) has recognized that not enough was being done to help animals during disasters. It was Belton Mouras, the president and CEO of UAN, who had the idea for the Emergency Animal Rescue Service Program (EARS) and hoped that it would someday grow to be a primary resource to relieve the suffering of animals in both natural and man-made disasters.

With limited financial resources and a full-time staff of only four, this nonprofit organization has managed since 1988 to mobilize the EARS Program during all the major disasters and some of the smaller ones, proving that "the little guy" *can* make a difference.

Besides myself, it has been staff members Deanna Soares and Deb Winslow, plus Belton Mouras, who have consistently worked so hard to ensure that the EARS Program remains on the front lines during disasters. Jeane Weston, the current chair of UAN's board of directors, has been a welcome supporter too, generously sharing her writing expertise and her thoughtful insight. Board members, Bob and Phyllis Roehs and Pat Harris, have been there from the beginning too.

What motivates this small group to continue giving so much of themselves is very simple: they genuinely believe in the need for the EARS Program and they know firsthand the difference it has already made for animals. I am reminded of this each time I look around at the animals we are caring for during a disaster and ask myself, "Would they be alive if the EARS Program hadn't shown up to help?" My answer is usually no.

The last few years seem to have been plagued by disasters, but in fact, they have always existed. It saddens me to think of the many animals that have died because of them. Bad timing, not enough money, a lack of trained people, a lack of awareness, inconvenience, no available supplies, or disagreements over jurisdictions have been some of the reasons given for a lack of support for animals during these times. In spite of facing some of these same obstacles, though, the EARS Program has somehow always managed to overcome them through creativity and an unwillingness to fail in our commitment to the animals and the people to whom they matter.

Each disaster leaves us drained of resources, since not as many people remember to support us when there is no major disaster on the evening news. Responding to a disaster *cannot* be an afterthought. To do the job right, ongoing efforts must be made to ensure that volunteers, supplies, and money are available *when* disasters strike.

An example of the desperate need for organized animal relief work occurred during Hurricane Erin, which hit Florida in August of 1995. In CNN's coverage of the disaster, it showed a police officer stopping at the home of an elderly couple to encourage them to evacuate. When he explained that everyone else in the neighborhood was gone, the woman quickly responded, "Yes, but they didn't have dogs they cared about. We couldn't leave them behind."

This situation repeats itself over and over in each disaster, and I think everyone agrees a solution *has* to be found. When evacuation orders are announced, people should not have to wonder what to do with their pets. The response and relief efforts for animals should always be automatic, just as they are for people.

I knew when I returned from the floods in the Midwest that I was never going to be able to expand the EARS Program while still working at Santa Clara University. It was going to take a full-time commitment on my part, and on the part of a lot of other people, in order to maintain the momentum the EARS Program had gained during the Midwest flood. We proved in this disaster what a difference an organized response effort for animals can make and that it was no longer acceptable to cheat the animals and their owners of the services they deserve.

I called Deanna Soares, UAN's comptroller, after I got home and said, "Pay me whatever UAN can afford. I don't care if it means I eat peanut butter and jelly sandwiches for the rest of my life. It's time this job gets done right!"

On September 1, 1993, I joined the staff of UAN as the first director of the Emergency Animal Rescue Service Program, and life has not been the same since, for myself or Deanna. Both of us have the gray hairs to prove it.

My first task was to assemble a team of individuals who recognized what the EARS Program was striving for and who would be willing to give their own blood, sweat, and tears to make it happen. In twelve years I'd learned that money alone does not support recovery efforts. Trained volunteers are themselves an invaluable asset. The Red Cross has long realized this, and they now have a nationwide force of 1.5 million volunteers.

In January 1994, I started conducting training workshops that would prepare individuals to properly rescue and care for animals during disasters. By January 1996 we had held forty-nine day-long workshops around the country, recruiting and preparing over twelve hundred individuals to respond to the needs of animals during disasters.

It takes all kinds of people, with a variety of skills, to make this program work, and I'm pleased that the classes have been composed of representatives from humane societies, animal control agencies, SPCAs, the Red Cross, law enforcement agencies, veterinarians, other national animal organizations, and individuals who have no particular affiliation—they just love animals and want to be sure that when the next disaster hits, they're not sitting on the sidelines doing nothing.

It will take *many* more training classes before we even get close to having the number of volunteers that the Red Cross has, but each workshop strengthens our team. If you would like information about becoming a volunteer with the Emergency Animal Rescue Service Program or how you can provide financial support, refer to page 388 for details on how *you* can become a part of this program too.

From this growing group of volunteers, we have carefully selected nine coordinators and three assistant coordinators who make up our Crisis Action Team (CAT). This initial-response-and-assessment team determines how the EARS Program can be used most effectively and how many volunteers and what supplies will be needed. Once the volunteers are on site, this group directs the different areas of operation and supervises the volunteers.

Each member of the Crisis Action Team has experience with animals, and each of them has been through at least two disasters, some as many as four. Experience builds upon experience. This group can make things happen a lot quicker with fewer mistakes, and it's the animals that benefit. Each of these individuals does his or her job without pay, which is something I hope to see change in the future. The Red Cross has a staff of thirty thousand paid employees, and as the EARS Program grows, we will need more full-time support than the present staff at UAN can provide.

As our team of volunteers grows and our response efforts expand, the EARS Program has gained recognition. As a result of this, in June of 1995, I was invited by the Federal Emergency Management Agency (FEMA), along with representatives of other animal interest groups to participate in a program on response and recovery efforts for animals during disasters. Even though FEMA's focus is on helping people during disasters, they are beginning to realize, as are other human disaster response agencies—that the needs of animals and people are interrelated.

·Our growing network of people has allowed us to respond to the following disasters since the Midwest floods:

October 1993, wildfires, southern, California. We worked with the victims in Altadena to remove harmful debris from burned-out barns and pastures so that horses could be brought back home. Staff and volunteers from the nonprofit organization Actors and Others for Animals gave generously of their time.

January 1994, Northridge earthquake, southern, California. EARS volunteers worked with employees of Los Angeles City Animal Regulations at its shelter in Chatsworth for nine days, working in the kennels, distributing water to horse owners who were without water for up to two weeks, matching arriving strays with lost-animal reports, answering phones, and transporting animals in need of medical care. Volunteers from Emergency Animal Rescue, based in Ramona, California, worked with the EARS Program.

March 1994, Georgia tornadoes, Jasper Georgia. The EARS coordinator worked with local poultry farmers, managing to save nearly three thousand chicks before a quarantine was placed on the area. The rescued birds were placed in homes where they were to remain free-roaming chickens.

July 1994, Georgia flood, Macon and Bainbridge, Georgia. EARS volunteers assisted Macon Animal Control in caring for some eighty animals that were evacuated from their shelter. EARS volunteers set up a temporary shelter in Bainbridge for eight days to house close to one hundred and twenty stray and owned animals, in addition to rescuing abandoned animals in the neighborhoods that flooded.

October 1994, Texas flood, Conroe and Liberty, Texas. EARS volunteers rescued stranded animals in a flooded neighborhood near Conroe and set up a temporary shelter in Liberty for seven days to house just one hundred stray and owned animals, in addition to rescuing abandoned animals in the neighborhoods there that flooded.

January 1995, Sacramento flood, Sacramento, California. EARS volunteers worked with the California Veterinary Medical Association and veterinarians in the Sacramento area to coordinate animal rescues, temporary housing of stray and owned animals, and distribution of pet food.

January 1995, Great Hanshin Earthquake, Kobe, Japan. Funded by United Animal Nations International and representing their Red Dove

Program, the former EARS assistant director and I spent nine days in Japan working with the World Society for the Protection of Animals, the Cat Fanciers Association, a local animal welfare group, and several local veterinarians to provide assistance to animals in the affected area.

March 1995, Monterey County flood, Pajaro, California. We assisted pet owners in the small farming community of Pajaro, retrieving stranded animals, providing proper carrying cages for transporting animals, and removing some dead animals for their owners.

May 1995, St. Louis area flood, St. Charles, Missouri. Three of the EARS coordinators and some EARS volunteers served as backup for local shelters. The volunteers scouted for abandoned animals. They also prepared the warehouse used during the flood of 1993 to receive animals should there be a need.

June 1995, Virginia flood, Madison, Virginia. An EARS coordinator and volunteers worked with the Animal Control Agency in Madison for three days, searching for stranded or abandoned animals, distributing pet food, and caring for the animals in the shelter.

There are so many stories to tell about animals and people from each of these disasters, and by the time *Out of Harm's Way* reaches the bookstores, I'm sure we will have participated in more disasters.

We're occasionally asked if we ever intend to expand our disaster response program outside of the United States. It troubles me that animals suffer in disasters all over the world and that in many instances there is no one there to help them, but because there is still so much catching up to do in this country, for now our focus must remain at home. There is hope, though, that more will be done in the near future to help animals affected by disasters in other countries.

UAN-USA already has an European connection, since we share common interests with UAN-International, located near Geneva, Switzerland. Under the leadership of Franz and Judith Weber, the international arm of this organization has furthered animal and environmental causes in Europe and Australia. We are pleased that the Webers have expressed an interest in expanding their services by developing their Red Dove Program into something similar to the EARS Program, working with other animal organizations to address the needs of animals during disasters outside of the United States.

The World Society for the Protection of Animals (WSPA) currently does international disaster work for animals, and we were delighted to work with them for the first time during the earthquake in Kobe,

Out of Harm's Way

Japan. John Walsh, the programs director, has made great strides in making the officials in other countries aware of the importance of figuring animals into their disaster plans. I commend him for *all* his hard work. His job is a tough one, with obstacles much greater than the ones we face in this country. If you are interested in finding out more about WSPA, they may be contacted at 617-522-7000.

On more than one occasion during the months that I worked on the stories for this book, I cried. But I also laughed as I remembered those times when volunteers or animals made me smile—a first sign that life would once again be better. I now know that time does lighten the grief, but the heart never lets you forget.

The EARS Program, in its brief life, has already allowed a lot of people to do things that have definitely made a difference for animals, and because they cared, there are dogs, cats, horses, birds, cows, pigs, chickens, rabbits, and one frog named Kermit that survived nature's rage.

I have shared a lot of their stories throughout this book, but there is one story in particular that continues to remind me why the EARS Program is so special. I share it with you as a final example of why this program is needed.

I want to tell you about a black-and-white dog.

In July 1994, the EARS Program set up a shelter in Bainbridge, Georgia, in response to the floods generated by Hurricane Alberto. We arrived in this small southern town located on the Flint River before the floodwaters had spread to the neighborhoods bordering the river. While out looking for animals that had been left behind, a team of EARS volunteers met a man who had two dogs, which he had no intention of taking with him when he finally evacuated.

When the volunteers offered to shelter the man's two dogs, he shrugged his shoulders and said, "Hey, it makes no difference to me."

When asked where the dogs were, he moved toward the elevated front porch of his tiny home and bent down. A minute later he dragged out from under the run-down house a large black-and-white dog. The man gathered the dog in his arms, walked toward one of our trucks, and deposited him in an airline crate. Then he turned and walked away, not bothering to even say "Good-bye" or something like "Don't worry, you'll be okay. I'll come get you soon."

Amy, one of the volunteers, asked the man some questions as she completed the animal-intake form. When she asked what the dog's name was, he replied, "He doesn't have one."

What's Next?

Unable to locate the man's other dog, a chow, the volunteers returned to the animal disaster relief center with just the nameless dog. When Amy went to the back of the truck and opened the door of the airline crate, the dog sat still, staring at the floor of his cage. No matter how much Amy coaxed, the dog would not budge. Concerned that maybe the dog was frightened by the height, Amy closed the crate door and had another volunteer help her lower it to the ground.

Another attempt at coaxing the dog out of the crate met the same response. The dog just stared at the bottom of its cage, displaying absolutely no reaction to the volunteer and not once showing any signs of aggression.

It was time to try something else.

Amy clipped a leash to the dog's collar, and then with the help of another volunteer lifted the back end of the crate so that the dog would slide out. When he landed on the ground, he just lay there.

"What's wrong with this dog?" the volunteer asked Amy as they both stared at the dog lying at their feet.

"I'm not sure, but my guess is he's been abused."

Amy was right. The dog had been abused, but it was not physical abuse that had made him this way. It was neglect.

A lot of the EARS volunteers have had to face animal abuse and neglect for the first time during disasters, and it's never easy to accept the reality that not everyone treats animals the way they should.

The reality hit Amy hard, but she determined she was going to do something to help the nameless dog. The first thing she did was name him Albert.

For the next two days Amy carried the sixty-pound dog around the compound, since he still refused to stand up or walk. One of Amy's jobs was to feed the other dogs who were housed in runs that lined our perimeter fence. As Amy moved from one pen to the next, she'd pick up Albert and move him along with her. In spite of all the barking and commotion the other dogs created, Albert did not react. He just sat on the grass, staring at the ground.

In an effort to save her back, we borrowed a golf cart from the neighboring country club. As Amy made her feeding rounds, Albert then sat in the front seat of the cart, staring at the floorboard, still not responding to any of his surroundings.

At night, Albert lay next to Amy's cot. When we ate, Albert sat next to Amy, refusing to accept any of the tidbits of human food she offered him. In the heat of the afternoon, Amy would find a shady spot and stretch out on the ground next to Albert. I remember, one of those afternoons, standing back and watching the two of them as Amy whispered something into Albert's black, floppy ear. I could only imagine what she was saying to the dog that still refused to respond.

Albert had been with us for four days when we had a late-night birthday party for one of the volunteers. I always come up with an excuse to have a party to relieve the tension and momentarily forget the pain and suffering present in disasters. Laughter and chocolate ice cream always do the trick. That is why we never travel into a disaster without our ice cream scoop.

The volunteers were gathered under the funeral tent loaned to us by Levy Funeral Home, each one wearing his own Barney birthday hat and acting like a five-year-old. There were outbursts of laughter, storytelling, and lots of chocolate being consumed, and sitting in the middle of it all was Albert, still at Amy's side.

"Look!" a volunteer suddenly shouted above the clamor as he pointed in Albert's direction.

The group immediately became quiet, unable to believe what it was seeing. Albert was still sitting in the same place, but for the first time the very tip of his long black-and-white tail appeared to wag, and as we all stared in amazement, Albert's entire tail started to wag. The next thing we knew, he stood up and his rear end began to switch back and forth. Then his head turned and his eyes started to blink, and his ears twitched. It was as if someone had suddenly pushed Albert's on-button. Albert had come alive for probably the first time in his life.

After that evening, the once nameless dog never stopped moving. His whole purpose in life was to keep up with Amy. Wherever she went, you could count on Albert being no more than two steps behind her. As she fed the other dogs, Albert trotted along with her responding to the other dogs as if to say, "I am finally happy."

Amy and Albert were inseparable. Even when Amy walked to the nearby fire station to take a shower, Albert had to accompany her. When Amy got into the shower, Albert hopped right in too, refusing to let Amy out of his sight.

I was beginning to notice, though, that Albert still did not have the energy of an eighteen-month-old dog. We decided it would probably be a good idea to have Albert pay a visit to Dr. Hight, the veterinarian in Bainbridge who had been such a great help to us. The vet confirmed our fear: Albert had heartworm. The good news was that because Albert was a young dog and the problem was not yet advanced, the doctor was willing to try to treat the frequently fatal illness.

This gave me the excuse I'd been looking for to call Albert's owner.

When I explained to him that Albert had heartworm and that it would cost at least three hundred dollars to treat him, I expected he'd say, "I don't have the money, so you keep the dog."

But I was wrong. He wanted Albert back.

"You understand that if the dog isn't immediately treated for the heartworm, he'll die," I told the man on the other end of the phone, still hoping I could convince him to release the dog to me.

"Yeah. I understand. That's what happens to all my dogs, and when I lose this one, I'll get myself another one," the man replied without the least bit of remorse in his voice. "Oh, yeah, my house didn't flood, so I'll be out shortly to pick up my dog."

And with that the man hung up.

In the distance I could see Amy and Albert, playing tug-of-war with a towel. "How am I going to tell Amy we have to give Albert back?" I said half out loud as tears streamed down my cheeks. "It'll kill them both."

An hour later a dark blue Camaro pulled up to the front gate, and I immediately recognized the man that stepped out of the car. In his hand he carried a heavy chain. As he came through the gate, Amy spotted him too. I had just explained to her that Albert's owner would be there soon to reclaim his dog. It was one of the most difficult things I'd ever had to do.

At that moment I wished I were not the director of the EARS Program. I wished more than anything that I could make one dog mysteriously disappear. Because of my responsibilities with UAN and EARS, I couldn't. Everything that I do during disasters now, every decision I make, has to be figured into the bigger picture of what the EARS Program is trying so hard to do. If we got the reputation of taking people's animals and not giving them back because we didn't like the way they were cared for, it could prevent us from helping animals in the future.

We have, during disasters, reported instances of animal abuse to local authorities, but as long as an owner is providing food, water, shelter, and not physically abusing the animal, the law *protects the person* from having his or her animal confiscated. Since emotional neglect is not considered abuse, Albert's owner was within the law.

When I remembered the shell of a dog that had arrived less than a week before and what Amy had done to bring him to life. How could we just let him die now?

"Where's my dog?" the man asked in a gruff voice when he spotted me near the intake tent.

"One of the volunteers is walking him right now," I replied, looking over his shoulder to where I could see Amy crouched on the ground next to Albert, her arms wrapped around his neck. This time I didn't have to imagine what she was whispering in his ear. I knew she was saying good-bye.

"Well, get him. I have things to do," he replied impatiently.

I had to ask one more time. "Are you sure you want your dog back?" I asked. "I expect he's not going to live much longer."

"Yeah. I want him back," the man said as he turned to survey the property. It took him only a second to spot his dog, still cradled in Amy's arms. "There he is," he said as he started toward the far end of the property.

That was when I reached my hand into my pocket.

"Wait!" I shouted, causing the man to stop and turn back toward me. "How about if I buy that dog from you," I offered, and then held my breath, waiting for his answer, the $50.00 bill scrunched in my hand.

I didn't have to wait long. Before I knew it, the man's hand was palm-up in front of him, and his reply was exactly what I wanted to hear, "Sure. I'll sell him."

Albert now lives with Amy and her family near Warner Robins, Georgia. He was successfully treated for the heartworm, and when I saw Albert about a month after the floods, it was hard to believe he was the same dog.

If there were not an EARS Program, Albert would not be alive today. If the EARS Program did not give volunteers a way to help animals during disasters, Amy would never have met the once nameless dog that will forever be her best friend.

Appendix

Basic Tips for Safeguarding Your Dog and Cat During Disasters

These are tips to help you keep your dog or cat safe during a disaster. Included are steps that you need to take *before* a disaster strikes to reduce the chances of your pet getting either lost or injured. Please take the time to prepare now. Your pet's life may depend on it.

Disaster Kits

Now is the time to assemble a disaster kit for *each* dog and cat in your household.

DISASTER KIT FOR CATS

Supplies should be stored in a plastic container with a secure-fitting lid and labeled "Disaster Supplies—Cat."

1. FOOD
   - Use the brand your cat is used to.
   - Have dry and canned if that is what the cat eats. (If you use canned food, buy the smallest size can available, as your cat's appetite may decrease during a disaster and you may not have a proper way to store half-used cans of food.)
   - Plastic lid to put on a half-used can of food. (Opened cans of food need to be stored in a refrigerator or ice chest.)
   - Have enough to last at least one week. (More can be stored if you have room, but be sure it is rotated at least once every three months to prevent it from going bad.)
   - Food dish.
   - Can opener. (Even if what you are storing has flip-top lids, you may not be able to obtain that type if you run out in the weeks following a disaster.)
   - Spoon to scoop the food out of the can.

2. WATER
- Have enough to last at least one week. (More can be stored if you have room, but be sure it is rotated at least once every three months.)
- Store water in a dark or shaded area, and not in direct sunlight, or bacteria will start to form that can cause diarrhea.
- Nonspillable water dish.
- Small container of bleach for purifying water.
- Sealed plastic container for storing purified water.

3. LITTER
- Have at least a one-week supply of scoopable litter stored in plastic jugs.
- Include a small plastic litter box and scoop in your disaster kit.
- Have a supply of plastic bags for disposing of litter that you have scooped.

4. CLEANING SUPPLIES
- Disinfectant cleaner for cleaning crates and litter boxes. (Be sure to rinse the crate well before putting the cat back in, and *do not* clean a crate while an animal is in it.)
- Paper towels for drying a crate or litter box after cleaning it.
- Dish soap for cleaning food and water dishes.

5. PHOTOGRAPHS
- Have recent pictures of all your animals. (Make at least ten copies, in case you have to distribute them to several shelters and post them where you last saw the animal.) Keep the pictures current, especially if you have a kitten that is still growing. (Be sure you include in the picture any distinguishing marks.)
- Include yourself in the picture, holding the cat. (This can assist in proving ownership of an animal.)

6. MEDICATION
- If your cat is on prescribed medication, be sure to keep a reserve supply in your disaster kit, along with directions on how to administer.
- Be sure the medication does not expire.

- Have enough to last at least two weeks.
- Include hairball paste if you have a long-haired cat or one that constantly spits up hairballs.

7. SHOT RECORDS
- Keep a record of all your cat's vaccinations in your disaster kit.

8. COLLAR AND TAG
- A breakaway collar and tag should be kept on your cat at all times, but an extra one of each should be kept in the disaster kit in case the permanent one gets lost during a disaster.
- Keep several spare tags in your disaster kit that can be personalized, so if you have to move to a temporary location, you can put that phone number and address on the tag.
- Include a proper-fitting cat harness and leash so that a cat that has to be confined in a crate can be taken out for exercise and can be safely controlled when cleaning the crate. (*Never* leave a cat unattended when it is on a leash, and do not tie it to something. Someone should always hold the leash when the cat is on it.)
- If you cat is microchipped or has a tattoo, be sure to have the national registry numbers in your disaster kit.
- Make up and store in your disaster kit preprinted "Lost Posters," in case your cat gets lost. (Include your phone number, an alternate phone number, and your address, and leave blank lines to write in the animal's description, where it was last seen, and any other pertinent information.)

9 VETERINARIAN INFORMATION
- Write on a piece of paper the name, address, and telephone number of your regular vet and an alternate vet.
- Write out a release form authorizing another party to get emergency medical treatment for an injured cat, in case you are not available to get approval during a disaster.

10. FIRST AID KIT
- Have a first aid kit in your disaster supplies. (A list of its contents is included later in this chapter.)

11. BRUSH AND COMB

- Include this in your disaster kit if your cat likes to be brushed. Otherwise leave them out, as a disaster is not the time to try and get your cat used to something new.

12. TOYS

- Include a few toys in your disaster kit if your cat is used to playing with them. Otherwise leave them out.

13. GROOMING SUPPLIES

- Dry shampoo, in case you have to give your cat a bath. Sometimes in disasters cats come in contact with substances that need to be cleaned off their fur. Dry shampoos work well because they do not require water (something that can be in short supply).
- Cloth towels for drying off a cat.
- Nail clippers. (Your cat will probably not have access to a scratching post for a while.)
- Flea powder. (Make sure it is a brand just for cats.)

14. CAGE

- If you have to confine your cat during a disaster, you can use a plastic crate. (Be sure it is large enough to hold a food/water dish, a small litter box, and allows ample room for the cat to stretch out.)
- Be sure the cage has a secure locking device, to prevent the cat from escaping.
- Another alternative is a wire collapsible cage. These are better to use in really warm weather because the cat will get better ventilation.
- For evacuating a cat, you can use an Evacsack, which takes up a lot less room. The cat cannot be housed in it for extended periods of time, though. (Information on ordering Evacsacks can be found in this chapter.)

DISASTER KIT FOR DOGS

Supplies should be stored in a plastic container with a secure-fitting lid and labeled "Disaster Supplies—Dog."

Appendix

1. FOOD
- Use the brand your dog is used to.
- Have dry and canned if that is what the dog eats. (If you use canned food, buy the smallest size can available, as your dog's appetite may decrease during a disaster and you may not have a proper way to store half-used cans of food.)
- Plastic lid to put on a half-used can of food. (Opened cans of food need to be stored in a refrigerator or ice chest.)
- Have enough to last at least one week. (More can be stored if you have room, but be sure it is rotated at least once every three months to prevent it from going bad.)
- Food dish.
- Can opener. (Even if what you are storing has flip-top lids, you may not be able to obtain that type if you run out in the weeks following a disaster.)
- Spoon to scoop the food out of the can.

2. WATER
- Have enough to last at least one week. (More can be stored if you have room, but be sure it is rotated at least once every three months.)
- Store water in a dark or shaded area, and not in direct sunlight, or bacteria that can cause diarrhea will start to form.
- Nonspillable water dish.
- Small container of bleach for purifying water.
- Sealed plastic container for storing purified water.

3 SANITATION
- Have a pooper-scooper for picking up after your dog. (A small plastic child's shovel will work.)
- Have a supply of plastic bags to dispose of the waste.

4. CLEANING SUPPLIES
- Disinfectant cleaner for cleaning crates. (Be sure to rinse the crate well before putting the dog back in, and *do not* clean a crate while an animal is in it.)
- Paper towels for drying a crate after cleaning it.
- Dish soap for cleaning food and water dishes.

5. PHOTOGRAPHS

- Have recent pictures of all your animals. (Make at least ten copies in case you have to distribute them to several shelters and post them where you last saw the animal.) Keep the pictures current, especially if you have a puppy that is still growing. (Be sure you include in the picture any distinguishing marks.)
- Include yourself in the picture, holding the dog or standing next to it. (This can assist in proving ownership of an animal.)

6. MEDICATION

- If your dog is on prescribed medication, be sure to keep a reserve supply in your disaster kit, along with directions on how to administer.
- Be sure the medication does not expire.
- Have enough to last at least two weeks.
- If your dog is on monthly heartworm medication, be sure to have a supply in your disaster kit.
- A muzzle, in case your dog is injured, to prevent getting bit. Practice putting it on your dog, before you are in a disaster.

7. SHOT RECORDS

- Keep a record of all your dog's vaccinations in your disaster kit.
- In order to board a dog at a kennel or shelter, it will need a Bordetella vaccination to prevent it from getting kennel cough.

8. COLLAR AND TAG

- A proper-fitting collar and tag should be kept on your dog at all times, but an extra one of each should be kept in the disaster kit in case the permanent one gets lost during a disaster.
- Keep several spare tags in your disaster kit that can be personalized, so if you move to a temporary location, you can put that phone number and address on the tag.
- Include a proper-fitting dog harness in your disaster kit. They work better when walking a dog. If the animal gets frightened, they cannot slip out of a harness as they can with a collar.
- If your dog is microchipped or has a tattoo, be sure to have the national registry numbers in your disaster kit.

- Make up and store in your disaster kit preprinted "Lost Posters," in case your dog gets lost. (Include your phone number, an alternate phone number, and your address, and leave blank lines to write in the animal's description, where it was last seen, and any other pertinent information.)

9. VETERINARIAN INFORMATION
- Write on a piece of paper the name, address, and telephone number of your regular vet and an alternate vet.
- Write out a release form authorizing another party to get emergency medical treatment for an injured dog, in case you are not available to give approval during a disaster.

10. FIRST AID KIT
- Have a first aid kit in your disaster supplies. (A list of its contents is included later in this chapter.)

11. BRUSH AND COMB
- Include this in your disaster kit if your dog likes to be brushed. Otherwise leave them out as a disaster is not the time to try and get your dog used to something new.

12. TOYS
- Include a few chew toys in your disaster kit if your dog is used to playing with them. Otherwise leave them out.

13. GROOMING SUPPLIES
- Dry shampoo, in case you have to give your dog a bath. Sometimes in disasters dogs come in contact with substances that need to be cleaned off their fur. Dry shampoos work well because they do not require water (something that can be in short supply).
- Cloth towels for drying off your dog.
- Nail clippers.
- Flea powder. (Make sure it is a brand just for dogs.)

14. CAGE
- If you have to confine your dog during a disaster, you can use a plastic crate. (Be sure it is large enough to hold a food/water dish and allows ample room for the dog to stretch out.)

- Be sure the cage has a secure locking device, to prevent the dog from escaping.
- Another alternative is a wire collapsible cage. These are better to use in really warm weather because the dog will get better ventilation.
- Wire exercise pens work well for confining small dogs, but be careful of them digging their way out.
- A spiral ground stake and 6-foot chain can be used to tie a dog outside. Be sure if you use this method of confining a dog that there is no risk of the dog hanging itself by falling off a porch, for example, or getting itself tangled around something. Be sure the dog also has protection from the weather (especially the sun). Don't tie a dog outside and forget it.

Identification for Your Pets

Keep a proper-fitting collar and tag on your pets *at all times.* This includes cats that never go outside. A collar and tag increases the chances of getting an animal returned should it get lost in a disaster. On the tag include your telephone number and address. If there is not room for both, you can write on the collar itself. Remember that during a disaster telephone service is often interrupted, so an address will help increase the chances of getting a lost pet returned sooner.

On cats, it is advisable to use the breakaway-style collars and the tag that can actually be attached flat against the collar and does not dangle. It is a common misconception that cats are prone to hanging themselves by their collar. It is actually more common with dogs.

You may also want to consider tattooing or microchipping your pets, as a more permanent form of identification. It is also a way to prove an animal is yours, should there be any question. Check with your veterinarian if you are interested in having this done.

Photographing Your Pet

Take at least ten colored pictures of all the animals in your household, and keep these pictures with your disaster supplies. It is necessary to have multiple pictures in case you have to leave the picture with different shelters in the area and post them in the area where you last saw the missing pet. Pictures are extremely helpful in identifying lost animals. Remember to update the pictures from time to time, especially if you start out with a puppy or kitten. Be sure to include any distinguishing marks. These pictures can help reunite you with a lost pet. Store the pictures in resealable plastic bags in case you have to post them during a time when it is raining.

Include several of your family members in some of the pictures, in addition to the pet. This can also serve as a way of positively identifying your pet, should there be any questions about ownership.

Proof of Vaccinations

With your important insurance papers, also keep the current health certificates of all the animals in your household requiring vaccinations. If you have to temporarily house your pets at a boarding kennel or veterinary office, they will require proof of current vaccinations, especially rabies and distemper. Your dog will also need to be vaccinated against Bordetella, which protects them from kennel cough.

Medication

If your pet is on long-term medication, always keep a backup supply on hand. Be sure it gets used before it expires, though. Your veterinarian may not be open following a disaster, and other vets in the area may be affected too. If the medication needs to be refrigerated, keep an ice chest on hand to store it in, in case the electricity is off and the refrigerator is not working. Ice can usually be obtained from a Red Cross Shelter or other emergency distribution centers.

Veterinarian's Disaster Plan

Ask your regular veterinarian if he or she has a disaster plan. Some state veterinary associations have a statewide disaster plan. Ask your veterinarian if one exists in your state and whether he or she is a participant. This is important to know in advance, should your pet be injured during a disaster and need emergency medical care. You may not have time to waste trying to locate a veterinarian during a disaster. It is a good idea to have at least two backups, in case your regular veterinarian is unable to provide emergency services during a disaster.

First Aid Kit

Included in your disaster supplies should be a first aid kit for pets. The quantities purchased should be based on the number of animals you have in your household. Listed below are the essential items recommended by veterinarians:

conforming bandage (3" × 5")   tweezers
absorbent gauze pads (4" × 4")   scissors
absorbent gauze roll (3" × 1 yard) instant cold pack
nonadherent absorbent dressing   zinc oxide tape (¾" × 1 yard)
cotton-tipped applicators (1 box)   latex disposable gloves (several
antiseptic wipes   pairs)
emollient cream

You should store these items in a watertight container. This container would also be a good place to store any special medication and the pet's medical records. Remember to replace any medication before it expires. In addition, you should have a pet first-aid guide to assist you in administering basic medical care. These can be purchased at most bookstores. For any serious injuries, it is important to get the animal to a veterinarian as soon as possible.

You may wish to take an animal first aid or animal CPR class. Check with local community colleges or adult education programs in your area. If you are unsuccessful in finding classes, check with your veterinarian. He or she may be able to tell you where a class exists, or maybe your vet would be able to provide you with some basic instruction. If so, you might want to ask if they would mind doing it for a group. You could also contact Animal Health Foundation at 203-535-3807. They conduct both CPR and first aid classes around the country.

Evacuating Animals

A rule of thumb when trying to decide whether to leave a dog or cat behind in a disaster is to ask yourself, "Is the situation safe enough to leave a child behind?" More than likely the answer will always be no. So in that case, never leave your pets behind, no matter who tells you it is safe to do it.

Listen to a radio station broadcasting emergency information. Pay attention to anything said pertaining to animals, and make note of locations where animals are being housed. You may need to utilize a facility at some time during the disaster.

Move your animals early! Do not wait until the last minute, especially if you have a lot of animals. Cats can sense danger early, and as they begin to feel unsafe, they will search out a hiding place. So as soon as you know you may have to evacuate, be sure to locate and confine your cats. Then you will know where they are when you get ready to leave.

If there is any doubt as to whether a disaster will affect you, don't take any chances—evacuate. It is better to have it be a false alarm than to have stayed behind and put the lives of your family and animals in danger. Besides, the more times you practice evacuating, the better prepared you will be when you really have to do it.

Red Cross shelters *will not accept pets.* The local health department is responsible for this rule, not the Red Cross. This is where people go to be safe, and there could be people at the shelter who are either afraid or allergic to animals. You don't want to do anything to increase their stress level. Also food is served to the public in shelters, which puts them in the same category as a restaurant, where animals are not allowed. The exception to this would be Seeing Eye, hearing, or helping dogs.

If you leave a mixture of dogs and cats behind, do not leave them confined in the same place, even if they normally get along. Animals become quite stressed during a disaster, and they will behave differently from normal.

If, for some reason, you absolutely must leave an animal behind, here are some things you should do:

Do not leave dogs and cats outside in a hurricane. The safest place to put them is in a basement. If you do not have a basement, leave them in the ground-floor bathroom. The bathroom walls are reinforced with plumbing, which helps that part of the house to better withstand the destructive winds of hurricanes. If your bathroom has a lot of windows, this will reduce the safety of this room.

In that case, you may want to put the animal in a closet in the innermost part of the house. Leave some of your clothing with the animal (preferably something you've worn recently and won't mind if it gets dirty) so they can smell your scent. This is comforting to a lot of animals. If they have a favorite bed or toy, leave that with them too.

Remember that when you return home, you will probably find a mess wherever you left your pet. Tiled floors are a lot easier to clean than carpeted areas, which is another reason to put the animal in the bathroom. If you leave a cat behind, leave them two litter boxes filled almost to the top. That way, if you can't return home right away, the cat will be taken care of.

Before you leave, fill the bathtub with no more than four inches of water. You don't want it so deep that the animal can get in the tub and drown, but you want them to have enough drinking water for at least five days. If you are leaving your pet in a room other than the bathroom, be sure and put their water in a sturdy, nontippable container. In addition to water, leave dry food to last the same amount of time. The slow-drop feeders are the best kind. Depending on the size of your pets, you may have to have several of this type of feeder. Choose a brand of food that your pet likes, but do not make it too tasty, or they will overeat in the first day or so, and then end up with nothing later. Do not leave any treat-type vitamins or mineral supplements for your pets. If they eat too many of these, it may cause salt poisoning.

In a flood, if you must leave a pet behind, give them a place to escape to that will be well above the expected flood level. Furniture can be stacked for dogs to climb up on. Clear dining room tables and countertops, as they are good flat surfaces that may remain above the waterline. If you leave a dog outside, do not leave it chained or confined in a run. Dogs can be put in garages or barns, loose, but again, provide them with a high, flat surface that they can reach that will be above the waterline.

Put dry food and fresh water out in a place the animal can reach. There should be enough of both to last at least five days. Keep it in a location where you think it will stay dry. Again, do not leave treat-type vitamins or mineral supplements for your pets.

If you leave a cat behind and it is indoors, provide the cat with a high place that it can reach to be able to remain above the floodwater.

The top of a refrigerator is a good place. If you use the refrigerator—or whatever other high, flat surface you select—be sure and leave at that spot food and water for the cat, plus a litter box. Another precaution, should the house flood to the ceiling, is to open the attic access and set a ladder up under it. If the cat has to, it can climb the ladder and seek safety in the attic. In the attic, you should provide food, water, and a littler box. In addition, lay a large piece of plywood across the rafters, so the cat doesn't have to lie right in the insulation. If there is a window in the attic, leave it open to allow the cat to get some air, especially if the flood is occurring during the summer months.

If you leave a cat outside during a flood, it will likely end up in a tree or on a roof. To be safe, on the closest roof to where the cat is used to being, provide the animal with food, drinking water, and shelter. Roofs can get really hot in the summer, so leave a piece of plywood on the roof so that the cat doesn't have to stand right on the hot roof. Roofs can get hot enough to burn a cat's paws.

Buddy System

Now is the time to start a buddy system in your neighborhood, so that you can check on each other's animals in the event there is an evacuation and you are not home. Let your neighbor know where you keep the dog's leashes and the crates for either a dog or cat. Set up a location where you can meet, should you have to evacuate each other's animals. Exchange information on veterinarians, in case one of the animals is injured, and have a permission slip on file with the vet authorizing your neighbor to get necessary emergency treatment for your pet should you be unreachable.

Vacation Planning

When you go on vacation, be sure that you check with the person or kennel caring for your pet to see if they have a disaster plan. It may take you a while to get home after a disaster has occurred, so you want to be sure that in that time your pet will be properly cared for. Make sure the pet's caretaker is authorized to get emergency medical care for an injured pet, should the veterinarian be unable to reach you to get permission.

Transporting Animals

Now is the time to purchase carriers for all the animals in your household. Each animal should have its own, and it should be the proper size, so that the animal is as comfortable as possible. Do not buy cardboard carriers. They do not hold up well, especially if it is raining, and if the animal should have to stay in it for an extended period of time, they do not provide enough room and cannot be cleaned properly. Buy crates that are made of plastic or stainless steel.

If your pet is not accustomed to being in a carrier, get them acquainted with one before a disaster occurs. The top and bottom of crates can be separated, and one half of the carrier can be used as a bed. Allow your pet to use it for a bed, and this will get them acquainted with it and get their scent on it.

The carriers also are a good place to store disaster supplies for your pets.

Have a cat carrier or an Evacsack (see page 386 for information about the Evacsack) for each cat in your household. If you will have to confine the cat for a long time, get a carrier large enough to hold a plastic, shoe-box-size litter box, a water/food dish, and for the cat to lie down comfortably. Make sure the carrier is not left in the sun and, especially if it is warm outside, the cat gets good ventilation. In cold weather, provide the animal with an old towel or even a sweatshirt of yours to curl up with. A personal clothing item of yours will have your scent on it, and that will help to comfort the animal. In cold weather, you can use a separate towel to drape over the cage if it gets cold.

If you take the cat out of its carrier while away from home, be sure to do so in a confined space. Should the cat escape, you want to be able to catch it again. It is not advisable to evacuate carrying a cat or allowing the cat to be loose in your vehicle. If you have to leave suddenly and don't have the proper means to confine the cat, another option is a pillowcase. It is not a secure way to transport a cat, though, and you have to be sure the cat is getting sufficient air to breathe.

If your dog rides in the car, always have a leash in the vehicle. A disaster may occur while you are away from home, and if you have to leave your car, you need a safe way to be able to control your dog.

You should have a large enough carrier for each dog in your household, allowing it room to stand up, turn around, and lie down. If the dog is kept in the carrier, be sure to take it out every few hours to get some exercise and relieve itself. Do not take the dog for a walk in a strange place unless it is on a leash.

Have a chain leash for each dog in your household. Walls and fences can come down during a disaster, and it may be necessary to keep your dog confined on a chain leash until repairs can be made. Be sure it is long enough for the dog to move around without getting tangled around something and perhaps choking itself. Do not chain a dog on a porch, where it might fall off the edge and hang itself. Make time to take the dog for a walk, being careful to keep to areas where it will not injure its paws on sharp objects. Shelter, food, and fresh water must always be within the dog's reach.

Temporary Housing for Displaced Pets

Know where the animal shelters are in your area. Call them now and find out if they have a disaster plan and whether it includes housing animals temporarily during a disaster. If they do, ask them how long they will hold them, if there will be any cost, and if they will implement a foster-home program should their facility become too crowded. If you take your pet to an animal shelter, be sure to keep in touch with them to update them on how much longer you will need your pet housed with them.

What you need to do before a disaster strikes is establish several alternative locations to house your animals in the event that you have to evacuate. It could be the home of a family member or friend. To ensure that they will not be affected by the disaster, find locations at least fifty miles away. Take into consideration how far inland from the ocean they are for a hurricane and how far away from waterways in the event of a flood. If you have a purebred dog or cat, there may be rescue groups for these animals in areas adjacent to where you live. Find them in advance of a disaster, and see if you can start a buddy system with them, agreeing to house each other's animals should one be affected by a disaster.

Locate boarding kennels in your area prior to a disaster to see if they would be able to board animals during a disaster. Keep the phone numbers of those that can with your important insurance papers. Also contact veterinarians in your area and see if they will be able to board any animals.

Call now to find out which motels in areas adjacent to where you live allow pets. Be sure to ask what their limit is on numbers of animals per room, what kind of animals, and what size. Add the names and phone numbers of those that do to the list of kennels that you have located.

If you leave an animal with a friend or family member, be sure they have a secure area to confine your pet. Most animals will try and return to their homes if given the chance. Before leaving your pet at its temporary residence, put a collar and tag on it (for a cat use a breakaway collar). On the tag, tape an alternate phone number in addition to your own permanent number. It's likely your phone will not be working during a disaster. If all you have on your animal is a rabies tag or the phone number of your vet, you should add a tag with your home information. The location where dog licenses or your vet's records are kept may be destroyed, reducing the chance of getting your pet back.

Food and Water

Have at least a week's supply of food and water on hand at all times for each of your pets. Store the food in containers that are airtight, waterproof, and insect proof. Be sure to rotate it at least once every three months. If you use canned food, buy the flip-top cans if possible to store along with the dry food. Be sure to have a can opener in your disaster supplies whether or not you are able to store flip-top cans.

Continue to feed your pet the food they are used to, and serve it as close to the normal time as possible. During the stressful time following a disaster, reduce the amount of canned food you feed normally by half. Canned food increases the chances of your animal getting diarrhea, which can lead to dehydration. Increase the dry food to make up the difference. If your pet is on a special diet, be sure and stock up on the brand you use. These type of foods are even more difficult to locate during and after a disaster.

If there is a "boil water" order in effect during a disaster, this means the water is not suitable for people to drink. This applies to animals too, so boil drinking water from the tap before you give it to them to drink. Another way to make water drinkable is to mix two drops of household bleach per quart of water, keep the mixture in a tightly sealed container for at least thirty minutes before you allow your pet to drink the purified water.

If you bring outdoor plants inside during a disaster, be sure they are not poisonous. It is a good idea to keep the plants in a separate room from all animals, just to be safe.

Animal Waste

Include in your disaster supplies at least a week's supply of cat litter. The brands that come in the plastic jugs are good for storing, especially during a disaster when things might get wet. Be sure to also have a litter box, scoop, and plastic bags in your disaster supplies.

Include in your disaster supplies, plastic bags to pick up after your dog. A small plastic child's shovel can work as a pooper-scooper, and it'll take up less room among your disaster supplies.

Disposal of Dead Animals

Following a disaster there is a good chance there will be animals that have died. If it is your own pet, there are several options you may wish to consider: burying it in your own yard, taking it to the local animal shelter, or taking it to the nearest landfill.

Following a disaster the normal disposal facilities for dead animals are not always functioning. If the electricity is off at the shelter, freezers will not work unless they are hooked up to a generator. Crematoriums will not work without electricity either. Rendering companies may not be able to reach shelters to pick up dead animals if roads are severely damaged or traffic into the area is restricted.

Euthanasia

Sometimes pets are severely injured during a disaster and the humane thing to do is to have the animal euthanized. People have come back to their homes after a disaster, and found severely injured animals that did not belong to them on their property. The first thing to do is to try to locate the owner. If you're unable to do this, then take the animal to a veterinarian or an animal shelter so they can make the decision whether to euthanize the animal. If you cannot find either, and the animal is in severe pain and appears unlikely to live, you may have to euthanize it yourself. Before doing this, if at all possible, photograph the animal, preferably on videotape, to verify the condition of the animal. Also get at least one, preferably two, witnesses that are not members of your family.

Comforting Animals

Be sure to comfort your pet during a disaster. They are frightened too. Having you near, to give them a hug or a pat on the head, will help. If your pet is not ready to be comforted, though, do not force them. Let them come to you when they are ready. If you have to leave your pet alone for a period of time, leave a piece of your clothing with them. Your scent will make them feel more relaxed. Also, be sure that when you leave, the animal is confined somewhere secure and safe. If you leave an animal, it may have a stronger urge than normal to find you, and if it is not properly confined, it will run away in search of you.

Animals display symptoms of stress during a disaster. These symptoms include loss of appetite, changes in sleeping behavior, diarrhea, aggressiveness, a need to be close to people, a desire to hide, nervousness, and a jumpy reaction to loud noises. If any of these symptoms persist for more than a week, consult your veterinarian, especially if your pet is not eating or has a case of chronic diarrhea.

Missing Pets

If you are missing a dog or cat during a disaster, be sure to check the permanent animal shelters in your area and any temporary shelters on a regular basis (at least once every three days). Take with you a picture of the animal that you are missing. If they have lost-animal forms, complete one before you leave. Also ask to check any listings of dead animals. This is a difficult thing to do, but if your pet has died, at least you know it and you will not go on indefinitely looking for that animal.

Basic Tips for Safeguarding Your Horse During Disasters

These are tips compiled to keep your horse safe during a disaster. Included are steps that you need to take *before* a disaster strikes to reduce the chances of your horse's getting either lost, injured, or killed. It is a lot more difficult to move a horse than a small pet to safety, especially when it has to be done in a hurry, so please take the time to prepare now. Your horse's life may depend upon it.

Before I list the tips, I want to share with you a few short stories that emphasize why it is so important to be prepared to evacuate a horse or other farm animals during a disaster. Most of these stories occurred in southern Florida during Hurricane Andrew, and they show how devastating this type of disaster can be to larger animals if they are not evacuated ahead of time.

One man who owned four horses had no way to evacuate them. He did have a four-horse trailer, but the hitch was broken, which made it impossible to pull the trailer behind his truck. In desperation, he finally decided to position the trailer between his barn and an adjacent building, with only inches separating the trailer from the buildings on either side. Then he loaded all four horses into the trailer, thinking they would be safe. When the man returned the next day, he found the trailer with all four horses in it a mile down the road. The horses were dead.

We got a report of a horse that was draped over a T-shaped utility pole, tangled in the wires. When we arrived at the location, we were horrified to discover the horse was still alive. For three days it had been hanging there, suffering terribly. On our way to help the horse we had passed a telephone company truck with a lift basket. One of the volunteers returned to see if the telephone company employee would let us borrow the truck so that we could get up to where the horse was. The man was kind enough to immediately stop what he was doing and return with us. A veterinarian then climbed into the lift basket and was positioned close enough to the dangling horse to be able to euthanize the animal. The wires were then cut and the dead horse fell to the ground.

Another man decided to leave his horses out in a big open pasture. When he returned he found his favorite horse lying on its side on top of the barn with critical injuries. Using his cellular phone, he was able to reach a large-animal veterinarian, who walked him through how to euthanize the horse, which was too severely injured to try to save.

A number of people returned home to find dead horses in their swimming pools. The horses had been blown into the pools and then were unable to get out. In their panic the horses drowned or were hit by flying debris, knocked unconscious, and then drowned.

Horses and other farm animals will instinctively search for the lowest spot to lie down in during a hurricane. If animals escape from their pasture, frequently they will take refuge in the ditches on either side of a road. Unfortunately, the utility poles also line each side of the road, and when the wind knocks them down, they fall on the animals. We found a lot of dead animals in these ditches who had been electrocuted under fallen utility poles.

One man had five calves, which he rounded up and put in the center stall of his barn. A neighbor of his reported the calves to us two days after the hurricane hit. It took another day to remove enough of the heavy, twisted debris to reach the calves. By then they were extremely hungry and dehydrated. We were able to keep only three of the calves alive.

A man who owned thirty goats had no choice but to leave some in the barn and put the rest out to pasture. When he returned, the barn had been reduced to a pile of rubble. Few of the goats inside had survived. A number of the goats were injured with broken legs and backs, and some were impaled by sharp pieces of wood. All but two of the goats left outside had died. The dead ones had been picked up by the wind and blown with such force against the barn that it was almost impossible to distinguish what kind of animal they had been.

In all these instances, a plan to evacuate these animals could have prevented them from getting hurt or killed.

DISASTER KIT FOR HORSES

Now is the time to assemble a disaster kit for your horses. These are items you should have on hand in case you are unable to evacuate your horse.

1. FOOD

- Always have enough food to last at least one week.
- Do not feed horses any food that has gotten wet or contaminated in any other way. Moldy hay can cause a number of serious illnesses.
- Have an extra supply of feed buckets or troughs, in case you have to leave and need to be sure your horse will have enough food while you are gone, being careful not to give more than necessary because, given an unlimited supply of food, horses will eat themselves to death.
- Get your horse used to eating from different types of buckets.
- Horses should eat twice a day, in the morning and at night, so continue to maintain this schedule the best you can.
- Try to avoid abrupt changes in the kind of food you feed or the amount.

2. WATER

- Because horses will drink between five and fifteen gallons of water a day, be sure to always have a supply to last at least three days.
- If you do not have the capacity to store large quantities of water, then be sure you have enough large, clean garbage cans to haul water to your horses.
- The water in swimming pools can be used as long as it does not have algae growing in it (pool water should not be used except in an emergency).
- Check with the local fire department to see if you can tap into the fire hydrants, if they are still functioning.
- Locate water distribution centers in your community set up during disasters.
- Make use of any nearby streams, rivers, or lakes, but be sure the water is drinkable.
- Find out if anyone in your area has a well you could pull some water from.
- It is important to always give water to a horse before you offer food. This allows the horse to get the most nutritional value out of its food, which is important when the horse has become stressed during a disaster.
- Get your horse used to drinking from different kinds of buckets.

3. CLEANING SUPPLIES

- It is important to keep your horse's stall clean following a disaster.
- Filthy surroundings added to any injuries the horse has sustained can cause medical problems to develop.
- Have at least a week's supply of shavings or straw at all times to replenish stalls once they are cleaned.
- Be sure your pitchfork and wheelbarrow are somewhere safe, so that you can find them during a disaster.

4. PHOTOGRAPHS

- Have recent pictures of all your horses. (Make at least ten copies in case you have to distribute them with "Lost" flyers around your community.
- Include yourself in some of the pictures.
- Keep the pictures with your important insurance papers and the bill of sale for each of your horses.

5. MEDICATION

- If your horse is on prescribed medication, be sure to keep a reserve supply in your disaster kit, along with directions on how to administer.
- Be sure the medication does not expire.
- Have enough to last at least two weeks.

6. VACCINATION RECORDS

- Keep a record of all your horse's shots and wormings with your insurance papers.
- Be sure your horse is current on its tetanus vaccination, since during a disaster there can be a lot of sharp metal objects, including nails, lying on the ground.

7. IDENTIFICATION

- You may want to consider microchipping your horse. This is a permanent way in which to be able to always positively identify your horse. Keep with your important insurance papers the telephone number of the company who maintains the microchip registry.
- Another permanent form of identification is tattooing. It is usually done inside the horses upper lip.

- If you need temporary identification on a horse, you can paint your driver's license number on the horse or weave a plastic band into the horse's mane or tail with your name, address, and telephone number on it.
- Use permanent ink and write your name, address, and phone number on all your halters, bridles, and saddles, in case your horse has any of these on it when it gets separated from you in a disaster.

8. VETERINARIAN INFORMATION

- Write on a piece of paper the name, address, and telephone number of your regular vet, and keep this with your important insurance papers.
- If you do not routinely use a mobile equine vet, locate one in your area to use during a disaster, in case your horse is too badly injured to be moved.
- Write out a release form authorizing another party to get emergency medical treatment for your injured horse, in case you are not available to give approval during a disaster. Keep this on file with your regular and an alternative veterinarian.

9. FIRST AID KIT

These are the basic medical items to include in your kit:

cotton balls	antiseptic pressure
10% iodine	spray
compression wrap	poultice
square gauze	glycerine
epsom salt	Elastoplast
Betadine solution	large syringes
wheat bran (Mixed with warm water	small syringes
this makes a bran mash that is good	liniment
for a stressed or traumatized horse. It	hypodermic needles
soothes the horse and helps to keep	rubbing alcohol
mobility in the stomach and intes-	peroxide
tines, hopefully preventing the horse	Visine eyedrops
from getting colic.)	Vaseline
antiseptic solution	Vicks ointment
antiseptic ointment	tourniquet

Appendix

These are the basic bandaging items to include in your kit:

rolled cotton	rolled gauze
compression wrap	elastic tape
medical tape	vet wrap
quilts	stable bandages
lilly pads	theoflex pads
easy boots	safety pins
butterfly closure tapes	

These are the basic items of equipment to include in your kit:

wire cutters	pliers
lead rope	rasp
halter	shoe puller
stethoscope	hoof testers
notepad and pens	blankets
duct tape	scissors
thermometer	tongue depressors
bucket for disinfecting feet	eyedropper
flashlight	towels—paper and
bulb syringe	cloth
twitch	

10. GROOMING

Be sure to keep the following grooming supplies in a safe place, so that they can be located and used if necessary during a disaster:

soft-bristle brush	hard-bristle brush
rubber curry	shampoo
mane comb	tail comb
sweat scrapper	hoof pick

If your horse should get loose during a disaster, it may be necessary to give the horse a bath when you find it, especially if it has come in contact with harmful substances floating in the water during a flood.

11. Temporary Housing of Horses

- Port-A-Stalls or livestock panels can be used to create temporary stalls.
- Picket lines are made by first securing a rope between two poles or two trees above the horses' heads and then tying the horses to the picket line with a lead rope and quick-release knot. Use 1000-lb. cotton or nylon test rope. Give each horse no more than three feet of rope, or else it may get its foot over it and get tangled. The horse should be able to comfortably move his head up and down and back and forth.
- When tying a horse out do not attach the lead rope to a bridle. Instead, you should always attach the lead rope to a halter.
- Horses can be tied to a sturdy fence, but be sure, if you are tying up more than one horse, that they are kept at least a horse length from each other to prevent them from kicking one another.
- Never stake a horse to something that is at ground level.
- Canopy tents, trees, or tarps can be used to provide a horse with shelter from the sun or rain.
- Have fly spray and wipes in your disaster kit to relieve the horse of these pests.
- It is important to make a horse feel safe, so that it will calm down, reducing the risk of it hurting itself, another horse, you, or someone else.
- Check with any fairgrounds, horse show arenas, or racetracks in your area to see if they are willing to temporarily house horses during a disaster.
- If your horse is not used to being kept in a stall, be sure you start getting him accustomed to it now, by putting him in one for short periods of time. During a disaster this may be the only way to keep your horse securely restrained.

Following are some other pieces of information that you need in order to be prepared to respond to the needs of your horse during a disaster.

Evacuating Horses

A rule of thumb when trying to decide whether to leave a horse behind is to ask yourself, "Is the situation safe enough to leave a child behind?" If the answer is no, do not leave your horse unless there is absolutely no way you can evacuate it. It is also important to go with your own gut feeling if there is ever a question. Never trust someone else when they say, "It's okay to leave the animal. Animals know how to take care of themselves during disasters."

Listen to a radio station broadcasting emergency information and take note of any information pertaining to animals. Make a note of locations where animals are being temporarily housed, in case you need to use these facilities at some point during the disaster. If there is any doubt as to whether a disaster will affect you, don't take a chance—evacuate. It is better to have it be a false alarm than to stay behind and put your own life and the lives of your family and your animals in danger. Besides, the more often you practice evacuating, the better prepared you will be when you really have to do it.

Move your animals early! It is difficult to evacuate large animals, and it will take time, especially if you have a lot of animals to move. Do not wait until the last minute, because you are taking the risk of leaving the evacuated area and then not being allowed back in to collect any remaining animals (this applies to floods, hurricanes, and wildfires). Horses can sense when you are stressed, so try to remain as calm as possible, to help ensure that the horses do not panic.

It is not advisable to sedate a horse before you get ready to evacuate it. A sedated horse loses its natural instinct to protect itself.

You will need a horse trailer to safely evacuate these large animals. If you do not have a trailer, check to see if there is someone in your neighborhood who has extra trailer space, or check with any local horse clubs in your area to see if they have members with trailers willing to assist in a disaster. Don't put off doing this.

There have been a number of instances during wildfires when horse owners waited until the last minute to evacuate their horses and as a result ended up adding to the confusion. A truck with a trailer hitched to it is not an easy thing to maneuver down narrow roads, and if it becomes necessary to suddenly turn it around because the fire has changed direction, you may find yourself and your horses in a lot of trouble. The fire departments are not very tolerant of horse owners who block the roads with loaded trailers. In one disaster, I watched a fire truck push an emptied truck and trailer into a ravine to make room so that the fire truck could pass.

If you have a trailer, be sure it is well maintained. Check the hitch, flooring, lights, and tires. You should also stock your trailer with some of the basic first aid items listed earlier and an extra halter, lead rope, leg wraps, water/feed bucket, picket line, five gallons of fresh water, and fresh food (rotate both regularly), and a blanket. If your horse is not accustomed to being trailered, you need to regularly practice loading the horse. It is best to do these practice runs both during the day and at night (use only a flashlight for lights), when you are tired and feeling stressed, and in different kinds of weather, especially in a thunderstorm. Wear protective rain gear with a hood when practicing trailering during a thunderstorm and a mask over your face in anticipation of a fire, so that your horse becomes accustomed to seeing you in different kinds of gear. This will also give you a more accurate idea of what it will be like during a disaster.

Remember that horses are herd animals, so wherever the lead horse goes, the others will follow. This can work in your favor if you have a number of horses to evacuate.

If you must leave your horse behind in a fire, remove the horse from the barn and *close* all the doors to the barn. Horses, once frightened, will seek out a place where they feel safe, and for most that will be a barn. Even if the barn is on fire, they will go back in it, so don't give them a way to do this. Do not put a horse in a confined area secured with barbed wire. If a horse panics, it might try to go through it, causing itself serious injury.

If you must leave your horse behind in a flood, once again remove the horse from the barn and *close* the doors. Horses are good swimmers, but if they get stuck in a barn or other building, they will drown. One of the most dangerous things for horses during a flood is deep mud. Horses can easily get stuck and then they will panic, risking serious injury to themselves. If you leave the horse outside in a pasture, choose one that is not likely to become one big mud puddle and that has elevated areas. If you have a padlock on your pasture gates, be sure you give a key or the combination to trusted neighbors, so that they can evacuate your horses if you are away from home when a disaster strikes.

If you must leave your horse behind in a hurricane, put the animal in the largest pasture available. Make sure there are no large trees in or near the pasture, that no power lines pass over the area, and that it is away from any building with metal roofs (metal roofs are easily blown off in a hurricane, and this flying metal can be deadly).

There should be some low-lying areas where the animals can take refuge. If you have no choice but to leave a horse in a barn, it should be an open pole barn, with a flat roof. If the barn has windows, you may want to invest in hurricane shutters. Otherwise, tape the windows to prevent shattered glass from flying.

Safety Tips for Evacuating a Horse During a Fire

- Blindfold the horse, using a wet towel tucked under the animal's halter.
- Be sure you cover both eyes.
- Never use a nylon halter, as it can melt if the fire gets too hot. Leather halters are the best thing to use.
- It is important to practice blindfolding your horse, so that it gets used to it.
- Use a piece of wet cotton fabric, such as a bandanna, to place over the horse's nostrils.
- Smoke inhalation can cause pneumonia, which can kill your horse.
- Wet the horse's tail and mane.
- Do not put a blanket on a horse's back when evacuating, as it can easily catch fire.
- Once you get your horse to safety, be sure to offer it water immediately, dehydration can come on quickly and can kill a horse.
- If a barn is already on fire and the horse is still in it, you have to evaluate the danger to yourself in going in and getting it. If you just open the door to the barn, the horse may not run out, so you will most likely have to go in and get it.
- Before you leave your property, be sure to turn off the gas and electricity and label any outdoor propane tanks.
- A little Vicks ointment in a horse's nostrils can reduce the horse's ability to smell smoke.

Safety Tips for Horses During a Hurricane

In the event of a hurricane it is better to leave horses and other large farm animals outdoors, rather than in a barn or other building. Injuries sustained outdoors from flying debris can be serious, but most are treatable. Whereas a building collapsing on your animals will probably cause much greater injury.

In addition, animals are likely to get trapped and be unable to escape to a safer location.

- You should start evacuating a horse or other farm animals far enough in advance to be on the road seventy-two hours before the storm is expected to hit. Otherwise, you run the risk of getting caught in traffic (this is particularly a problem if the temperatures are extremely hot) and being caught in high winds (horse trailers are susceptible to being flipped in high winds).
- Make your property as hurricane safe as possible. Remove or secure anything that can become airborne and cause injury to an animal.
- Before leaving your property be sure to turn off the gas and electricity. If you have propane tanks, secure them to the ground with tie-down stakes. Label any outdoor propane tanks.

Horses are not affected by earthquakes unless a barn or other building falls down and traps or injures them. Immediately following an earthquake, be sure to check that any pasture fences are still standing and that support posts have not been loosened by the shaking. During the Northridge earthquake in January 1994, the biggest problem for horses was dehydration. In some areas the water remained off for as long as two weeks.

Medical Concerns for Horses During a Disaster

These are some of the common medical problems to look for in horses during a disaster:

cuts and abrasions
burns
respiratory problems (especially in fires)

lameness
eye injuries
nails or other sharp debris in the feet
abscess in the foot area
foot infection from standing in water or mud
    for prolonged periods of time
difficulty breathing
discharge from the nose

Another possible problem, which is brought on by stress, eating bad food, changes in diet, or unclean stalls/pastures, is colic. The first signs of colic are:

restlessness
pawing with the front foot
biting at their side
kicking under the belly with a hind foot
repeatedly lying down and then getting back up or rolling
heart rate may be elevated (normal heart rate for a horse is 28 to
    42 beats per minute—you check this by placing three fingers
    over the submaxillary artery in the inner aspect of the lower
    jaw bone)
excessive sweating (in extreme cases)

If you notice any combination of these symptoms, contact an equine veterinarian immediately.

Returning an Animal to Devastated Property
IN AN EARTHQUAKE
- Check the stability of a barn before putting a horse inside.
- Remove any fallen objects.
- Check to make sure the electrical wiring has not been damaged before using it.
- Check the stability of pasture fences before allowing a horse into the area.
- Check for any gas ruptures or leaks before allowing a horse back into the barn or surrounding area. Do not light any matches until it is determined to be safe.

Appendix

IN A FIRE

- Remove any burned wood.
- Disassemble what remains of burned barns or stalls.
- Remove any debris from the ground, especially nails.
- Any metal pasture fences need to be wiped down. Heat causes the galvanizing to come to the surface, leaving a yellow residue that is toxic for the horse should the horse lick it.
- Turn over the soil in the pasture where it has burned and look for hot embers. Bury as much of the ash as possible.
- Get rid of any food covered with ash.
- Do not turn on the electricity in a barn until the building has been checked for any damage to the electrical wiring caused by the fire.

IN A FLOOD

- Look for any poisonous snakes that may have gotten trapped inside barns or stalls.
- Remove any debris that has collected in the barn or stalls.
- Remove any mud to prevent horses from having to stand in it for prolonged periods of time, causing foot problems.
- Check to make sure all the perimeter fences are still standing and secure.
- Get rid of any feed and hay that has gotten wet. Moldy food can make a horse sick.
- Feed hay in a hay net or a manger until the ground is dry to prevent the hay from getting moldy.
- Empty any water containers, in case contaminated water collected in them during the flood.
- Check any wooden floors for weaknesses caused by water damage.
- Do not turn on the electricity in a barn until the building has been checked for any damage to the electrical wiring caused by the floodwater.
- Do not use any water piped into the barn until it has been determined that the water is safe to drink.
- Do not light any matches in the barn or around the building until it has been determined that there are no flammable liquids on the ground, brought there by floodwaters.

Appendix

IN A HURRICANE OR TORNADO

- Be sure to check for and remove any debris that could cause injury to a horse's feet before putting them back in a pasture.
- Check a barn for its stability before placing a horse inside.
- Remove any debris from inside the barn and stalls.
- Check to make sure all the perimeter fences are still standing and secure.

Basic Tips for Safeguarding Your Bird During Disasters

These are tips to help you keep your bird safe during a disaster. Included are steps that you need to take *before* a disaster strikes to reduce the chances of your pet getting either lost or injured. Please take the time to prepare now. Your bird's life may depend upon it.

DISASTER KIT FOR BIRDS

Now is the time to assemble a disaster kit for *each* bird in your household. The kit should include:

1. FOOD
- Use the brand food that your bird is used to.
- Include a supply of gravel and a cuttlebone.
- Store food in waterproof containers.
- Have enough food to last at least two weeks. (More can be stored if you have room, but be sure it is rotated at least once every three months.)
- Food dish for transport cage.

2. WATER
- Have enough to last at least one week. (More can be stored if you have room, but be sure it is rotated at least once every three months.)
- Store water in a dark or shaded area, and not in direct sunlight, or bacteria that can cause diarrhea will start to form.
- Have a small container of bleach for purifying water.
- Have a sealed plastic container for storing purified water.
- Water container for transport cage.

3. CLEANING SUPPLIES

- Have disinfectant cleaner for cleaning a bird cage. Before putting the bird back in the cage, be sure the cage is rinsed well. *Do not* clean the cage while the bird is in it.

4. PHOTOGRAPHS

- Have recent pictures of all your birds. (Make at least ten copies, in case you have to distribute them to several shelters and post them in the area where you last saw your missing bird.)
- Include yourself in the picture, holding the bird. (This can assist in proving ownership of a bird.)

5. MEDICATION

- If your bird is on prescribed medication, be sure to keep a reserve supply in your disaster kit, along with directions on how to administer.
- Be sure the medication does not expire.
- Have enough to last at least two weeks.

6. IDENTIFICATION

- If your bird is microchipped, be sure to have the national registry number in your disaster kit.

7. VETERINARIAN INFORMATION

- Write on a piece of paper the name, address, and telephone number of your regular vet and of an alternate vet.
- Write out a release form authorizing another party to get emergency medical treatment for an injured bird, in case you are not available to give approval during a disaster.

8. FIRST AID KIT

- Have a first aid kit in your disaster supplies. (A list of its contents is included in this chapter.)

9. CAGE

- Transport cage. (If you have a large-beaked bird, make sure the transport cage is strong enough to withstand the bird's trying to chew its way out.)

10. TOOLS
- Pliers (to use in case the bird's cage is damaged and bars need to be repaired).
- Wire (to repair a damaged cage).

11. MISCELLANEOUS SUPPLIES
- Have a long-handled net for capturing birds that have escaped.
- Have a cloth towel to throw over an escaped bird when it has landed.
- Free-standing flashlight and extra batteries to help regulate light hours for birds.

Identification for Your Bird

You may want to consider microchipping your bird, in case it gets loose. This is also an easy way to prove ownership should there be any questions as to whom a found bird belongs to. If you want more information on microchipping, contact your veterinarian.

Photographing Your Bird

It is important to take pictures of your bird and keep them with your disaster supplies. If the bird escapes during a disaster, you will have pictures to take to the local animal shelters and to post in the area where the bird was last seen. You should keep a minimum of ten color photographs and update them if the appearance of your bird changes.

Medication

If your bird is on a long-term prescribed medication, be sure that you have a backup supply in the event of a disaster. Your veterinarian and other ones in the area may be affected by the disaster and be unable to refill a prescription.

Veterinarian Disaster Plan

Ask your regular veterinarian if he or she has a disaster plan. Some state veterinary associations have a statewide disaster plan. Ask your veterinarian if one exists in your state and whether he or she is a participant. This is important to know in advance, should your bird be injured during a disaster and needs emergency medical care. You may not have time to waste trying to locate a veterinarian during a disaster. It is a good idea to have at least two backups, in case your regular veterinarian is unable to provide emergency services during a disaster. Make sure they have someone on staff that specializes in birds.

First Aid Kit

Included in your disaster supplies should be a first aid kit for your bird. The quantities purchased should be based on the number of birds you have in your household. Listed below are the essential items recommended by veterinarians:

Kwik-Stop and/or cornstarch   tweezers
a first aid book on birds   disposable gloves
heavy-duty gloves (to prevent
  getting bit)

Evacuating Birds

If your neighborhood is under evacuation orders, it is important that you not leave your bird behind. Once an area is evacuated, the gas and electricity is usually turned off. Birds are sensitive to drafts and cold, and the indoor temperature will no longer be regulated. In a hurricane, walls can be blown in and land on cages, crushing the bird or giving it a way to escape. An escaped bird runs the risk of injury or death outside of the cage.

Have a transport cage to put your bird in for evacuation purposes. Make sure it is small enough to fit in a vehicle but large enough to give the bird room to move about. Include in the cage food and water. It would be best to put the water in a nonbreakable dispenser. Be sure the water dispenser is securely attached to the cage too, so it doesn't fall and spill the water. This could be a problem if water is in short supply.

Buddy System

Now is the time to start a buddy system in your neighborhood, so that you can check on each other's birds in the event there is an evacuation and you are not home. Let your neighbors know where you keep the bird's transport cage. Set up a location where you can meet, should you have to evacuate each other's birds. Exchange information on veterinarians, in case one of the birds is injured, and have a permission slip on file with the vet authorizing your neighbor to get necessary emergency treatment for your bird should you be unreachable.

Vacation Planning

When you go on a vacation, be sure that you check with the person or kennel caring for your bird to see if they have a disaster plan. It may take you a while to get home after a disaster occurs, so you want to be sure that in that time your bird will be properly cared for. Make sure the bird's caretaker is authorized to get emergency medical care for an injured bird, should the veterinarian be unable to reach you to get permission.

Transporting Birds

Now is the time to purchase a transport cage if you do not already have one. Each bird should have its own, and the cage should be the proper size, so that the bird is as comfortable as possible. If your bird is not used to the transport cage, put it in the cage for at least an hour each month. You may want to put the bird in the transport cage while you are cleaning the bird's regular cage.

While the bird is being evacuated, be sure to keep the cage out of direct sunlight if it is hot and away from air-conditioning vents that are blowing cold air. Do not leave the bird in a hot car.

Temporary Housing for Displaced Birds

When you get situated in a temporary shelter, be sure the cage is out of drafts too. If you are in a shelter with a lot of other people, be sure to keep the bird as secluded as possible. This will reduce stress on the bird. Keep the bird away from people who may have colds, which can be passed on to birds. In shelters, the lights are not always turned off completely at night, making it more necessary to cover the bird's cage. Birds need a balanced number of daylight hours and dark hours to remain healthy.

Food and Water

During a disaster it is advisable to feed birds only dry seed mix. Soft foods, pellets, and fresh fruit or vegetables are susceptible to bacteria and mold that could go undetected during disasters, when routines get changed and things are hectic.

If there is a "boil water" order in effect during a disaster, this means the water is not suitable for people to drink. This applies to birds too, so boil drinking water from the tap before you give it to them to drink. Another way to purify water is to mix two drops of household bleach per quart of water; keep the mixture in a tightly sealed container for at least thirty minutes before you allow your bird to drink the purified water.

Euthanasia

Sometimes birds are severely injured during a disaster and the humane thing to do is to have the bird euthanized. Local animal shelters and veterinarians can provide euthanasia during a disaster.

Missing Birds

If your bird should get loose during a disaster, be sure to check the permanent animal shelters and any temporary shelters in your area, on a regular basis (at least once every three days). Take with you a picture of the bird that you are missing. If they have lost-pet forms, complete one before you leave. Also ask to check any listings of dead animals. This is a difficult thing to do, but if your bird has died, at least you know it and you will not go on indefinitely looking for your pet.

Additional Concerns About Birds During A Disaster

In a disaster, light and dark hours can get scrambled for birds, especially when there is no electricity. If the bird spends too many hours in the dark, especially if its cage has to be covered additional hours to keep it warm and prevent drafts from blowing on it, you may have to use a flashlight to give some additional hours of light at night. Providing light when it has been in the darkness more than normal can have a calming affect.

Birds are extremely sensitive to smoke. If you are being evacuated during a fire, make sure the bird is the first to be removed from the area, even if the fire is still a considerable distance away. While transporting the bird, be sure to cover the cage to block out as much smoke as possible, but still allow some air to reach the bird.

When birds become extremely frightened, they can start panic-thrashing and cause injury to themselves. In addition to breaking blood feathers, they can cause flight feathers to be pulled out and the flesh under their wings to be torn. If a bird is in this state, cover its cage with a towel or anything else available. When the bird assumes a defensive posture, reach in with a towel and remove the bird, careful to fold its wings against its body.

Once you have the bird in your hand, you need to stop any bleeding. A simple solution is to pack cornstarch or flour onto the wound. The combination of flour or cornstarch and blood will congeal into a cast-hard compound that stops the bleeding. It is important to then get the bird to a veterinarian as soon as possible.

Microchipping: A Permanent Form of Identification for Pets

Every day pets are lost, especially in the aftermath of disasters. Tragically, millions of these animals never make it back home because the collar and tag they were wearing was somehow removed. Now there is a more *permanent* form of identification available for dogs, cats, horses, birds, rodents, reptiles, and non-food farm animals—the microchip.

The microchip is a tiny computer chip into which an identification number is programmed. The chip, encapsulated in a biocompatible material, is small enough to fit inside a hypodermic needle and can simply be injected under the skin of an animal (of any age), where it will remain for the rest of the animal's life. This procedure is performed by a veterinarian, and takes just seconds. Since there is only minimal discomfort to the animal, anesthesia is not required. Once injected, the microchip becomes encased by a thin layer of protein, which anchors it in place. The microchip itself has no power supply to replace or moving parts to wear out, so there is never a need to remove it.

A microchip reader is used to scan animals to detect the number assigned to a chip. Through a national registry, the number is used to track down the animal's owner. In this country, there are now over

Appendix

15,000 scanners being used by animal shelters, rescue groups, police departments, agricultural departments, and veterinarians.

If you would like more information about the microchip or the national registry, you may contact AVID at 800-336-2843. Take the time to look into this! If more animals arrived at the temporary shelters we set up during disasters with microchips implanted, reuniting them with their owners would be much easier.

Feral Cats: Moving From Pest Control to Birth Control

It doesn't take a disaster for feral cats to become victims ... they suffer daily.

Feral cats are cats that are no longer domesticated or never were. There are an estimated thirty to sixty million of them living in the United States today. They make their homes in cities and rural areas, congregating near food sources to survive.

Feral cats instinctively form colonies. Since they are not sterilized, the unneutered male cats will fight over mates and unspayed females will caterwaul when in heat, often making a nuisance of themselves. The more serious concern is the number of kittens that are born in these colonies. Even though on average over fifty percent of a feral cat's offspring die soon after birth, enough survive to perpetuate the overpopulation problem.

The response of some people is to euthanize these cats in an effort to control their numbers. However, studies indicate that when an entire colony is removed, other stray cats will soon move into the vacated territory, and the breeding begins all over again. There is another alternative to euthanasia to consider.

The "trap and release" method involves humane trapping, sterilization, vaccination, and release of the ferals back into the environment where they came from under the supervision of a responsible care-taker. In the United States there are thousands of documented cases of individuals who are successfully maintaining colonies of feral cats.

It is almost impossible to tame adult feral cats. There is a greater chance of domesticating kittens that are less than eight weeks old, but it requires a great deal of patience. (See Chapter 20, "Elvira," in this book to see how one person tamed a feral kitten.)

If you would like more information about feral cats, contact:

Alley Cat Allies
P.O. Box 397
Mt. Rainier, MD 20712
Contact persons: Louise Holton or Becky Robinson, codirectors

Alley Cat Allies operates a network that links individuals concerned about the well-being of feral cats. This national organization helps educate the public on the humane techniques available for feral cat control.

Modeled after successful programs in the United Kingdom and parts of Africa and Europe, Alley Cat Allies advocates a trap-neuter-release program that stabilizes populations, reduces birth rates, and improves the overall health of the maintained cat colony.

Alley Cat Allies has publication and fact sheets on the following topics:

- Feral Cat Population Control: Implementing a Humane Sterilization Plan
- Relocating Feral Cats
- Taming Feral Kittens
- Notes for Veterinarians Treating Feral Cats
- Rabies and Feral Cats: Facts and Control
- Health Care for Feral Cats and Zoonoses: Potential Health Hazards for Humans
- Do-It-Yourself Cat Fences for Domestic and Homed Feral Cats—Inexpensive and Effective for Confining Cats to Yards
- Build an Inexpensive Feral Cat Shelter
- Guidelines, Facts, and Myths About Colony Management and Wildlife Predation

Humane Cat Trapping

There is one thing that you *must* have to successfully trap cats ... patience.

Besides patience, you need humane traps designed specifically for catching cats. There are several companies that sell a variety of traps, and they are:

- Animal Care Equipment and Service
  800-338-ACES
- Animal Management Inc.
  800-745-8173
- Tomahawk Trap Company
  715-453-3550

Cat traps are sold in three sizes, kitten, standard, and large. The kitten trap is for cats under the age of eight weeks. Standard traps are used to trap almost all adult cats. The large trap would be for Toms. A good rule to use when judging what size to use is that a cat should not have to crouch down when it walks into a trap. Some humane societies and animal control agencies rent traps and transfer cages, so check with the ones in your area if you do not want to purchase the equipment. If you live in an area prone to attract feral cats, though, it may be cheaper in the long run to invest in a trap.

Out of Harm's Way

Do not try to make your own trap. Cats are more likely to escape from a homemade trap, which may result in the cat and/or you getting injured. If a cat escapes after it has been in any type of trap, it is very unlikely that you will capture that cat again. So use a trap that will safely catch the animal the first time.

Trapping is primarily done when a cat is too wild or frightened to be safely caught by hand. If in doubt, always use a trap. Cats can cause severe injury with their claws, and they will bite. If you are not sure if the cat you plan to trap has been vaccinated, especially for rabies, do not take a chance—use a trap.

Remember, young kittens can bite and scratch too. *Do not* attempt to catch them by hand, even if they look harmless. You should always use a trap, which will prevent you from having any hands-on contact with the cat and from getting hurt.

Use the following checklist of equipment needed to successfully trap cats. Take everything on the list with you, even though you may not use all of it. It is better to have excess equipment than to discover once you begin trapping that you have forgotten something really important.

	cat trap(s)—kitten, standard, and/or large
	transfer cage(s) that are designed to work with the trap being used
	canned cat food
	can opener
	spoon for scooping the cat food
	towels to drape over the cage after the cat has been caught
	newspaper for traps and to put under traps while transporting cats
	heavy gloves
	first aid kit, in case you get scratched or bitten
	flashlight with fresh batteries
	catnip (optional)
	jug of water and small bowl (for use during hot weather)

Appendix

Cats are nocturnal, so trapping is usually done early in the morning or starting at dusk, especially when the weather is hot. During the hottest hours of the day, cats find a cool spot to sleep and there is little chance of luring them into a trap then. Trapping effort are usually not productive when it is raining, either.

In selecting a place to set a trap, the best location is where the cat is accustomed to eating. Try and set the trap close to the time the cat is used to eating, which will be either first thing in the morning or in the evening. If you are not sure where the cat eats, set food out in a location where you frequently see the cat and at the time of day you intend to try to trap the cat. Usually after three days of your setting out food, the cat will fall into the routine. When it comes time to trap, the cat should be waiting for you. Only this time you will put the food in the trap.

Another consideration when placing the trap is finding a location where there are not a lot of people or automobile traffic. If you have to trap during the day or when the sun is still hot, place the trap in the shade. Be sure there are no automatic sprinklers set to go off in the area when you are trapping. The sudden burst of water will frighten the cat, and you will have to find a new location to reset the trap.

It is best to place the trap on grass, dirt, or thin coverings of leaves. Be sure you *do not* set the trap down on an anthill. You are trying to create a natural surface for the cat to walk on and at the same time concealing, as much as possible, the bottom of the trap. If the cat seems reluctant to walk on the wire trap bottom, take a section of newspaper and fold it so that it covers the bottom of the trap. Make sure the paper will not interfere with the trap closing.

Do not place the trap on cement unless that is the only flat surface available. Make sure the trap is level and does not wobble. If it wobbles, find another location for it or place something under one corner to level it. Be sure the trap is not off the ground. You do not want the cat's paws falling through the openings in the bottom of the trap.

The cat's greatest motivation for going into a trap is food. If they are not hungry, there is no reason for them to go into one. The day before you intend to try and catch them, *do not* feed the cats their usual meal. If you plan to trap on Wednesday night, for example, do not feed the cats all day Tuesday or before you set the trap on Wednesday. If you know of other people in the area who feed the cats, let them know what you are doing and ask them to hold back the food too. You can still put out water for the cats.

Appendix

If you aren't feeding the cat and do not wish to do so, the best time to set out the trap is early evening. That is when cats start to prowl for food, so put the trap in their path where they will find it.

Bait the trap with the smelliest tuna that you can buy. Generic cat-food brands work very well. *Do not* use dry food unless the cat is not responsive to the canned food and is used to eating only dry food. If the cat still seems to be finicky, try sardines. Sometimes placing a few sprinkles of catnip on the food will entice the cat inside the trap too.

When baiting the trap, put no more than a couple of bites of the canned cat food right outside the entrance to the trap. This is to help the cat locate the door. Trail in several more bites of the food, leading to the back of the trap. Lift the back end of the trap and, underneath it, put a mound of the food. Then set the trap back down on top of it. *Do not* put any food in a dish in the back of the trap, and this includes the can that the tuna was in. You want the cat to work at getting the food. If it is too easy, they can walk in, stretch over the "trip" mechanism, eat what they want and back out of the trap without tripping the door. Do not worry about putting water in the trap. When it is real hot outside, put a dish of water near the entrance to the trap, and if the cat is thirsty, the water may lure them to the trap.

If you have multiple cats to trap, you can set more than one trap at a time if you have them. Leave at least three feet of space between the traps or spread them out in different areas where the cats are seen. Do not spread them out so far that you cannot closely monitor them, though. For example, if you are trapping cats that roam between several backyards, set traps in one yard at a time.

After you set the trap, move out of sight, but stay close enough to monitor the trap. Limit peeking to see if any cats are nearing the trap. *Do not* check on them more than once very fifteen minutes, unless you hear the trap's door close. If you are using more than one trap, remove the trapped cat as quickly as possible from where the other traps are set unless there is another cat working its way into a trap. If this is the case, let that cat get caught and then remove both traps.

If a cat gets trapped and other cats witness it being trapped, the other cats will still go into the trap. At first they may scatter at the sounds of the trap closing and the trapped cat reacting to being caught, but the other cats will come back, usually within a half hour at the most.

After you have caught the cat, drape a towel over the trap. This will help the cat to calm down. When you remove the trap, be sure to use the handle on the trap and wear gloves. Some traps have a sliding door at the rear of the trap. Be sure that the door is hooked before you pick up the trap. Otherwise, you may lift the trap and accidently pull up the door, allowing the cat to escape.

In most cases, cat trapping is done either to have the cat spayed/ neutered, vaccinated, and then returned to where it was caught *or* to have it removed permanently from the area where it was living. People's objections to feral cats include:

- They continue to reproduce (this is the biggest objection).
- They howl and fight at night.
- The males spray on such things as car tires, patio furniture, and flower boxes.
- They dig in gardens and flower beds, using them as litter boxes.
- They attack pet cats.
- They leave paw prints on cars.
- They get sick or injured, and people hate to see them suffer.

If you decide to trap a cat to have it permanently removed, *do not* take it somewhere else and "dump" it. You are just relocating the problems. And remember, once a cat has been through the experience of being trapped, it is unlikely that cat will ever be trapped again. Humane societies and animal control shelters will take feral cats. Unfortunately, they are almost always euthanized, but the majority of the shelters will do it with a painless injection. This is a more humane solution than shooting, poisoning, electrocuting, setting on fire, beating, or drowning the cat, which is what some people will do to get rid of the animal.

If you have a lot of cats to trap, it will go faster if you have several traps and transfer cages. Transfer cages are designed to fit up against the back sliding door of the trap. They too have a sliding door, and when you pull both doors up, you create an opening for the cat to move between the cage and the trap. When you are moving a cat from a trap into a transfer cage, *always* set the transfer cage up against something that will not move, such as a curb, a wall, or the tire on a car. If you do not, cats (particularly large ones) can lunge into the transfer cage and send the cage flying with the cat in it, providing a way for the cat to escape. (See diagram.)

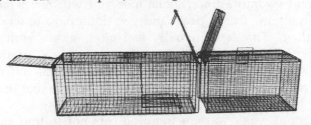

If you do not have transfer cages available, *do not* try to move the cat from the trap into a box, an airline crate, or any other type of cage. If you do, there is a very good chance that the cat will escape, and it's amazing how tiny a space a cat can slip through. You also increase your chances of having hands-on contact with the cat, which is how people get bitten and seriously scratched. Take the trap, with the cat in it, to a shelter if you are not keeping the cat or to a veterinarian if you are going to keep it. They will do the transfer using the proper cage.

If it is hot weather and you have multiple cats to trap in an area, *do not* load the cats you have already caught into your vehicle until just before you are ready to leave. Put the occupied traps in a cool and shady location where you can keep your eye on them at all times. Sometimes people don't understand why you are trapping, and if they see the cat in the trap, and you are not around, they may release it. Then you have considerably reduced your chances of ever catching that cat again.

If you trap a seriously injured or sick cat and there are still more cats to be trapped, remove all the traps and take the sick/injured cat either to a shelter or a veterinarian.

If you know a female cat has nursing kittens, trap the kittens first, then the mom. *Do not* trap the mom until you are sure you have gotten all the kittens. If you think a female cat may have kittens, but you cannot locate them, discourage the mother from entering the trap by approaching her when she gets near it. If you should catch her, leave her in the trap while you search for kittens. If it is at night, use a flashlight. The light will pick up the reflection from the kittens' eyes.

Some favorite places for cats to hide their kittens are woodpiles, thick bushes, barn lofts, seldom-used sheds, and under houses. When looking for kittens, wear gloves and be on the lookout for poisonous snakes and spiders that may live in your area.

If you do not find the kittens, free the mom, and try trapping her again in several weeks when the kittens are old enough to eat on their own and go into a trap. Sometimes you will catch more than one kitten in a trap. This is okay, and you don't have to worry about separating them. They will actually feel more secure with some of their littermates. If you have trapped the mother in a separate trap, *do not* try to put the mother and kittens together in one transfer cage. Keep them separate, but put the cages side by side so that the mother can see her kittens.

It is important when you are trapping cats not to trap someone's pet. Here are some ways to distinguish between a feral or a domesticated cat that has been trapped.

Common Feral Cat Behavior in a Trap
(Cats may display some *or* all of these behaviors)

- They will pace back and forth.
- They will no longer eat any food that is still left in the trap.
- They will urinate.
- They will lunge at the side of the trap if a person approaches.
- They will try squeezing through the end of the trap that they entered through.
- They will hiss and growl.
- Their ears will be laid back.
- Their eyes will be full of fright.

Common Domesticated Cat Behavior in a Trap
(Cats may display some *or* all of these behaviors)

- They will just sit still.
- They will not hiss or growl.
- Sometimes they will meow, but it will be a friendly sound.
- If all the food in the trap has not been eaten, they will continue to eat.
- If a person approaches, they will allow the person to touch them through the trap.

If you are going to be doing a lot of trapping in an area, you should notify the people within that area, especially people who own cats. Try and be specific as to when you will be setting the traps, and people who have cats that are allowed outdoors can perhaps bring them inside or put them in a garage temporarily.

If you are trapping cats that you intend to have spayed/neutered, vaccinated, and released back to where they had been living, be sure you take any cats you catch to a veterinarian who is prepared to handle feral cats. Not all veterinarians will work with them. Also, *do not* trap on a Friday or Saturday night, because veterinarians usually will not do spays/neuters on Saturday and Sunday, and that would necessitate keeping the cat confined in a trap for too long a period of time.

When you take a female cat in to be spayed, it is advisable to let the cat stay an extra day at the veterinarian's office. Be sure, too, that the vet puts in dissolvable stitches, because there is little chance of retrapping the cat to take her back in to have her stitches removed. Once you get the female cat home, if you can keep her confined in a garage for a couple of days, that will give her a few more days to recuperate in a safe place. During that time, restrict your interactions with her to just putting fresh food and water out for her. Remember to give her a litter box.

Information on Wildlife Rescue and Rehabilitation

Most people are not aware that it is illegal to transport and care for wild animals or birds unless you are properly licensed. If you find an animal or a bird in need of help, you should contact an accredited rehabilitation group. They know

- how to safely transport an injured bird or mammal
- what dangers to be aware of while handling wildlife
- how to administer medical care
- how to provide the proper food
- how best to protect themselves and the bird or mammal from additional harm

Many communities have wildlife rehabilitation programs that handle day-to-day emergencies. If you are interested in this area of animal rehabilitation, I encourage you to contact the experts in this field. There are probably some in your own community, or you may contact one of these organizations:

Appendix

International Wildlife Rehabilitation Council
4437 Central Place, Suite B-4
Suisun, CA 94585
707-864-1761

National Wildlife Rehabilitators Association
14 N. 7th Ave.
St. Cloud, MN 56303
612-259-4086

If you are looking for information on how to respond to the needs of oil-covered birds or mammals, you may wish to contact one of the following organizations for more information:

International Bird Rescue/Research Center
699 Potter Street
Berkeley, CA 94710
510-841-9086

International Wildlife Research
2661 Concorde Circle
League City, TX 77573
409-740-4528

Tri-State Bird Rescue and Research
110 Possum Hollow Road
Newark, DE 19711
302-737-9543

If you find an oil-covered bird, here are some emergency instructions:

1. Keep the bird warm (80 to 90 degrees).
2. Handle the bird with gloves and/or a towel, minimizing human contact as much as possible.
3. Confine the bird in something that is dark, such as a cardboard box with a lid and air holes poked in it *or* an airline crate draped with a towel.
4. Reduce the noise around the bird as much as possible.
5. *Do not* make any attempt to wash the oil off the bird.
6. *Do not* give the bird any food *or* water.

Appendix

7. Contact an agency in your area prepared to handle oil-covered birds for further instructions. This could include:

- a wildlife rehabilitation group
- Fish and Wildlife or Fish and Game agency
- a marine mammal/bird sanctuary
- a Humane Society or SPCA
- an Animal Control Agency

Evacsack: An Alternative
to a Cat Carrier

During the 1993 Midwest flood, the rescue teams tested a new product called an Evacsack. It is an orange, rubberized mesh sack that measures 20 inches across and 24 inches deep. At the top is a drawstring with a locking mechanism. The Evacsack was used on the rescue boats during the flood to transport kittens, cats, and small puppies. When rescuing from a boat, you are working within limited space and the Evacsack took up a lot less room than a wire transfer cage or airline carrier.

If you are involved in any type of animal rescue work, I highly recommend Evacsacks. They are durable, the animal gets good ventilation, and they are easy to clean. You may also want to consider having an Evacsack for each of the small animals living in your household. You never know when a disaster may strike, and this is a fast and effective way of getting your animal to safety, without the risk of injuring it or losing it. When not in use, it can be folded and stored in a drawer. This is a real advantage over cat carriers, which can take up a lot of room and may have to be assembled before you can use them.

The Evacsack can be ordered from Animal Care Equipment and Services. If you tell them you heard about the Evacsack through this book, they will donate $1.00 to United Animal Nation's Emergency Animal Rescue Service Program fund. For more information about the Evacsack or to place an order, contact:

Animal Care Equipment and Services
800-338-ACES.

How to Become an Emergency Animal Rescue Service Volunteer

1. Contact United Animal Nations (information on how to do this is found on page 390), and they will send you a volunteer training registration form, which you complete and return to UAN. On that form you will list three cities in the United States that would be convenient for you to attend a workshop in. Once a workshop is scheduled in one of the cities you have listed, an enrollment form will be sent to you at least thirty days prior to the date of that workshop.

2. After you have completed a volunteer training workshop, you will be added to the Active Volunteer data base. When a disaster occurs in the region(s) where you have indicated you are willing to volunteer, you will be contacted and told whether or not you need to report.

Information About the Volunteer Training Workshops

The goal of the Emergency Animal Rescue Service volunteer training workshops is to prepare people to help animals during a disaster. There is never a shortage of individuals who want to volunteer their time to help animals after a disaster has struck, but if they are not already trained, good intentions can impede relief efforts.

If you work for a Humane Society, Animal Control Agency, SPCA, animal rescue organization, or have no affiliation with an organization but would like to do something to help animals during a disaster, this workshop is the first step toward being prepared.

Listed below is an outline of what is discussed in the EARS Volunteer Training Workshop:

- Information about United Animal Nations and the development of the Emergency Animal Rescue Service Program
- The need for a national disaster-relief program for animals
- Services provided by the EARS program for animals during a disaster
- How the EARS program is funded
- How the EARS program works with other organizations during a disaster
- How to set up an Animal Disaster Relief Center
- Acquiring supplies, rescue equipment, and animal food during a disaster and in nondisaster times
- The forms that the EARS program has available to use during a disaster
- The importance of communicating during a disaster
- How the media can assist animals during a disaster
- Volunteer positions
- Insurance coverage for volunteers
- Safety for volunteers
- Gearing up volunteers
- Who rescues the animals during a disaster
- What steps you need to take to ensure that you are prepared to take care of your own animals should a disaster strike where you live
- The emotional aspect of being a volunteer during a disaster
- What a volunteer can do in nondisaster times
- Steps to mobilizing volunteers

The volunteer training is supplemented with videos and slides taken during actual disasters that the Emergency Animal Rescue Service program has participated in. Each volunteer will receive a volunteer packet with detailed information to prepare them to help animals during a disaster.

Appendix

A training exercise will be done in the morning to help the class participants understand what is involved in setting up an Animal Disaster Relief Center. The group will be divided into smaller working groups, and each one will work together to create an Animal Disaster Relief Center based on information that is given to them in a handout.

There will be no hands-on animal handling offered in this class because of the constraints of being in a classroom situation. United Animal Nations hopes in the future to offer additional classes for volunteers, which would include an animal-handling class. In the meantime, we suggest you look into volunteering with a humane society or animal control shelter in your area to pick up animal-handling experience. It takes repeated exposure to animals of different temperaments to learn the techniques of animal handling. A one-day class cannot teach you this.

Each training class is limited to fifty people to allow all the volunteers ample time to ask questions, so don't delay in registering. The classes are usually full. Because of insurance reasons, you must be at least sixteen to become a volunteer.

In order to receive registration forms and more information about the training workshops, please write to:

> United Animal Nations
> Emergency Animal Rescue Service Workshop
> P.O. Box 188890
> Sacramento, CA 95818

If you have any additional questions about the workshop, you should contact UAN at 916-429-2457. Or fax them at 916/429-2456.

Emergency Animal Rescue Service Program Wish List

These are some of the supplies that the Emergency Animal Rescue Service Program needs in order to be prepared to respond when disasters occur. Any assistance you can provide would be greatly appreciated.

air compressor
bandaging supplies (for animals and humans)
beekeeper hood
beekeeper smoker
binoculars (compact size)
bolt cutters (heavy duty)
bristle brushes (hard and soft)
buckets (collapsible—can be bought at sporting goods stores)
bug zapper (electric)
bullhorns
clipboards (wooden, 8-½" × 11")
collapsible wire cages for dogs (large and extra-large sizes)
collars for dogs and cats (various sizes)
communication equipment (handheld radios, CBs, cellular
    phones, pagers)

copying machine (portable)
cots (aluminum frame)
cupboards (Rubbermaid, portable with lock)
dog chains (heavy duty, 6' long, clips at both ends)
dog runs (portable, 5' × 5' square)
duct tape
extension cords (outdoor approved, 50')
fans (industrial-size, portable)
fax machine (portable)
fire extinguishers
fire retardant clothing (various sizes of pants and shirts)
first aid kits for rescue teams
flashlights (heavy duty, waterproof)
flatbed trailers
flat tire inflator (aerosol cans for temporary repair)
flip charts and easels
fly strips
garbage bags (plastic, heavy duty)
generators
gloves (disposable—surgical)
gloves (heavy duty—work gloves)
grooming table
grooming shears
halters (horses)
hard hats with lights
heating pads
hoof picks (horses)
horse trailers
hoses (garden type, 75')
ice chests (with wheels)
johnboats (flat-bottom boat)
jumper cables
ladders (extension style)
lanterns (Coleman)
laptop computers
lead ropes (horses)
leashes
life jackets
litter scoops

metal detectors
padlocks (heavy duty)
pitchforks
Polaroid camera
police tape (yellow spools)
pooper-scoopers
printer (portable for laptop computer)
radios (portable with weather band)
refrigerator (small portable)
rock-climbing equipment
rope (nylon, heavy-duty 1000-lb. test)
rubber boots (various sizes, knee-high)
shelving (plastic and that can be broken down and reused)
Shop-Vac (heavy duty, wet/dry)
shovels (heavy duty)
shower curtain rings (metal)
sink (freestanding, portable)
snake-bite kits
sponges (heavy duty)
spotlights (freestanding, portable)
spotlights (plugs into cigarette lighter)
stove (Coleman, portable)
stretcher (for animals)
tarps
telephones (cordless)
telescope
tents (two- and three-room)
tents (awning type)
tick-remover kit
toilet (portable)
tool kits (basic sets: hammer, pliers, screwdrivers, wrench, small
saw)
totes (Rubbermaid, heavy duty; 27 gallon size)
tree-climbing equipment
trolling motors
vests (reflective, bright orange)
waders (chest-high with straps)
water bottles (for rabbits and other small caged animals)
water-purification tablets

wet suits (various sizes)
wheelbarrows (plastic)
white boards (4' × 5') erasable
Ziploc bags (largest size)

In addition to supplies, the following services are always needed from either companies or individuals:

airline tickets for getting volunteers to disasters
carpenters
cellular phone time during disasters
electricians
fencers (who can loan us chain-link fence panels)
food (to feed volunteers)
ham radio operators
helicopter pilots
motor-home rentals (to house volunteers)
pilots (airplane)
plumbers
printing (banners, disaster forms, hats, magnetic vehicle signs, signs, T-shirts)
rental cars (vans and trucks)
telephone installers
telephone service during disasters
truck drivers for transporting supplies to a disaster location

If you would be interested in donating any of the items or services mentioned above, please contact (donations are deductible for tax and estate purposes):

United Animal Nations
P.O. Box 188890
Sacramento, CA 95818
916-429-2457